Also by Thomas Parrish

Great Battles of History: The Bulge
Victory at Sea: The Submarine
The Simon and Schuster Encyclopedia of World War II (Editor)

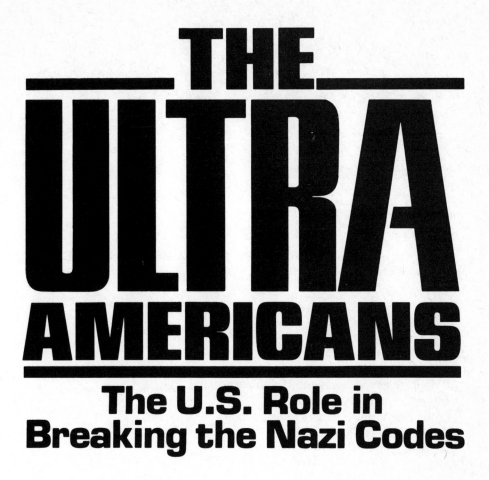

THE ULTRA AMERICANS

The U.S. Role in Breaking the Nazi Codes

THOMAS PARRISH

STEIN AND DAY/*Publishers*/New York

First published in 1986
Copyright © 1986 by Thomas Parrish
All rights reserved, Stein and Day, Incorporated
Designed by Louis A. Ditizio
Printed in the United States of America
STEIN AND DAY/*Publishers*
Scarborough House
Briarcliff Manor, N.Y. 10510

Library of Congress Cataloging-in-Publication Data

Parrish, Thomas (Thomas D.)
   The Ultra Americans.

   Bibliography: p.
   Includes index.
   1. World War, 1939-1945—Cryptography.   2. World
War, 1939-1945—Electronic intelligence—United States.
I. Title.
D810.C88P36   1986   940.54'86'73   85-40583
ISBN 0-8128-3072-5

Know the mind of the opposing generals in order better to divine their actions, to know how to force your actions upon them, and to know what traps to use against them.
—Frederick the Great,
from *Military Instructions*

They were such a damn good group of people.
—Gordon Welchman,
first head of Hut 6,
Bletchley Park

Contents

Illustrations

Preface

In the last decade the reading public has learned that during World War II the Western Allies possessed a remarkable secret weapon called Ultra that gave them the ability to look over the shoulders of Adolf Hitler and his generals and read the high-level radio communications of the German armed forces. This book tells the story of the Americans, most of them young men, who took part in this hidden war as code-breakers and intelligence officers. They did their work in England, in Washington, and with U.S. forces in the field.

The theme of the story is cooperation between men of diverse nationalities, backgrounds, and personalities. Beginning in places as far apart, mentally and politically, as Washington and Warsaw in the early 1930s, battling prejudices and national egotisms, learning and working through the twists and turns of one of history's most troubled eras, the characters in this story welded a partnership more intimate and more effective than anything ever seen before in war, bringing it to full strength under the supreme need to squeeze the life out of Hitler. And the partnership so begun has ever since constituted a vital link between the United States and Great Britain. The story here is one of generally rising success in communication, and yet communication sometimes failed and disaster threatened or even won out; triumph, as often, was only a step or two ahead of tragedy. And finally at the end of the war the intelligence that the British and Americans had welded together was to achieve one last startling success—a success that must be considered one of the first developments in what was to be known as the Cold War.

The advances in radio in the decades before the war meant that armies could now take to the air waves for quick and close exchange of

9

orders and reports; the method of war called the blitzkrieg would not otherwise have been possible. But this new development held advantages for enemies as well, since what is put on the air can be heard by any would-be eavesdroppers within range. Countries around the world began creating teams of code-breakers and eventually agencies to exploit the intelligence the code-breakers produced, although it took the pressures of war to teach some governments that code-breaking without properly organized exploitation is a menu rarely followed by a meal. On its own, in the decade before Pearl Harbor, a small agency of Americans, most of them not long out of college, produced remarkable secret victories that play an important part in this story. The Americans came to the wartime intelligence alliance not empty-handed but bringing gifts that were some of the finest achievements in the history of hidden warfare and that were to take on new importance in the great struggle.

Even persons who have no special interest in the details of World War II know something about the role performed by the Allied reading of German code and cipher messages, but it must be said that much of what these persons think they know is not so. There often appears to be some idea that the Allies "broke the German code" and that this triumph was a one-shot affair, really all that needed to be done. From that point on, so the notion runs, the Allies could sit back in their armchairs and read German messages as readily as if they were dispatches in the morning paper. The truth is vastly different and more admirable. Faced with continual challenges, the codebreakers could never sleep. They were dependent on constant vigilance and on the development of marvelous machines, contributed to by the ingenious mathematicians and technicians of four countries. The triumph was truly international, hence the characters in this story: Polish graduate students, bon vivant French intelligence officers, and idiosyncratic Cambridge dons, as well as all the young American mathematicians and linguists, lawyers (including a future Supreme Court justice) and teachers, who fought their war offstage and kept the secret to themselves for thirty years.

The accounts of the events and the plans and the inventions given here come chiefly from conversations and correspondence with surviving participants and from the written record left by those who knew, much of which has only lately become accessible. One important figure, in fact, made himself available partly because of his wish, as he expressed it, to "set the record straight." Every conversation in this book has been presented as it was reported by someone who took part in it. As a result, the background to certain events will be seen in an entirely different light from that found in previous books. One reason for this is government disinformation procedures. After the breaking of the Ultra story in 1973 and 1974, the governments concerned seem to have felt that parts of it still needed to be cloaked in cover stories; hence, extravagant and groundless accounts of thefts and smugglings were put into circulation and have sometimes appeared in print. Nobody writing in the field of intelligence can ever be in the position of saying that he has in hand the ultimate and unalterable truth, but the information in this book is not only the latest available from declassified documents, it is the result of listening to the participants themselves, comparing their statements with the words of others, and weighing the evidence all up.

Any writing about the happenings of even the recent past depends, of course, on the advantages conferred by hindsight, but the story here is nevertheless told from the point of view of the characters in the circumstances of their time. Before Pearl Harbor, a person might reasonably have supposed that Japan would become an active enemy of the United States, but supposition became reality only on December 7, 1941.

The older characters in these pages were the contemporaries of our grandfathers, and many of the junior figures are still in their full vigor today. Yet the era of the bucket-helmeted Wehrmacht infantrymen striding down the Champs-Elysées, of sausage balloons bobbing in the London sky, of the day of infamy and To Hell With Japan—KO Tokyo, of B-17s exploding into flame in the flak above Schweinfurt, of silent soldiers in snow capes creeping forward in the Ardennes dawn ... that era in many ways has for us now the remoteness and hence the romance of Chancellorsville and Gettysburg. Sometimes it is hard to remember that it was all a dirty, savage war, a business of death.

But the men who broke the ciphers and decided what the messages meant knew that they were not merely playing with letters and numbers, they were giving military commanders tools with which to affect men's lives in battle and, as a result of those battles, millions of human lives in the war's aftermath. They were persons of great ability and, like us, of many types and temperaments. Fortune gave them the rare opportunity to do wondrous things.

Thomas Parrish

Acknowledgments

One of the most pleasant discoveries a writer makes in pursuit of information is the remarkable readiness with which requests for help are met—a readiness that has no motive other than a genuine wish to aid in making the book as truthful, and as interesting, as possible. It can never be said too often: a book of this kind cannot come into being without the active participation of a great many persons. I am deeply grateful to all those who made contributions.

I must first mention Dr. Paul K. Whitaker. It was in conversations with this scholarly gentleman that the idea of *The Ultra Americans* was conceived, and it was through such talks, and as a result of Dr. Whitaker's willingness to answer all sorts of questions, that the story began to take shape. He also made available his diaries and journals, his copies of orders, and his photographs. This material naturally suggested lines of inquiry to follow and persons to seek out.

The heart of the book is the material that came from interviews and from correspondence with Dr. Whitaker and all the other persons who offered me their firsthand knowledge of the Ultra story. These persons are listed under Sources, on page 313; this listing is as much an acknowledgment of valuable services provided as it is a bibliographic statement. Many of these contributors were available for conversation not once but several times, and they supplied various kinds of written information—answers to queries, and their documents, memoranda, and reminiscences. Among these persons special mention should be made of the American master cryptologist Frank Rowlett, whose word processor seemed always ready to pour forth the information I requested, and Gordon Welchman, the pioneer of Hut 6 who supplied answers to the most minute questions about his work, and who invariably did so with the greatest good cheer. Among the persons

13

interviewed, those besides Mr. Rowlett who gave or lent written material, or supplied written answers to questions, were William P. Bundy, Brig. Gen. Carter Clarke, Mrs. Benjamin A. Dickson, Lt. Col. Melvin C. Helfers, Justice Lewis F. Powell, Edmund Kellogg, Louis Smadbeck, Telford Taylor, and Doris E. White. Maj. Gen. John W. Huston paid a special visit to the National Archives on my behalf. I am especially indebted to Beverly Kitchen Almond for the loan of her irreplaceable scrapbooks from the Bletchley Park era, and for permission to include some of the photographs in this book. I thank, too, all others who supplied photographs. I am particularly indebted in this regard to Louis Kruh. And special thanks for hospitality are due to Arthur Levenson, Mr. and Mrs. Edmund Kellogg, and Beverly Almond and her husband, the Rev. Harry J. Almond.

Other persons who helped with spoken or written information were James Bamford, Ernest L. Bell, Anthony Cave Brown, Joseph B. Cornelison of IBM, James T. DeVoss, Arthur A. Durand, Graydon Lewis of the Naval Cryptologic Veterans Association, Greg Mellen of the Sperry Corporation and *Cryptologia,* Forrest C. Pogue, Paul Stillwell, and Wallace Winkler.

I am indebted to archival collections as sources of information. Like many another author writing about an aspect of World War II, I am indebted for thoughtful help to the unusually conscientious and refreshingly unbureaucratic John E. Taylor of the Modern Military Branch, National Archives, in Washington. At the George C. Marshall Library and Research Center in Lexington, Virginia, I have been made to feel absolutely at home by Royster Lyle, Jr., and I thank Mr. and Mrs. Lyle for their hospitality and friendship. Thanks for his help are also due to John Jacob of the Marshall Library. I also wish to express my appreciation to my very efficient research associate in London, Marco Rimini, to Richard Natkiel of the *Economist,* and to Mrs. H. E. Forbes of the Cabinet Office Historical Section.

One of the anchors of our present civilization is the comprehensive and efficient mechanism known as interlibrary loan; my thanks to Phyllis Hughes and her associates who conduct this operation at the Hutchins Library of Berea College and to the director of the library, Thomas Kirk. I have also made use of the libraries of the University of Kentucky and Eastern Kentucky University; I am indebted to the respective directors, Paul Willis and Ernest Weyhrauch, and to their staffs.

I am happy to have the occasion once again to thank Ann Pollard for her many labors, which are inadequately described as secretarial; I also thank Lillian McGuire for her work in transcribing the mound of tapes I presented to her.

I wish to acknowledge a debt to Professor Barry Machado of Washington and Lee University for his advice and suggestions; he will very likely differ with some of the points made in this book, but I hope he will enjoy it.

Fortunate is the author who has an effective and devoted agent. I am most pleased to have this opportunity to record my appreciation to Patricia Berens of the Sterling Lord Agency for her work on my behalf and, beyond that, my gratitude for her continuing faith in me. I also thank her associate, Norman Kurz, for his interest and helpfulness.

I also acknowledge with pleasure both the work and the cooperative spirit of my editor at Stein and Day, William Fryer. And, of course, I thank Sol Stein for his interest in the book.

Among my most profound debts are those to two good friends and fellow authors: to Charles B. MacDonald for his invariable willingness to be of help in all kinds of ways, with respect both to this book and to my earlier *Encyclopedia of World War II,* and to Charles Bracelen Flood, to whom I owe more than I can express; his encouragement and suggestions have been of enormous help to me throughout my work on *The Ultra Americans*; he also gave the manuscript a critical reading but is, of course, absolved of any responsibility for the statements herein—as are all the other persons who made contributions.

Finally, I acknowledge with pleasure a special debt to my dear friend Nancy Coleman Wolsk, who is an art historian but was perfectly ready to become absorbed in a subject that cannot be said to have been among her previous fields of study or interest. I am grateful for her encouragement and her sound advice, for her active help in research, and for her never failing love and support.

PROLOGUE
Assignment: "Something Special"

SHORTLY BEFORE NOON on a sunny August day, a small black sedan drove up to the closed iron gates of a nineteenth-century mansion in the English midlands. A soldier stepped out of the sentry box beside the gates and extended his hand for identification papers. The driver of the car needed none; the guard recognized him right away. But it was different with the passengers, three U.S. Army second lieutenants whom the soldier had never seen before. No matter who their escort was, they would have to prove themselves.[1]

As the guard checked their papers, the newcomers studied the scene in front of them. Through the gates they could see, across a lawn and behind a line of scattered trees, a sprawling red-brick house with sharp gables and large bay windows framed in stone, everything embellished with spikes and swirls and looking all the more Victorian because it was supposed to be Tudor Gothic. A forest of fluted brick chimneys sprouted from the peaked roof. It was an enormous building, and one did not have to be a student of social history to know immediately that it stood as some tycoon's monument to his prowess in making and selling bricks, beer, buttons, or whatever. To the right, across the drive, was a small pond in which a few ducks cruised idly. The house was flanked by long white wooden one-story buildings like army barracks, and other temporary-looking structures took up much of the space among the fine old trees nearby.

One of the gates bore a black plaque with a cryptic message in gilt: GC&CS. While they waited, one of the Americans wondered aloud what this row of capitals with the ampersand might stand for.

"Government Code and Cipher School," the Englishman explained casually.

What? Government Code and Cipher School? The Americans were

17

shocked. What kind of security was this? Although they did not know exactly what went on behind those gates, they had a general idea, and they were damned sure that the place was far more than a school. What could the British be thinking of, revealing even by initials the fact that the establishment inside dealt with such hush-hush matters as codes and ciphers?

The Americans had come from "an atmosphere where security with a capital *S* was almost a pathological fetish,"[2] and the method they were accustomed to was silence rather than deception. GC&CS! The British, with all their experience, were said to possess excellent security procedures. Was this an example? Inside the great brick house and the array of buildings around it was a Top Secret community, one about which the three American lieutenants had been told nothing but could guess much, and one of their guesses was that the establishment ought to have all the security it could get.

EXACTLY ONE MONTH earlier, on July 28, 1943, the three lieutenants—Arthur Levenson, Selmer Norland, and Paul Whitaker—together with seven other U.S. Army signal intelligence officers, had been put on orders directing them to report to the New York Port of Embarkation for shipment to the 10th Replacement Depot in England. Although he had no military background, having been in the army only five months, Whitaker in particular brought exceptional credentials as well as fascinating personal experience to this European Theater assignment. A trim, brown-haired man, standing about five-eight, he was a university professor of German in civilian life. At the beginning of the year he had applied for a direct commission in intelligence. (If he was accepted, he would become an officer the moment he took the oath, without having to undergo any training.) His qualifications had won quick approval for his request, and he had been ordered to report to Arlington Hall, across the Potomac from Washington, the headquarters of the army's Signal Security Agency.

What made Whitaker so attractive to the army was a knowledge of the German language and German culture remarkable in a person who was not of German descent. A small-town boy from north-central Pennsylvania, he had graduated from the University of Michigan in 1929, with a major in German. The next year he won a German-American exchange fellowship, good for a year's study at the University of Munich, and once there he did well enough in picking up teaching jobs on the side to enable him to spend a further year in Munich on his own. He had a position at the American Institute, and he also had private clients. In the late spring of 1931 he was hired as tutor for her children by a restless, roaming American woman, Mrs. Ethel Clift—"very proper and aristocratic in manner"—who managed, in spite of her husband's business problems in the aftermath of the Wall Street crash, to go on spending a good deal of time in Europe. One of her youngsters, Montgomery, was the future actor.

On returning to the United States in 1932, in the depth of the depression, Whitaker was lucky enough to be offered a teaching job as an instructor in German at the University of Kentucky. In 1933 he finished work for his master's degree at Ann Arbor and, now a married man, settled in to life on campus. Then, four years later, came a major event: he won a fellowship for doctoral study at the University of Vienna. He wrote his dissertation while in Austria, but after returning to Vienna in the nervous summer of 1939, had to come home—for reasons that will be explained—without his degree. In 1941 he went to Ohio State as a graduate student, and he received his Ph.D. the following year.

It was shortly thereafter that he applied for the direct commission. Since his knowledge of German was, he knew, unusual and potentially valuable, he felt that there might be a place for him in some kind of intelligence work. The speed and the appropriateness of the response to his suggestion certainly contradicted the common idea of the army as a perverse institution dedicated to turning surgeons into truck drivers and linguists into mess sergeants.

As a result of all his study and experience, Whitaker read and spoke German like a well-educated native, and he had enjoyed the fringe benefit of extensive exposure to German and Austrian political life and politicians in the 1930s—some of it highly unusual. In his Munich days, notably, he had developed the habit of dining at the Osteria Bavaria, a restaurant popular with the students. As its name suggests (*osteria* is the Italian for "tavern"), it was not the typical sauerbraten-and-kartoffelpuffer establishment but featured Italian dishes, which were supplemented by house special delicacies like Königinpastete (chicken and peas in a patty shell) and russische Eier (deviled eggs with caviar); life was not all austerity for Munich students, even in the leanest days of the early 1930s. Yet the plain wooden tables and the uncarpeted floors made the Osteria look like any ordinary tavern, and the prices were reasonable.

A regular fellow patron, also attracted by the food, or the prices, or both, was a rapidly rising local politician named Adolf Hitler. Whitaker usually sat at a table just inside the door from the vestibule into the dining room. About ten feet away, on a dais raised one step and lightly screened by a plain wooden railing, stood a round table with room for seven or eight people; this special spot was regularly reserved for the man whom his followers in the fast-growing National Socialist Party solemnly called the Führer. Hitler tended to be a late diner, appearing when most of the customers were well along with their meals or had finished, moving into the restaurant in a cluster of brown-shirted associates and cronies. He was a rather quiet fellow, talking earnestly but not loudly, not seeming to demand any unusual attention, though he was clearly the dominant figure in the circle around the table. He also had the true politician's touch: it was known that when Resi, a good-looking young waitress at the Osteria, was having trouble finding money to pay for her forthcoming wedding, the Führer had produced the needed cash. Although somewhat curious about the aims and ideas of this odd-looking fellow with the faithful entourage, Whitaker, absorbed in his own study and work, did not, at the time, give him a great deal of thought.

But the world had changed by 1938, when Whitaker was in Vienna working for his doctorate. One evening, he and his wife were having dinner near the university, and they heard the sounds of people marching and making a commotion outside.[3] Curious, the Americans headed for the square in front of the chancellery and, when they reached it, saw a fellow climbing up the face of the building. "There was a balcony up there, and he planted the swastika flag on it. Then Arthur Seyss-Inquart, an Austrian Nazi leader, came out and made an announcement: the old order was changing, things were going to be different from now on. They were asking their brethren from the great German Reich to come in and "maintain order."

Whitaker had one more look at Vienna and the German world in the summer of 1939, when he returned for the Ph.D. final examinations. During the year since the *Anschluss* the Nazis had completely taken over the Austrian educational system, and when Whitaker presented himself at the university he was surprised to be told that he could not be readmitted. Why not? It was simple. Where was his documentary proof that he was of Aryan blood? Well, Whitaker said, it hadn't occurred to him to bring along any such evidence, whatever it might be. The officials shook their heads, and not in sympathy: he ought to have known better.

This bizarre roadblock kept Whitaker from receiving his doctoral degree in Vienna, but even though his studies there had not won him the standard badge of academic acceptability, they and his earlier experiences had prepared him for an unforeseeable kind of usefulness outside of the academy.

WHITAKER, OF COURSE, knew nothing about being an army officer, a deficiency that did not seem to perturb the men who directed the Signal Security Agency. He and others of similar background were given some training in basic military mysteries—how to salute, even a bit of marching—but the main thing he did was work. As soon as he got to Arlington Hall he was installed in the German section, and immediately he was translating messages that American listening stations had plucked from the air—exchanges in the German diplomatic code between Berlin and German embassies and missions in Buenos Aires, Dublin, and other capitals all over the world. Although he was being employed as a translator, he, like the fledgling cryptanalysts at Arlington Hall, was ordered to take home-study courses in cryptography. This pursuit was not to interfere with his regular duties; the idea, in his case, seemed to be to make him aware of what was involved in solving encrypted messages, not to teach him how to do it.

The beginning point here was the distinction between codes and ciphers. (Although this distinction is not clear-cut and absolute, and some present-day dictionaries tend to fuzz it, it nevertheless has much practical importance in the world of cryptology.) In general, a code is quite a straightforward mechanism; it substitutes a word (cabbage) or a number (14923) for a word or a phrase (aircraft carrier) in what is called the "plaintext," the plain-language message that must be disguised. Code books, like the ones you read about in spy novels, consist of columns of words or number groups with their plaintext equivalents alongside. It is different with ciphers. Those of the kind Whitaker was concerned with operate letter by letter, turning a plaintext message into what appears to be utter gibberish. Cipher instructions give the operator the key, or keys, for transforming the letters of the plaintext alphabet into cipher equivalents; they tell him, that is, what he is supposed to do with a *J* so that it will become a *Q*, or a *Y*, or whatever the particular system calls for at that moment. By the time Whitaker was learning these principles, enciphering was being carried out by ingenious machines, and an encrypted message tended to be an extremely complicated affair, very often a coded text wrapped in a cipher, or "superenciphered."

Having spent several months in translating decrypted German messages, Whitaker was able to make a pretty good guess about the probable nature of his overseas assignment, though neither he nor any of the other men, with the exception of the young officer who was to be in charge of the group, was told anything about it. The only thing the security-conscious people of the Signal Security Agency would say was that the work would be "something special."

AND NOW SECOND Lieutenants Whitaker, Norland, and Levenson were at the gates, waiting, pondering those letters: GC&CS. The three were the first members of the group from Arlington Hall to report. The guard returned the papers to the driver, the gate swung back, and the little black car carried the newcomers forward into a secret world.

The opening of the gate was in itself a simple act, easily performed by an RAF enlisted man, but the obvious symbolism was profoundly fitting. When that gate swung wide, history swung with it. Something utterly new was happening in the world of secret intelligence. A kind of relationship never before seen between allies was being inaugurated by Britain and the United States. The greatest hidden treasure of the war, code-named Ultra, was becoming joint property.

On another level, this entry into the Government Code and Cipher School was for American signal intelligence a rite of passage, a first step toward full participation in the mighty events being planned and prepared by the Allies—a first step, yet one preceded by a hundred steps along a hard, secret trail that had already known its own special triumphs. It was a trail that had begun thirteen years earlier, on a spring day in Washington.

1

Four Young Men

I

EIGHT O'CLOCK ON a warm April Fool's morning in Washington, D.C.: for several minutes the tall, strongly built young man in the neat blue suit had been standing on the sidewalk in front of the Munitions Building, a large and unprepossessing structure that had been run up during the World War. The unattractiveness of the building did not concern the young man; its size was another matter. He was supposed to report to Room 3406, but he was a "country boy."[1] How on earth did you go about finding an office that was designated by so many numbers? Finally he decided to seek help from the guard standing by the front doors.

Tuesday, April 1, 1930, was a promising day. There was some evidence that the American economy might be on its way to recovery from the great stock market collapse of nearly half a year earlier. On Monday, an accumulation of buying orders that had piled up over the weekend had pushed prices sharply higher on the New York exchange; in fact, it had been the biggest trading day of 1930 so far, and *The New York Times* index of stock prices reached 240, a long way from the precrash peak of 307, but even further from the mid-November low of 166,[2] when the initial panic had finally subsided. A Wall Street firm was celebrating what seemed to be a rebirth of the bull market by moving into new offices paneled throughout in walnut and said to be among the most sumptuous in the financial district; the inlaid table around which the board of directors would convene had been imported from England at a reputed cost of $30,000.[3] President Herbert Hoover, Secretary of the Treasury Andrew Mellon, and leading business figures, like Henry Ford and Owen D. Young, were assuring the worried public that not only was this simply another recession, but that the economy would soon resume the upward march that had been interrupted by the regrettable break of late October. Julius H. Barnes, a spokesman for the president, was particularly soothing: "The spring of 1930 marks the end of a period of grave concern.... American business is steadily coming back to a normal level of prosperity."[4] Still, more than four million people in the United States were out of work, and the number was increasing;[5] and no one, in business or in government, seemed to be taking any steps beyond incantation to relight the fires in the smokeless factories.

However the economic picture might look to the politicians and the experts, the young man on the sidewalk was sure of one thing: the offer of a steady government job paying $2,000 a year was one he simply could not refuse; he and his wife of seven months had agreed on that. It was not even important that they had no idea what the job was. The young man had been curious about it, of course—he had asked around—but his failure to advance beyond guesswork had not kept him from accepting the offer, and without much hesitation.

The young man's name was Frank Rowlett. Twenty-one years old, he was a native of a tiny Appalachian town in Virginia called Rose Hill, in the extreme southwestern part of the state, near the Kentucky border. The town was an isolated spot in the days just before the World War when Rowlett, walking a mile and a half to the one-room schoolhouse, began his formal education. He showed a consuming eagerness to learn, accompanied by a willingness to work. He proved to be a demon in the spelling bees, his most resounding victory coming as a fourth-grader when he beat back a seventh-grade challenge by successfully spelling "chrysanthemum." His mental day actually began very early, as he and his father would play checkers "from fire-building until break-fast time."

His greatest love and main after-school pursuit, however, soon became science. He approached it by way of photography, and from the age of eleven was absorbed not only in snapping pictures but in developing and printing them—an interest that led him into chemistry. With help from his father, who owned a general store and could get chemicals at wholesale cost from his supplier, Rowlett set up his own laboratory at home. From chemistry he moved into electricity, teaching himself from the family's set of the *Britannica* and from textbooks he read on his own. The inspiration for all the experimentation, for Rowlett as for thousands of other American boys of the late nineteenth and early twentieth centuries, was Thomas Edison. The great inventor, like other kings temporal or intellectual, was bound to have a successor, somebody yet unknown. Why should it not be Frank B. Rowlett?

Constrained by the family budget, Rowlett went to college at a little school called Emory and Henry, two counties away from Rose Hill. After his freshman year, during which he had decided, rather surprisingly, to major in Latin—languages interested him too—his father gave him the drab news that the family business was in a real slump; there would be very little money for further college. Rowlett, who had long been used to creating not only his own amusements but the greatest part of his own education, saw the financial problem as a fresh challenge. He discovered that Emory and Henry was in search of somebody to do remedial tutoring of freshmen in algebra and geometry, and since he had by this time absorbed a great deal of mathematics, he was able to convince the department chairman that he was highly capable of explaining x and y and angles to puzzled beginners. The job paid enough to enable him to stay in school. During his junior year he taught regular beginning courses in mathematics and was also laboratory assistant in both chemistry and physics. But his main source of income in the last two years (he was now entirely self-supporting) was actually his photographic developing and printing business.

After graduating from Emory and Henry, he planned to go to the University of Virginia, at Charlottesville, for graduate work in mathematics. By now his adolescent dream of becoming a second Edison had been replaced by a vision of himself as a college professor and mathematical theorist; he would be a pure thinker, he thought, rather than somebody who developed new mechanical devices. But late in his senior year one of his bosses, the head of the Emory and Henry math department, called his attention to an announcement of a U.S. Civil Service examination to be held in August for a junior mathematician post. He could take the exam at Middlesboro, Kentucky, just on the other side of Cumberland Mountain from his home. Why not go over there and see how well he could do?

At this point—it was the summer of 1929—Rowlett's life was complicated by the need to make some fundamental decisions. His father wanted him to take over the family store, but "slinging those feed bags was too much work"; life was bound to hold better things than that, especially for a young man who was a mathematician, a chemist, a physicist, and a Latin major into the bargain. And he also wanted to get married. In any case, he was perfectly agreeable to taking the Civil Service test. What harm could it do?

Rowlett was married on Friday, September 13, 1929, just a little more than a month before the market crash, and was offered a job teaching chemistry and mathematics at Rocky Mount, a Virginia county-seat town farther east in the Blue Ridge foothills. The pay was small, no more than enough to support one person in minimal style, and his bride ended up with her own teaching job two hundred miles away—a state of newlywed affairs that could hardly be called satisfactory. In the ensuing months came two government telegrams, each offering work for three or four months. Evidently the results of the exam he took before his marriage had been satisfactory. But even without the stock market crash, it would not have seemed a prudent idea to give up a regular job for a temporary one, and Rowlett stayed put.

In March 1930 something different happened; a telegram arrived bearing the offer of a permanent job at a respectable salary. Rowlett's principal looked up from reading the wire: "What's a . . .a cryptanalyst, Frank?" Rowlett could only shrug; he had never heard the word either. He telephoned his wife. The offer of $2,000 a year sounded fine to her, too, but . . . what kind of job was it? Rowlett still did not know, but before making the call he had spent a little time with the dictionary. "Cryptanalyst" was not in there, but "crypt" of course was, and anybody could tell you what *that* meant. After the World War, as Rowlett knew, the United States had established a number of military cemeteries in France; accounting for all those bodies must raise statistical problems. His new job, therefore, would likely have something to do with the Graves Registration Service. But whatever it was, it was bound to be better than what he had.

HE CLIMBED TWO flights of stairs, went through double doors, and found himself in a very large room, perhaps sixty feet wide. A briskly efficient woman took charge of him as soon as he gave his name, helped him fill out a number of forms, and without any frills swore him into the service of the United States. Then a man of about fifty, a civilian in a blue suit, approached the desk. He had caught Rowlett's attention by the way he walked, swinging his arms in cadence with his footsteps and at the peak of each swing clapping his hands; characteristically, Rowlett, who liked to find a mechanical analogue for everything, tried to think of some machine the man resembled.

"Who's this?" the man asked the head clerk. She introduced Rowlett, explaining that he was the first person to come to work for Mr. Friedman. The man nodded, then crooked his finger: "Come with me, Rowlett," and swinging and clapping, off he went through a half-door into another office, occupied by a man neatly dressed in a light gray suit. Introduced as Major Crawford, this man had an easy and pleasant manner; his eyes seemed to twinkle behind the glasses he wore.

"You and two others will be working under Billy Friedman's direction," Crawford told Rowlett after the first man had left. "It should be interesting." He explained that it was a new project, that Friedman was the army's senior cryptographer, and that cryptography was now being centralized. "Your being hired," he said, "is the most significant step so far." The room held three desks, and Crawford pointed to one he said would be Rowlett's.

The major handed him the morning's *Washington Post*. "Billy will be here soon to explain things to you," he said, and stepped out of the office, leaving Rowlett alone. The room was plain, simply furnished with the desks, a table in one corner, and two file cabinets in another. The doors were slatted, like café doors, as though to combine privacy with ventilation; there were four steel-framed casement windows, all in a row. In one wall was a formidable steel door, like those in banks, with a combination lock; Rowlett stared at it, wondering what sort of valuables might be piled up behind it. Nearby hung a small sign: THINK. What in the world was this enterprise all about?

After half an hour or so, spent alternately in reading the paper and in speculating about the shape his fate might take, Rowlett heard the twangy voice of the man with the swinging arms, and in a moment in he came, accompanied by a man of middle height, neatly dressed, almost dapper. Everything about him seemed precise, even his tiny mustache. This, Rowlett was told, was Mr. Friedman. Friedman apologized for not having been on hand when Rowlett had arrived. Then he smiled. "Well, you're the first one of three young men, all mathematicians, who will be junior cryptanalysts."

"What am I going to be doing, Mr. Friedman? Please tell me," Rowlett said.

Friedman must have thought his new arrival was, rather prematurely, asking for a full rundown on his duties; and he said, "Why do you ask?"

"Well," Rowlett said, "I've asked several people what a cryptanalyst is. No one knows, and the dictionary didn't say."

Overcoming his astonishment, Friedman explained. The word "cryptanalyst" had only been in use a few years, he said; its adoption by the Signal Intelligence Service (SIS) was its first official employment anywhere.

"Are you familiar with Edgar Allan Poe?" Friedman asked. "'The Gold Bug'?"

"Yes."

"Did you ever try to break a code message yourself?"

"No."

"We'll soon change that."

Saying that he had some material for Rowlett to read, Friedman went over to the steel door. Shielding the combination lock with his body, he twirled the knob back and forth; the door clicked open, and then, with a key, Friedman opened an inner steel door. Could Rowlett read French as well as German? Yes, he said, he could. Presently Friedman emerged from the vault with two books in French and two in German, and having launched Rowlett on the reading of them he went off to attend to other duties.

Rowlett first tackled a compact volume, *Die Geheimschriften und die Dechiffrirkunst,* a nineteenth-century work by one Friedrich Kasiski. Enciphering and deciphering—so that really was what it was all about! He quickly found his reading to be "more like fun than work," though penetrating the author's densely expressed thoughts demanded some real effort.

About four o'clock, Friedman popped back into the office. "How are you getting along, Rowlett? How would you like to translate Kasiski?"

After receiving something less than an enthusiastic response, Friedman took the books back into the vault. Polite leave-takings were exchanged: "Good night, Mr. Friedman." . . . "Good night, Mr. Rowlett."

The young man's first day in the service of the U.S. Army Signal Intelligence Service was over. He returned to his temporary residence, the house of a cousin who was originally from Jonesville, fourteen miles from Rose Hill.

II

A DECISION THAT could have been made in no other country of the world had produced the crystallization of the Signal Intelligence Service in 1930. The American declaration of war on Germany in 1917 had, in spite of reluctance deep-seated in the national character, thrust the United States officially and thoroughly into the main current of world affairs. The deaths by battle of 50,000 young men and the wounding of 200,000 others, and the financial bill—$32 billion in dollars of the day,[6] an enormous cost for a year-and-a-half's participation in the war—had dramatized in blood and treasure the extent of the American involvement. Certainly the British and French casualties were far higher, proportionately as well as in total numbers for each; the United States had come in late, though decisively. As an element in this American involvement, on the urging of a bumptious and enormously clever young Hoosier named Herbert O. Yardley, the army had created a cryptologic service, designated MI-8, in the Military Intelligence Division. Certainly the United States would not wish to be wholly dependent on her allies for cryptographic intelligence, far more important now than ever before because of the development of radio—and, besides, the possession of such a service was one of the identifying characteristics of a modern great power, like the possession of howitzers and battleships.

But it was after the war was over that Yardley was to know his special moment. First, struggling against the push for disengagement and demobilization, soon to be unforgettably characterized as "normalcy," he played a large part in the creation of a successor organization to MI-8, to be funded jointly by the State and War Departments. On a wartime mission to London he had been inspired by the "power, tradition, and intrigues" of the British cipher bureau; clearly, "MI-8 in Washington must not die at the close of the war."[7] The United States could not hope to find her way in the new postwar world if she had to proceed haltingly, blindfolded, while other countries at least sometimes could see where secret paths were leading. Yardley was strongly, and usefully, supported in his fervor by the director of U.S. military intelligence, the splendidly named General Marlborough Churchill.

Since the United States had never mounted such an un-American, old-worldish operation in peacetime, the snooping would have to be carried out in the deepest secrecy, out of sight of most of the politicians as well as, of course, all of the public. For oddly legalistic reasons, the office could not be based in Washington; it therefore opened shop in a four-story brownstone just off Fifth Avenue in New York, a location that brought with it the advantage of being more than two hundred miles from Capitol Hill and its perennially issue-hunting occupants. The operation was known to initiates as the American Black Chamber (the term "black chamber" having had a long, if not necessarily honorable, history in European intelligence circles).

Yardley's moment came in 1921. He and his fellow gnomes of the Black Chamber had made an all-out assault on Japanese ciphers, with such success that at the Washington Naval Conference, called to discuss the limitation of naval armaments, in dealing with the Japanese "the American negotiators were essentially in the position of knowing the other side's stand completely," as a U.S. cryptanalyst later said; it was "like playing a card game with your opponent's cards visible to you."[8] Secretary of State Charles Evans Hughes had to do little more than sit back and wait for the Japanese representatives to offer the compromises he had already read about in their telegrams from Tokyo. The outcome of the conference was regarded by all the diplomats as a triumph for American diplomacy.

The Black Chamber worked energetically throughout the 1920s, attacking the codes of countries, large and small, around the world, from El Salvador to the Soviet Union. It moved from the brownstone to a midtown Manhattan office building, where it presented itself as a regular business firm dealing in commercial codes; Yardley was president of this venture, which actually did provide services to some corporate clients.

Brilliant and innovative, Yardley worked with zeal, sparing neither himself nor his associates. But, in some eyes at least, he was working more for Herbert Yardley than for the United States. He was a hedonist, openly devoted to gambling and girl friends, and a third of the appropriations for the Black Chamber went to pay his salary. Yet, however much grumbling there may have been, it was not rivals and malcontents who brought Yardley down. Nor did his personal failings figure in his fall.

In 1929, when President Hoover assumed office, he installed at the State Department a veteran public servant, Henry L. Stimson, who had been secretary of war under President William Howard Taft and, later, governor general of the Philippines. All his years in government—and on Wall Street, where he had been a partner in Elihu Root's eminent law firm—had not made Stimson jaded and cynical. He was brought up with strong principles, and he had remained a figure of probity. When Yardley, seeking the new secretary's favor—as it was not unreasonable to do—caused him to be sent an impressive bundle of Japanese decrypts, the reaction was disastrous. It was Stimson's first intimation of the existence of such an activity, and he was aghast: why, this was as bad as cheating at cards! His feelings were immortally summed up in the dictum he later uttered: "Gentlemen do not read each other's mail."[9] Favoring, instead of sneakiness, the "principle of mutual trust"[10] in international affairs, he ordered State Department funding of the Black Chamber brought to an end, and since State had furnished more than two-thirds of its budget, that was the remarkable end of the Black Chamber itself.

But it was not the end, even temporarily, of American codebreaking. For one thing, there were the navy's activities. In 1924, a Communications Intelligence Organization had been established in the Code and Signal Section of the Office of Naval Communications. It was given the name Research Desk, a designation that was intended to serve as a cover name. It was also literally accurate, the organization consisting at first of only Lieutenant Laurance F. Safford, a lean, young New Englander whose last previous assignment was as skipper of a mine-sweeper based at Manila. Safford sat at a venerable desk in room 1649 of the Navy Building, and four civilian helpers were also authorized by the founding order. Safford was a good chess player but no cryptographer. He was, however, addicted to tinkering with gadgets. Soon—revealing that he was a man of vision and energy—he began pushing in two directions. The navy must set up a chain of intercept stations in the Pacific, where it could eavesdrop on the Japanese, and in Washington it must recruit, train, and put to work a team of crypt-analysts. The latter would have something juicy into which they could sink their teeth, because a few years previously American agents, including naval-intelligence operatives, had broken into the Japanese consulate general in New York and photographed an Imperial Navy codebook; cracking the ciphers used with the code would be a fine first assignment for Safford's cryptanalysts. In the hallowed American tradition, the army and the navy observed the tightest security with respect to each other. As far as the army was allowed to know, Safford's Research Desk might as well have been on a different planet whirling about its own sun; and for its part, the army was less likely to reveal to its sister service than to anybody else that such an enterprise as the Black Chamber existed.

There was also, as an American code-breaking activity, the army's immediate response in 1929 to the Stimson crisis. When the director of military intelligence had managed to convince himself that, incredi-bly, the Secretary of State meant exactly what he said, he sought out the chief signal officer. Cryptanalysis must continue, Stimson or no Stim-son; therefore, G-2—military intelligence—and the Signal Corps must get together; G-2 would contribute the money that had previously gone to the Yardley Chamber, and the Signal Corps, which was quite openly and legally concerned with the making of codes and ciphers, could develop a new and less-public line of work. Secrecy, of course, was absolutely vital; if the Secretary of State got wind of the new cryptanalytic activity, he might well use his considerable influence to see that it was put out of business before it got started.

On July 19, 1929, a small group of men—three Army officers, one civilian—met in the office of the chief signal officer to discuss and plan the "organization of the Signal Intelligence Service, consequent upon taking over the Code and Cipher Solution and Secret Ink Services"[11] from the Military Intelligence Division; that is, the new service would consist of a consolidation of the Black Chamber with the Code and Cipher Compilation Service, which the Signal Corps had been operat-ing, as required by law, throughout the 1920s.

Who was to take charge of this new, consolidated service? It was clear who was *not* wanted for the job. The ranking officer at the meeting proposed that a definite offer be made to Herbert Yardley "at a salary considerably below his present." Yardley would be told that he could bring with him from the Black Chamber any associates he wished but that they would all have to get along within a total budget for salaries of $10,000 (Yardley's pay alone had been $7,500). The offer would surely be rejected, "in which case this office is free to go ahead and reorganize from the very bottom, with no entanglements from the past."[12] Unfortunately, as is common in disputes that have a factional quality, the disciples would suffer with the master; none of them would be called to Washington. The collective experience of ten years was thus tossed away.

One of the persons least grieved to see Yardley go, and most active in hurrying him on his way, was the lone civilian at the July 19 meeting, William F. Friedman. Since 1922, Friedman had been head of the one-man band called the Code and Cipher Compilation Service, in the Office of the Chief Signal Officer. His official duty had been to create codes and ciphers for the use of the U.S. Army, not to crack the secret traffic of foreign powers. But even before Secretary Stimson's decree, he and other Signal Corps personnel concerned with cryptology had looked to the kind of consolidation that took form in the July 19 meeting—a consolidation that would rid army cryptology of the flamboyant, credit-hogging Yardley and his independent operation off in New York. Although officially a codemaker, Friedman was a cryptanalyst at heart, one already renowned in the field through his writings, and he was to take charge of the new service.

As Frank Rowlett was to do in his turn, Friedman had entered the world of cryptology without having any such intention. The child of Russian Jewish immigrants, he grew up in Pittsburgh, and after flirting for a time with the unlikely idea of becoming a farmer, he went off to Cornell to study genetics.[13] In 1915 he was hired, fresh from graduate school, by one of the most colorful entrepreneurs of the day, "Colonel" George Fabyan, who operated a variety of laboratories and experimental facilities on his estate, called Riverbank, some forty miles west of Chicago. What the colonel had in mind was for Friedman to apply his knowledge as a geneticist to improving the mating selectivity of the Riverbank stock of fruit flies. But it happened that Fabyan was a committed member of that large and seemingly perpetual band of obsessives who believe that the plays traditionally ascribed to the hand of William Shakespeare were in fact written by somebody else; the colonel was an adherent of the Baconian school—a belief that suggests his lack of acquaintance with any of the works of Francis Bacon. So enthusiastic a believer was Fabyan that he maintained at Riverbank a cryptological department whose members were supposed to read and reread the plays in a concentrated search for Baconian ciphers, clues that would reveal the true authorship of the Shakespearean canon. It quickly grew into a case of fascination by association, Friedman becoming more and more involved in the cryptological work.

With the United States having just entered the world war, the Riverbank cryptologists found themselves concerned with more pressing problems than the hidden whereabouts of Baconian signatures in *The Tempest* and *Macbeth*. Cryptanalysis was so little practiced in this country that anybody who presided over a stable of code-breakers naturally came into great demand. Not only did Fabyan begin providing cryptanalytic services at the request of various government agencies, but Riverbank also became a training center for army officers who were to be transformed into cryptologists. During this period, Friedman, whom the colonel placed in charge of this pioneering school, wrote a series of training manuals on ciphers and methods for their solution, manuals that actually were original works of cryptanalytic theory and practice. In 1918 he took this experience to France, where he served as a lieutenant in the Code and Cipher Solving Section of G-2 at American Expeditionary Force headquarters.

After the war, having fallen out with Fabyan and his Baconian obsession, Friedman accepted an offer to work for the government, compiling codes and ciphers. During the twenties he wrote, devoted much attention to technical developments related to enciphering machines, represented the United States abroad and viewed the activities of Yardley and his Black Chamber with longing and frustration. And he waited.

At last 1929 came. The creation of the Signal Intelligence Service, combining the making and the breaking of codes and ciphers—cryptography and cryptanalysis—represented the fulfillment of a dream. Even if it had been necessary to act as if the two activities were separable, they were so closely related that living apart could not constitute a satisfactory arrangement. They had to be combined if the United States was to protect herself and her interests. The Stimsonian view of international affairs, with its "gentlemen" and its "principle of mutual trust," might not yield the field quickly, and certainly would not do it publicly, but a long first step had been taken into the real world.

The real work, however, had just begun. One of the director's first tasks would be to acquire persons to staff the new service. What precise form the organization would take would have to be seen in practice, but the planners did suggest the hiring of "four young men," who by definition would be utterly inexperienced, since Black

Chamber alumni were not being sought. The young men should, the planners said, "be college graduates or equivalent," and "they should form good material for commissioning in the Signal Reserve";[14] their salaries, together with that of a cryptographic clerk, would exhaust the G-2 contribution. Friedman knew, or soon decided, that he wanted men who combined mathematical proficiency with knowledge of languages. Cryptanalysis—this was where the emphasis of the service would lie—being, essentially, a statistical procedure, dealt with numbers, but the medium was words. Where to find these paragons of promise? The director decided to try the established federal hiring procedures. Civil Service examinations were regularly given in various fields; persons were hired on the basis of test scores, which were published in a register available to the different bureaus and agencies. Anyone needing an employee in a particular specialty could pick from the top three names listed in the register for that category. When he was ready for his young men, Friedman decided, he would go to the listings for junior mathematicians. Each person he hired would be a top scorer who also had a good knowledge of a foreign language; the director would take care of teaching him to be a cryptanalyst. In March 1930, at Friedman's instruction, the Signal Corps began sending telegrams of notification. The first one went to Frank Rowlett.

III

AFTER A WEEK spent in reading about codes and ciphers, Rowlett came to the office on the following Monday ready for more of this scholarly routine.

"Now," Friedman said to Major Crawford, "since Mr. Rowlett is going to be working in the vault, I think he should start today. Let's show him what's off-limits." He led Rowlett inside and pointed out some cabinets and a table that he was to have nothing to do with. "Do you understand?"

Rowlett understood.

"Billy," Crawford said, "leave the door open for ventilation . . . and so you can keep an eye on him."

This was secrecy indeed . . . a long way from the Graves Registration Service.

On the following Thursday, April 10, the second of the "young men" arrived. Rowlett was introduced to a short, slender New Yorker, notable for a pair of "cheery and twinkly eyes."[15] This was Abraham Sinkov, a math teacher in the New York City school system. Sinkov, it turned out, had taken the Civil Service examination for junior mathematicians, with the idea that it might lead to a good job with the Census Bureau, but when the Signal Corps offered him an appointment as a cryptanalyst he thought that sounded interesting—though he "had no awareness of what kind of thing this would be." In about ten days Sinkov was followed by an intimate friend of his from high school, undergraduate days at CCNY, and graduate school—Solomon Kullback, who had a "happy face"[16] and could have been taken for a football player. With these three, the team now had an abundance of mathematical capability and adequate strength in German, French, and Spanish (Rowlett, Sinkov, and Kullback, respectively). But the director still had a big problem, one on which the Civil Service register gave him no help. Where was he to find a potential junior cryptanalyst who was fluent in Japanese? He would have to leave a spot open, while looking and hoping.

Near the end of his first month Rowlett received his first biweekly paycheck: $83.33, only about eight dollars less than his monthly wage as a teacher. Immediately, he hurried out and rented a one-room, Murphy-bed apartment on New York Avenue, within walking distance of the labyrinthine Munitions Building at Twenty-First and B Streets, NW. Now his wife could join him and, as a bonus, he could go home for lunch sometimes and thus escape the unimaginative austerities of the navy cafeteria.

As the depression deepened, austerity become the norm in the office. So shrunken did the budget become that the young cryptanalysts sometimes had to furnish their own scratch pads and penny pencils. Once they had to take a temporary cut in pay. Later, when for a time the money completely dried up, they were forced to go on a month's unpaid leave. It was springtime, and Rowlett and his wife simply took a vacation down on the farm. The "little bull market" on Wall Street that was being talked about his first day on the job had long since had its own crash.

Aside from the economic problems, however, the SIS was a scene of harmony. Friedman impressed Abe Sinkov as a "fine administrator, besides being a splendid technician," and the group "got on very pleasantly together."[17] The director was not a man to whom one related in a casual fashion; he was "Billy" only to his superiors, like Major Crawford, and his peers, but never anything other than Mr. Friedman to his staff. Friedman's writings of the Riverbank period and the twenties served as the textbooks for the small and highly specialized graduate school of which he was dean and sole professor. "It was essentially a kind of problem-solving session all the time—not greatly unlike dealing with mathematical problems."[18] The training materials described cryptographic systems and presented suggestions about attacking them for solutions. The students learned to develop techniques and analytical procedures for approaching particular types of problems. They learned, as well, that though the basic techniques were completely scientific, depending on systematic analysis, there were times when they would have to call on guesswork and hope for a flash of inspiration.

One muggy morning in late June, after his team had been working for a little more than two months, Friedman, like the Pied Piper, led the young men out of their quarters and through a maze of corridors and stairways to room 2742 of the Munitions Building. There he pulled a card from his pocket, read it, and then began working the combination lock on the heavy steel door; Rowlett, Sinkov, and Kullback looked on, fascinated. What was the director up to? After he opened this door, he produced a key for the lock on the inner steel door and swung it open with a flourish, revealing nothing but a pitch-dark area. Friedman next struck a match, located the pull cord of a ceiling light, and yanked on it. The junior cryptanalysts saw that they were standing on the threshold of a room about twenty-five feet square, crammed with filing cabinets arranged back-to-back in double rows, with barely enough room between them for the drawers to open. Turning on more lights, summoning his young men inside, and closing the door, Friedman said solemnly, "Welcome, gentlemen, to the secret archives of the American Black Chamber."[19]

The American Black Chamber? Trying to look appropriately awed, the young men stared around the dusty room. None of them had ever heard of the Black Chamber. But now, they quickly found, they were going to learn everything there was to know about it; their assignment was to organize and catalogue this array of files. They were to begin, Friedman told them, by trying to locate all the information they could about German army field ciphers and Japanese diplomatic codes and ciphers. Then, in the way they had come to know, he left them on their own, saying that he would be back by lunchtime.

Yardley's files were dazzling. To Rowlett, "King Solomon's mines could have offered no greater treasures." The three young men soon lost all track of time, hypnotized by the decrypts of German field ciphers from 1917 and 1918, the worksheets that had been used in the cracking of Japanese high-level messages and the translations of these messages, as well as copies of codes and ciphers from other countries around the world. When Friedman came back he found "three sweaty and grimy but nonetheless starry-eyed junior cryptanalysts. Kully had a dirty streak across his forehead. Abe's shirt was spotted with smudges of dust and soaked with perspiration," and Rowlett's own "brand-new pin-striped trousers were no longer white; they were a dirty mess." But nobody cared; they now saw where the work they were entering on might—no doubt, *would*—lead.

Studying his grimy staff, the director suggested that they clean up and go to lunch. And he added a wry comment. Now they could see, he told them, "what a dirty business cryptanalysis is."[20]

IV

THERE WAS ANGER and dismay in the office of the Signal Intelligence Service. Less than a year after the revelation of the Black Chamber files, Herbert Yardley was claiming fresh attention, this time on his own initiative. Leading off the April 4, 1931, issue of the *Saturday Evening Post,* the country's most popular weekly magazine, was the first of what was to be a series of articles on codes, ciphers, invisible inks, the whole secret business, by no less an authority than the former head of the American Black Chamber. And among the secrets given away was, of course, the very fact of the existence of American cryptanalytic activities. Crawford and Friedman were grim.

And that was not the worst of it. On the first of June appeared a book by Yardley containing the material in the articles (one article had yet to be published) and more sensational disclosures than any that had appeared in the magazine. The incredible chapter fifteen was called "Japanese Secret Codes"; it was followed by others, complete with translated telegrams, giving the whole story of the Black Chamber's eavesdropping on the Japanese negotiators in 1921. How the Japanese cryptographic chiefs would react to Yardley's revelations was obvious. Any success the SIS had won with Japanese ciphers could now be forgotten. It was back to the starting line again.

The Signal Intelligence Service did, in fact, by this time have a Japanese capability. It had come in an odd manner. Try as they might, Friedman and Crawford had been getting nowhere in their search for a young man who knew Japanese well—in a functional, useful way—and also had mathematical talent and training. Another criterion had been that the person be a clearly loyal American, and since no kind of security-clearance procedure existed to show which Japanese-Americans were devoted to the United States, this meant, in practice, that the person must be Caucasian.

One day in early May 1930,[21] Crawford received a caller in his office—Congressman Joe Shaffer, of the ninth district of Virginia. The congressman had approached the secretary of war, who had passed him on to the chief signal officer, who in turn had sent him to Crawford. He understood they were looking for somebody who knew Japanese, Shaffer said (word had a way of getting around, however secretive you tried to be), so he had come to tell them about his nephew. The major listened politely as his caller expatiated on his nephew's linguistic knowledge; that, after all, was what you did with congressmen. No one knows whether Crawford was aware of the literal meaning of "nepotism," but after Shaffer went on his way Friedman and Crawford, conferring, agreed that the congressman was undoubtedly trying to use the suggestion of political muscle to land a good job for his nephew.

But Friedman said all right, he would talk to the boy, whose name was John Hurt. The interview was not promising. Far from being a mathematician, Hurt said, he hated the subject. He had dropped out of the University of Virginia after twice flunking trigonometry; when it came to math, he was, unquestionably, "a complete washout."[22] As for the linguistic side, Friedman, who had no knowledge of Japanese, reserved the right to be skeptical, but just because he had said he would, he sent Hurt to see a G-2 Japanese specialist, Maj. Harry Creswell, the compiler of a Japanese-English military dictionary. A while later Creswell appeared in Crawford's office.[23] He had quizzed young Hurt thoroughly, he said, and even if the boy *was* a congressman's nephew he had the most remarkable knowledge of the Japanese language of any non-Japanese he had ever met.

"He's unbelievable. He's fluent in conversation, he can read both forms of the written language, and his vocabulary is fabulous." Looking at Crawford squarely, Creswell said, "Dave, if you don't hire him, I'm going to."

"But what about math?"

Forget it, Creswell said. "You'll never find another fellow like this one."

Yet Hurt had never been to Japan. As a boy in Wytheville, Virginia, a mountain town a few counties east of Frank Rowlett's home, he had lived next door to a returned missionary family named Patton; out of interest in the unusually bright lad, Mrs. Patton undertook the remarkable project of teaching him Japanese—and, more remarkably, the project was an absolute success. The boy was simply a natural linguistic whiz, although later he never seemed to find himself in college, attending both Roanoke College and the University of Virginia, but not graduating from either. His time on campus was hardly squandered, however. Each year at Charlottesville he roomed with a Japanese student and thus refined his knowledge of the language, although his major was French, which he learned thoroughly, well enough to compose poetry in it; he also acquired a good knowledge of German and became respectably acquainted with various other languages. He was a lively, rather strange fellow, witty, and in many ways destined to be the exotic plant in Friedman's orderly hothouse. Clearly he was a priceless addition to the team (at a salary of $1,800 a year), even without any competence in math. At Friedman's request, he began teaching his colleagues the rudiments of Japanese; Japan, the director explained, was to be the number one priority of the SIS.

DURING THEIR FIRST two years, a period neatly halved by the publication of Yardley's revelations, the young men made substantial progress, turning, in fact, from potential cryptanalysts into the real thing.[24] They were working primarily on hand-cipher systems, called tables. The Japanese seizure of Mukden in Manchuria in September 1931, with all that this move signified of the ascendancy in Tokyo of military over civilian influences, gave new urgency to cryptanalytic efforts directed against Japan. This was not so, however, in the thinking of the State Department, which, at least cryptologically speaking, seemed to regard the Japanese sword-wielders as nothing more than gentlemen in uniforms; their mail was still to be inviolate. So well were the members of Friedman's team developing their skill and so great did the possibilities of their usefulness seem that in October the chief signal officer put in a request for four more slots in the SIS; but the depression-squeezed budget would not allow for it. In any case, the fact that stood out with respect to Japan as 1932 advanced was that Yardley had chanted the requiem not only of the old secrecy but of the old ciphers. The Japanese, it was obvious, were now using electrically powered machines.

This was not welcome news to the cryptanalysts of the U.S. Army and Navy, but neither was it shocking. For almost twenty years now, the electromechanical enciphering machine had been casting its shadow before it. In 1915 a Californian named Edward Hebern had designed what he called an "enciphering device," consisting of two electrically driven typewriters hooked together by twenty-six randomly connected wires; plaintext typed on one machine came out ciphertext on the other. Although this was indeed a pioneering development, in itself it was nothing that would have baffled a cryptanalyst for long. But within a few years Hebern had complicated the device by adding a series of intricately wired rotors through which the current flowed. The effect was to scramble the original plaintext message in quite a complex fashion. It was the invention of these "code wheels" that moved mechanical cryptography into a new dimension. Similar work was independently being carried on in the Netherlands and Germany, leading, in the early 1920s, to the development of the cipher machine called the Enigma. This machine, the manufacturer believed, would have a great commercial future, since it could enable business firms to transmit trade secrets by radio to overseas branches in what appeared to be unassailable safety. But when the Enigma was put on the market, it attracted the eys of others besides businessmen. Among those showing an interest was Billy Friedman, who, working through the U.S. military attaché in Berlin, obtained a model for study by the Signal Corps.

The Japanese, it was clear, had now been attracted to code-wheel encipherment. If the fact that they had advanced to the use of machines was not shocking to Friedman and his associates, it nevertheless meant that a new era in cryptanalysis had arrived, and that new kinds of efforts would have to be added to the old. For high-level communication, hand ciphers were now dead. It had become a machine age, around the world.

2

Enigma with Red and Purple

I

ALTHOUGH IN THE early and middle 1930s the U.S. Signal Intelligence Service was not exclusively concerned with Japan (Abe Sinkov, in fact, was beginning to work on Italian ciphers, and Solomon Kullback on German), the expanding, increasingly militaristic Empire of the Rising Sun was by far the most proximate source of possible conflict; Orange, as U.S. planners code-named her, seemed to be trying to burst out of her skin. Even so, the attack on the new Japanese diplomatic cipher system,[1] which its users called Angooki Taipu A (Cipher Machine, Type A) did not have top priority in the SIS office. The army had at least equal concern with the development of American cipher systems. But in 1935, when the army intelligence chiefs realized that, properly exploited, the traffic on Cipher Machine, Type A, could enable them to listen in on Japanese negotiations with Germany and Italy concerning a tripartite treaty, the SIS team was ordered to make the decryption of Japanese diplomatic messages its first concern.

A more in-house concern, expressed by Friedman, was that the habit of referring in talk and official reports to the Japanese system as the "A Machine" represented lax security. Picking up the color cue, after some discussion, the SIS team chose the first color of the spectrum as a cover name, and Type A became the Red machine. Friedman assigned Frank Rowlett,[2] the most mechanically inclined of his group, and Kullback to the task of breaking the Red machine, with Johnny Hurt as their linguistic associate.

A similar device to the Red machine, used by the Japanese navy, had been a preoccupation of U.S. navy cryptanalysts, but not, unfortunately, of their chief organizer and inspirer, Lieutenant Safford, who no longer presided over the Research Desk. He had spent three years back in Washington, but the inexorable navy pendulum—working as mechan-

43

ically as a grandfather clock, completely unconcerned with this man's unusual personal qualities and achievements—swung him back out to sea, leaving the navy team without its leader. The road to promotion, it was true, did not, in either of the services, pass through the slough of secret intelligence,[3] but it perhaps represented a bit less of a detour for the army than for the navy. For the admirals, the only operative word was "deck," never "desk"; but the army, as well as the navy, considered intelligence (of the military, not the cerebral, variety) to be of little importance, compared with training in leadership.

Friedman's team had had to work with its own kind of handicap. One day, distressing news had come. Johnny Hurt, hitchhiking back to Washington from Wytheville after a visit to his family, had been found, in a state of collapse, by the side of the road. He had suffered a severe hemorrhage of the lungs—from tuberculosis. He would have to spend some time in the hospital, and, when he got out, he would be no better than convalescent for an unforeseeable period. How to parry this blow of fate? Where could a replacement be found? Certainly no other congressman was likely to have a suitable nephew; that bizarre recruitment source had seemed like a miracle, but, like most miracles, it was a one-time affair. Friedman and his team conferred, and the young men said that they believed Hurt to be so valuable that if he could work part-time—half days, maybe—they would be willing to take on his routine duties among themselves.[4] Friedman agreed.

While Rowlett and Kullback were studying groups of intercepts that had been encrypted on the Red machine, Friedman discussed the project with the head of navy cryptanalysis at the time, Cmdr. Joseph N. Wenger.[5] Wenger told the army cryptanalyst that the navy had been successful in its attempts to break into Japanese naval machine cipher, but he would not provide any details, either of the system or of the techniques that had solved it. Friedman wondered who was his adversary, the Japanese or the navy? Fortunately, his team did not wait for the navy to give answers to the problems raised by Japanese machine encipherment; paying close, analytical attention to the telegrams, the team discovered that the system used two sequences, enciphering vowels and consonants independently—a vowel for a vowel and a consonant for a consonant. Proceeding from this point, divining the overall pattern that governed the mechanical advancement of the sequences, Rowlett and Kullback began recovering Japanese plaintext. Friedman was delighted; his disciples had solved a cipher machine they had never seen, solely through making good use of analytical principles on intercepted messages. And perhaps they were to be most congratulated for having demonstrated "that the Signal Intelli-

gence Service does not need cryptanalytic assistance from anyone"—
not even the U.S. Navy.

Thus, after switching its priorities, the SIS team had triumphed.[6] The
staff of the office had expanded since its beginning days. The director
had made "special arrangements for the assignment to the office of a
couple of Signal Corps officers, to be trained in cryptographic work."[7]
The first of these officers was Lieutenant Mark Rhoades, who came in
1931 for a year's training but stayed a further year; then officers began
coming in pairs. Among them were Capt. Harrod Miller and Lieut.
Preston Corderman, the latter later becoming an instructor in this new
school for cryptographers and cryptanalysts.

In 1935, the far-flung network of radio interception stations foreseen in the 1929 memorandum began to come into being. Rhoades
went off to the Philippines on this mission, followed during the next
year by Sinkov to the Canal Zone and Kullback to Hawaii; the role of the
SIS men was "to assist in collecting material and providing it to
Washington."[8] Rowlett, with Japanese ciphers his prime assignment,
stayed in the Munitions Building. Even with its increasing success,
however, the SIS was woefully understaffed. In May 1936 the navy had
some forty persons involved in cryptologic work, the SIS only seven or
eight. In spite of pleas from Friedman, the budget makers held the line;
of course, the director was hardly in a position to buttonhole the fiscal
authorities and tell them what wonderful work his boys were doing.

II

PARALLEL WITH THE efforts of the SIS, wonderful work was also being
carried out in Poland by a young mathematician, Marian Rejewski,[9] and
a group of associates who were attacking the Enigma cipher machine,
which had been adopted by the German Army. This group proceeded
in much the same careful, laborious manner as the American team, and
it received valuable help from French intelligence, which was given
technical information by a German traitor working in the *Chiffrier-
stelle*—the cryptological service. A series of rendezvous had begun
between a French team headed by a shortish, plump intelligence
officer, Capt. Gustave Bertrand, and the informer, whom the French
knew by the code name of Asché. These meetings were held around
the periphery of Germany, as close as possible to the Reich, because
Asché, a working bureaucrat, only had the weekends off, and the
French thought it pointless for him to spend any of his limited time in
traveling needless miles. For Bertrand, those special weekends began
with "departures from Paris in the evening, in a taxi, across the city

through the neon lights to the gare du Nord or the gare de l'Est."[10] The meetings would take place in high-class hotels, complete with cocktails and dinner. The important work would be done in a bathroom, with Bertrand turning the pages of a sheaf of documents while his photographer clicked away. Bertrand would then take the material to Warsaw, where it was turned over to the head of the Polish Cipher Bureau, Maj. Gwido Langer, a roly-poly man who looked like a cheery chef.

What Bertrand gave the Polish Cipher Bureau was a group of documents, including the *Gebrauchsanweisung,* or operating manual, complete with drawings. Other material included the *Schlüsselanleitung,* a list of instructions for setting the machine, and some sets of daily keys (machine settings).

The machine described in the Asché documents was, in appearance, quite similar to the commercial Enigma,[11] with a typewriterlike keyboard and, instead of keys themselves, a second set of twenty-six letters painted on small round holes lit by flashlight bulbs. The rest of the machine, the guts of it, was a series of mazelike pathways through which an electric current from a battery pursued its way from the depressing of a letter on the keyboard to the lighting up of one of the little lamps. Copying down the illuminated letters as they appeared would give the cipher team the encrypted message to transmit. These pathways constituted the enciphering elements of the Enigma. The most important of them, certainly the most characteristic, were three removable rotors and one stationary wheel of the same size; all four were lined up behind the light panel. Each of the rotors had a serrated metal circumference so that it could be moved by hand, and to each was attached a movable ring bearing the letters of the alphabet. Inside each rotor, which was made of hard rubber of the kind once used for combs and buttons, was a jumble of tiny wires connecting, in random fashion, twenty-six metal contacts on one side of the disc with twenty-six protruding metal pins on the other. These pins would move as the ring with the letters of the alphabet was turned.

When the cipher clerk hit a key, the current would flow through the three rotors, linked by the pins and the contacts, to the stationary wheel (called the *Umkehrwalze*), which served as a reflector sending the current *back* through the three movable wheels; it thus passed twice through each jumble of wires and once through the reversing wheel. The intellectual challenge so far presented by the Enigma, then, was the nature of the connections of the wires inside those wheels. It was not a problem to be tackled by the faint-hearted, since the number of possible differently wired rotors was equivalent to factorial 26

(26!), or 403,291,461,126,605,635,584,000,000, and the number of possible different *Umkehrwalzen* was 7,904,853,580,025.

For Rejewski, of course, these calculations were less than elementary, but the numbers were certainly awesome. Naturally, the Germans would not wish to produce all of these drums, or even very many of them, since the machines had to be able to talk to each other, which meant that during a given period of time their rotors and *Umkehrwalzen* had to be identical. So the operative question was this: Out of all these almost limitless possibilities, what had the Germans actually done?

But there was much more. Since the three rotors could be removed, their arrangement could be shuffled. And before sending any message, the Enigma operator would have to set his machine, which meant that he would have to pick a starting point for each rotor. He could turn the rotor he had placed in the right-hand slot so that *B,* for instance was on top, and then move the middle rotor to *X,* and set the third at *L.* The total number of possible settings was 26^3, or 17,567, a number that, when multiplied by the six different possible left-to-right arrangements of the three rotors, grew to 105,456.

The specifications of the Enigma contained yet another feature—a small panel that looked like a miniature telephone switchboard. This plugboard, which had not been a feature of the commercial versions of the machine, could be connected by patch cords to the keyboard and the series of rotors; several pairs of letters were provided for in this aspect of the Enigma. The current that was set in motion by the hitting of a key went first through the plugboard, then through the three rotors to the *Umkehrwalze,* back through the rotors, through the plugboard again, and finally to the light panel. A further factor was that the movable wheels did, in fact, rotate. When a key was pressed, the first rotor advanced one position, and so on; after twenty-six advances had brought it to a complete rotation, the second wheel then began advancing, and in due course the third rotor went through the same process.

All in all, the Polish team appeared to be confronted by a fiendishly difficult problem. The Germans seemed to have thought of everything to frustrate hostile eavesdroppers. No one could doubt that they felt quite secure with their modified Enigma—a machine-age triumph.

Like any other cryptanalyst, Rejewski would study a message carefully and patiently, drawing on his mathematical knowledge to treat it as a problem in statistics, searching for parallels, repetitions, and other patterns that might be revealing. Special attention would be paid to the beginnings and endings, which, consisting of call signs, titles, formalized closings, and the like, would tend to involve far more repetition from message to message than would the actual body of the message itself. Before he had tried to go very deeply into the messages themselves, Rejewski had paid close attention to the beginnings and endings, and simply by looking through sheafs of telegrams he had come to realize that the first six letters of a message were of particular importance.

The concept of "key" was, indeed, the key here. It was obvious that a German cipher clerk would have some sort of instructions, or key, for setting his machine each day; if the machine was in fact the Enigma, the key would include the arrangements of the rotors, the setting of each, and any other factors (Rejewski at this point could not be sure of the details). But beyond this daily key, Rejewski had seen that the German operator used another key, an individual message key, changing for each message, and it was this key that he found in the first six letters of each. His breakthrough came when he realized that the key consisted of three letters—rotor positions, obviously—but that the German procedure called for enciphering it twice. This was a grave mistake on the Germans' part. If the operator had decided on, say, *BJQ,* the ciphertext might be *LVC,* if the key was enciphered only once; enciphering it again, so that the eavesdropper had three more letters to work with—*DXP,* for instance—was equivalent on the Germans' part to leaving a small door open into their secrets. Rejewski would know that whatever they were, the first and fourth cipher letters stood for the same plaintext letter, and the same for the second and fifth and the third and sixth. It was a beginning.

After combining the first information brought by Bertrand with his own previous insights, Rejewski, within a few days, managed to divine the wiring (the internal hookup of the twenty-six pins to the twenty-six contacts) of one rotor. It was one that had been in the right-hand position for the encipherment of a group of telegrams, and, within a few weeks, he had solved all three rotors and the *Umkehrwalze.* This breakthrough gave BS-4, the German section of the Cipher Bureau, enough knowledge to build its own Enigma (or, in practice, to take apart and rewire a commercial model). Rejewski's success seemed to have an almost foreordained quality, coming as it did just a few weeks before Adolf Hitler took the oath as Chancellor of the German Reich on January 30, 1933.

Although Rejewski's solving of the connections inside the rotors was his greatest accomplishment, it did not yield immediate success. Victory had to await a nonmathematical insight, one having to do with so seemingly simple a matter as the arrangement of the letters of the alphabet. In the commercial Enigma, the letters on the keyboard went *QWERT,* and so on, like those on any ordinary office typewriter; there was every reason to suppose that the keyboard of the military Enigma was arranged the same way. Since the commercial model had its keyboard wired into the rotor sequence in the same QWERT pattern, Rejewski took it for granted that this was also true of the military machine, but as long as he worked on this assumption be produced no results—only gibberish and extreme frustration. What was the trouble? Perhaps his whole approach was wrong, and he had not really solved anything, however promising his efforts seemed to have been. Then came a gleam of an idea, which he decided to consider even though he actually had very little faith in it. Had the Germans switched for the military Enigma to alphabetical order for wiring the keyboard into the enciphering elements, as if it were arranged ABCDE instead of QWERT? Testing this hypothesis brought quick and surprising results. It was exactly what the Germans had done.

The Polish cryptanalysts now had the equipment and the understanding to read German messages enciphered on the military Enigma. But this triumph did not mean that the battle of the ciphers had once and for all been won. Aside from any other problems that might come up, what the cryptanalysts would face in the ensuing years was the recurring puzzle presented every twenty-four hours by the change in the daily keys.

The Polish team enjoyed consistent success until the autumn of 1938, when the Germans introduced changes in the rotors and in the ways of setting the machine. The Poles had to find some method of checking rotor and plug positions at high speed. Rejewski's solution was to hook a number of Enigma machines together, with added features, and whirl them through their paces. The resulting creation, consisting of six linked machines, was christened the *bomba* by Jerzy Rozycki,[12] a member of the team. The title was suggested not by an explosive device, but by an ice cream treat that Rejewski and his colleagues were enjoying when the idea first arose. Successive modifications by the Germans began to produce such complex problems that the frail, understaffed craft of BS-4 was swamped. In the summer of 1939 as war approached, Gen. Waslaw Stachiewicz, the Polish chief of staff, ordered Colonel Langer to invite British and French intelligence officers to a meeting in Poland.[13] It was time to share the Enigma secret, successes and failures alike.

DILLWYN KNOX, A member of a family that included the editor of *Punch* and the distinguished Catholic convert Monsignor Ronald Knox, was a veteran of the famous world war British naval code-breaking operation known as "Room 40," and he had continued after the war on the staff of the Government Code and Cipher School. In 1931 he had suffered a broken leg in a motorcycle accident and walked thereafter with a limp; he was also plagued with stomach problems. In 1936 he had been on the point of retiring from GC&CS: He wished to return to Kings College, Cambridge, where before the world war he had been a fellow, studying Greek literature, but he had agreed to stay on in government service and take charge of an important new project—the British effort to break the German Enigma. His success had been limited, and even in the summer of 1939 it was hard for him or anyone else in England to believe that the Poles might really have succeeded where the British had made little progress. The Poles?

Now, unlikely as the whole thing was, came an invitation from Warsaw. Commander Alistair Denniston would go, and Knox with him. What would they find? It was a puzzling question. Certainly Knox would have been incredulous had he been told that in Poland he would learn a fact that would make him absolutely furious. He might have anticipated something on the order of mild surprise, but hardly anger.

On July 24, the British party flew into the Polish capital, where they met the French representatives, Bertrand and Capt. Henri Braquenié of Air Force intelligence, who had come by train. Bertrand, as the old Warsaw habitué, took it on himself to create a convivial atmosphere; on the first evening, he escorted the British group to a leading restaurant, the Crystal. During the evening, Denniston maintained a professional detachment, and Knox appeared "*froid, nerveux, ascète,*" saying little. The conviviality, what there was of it, was all on the part of a naval officer who had accompanied the British delegates and managed to stuff himself with the excellent food and far more than enough liquor.[14]

The next morning, the foreign representatives were taken to Pyry, a spot a few miles south of Warsaw, where for some time now the Poles had lodged their cryptanalytic center in a bombproof concrete shelter—"the house in the woods"—hidden in a dense forest. Langer was awaiting his guests at the foot of a flight of dank steps. One member of the British group, present in addition to the official cryptological representatives, was introduced as Professor Sandwich, a mathematician from Oxford. The professor was described as an observer who would not participate in the technical talks. Why had he taken the trouble to come at all? The British were evasive, but this "observer" displayed a quietly military manner and little knowledge of mathematics. He appears to have been no university don, but Colonel Stewart Menzies, holder of the Military Cross won as a Guardsman in the world war and deputy head of British intelligence (in fact, owing to his superior's serious illness, Menzies was acting head of the service). The chiefs of British intelligence, whether or not their technicians were "omniscient," were taking this unprecedented meeting with unprecedented seriousness. No one could know whether war would break out soon, but few doubted it; even a dubious venture like this foray into Eastern Europe ought not to be passed up.

The host showed his visitors into a room where there reposed a Polish-built Enigma; the switch was thrown, and the machine proceeded to put on a dazzling performance, flashing lights, one by one, proclaiming the decryption of a ciphertext. Bertrand was amazed. Whatever he may have suspected during the years of his cooperation with the Poles, he had been told only the previous evening of their success in actually building such a machine, and it was his first look at an example of it. Denniston and Knox were "speechless, and it was there that, perhaps for the first time, the pride of the British experts collapsed in the face of the results achieved by the Polish experts."[15]

The French officer did not know that Knox was speechless for another reason as well. For a year now this bald and bespectacled classical scholar, the very paradigm of the rumpled and remote academic, had been grappling unrewardingly with a problem that had to be solved if he and his team were going to crack the Wehrmacht-model Enigma: How was the keyboard of the Enigma wired into the rotor sequence? What was the order of the letters? It was the exact problem confronted—and, in the face of his doubts, solved—by Marian Rejewski at the beginning of 1933. And here, right in front of Knox, sat the maddeningly simple answer: ABCDEF ... Knox was furious. "It was a swindle, not because he had failed to solve it, but because it was too easy. Games should be worth playing. The keyboard was, it turned out, not a significant factor at all."[16]

At lunch the British cryptanalyst was still so put out that he was unable to enjoy the meal,[17] which was taken at the promisingly named Restaurant Bacchus. The best he could do by way of conversation was to utter a few quiet groans. Again, as during the previous evening, the day was saved for British conviviality by the naval commander, who this time managed to stow away enough of the restaurant's offerings to make himself sick.

Aside from his childish pique, Knox, along with Denniston, was enormously impressed by what the Poles demonstrated. Besides the Enigma, remarkable enough in itself, there was the *bomba*. There were also stacks of perforated sheets, devised primarily by Henryk Zygalski, the third of the young men, which could be piled on a light table in such a way as to give clues, through the illuminated gaps, to the new individual message keys used by the Germans. It was clear that the difficulty faced by the Poles was not nearly so much with their ideas as with the need for time, equipment, and trained people to take advantage of them. At this meeting in the little house in the woods, the men of the Cipher Bureau "told everything we knew and showed everything we had";[18] thereby, they offered a challenge to the British and the French, with their far greater resources of manpower and material.

EARLY IN THE evening of August 16, 1939, a dapper figure in a dinner jacket, with the rosette of the Legion of Honor in his buttonhole, stood waiting on the platform at Victoria Station. Colonel Menzies was on his way to dine, but he had made this stop in order to give a personal greeting to a foreign acquaintance, who was arriving with some highly unusual baggage. The Poles, making a gesture of a sort rare in the annals even of friendly relationships among nations, were turning over one of their precious Enigma machines to the French and another to the British; Major Bertrand, who had been given custody of both, was himself bringing the British machine across the Channel; he also carried detailed drawings of the *bomba*.

Within little more than a month of delivering the Enigma goods to their Western allies, the men of BS-4 saw their country—put to flames by a German blitzkrieg, encroached on more quietly by the Soviet Union, and divided between the two dreaded powers—disappear once again from the map of Europe. Fortunately, Marian Rejewski, Jerzy Rosicki, and Henryk Zygalski all escaped to France.

III

THE RED MACHINE, once Rowlett and Kullback had broken it, had proved to be an open faucet. Hundreds and hundreds of diplomatic messages poured in, overwhelming the handful of linguists available to the SIS. But, as everyone realized, some of these signals might be of high significance; they dealt not only with the treaty negotiations with Germany and Italy but with every other aspect of Japanese foreign policy. Japan was the rising adversary in the Pacific. Important messages must not be lost in the flood, but how was it to be prevented?

The solution that was adopted was highly logical and commonsensical and, so far as is known, without precedent in American annals. Laurance Safford, fortunately, was back in Washington now[19] (he had been ordered ashore again in May 1936 to be director of the Navy Department Communications Intelligence Unit) and more inclined than most officers toward interservice cooperation. The army and the navy agreed to work together, share the burden, and let each other in on some of their secrets—a decision that, in truth, represented something of a sacrifice for the navy, which "always recognized that its proper targets were the major navies of the world."[20] Diplomatic systems were a side issue. The agreement provided that the "Navy would decipher and translate all messages originating on odd calendar days and the SIS would deal with messages originating on even calendar days."[21]

Shocking as it no doubt would have been to many veterans of each service, had they known about it, the approach was put into practice, and it worked. It was even applied to the translation of any manually enciphered messages that were intercepted, though interception itself and cryptanalysis—cracking of the key for the day, the preliminary to decryption—remained separate.

But triumphs in cryptanalysis, it was already clear, tend to be impermanent. As in any other branch of military science, offensive and defensive weapons exist in a dynamic relationship. In the realm of hardware, today's stockpile becomes tomorrow's junk pile; in intelligence, today's answer will not often fit tomorrow's question. It was, therefore, with no pleasure but with no great surprise that late in 1938 American code-breakers saw Red Machine decrypts "giving the authorization for travel for a 'communications expert' named Okamoto, in order that he might put into service certain cryptographic paraphernalia termed by the Japanese diplomatic offices as the Type 'B' cipher machine."[22] The new machine was to replace Type A in all the important Japanese embassies, including Washington and the chief European capitals. The Red machine was thus confessing to Rowlett and the other American listeners its own obsolescence for the highest level purposes.

In March 1939 the SIS team was handed the first intercepts in the new Japanese cipher language, which received the code name Purple. Within a month, it became clear that all the important diplomatic traffic had changed color, and a deeper color was appropriate, since it was the designation for what was quickly seen to be a deeper mystery. Purple was not only a new machine, it was radically different from Red. Techniques of analysis that solved Red cryptograms were only about 25 percent effective with the complex new cipher.

As a student of the electromechanical principles that applied to the cryptographic process, Safford was fascinated and piqued by the new machine the Japanese were using for diplomatic messages, but the navy, in fact, had its hands full with Japanese—one could not at this point say enemy—naval ciphers. As 1939 waned with no real progress toward cracking the Purple machine, the navy, perhaps deciding that the mystery was beyond solution, switched the cryptanalysts who were working on it to the analysis of Japanese naval intercepts. The move was made without any consultation with the army team, the navy's contribution to the attack on Purple being limited from this point on to its continuing intercept coverage of the Japanese Far Eastern diplomatic net.

By this time some problems had arisen between Friedman and his team. For one thing, in a flawless demonstration of the working of the Peter principle years before that notion received its name, Friedman had been turned into an administrator, and he was sometimes remote from the technical work of the office. This evolution had already been under way when the Red machine was the object of SIS concern. Aside from the lessening of the return on Friedman's technical talents (although not a mathematician, he was blessed with a cryptanalytic flair, as was Dillwyn Knox, the classicist, in England), this was perhaps no tragedy. But Friedman had become increasingly moody and diffi-cult, and he appeared self-conscious about sometimes not being able to grasp what he was told about the work of the group.[23] Whatever it was that disturbed him made the ordinary office dealings take on an unforeseeable complexity.

The Purple machine presented enough complexity of its own. By this time the Americans were veteran sophisticates when it came to applying analytical principles to ciphers so as to be able to infer the wiring of the rotors, or code wheels. But three-quarters of Purple continued to be shrouded in midnight black. Rowlett, who was chief of the Purple team, would go home after the day's work, sleep for a while, awake sometime around two o'clock, and call up to his mind's eye the day's worksheets, going over them, looking for an opening, a gleam of light—and sometimes spotting one. A worksheet from Genevieve Grotjan, a junior cryptanalyst, offered one such breakthrough during office hours.[24] And late in the summer of 1939, a concept crystallized. Rowlett told Friedman that he needed a particular kind of device; fine, Friedman said, put Leo Rosen on the problem. In a few days Rosen, who was an electrical engineer, came in with a new kind of design, based on the use of stepping switches of the type employed in an ordinary telephone exchange.[25] Rosen's proposal led the army crypt-analysts, after some reflection, to the conclusion that the Japanese had, indeed, not used rotors in the construction of their Purple machines, but had done the job with such telephone switches. Still, it took about a year for the SIS team to develop enough analytic information to enable them to design a machine, based on the use of stepping switches, that could actually decipher Purple intercepts. Once the design was completed, around Labor Day, 1940, creation of an operational machine took only a few days. In putting the device together, the wiring team worked fourteen-hour days, building and testing the banks of stepping switches, each one of which demanded more than five hundred different soldered connections. Then came the moment when the machine was plugged in. Contrary to legend, it neither hummed nor crackled, nor did it throw sparks. But there on the table before the American team was a cipher machine that might, or might not, look like the Purple machine in the Japanese embassy over on Massachusetts Avenue—or those halfway around the world in Tokyo—but that was capable of doing exactly the same work.

Without ever having seen a Purple machine or any part of one, the Americans had created their own. Friedman and Rowlett sought out General Mauborgne, who had been the chief signal officer since 1937 and was a pioneer in radio intelligence and a driving force behind the work of the SIS. They wanted permission to reveal their success to the navy. It was important, they felt, that navy cryptanalysts be made aware of the cryptographic concepts that had been uncovered and the analytical techniques that had been developed in the successful attack on Purple. By all means, agreed the general.

Friedman telephoned Safford, inviting him in a more or less casual way to come by the office the next morning. When the commander arrived, he was led into a room with a table on which sat an object covered with a black cloth. They had something to tell him about Purple, Friedman said; they'd done some work and were ready to share the results. Then Friedman turned the floor over to Rowlett, who stepped to the table, grasped the black cover, and lifted it from the machine. Safford's lean face was tense; his eyes seemed to pop.

"My God! Where'd you steal it?"

Friedman turned a bit lofty. "We built it ourselves."

"Unbelievable!"

Rowlett now switched on the machine. Safford, intently watching and listening, "exuded praise from every pore." He was amazed, he said, that the SIS team had succeeded in breaking such a complex cryptographic system, and he was greatly impressed by the quietly efficient electromechanical performance of the reconstructed model in front of him.[26]

The scene was the perfect counterpart of the little drama staged in the house in the woods outside Warsaw, just a bit more than a year earlier. But now, not only had Poland been destroyed, but the Low Countries and France had fallen, and the British, bracing for possible German invasion, were fighting the supreme battle to save their skies from the Luftwaffe. The United States might soon find herself alone in a malevolent world. Solving the mysteries of Purple had been a matter of the highest importance.

As Rowlett conducted Safford back down the hall, the commander was shaking his head all the way.

SO WONDROUS WERE the results of the efforts against the Red and the Purple machines, and so arcane were the processes by which they had been achieved, that General Mauborgne developed the agreeable habit of referring to his cryptanalytic team as "magicians"—from which came the U.S. designation of intelligence produced by cryptanalysis as "Magic."[27] In Safford's later view, "the army's solution of the Purple machine was the masterpiece of cryptanalysis in the war era."[28] And welcoming this masterpiece in September 1940 was the new Secretary of War. In office barely two months, the veteran statesman Henry L. Stimson now believed that gentlemen should read any useful mail they could get their hands on; "the world was no longer in a condition to be able to act on the principle of mutual trust."[29]

3

Courtship

DURING THE SUMMER of 1940, after France had collapsed like a balloon under the skillful thrusts of the German panzers, American policy makers and military planners had taken a new look at Great Britain. No longer did the United States have the French army as the first line of defense against the Nazi barbarism; that role had fallen to the embattled island, whose army had left its weapons on the Channel coast at Dunkirk. Could the British stand up against all-out air attack? Would they be able to resist an attempted invasion? Was it in the true interest of the United States to send any of her very limited war materiel across the Atlantic to help a Britain that might soon follow France into defeat?

President Roosevelt deeply believed that the answer to each of these questions was yes, but he nevertheless deemed it desirable to get a private, expert opinion. In line with his fondness for personal "eyes and ears" observers functioning outside the official structure of government, he dispatched a New York lawyer and World War I hero, William J. Donovan, to England to take a hard-headed look at the situation and also to try to establish liaison with British naval intelligence. Whoever he was, Donovan, in the circumstances, would surely have been warmly received by his transatlantic hosts because he bore, if not gifts, at least the possibility of gifts; but, beyond that, as Bradley Smith has observed, "his focus and apparent restraint impressed the British, who customarily had trouble getting the words 'Yank' and 'restraint' into the same sentence."[1]

When he returned home early in August, Donovan reported that the Royal Air Force would win the battle with the Luftwaffe, though it would certainly be a close-run thing, and that sending war supplies to Britain would, indeed, represent for the United States an investment in her own security. Besides that, he had reached agreement with Vice Adm. John Godfrey, the British director of naval intelligence, that cooperation between the two countries with respect to naval intelligence was both desirable and possible. The sealing of the famous "fifty-destroyers deal," developed in detailed correspondence between Prime Minister Winston Churchill and President Roosevelt, followed Donovan's mission. Earlier, emblematic of his own faith in the British, the president had approved the dispatch to England of half a million U.S. Army rifles that had been stored in cosmoline since 1919. The relationship between the two leaders and the two countries clearly was becoming unique: they acted like a pair of allies, with the difference being that only one was officially at war.

By this same summer, a number of leading British scientists had become convinced, in the words of C. P. Snow, that "there were overwhelming arguments for telling the American scientists the whole of our radar and other military secrets"[2]—this at a time when the British lead in radar was proving itself against the massed attacks of Hermann Göring's imposing plaything, the Luftwaffe. "Nearly all the English scientists agreed—Cockcroft, Oliphant, Blackett all pressed the matter. Nearly everyone else disagreed."[3] For one thing, said the dissenters, American security simply could not be trusted. The United States had no Official Secrets Act; newspapers could print whatever they chose and get away with it, and, besides, Americans talked a lot. Others suggested that it would be a one-way bargain. What did America have to offer?

But, led by Sir Henry Tizard, for many years the scientific adviser to the Air Ministry, the scientists won their case, or a great deal of it—which actually meant that Churchill agreed with them, although not without some reservations. A scientific mission would be sent to the United States; Tizard himself would lead it.

Tizard arrived in Washington on August 22, as it happened just before the Purple team worked its magic. He spent a month and a half in the United States, meeting with civilian officials, army and navy officers, and scientists. In the nature of things, he spent time with General Mauborgne, who throughout his entire career had been involved with the military applications of radio, particularly with respect to aircraft.[4] Whether or not their first meeting was intended merely as a formality, it did not turn out that way, Tizard noting that the general "got interested and went on until lunch time."[5] After this long and detailed talk, General Mauborgne promised a full interchange of information with the British.

Cryptology was nowhere mentioned in the record of this conversation, or any other that Tizard held, nor did he have any known mandate to discuss the subject, though it was, of course, one of the general's prime concerns, as well as an early personal interest. But in view of the purpose of Tizard's trip and of the backgrounds of the two men, it is not unlikely that some mention, however broad, was made of the work of the two countries in this field in relation to the contemplated full exchange of intellectual goods. No one knows this, but many believe so.[6] What *is* known, however, is that Tizard and those who came with him found a great many Americans able and ready to talk scientific business. New lines were established, new connections made, and it was certainly Tizard who threw the switch that started the cooperative current flowing. The partnership thus created was capable of taking all sorts of shapes, some foreseeable, some not.

The satisfaction over the results of the Tizard mission was not universal. Just as there had been Britons who were skeptical of the worth of any exchange with the Americans, so there were Americans who returned the compliment. The officer corps of the U.S. Army and Navy had, at all levels, men who were constitutionally antipathetic to England—"by nature," as Gustave Bertrand once said of the hostility between the Poles and the Czechs. In addition to these anglophobes, some officers were so focused on the Pacific that they feared the weakening effects in this critical arena of any pull toward involvement in Europe; Hitler posed no real threat to the security of the United States, whereas Japan was an imminent menace. Why should we fool around making deals with the British?

This, however, was not the opinion of the officers at the top, of the Chief of Staff, Gen. George C. Marshall, and of the Chief of Naval Operations, Adm. Harold R. Stark (who was known to his intimates, lamentably, as "Betty"). Even before Sir Henry Tizard began his conversations in Washington, these commanders had dispatched their own observers to the big show in Britain. Although they were given little in the way of precise instructions, the American observers would see for themselves just how well the partner the United States seemed to be acquiring was bearing up under the onslaught of the Luftwaffe. They would enter into informal conversations with representatives of the British Chiefs of Staff. Three officers—Maj. Gen. George V. Strong, Maj. Gen. Delos C. Emmons, and Rear Adm. Robert L. Ghormley—sailed on August 6 aboard the liner *Britannic* on "what was supposed to be a secret mission; two days later the ship's radio picked up a news broadcast announcing the mission."[7] It is to be hoped that Sir Henry, not to mention the scientists who were skeptical of American security procedures, never heard of that particular lapse.

Head of the army planning staff, General Strong, a sixty-year-old native of Chicago, did not enter on the mission as any glowing optimist. On June 17, the day after Marshal Philippe Pétain had accepted the premiership of France and shocked the civilized world by telling his countrymen that it was "necessary to try to end the fighting,"[8] Strong had sent General Marshall a memorandum recommending radical changes in U.S. policy. He advised including no further commitments to send supplies across the Atlantic, in "recognition of the early defeat of the Allies."[9] The Chief of Staff found this conclusion a bit premature. Now in August, with Britain still in the struggle, still uninvaded, with the great air battle at its height (Göring's all-out offensive began two days before the arrival of the American party), the British Chiefs of Staff talked not of defeat but of future strategy, making it plain as they did so that in formulating their plans they were "certainly relying on continued economic and industrial cooperation of the United States . . ."[10]

A former cavalryman, General Strong cultivated a gruff, old-soldier style with a facial expression to match. But behind the facade was a listener who was willing to be convinced. Not only should the United States continue to supply Britain, in fact, but matters ought to be more thoroughly organized and better coordinated. And Strong, agreeing that a periodical exchange of information between the two governments would be desirable, "thought that the time had now come when this exchange of information should be placed upon a regular basis."[11] The general's principal negative reaction to the situation he found in London seems to have had to do with the lack of good food at the Dorchester Hotel, which had suffered from a bomb hit. In compensation, the U.S. military attaché, Colonel Raymond E. Lee, took him one evening to a restaurant that was yet untouched, where the general dined on pâté de foie gras, filet of sole, and roast pigeon, accompanied by a bottle of Pommard and postprandial Armagnac. Somewhere between the pâté and the brandy, a bomb exploded just outside the restaurant, but dinner was not interrupted.[12]

At some point in the autumn, London was made aware of the triumphs of the Washington Purple "magicians." Who did the telling and to whom is a matter for debate, but it is reasonable to assume that the information was not conveyed, as one officer opposed to sharing the information put it, through the medium of Strong and Ghormley "blabbing the secret all over London."[13] Whether it was blabbed or discreetly whispered, the news that the Americans could now read the Japanese diplomatic cipher, on which the British themselves had made no progress, was of profound interest to the British, with their great commitments around the Asian arc from Hong Kong to India.

II

IN LATE JANUARY 1941 HMS *King George V* arrived off Annapolis, Maryland, on her maiden voyage, bringing with her the new British ambassador to the United States, Lord Halifax. President Roosevelt did the Englishman the signal honor of sailing out to meet him (though some who knew FDR well suggested that the President was "impelled by an irrepressible desire to have a good look at the new battleship.").[14] Before KGV, as she was called, weighed anchor for her return trip, she took on four Americans as special passengers: Abraham Sinkov and the engineer Leo Rosen from the Signal Intelligence Service, and two young navy communications officers, Lt. Robert H. Weeks and Ens. Prescott H. Currier. One notable person was missing from the group: the chief cryptanalyst of the SIS, Col. William F. Friedman. In November the United States and Great Britain had reached a general agreement to establish cryptographic cooperation (the British used "cryptographic," not "cryptanalysic," as the explicit label for the decrypting of messages sent by the other side). Once it was decided that a technical mission ought to be sent to England, Friedman was appointed to lead it, and in December he was put on active military duty for the purpose.[15] But just after New Year's his prickliness, depression, and suspicion of others combined to produce a nervous collapse; his subordinates had "no real awareness of what caused those problems,"[16] but they did not appear to be connected with the work— although the push to solve Purple had been a strain for everybody involved in it. Instead of going to England, Friedman went to Walter Reed Hospital.

The chief cryptanalyst's being ordered into the hospital resulted in the taking of the first steps toward his retirement from the Army Reserve, a move that could have led to a bureaucratic tangle niggling enough to delight the most punctilious paper shuffler. Because Friedman would now be a civilian, and because the mission was, of necessity, going to travel on a British ship, the chief cryptanalyst would be unable to make the trip—even if it should be postponed—since the law at the time forbade American private citizens to travel on the vessels of belligerents.

Application of the law also meant that the persons who did go on the mission would have to be in uniform; Sinkov thus became a reserve captain. The official mechanism making the whole enterprise possible was the appointment of Sinkov and the others as assistant attachés, military and naval, to the U.S. embassy in London, and they were provided with diplomatic passports.

Frank Rowlett, as the senior of Friedman's "young men," would stay home in charge of the office, a role he often filled. Besides, the Chief Signal Officer felt that Rowlett's involvement in cryptographic labors —the devising of American ciphers—was so important that he should not leave it.[17] If the United States found herself engaged in the war as an active belligerent, she would not only need a greatly increased production of aircraft and tanks and shells, she would in the same way need many new codes and ciphers.

As seems to have been the pattern with American missions at the time, Sinkov and his fellow officers had been told nothing about the high-level negotiations that had led to their trip, nor had they been given any detailed information about what they might expect to see and hear in England. They knew they were to keep their eyes and ears open, and they knew they were to deliver the package they took with them, a box making a cube about two feet on a side—for the Americans had not left Washington without a gift for their hosts-to-be, a gift that ensured their being eagerly awaited on the other side of the Atlantic.

It was a cold crossing. For almost two weeks *King George V* plowed through the wintry seas, making a far-northerly track to cut down the chances of encountering any U-boats, anchoring finally in Scapa Flow, the Home Fleet's desolate base in the Orkneys. Escorted off the battleship to two cars parked on the quay, the Americans were impressed by their reception. Waiting at the cars was a trim, "very smart-looking officer,"[18] introduced as Brig. J. H. Tiltman. So a general had made the trip to this spot, almost as far north in the United Kingdom as you could get, to greet a group of American junior officers. Not bad! Although Sinkov and his companions were, indeed, gratified by the courtesy, they were mindful, too, of the attractiveness of the package they had brought with them. The brigadier and the Americans and the box were installed in the cars, which transferred the party to another dock, where lay a Royal Navy destroyer that was to take them down the coasts of Scotland and England to the Thames.

Tiltman, it quickly became evident, was not simply an officer drawn out of a hat to perform a ceremonial function, although his unusual charm and affability would have made him an excellent choice for such duty. He was to be the Americans' working host during their stay and, despite the fact that he looked exactly like the layman's picture of the smartly turned-out British officer, suggestive of scarlet mess jackets and polo, he was a brilliant cryptanalyst—in a sense the dean of British cryptographers.[19] He was a veteran of Denniston's prewar Government Code and Cipher School, which was pretty much a British analogue to Yardley's Black Chamber and Friedman's Signal Intelligence Service, except that it was an interservice operation and it was under the administrative control of the Foreign Office. Although perhaps not greatly interested in their work, the Foreign Office had never doubted that most "mail" the cryptanalysts were reading was not written by gentlemen. Tiltman, who was in charge of army decrypting operations, was "probably the greatest expert on nonmachine ciphers,"[20] said an American liaison person, though he was given to remarking that "the machine age left me a little behind."[21] This bit of self-deprecation, however, did not mean that Tiltman was unable to appreciate the importance of the gift that Sinkov and the other members of the American mission had brought with them, or the significance of the fact that they had brought it.

In London, the Americans reported to their respective contact persons; the army representative was General Strong, who had returned to England as an observer. Sinkov handed the general a sealed envelope. Nobody had told him the contents of the letter inside, but he suspected that it, in effect, told the recipient that the group was on a very special mission and would be working with the British and that he need not concern himself about them: "He was to greet us and send us home."[22] That, at least, was what happened. Although Strong certainly knew about the Magic operation and may well have been the person who first told the secret to the British, neither he nor Sinkov and Rosen made any mention of it. After the meeting, the younger officers were returned to the charge of Brigadier Tiltman, who told them they would be leaving London right away, that same afternoon.

By the time the party got started, again in two cars—Sinkov and Rosen being assigned to one driven by a young Scot, an enlisted man—the short February day was drawing in. The blackout was total, and when darkness fell, the only light the driver had to go by was the tiny ray that escaped through the slit scratched in the paint over each headlight. All the road signs had long since been taken down, so that in the event of a surprise enemy airborne attack they would not supply the invaders with information about places and directions. Somewhere northwest of the city, the driver, who was rather new to his assignment and not very sure of his way, got lost. Stopping the car, he hailed a dark shape that was, indeed, a pedestrian. Just where was he?

No answer. The good citizen obviously had no intention of giving aid to somebody, Scot's burr or no, who might be a Hun in cunning disguise. A few minutes later, the same thing happened, or failed to happen, again. Finally, proceeding, the driver blundered into a fork in the road. Which way to go? The boy shook his head; he couldn't see far enough in the darkness even to have an idea about which route looked more promising. Some position for two American intelligence officers, crackers of most-secret ciphers, to find themselves in—helpless as children who have wandered away from their mother in Macy's. What ignominy! Or was it the British who should be embarrassed? They, after all, represented the heedless mother. Anyway, it was funny, whatever else it was.

The driver called out to a man walking nearby. Fortunately, the fellow did not seem to regard the young Scot as the possible spearhead of a German landing party, and, in answer to the driver's question, said, "Oh, it won't matter. You can go there either way." That was even funnier, and it turned out that it was literally true. Thus, the driver finally got his party to their destination, a country mansion standing in large grounds.

The following morning the Americans were driven a few miles through the countryside to another mansion that also stood in extensive grounds, but otherwise presented a very different picture. With soldiers guarding the fences and the lawns, it looked like a village of temporary military buildings. This was the Government Code and Cipher School at the town of Bletchley. The four visitors, the first Americans to be shown "the Park" and some of its wonders, were introduced to various members of the integrated army-air force-navy-civilian staff. The degree of this integration, though not one hundred percent, was striking, as it would appear to be to all the Americans who came after Sinkov and his group in later years. No doubt the high level of interservice cooperation seemed all the more remarkable when looked at in contrast to the dogged divisiveness with which the Americans had pursued their own cryptological—in fact, all of their military—goals, as witness the separate army and navy attacks on the diplomatic Red machine and the similar Japanese naval device. Only the navy's wish to devote all its efforts to later Japanese naval ciphers had made possible the single and successful effort on Purple. Perhaps the British were profiting from the fact that the athletic event of greatest interest to their generals and admirals was not an army-navy football game with all its encrusted hostilities more profound and more permanent than many of those waving banners and cheering realized. Or, as the military attaché Colonel Lee observed after taking

Admiral Ghormley to lunch, while the latter was in London in October 1940, "He is very agreeable and pleasant, but not inclined to express himself very freely on any subject except the weather."[23] At least, not to an officer of the other service.

Sinkov and his companions had not known what to expect at Bletchley Park; they were literally seeing for themselves. It was the first look by any Americans at the British most-secret cryptanalytic effort; Sinkov quickly decided that it "was a very efficient organization. It seemed to be doing quite a job."[24] But the main purpose of the mission, so far as Sinkov knew, was for the Americans as representatives of the magi in Washington to convey their gift, a Purple machine, to the British, and to demonstrate its abilities. If any other high-level agreements had been made and expectations raised, he had not been told of them.

Since Sinkov had not been involved in the work on Purple, he left the discussion of Magic to the other members of the team, spending a good deal of time with the British cryptanalysts working on Italian ciphers. And the Americans had "one or two occasions to listen to some of the cryptanalytic details"[25] with respect to the German Enigma, but this kind of presentation was essentially an account of some of the British achievements; "it was far from enough to enable us to get into the actual process of producing information."[26] So Sinkov and the others were, in a general way, made aware of some British successes, but they were not given any hardware to take back home in return for the Purple machine. Cryptological cooperation had been launched, and the Americans had given a notable earnest of good faith and good intentions. Were the results enough from the American point of view?

A number of persons in Washington felt not. The Purple machine was a rare achievement, a triumph that could turn out to be of vital importance to the United States and Britain alike. Surely the British ought to reciprocate in kind. And, in fact, were they not welshing on a deal that was supposed to see the Americans returning home with an Enigma machine and the knowledge to put it to use?[27]

If such an arrangement had been agreed to at some level, it may be that it was later repudiated at a higher level. In any case, the British were proving reticent. There were the old nagging questions about American security; besides, the work on the Enigma ciphers, however far it had progressed at this point, was a "most precious secret,"[28] and the United States was not yet, and might never be, actually in the war. To some Americans, the argument was academic. The United States was not ready to undertake her own work on the Enigma ciphers and, in fact, being in no armed confrontation with Germany, had little reason to do so. The most important point was for the two countries to move past a kind of first-date stage of restricted intimacy—for them not to engage in cryptological competition, but to think out and develop ways in which they could cooperatively use their resources to best effect. Another consideration was that the situation with respect to Purple was quite different from that of Enigma.[29] Given the blueprints and the wiring diagrams, the Americans had the people and the resources to build plenty of Enigmas, if and when the need arose. The British, on the other hand, were short of the materials required to build Purple machines, and their technical facilities were, in general, stretched tight. Those in favor of the movement toward a closer relationship with the British regarded the turning over of one or more Purple machines as representing no great sacrifice; ample parts were available and, now that the trick was known, a machine could be assembled in four days—at a cost of only about $1,000.

Still, however "regally treated"[30] the American party had been in the humming world of Bletchley Park, there had certainly not been anything that could be called an even swap.[31] Had a lid been put on the British revelations by Lord Halifax, who was still Foreign Secretary and, the official master of the Government Code and Cipher School, when the mission was agreed upon? Was it the First World War all over again, with the frank, open, and helpful Americans being bamboozled and having their pockets picked by the wily and sophisticated representatives of perfidious Albion?

The Americans and the British seemed to be edging into a common-law marriage, but, clearly, they were a long way from enjoying a honeymoon.

III

ON MAY 5, 1941, the Japanese ambassador to the United States, Adm. Kichisaburo Nomura, received a politely worded but shocking telegram from Foreign Minister Yosuke Matsuoka in Tokyo.

> According to a fairly reliable source of information, it appears almost certain that the United States government is reading your code messages. Please let me know whether you have any suspicion of the above.[32]

The messages referred to by Matsuoka were the traffic to and from Tokyo, first put into code and then enciphered by the Cipher Machine, Type B, the machine the Americans called Purple. Nomura fired back a message the same day, under "most guarded secrecy." "The most stringent precautions are taken by all custodians of codes and ciphers, as well as of other documents,"[33] he stiffly assured the Foreign Ministry, but he would, of course, investigate. Meanwhile, would Tokyo tell him what concrete details they had?

Two days later Matsuoka answered. Well, no, he had no specific details.

> This matter was told very confidentially to Ambassador Oshima [Hiroshi Oshima, the Japanese ambassador to Germany] by the Germans as having been reported to them by a fairly reliable intelligence medium; but to our inquiry they are said to have refused to divulge the basis on which they deemed it to be practically certain.[34]

The Germans, that is, had said all they were going to say. Presumably feeling that they had little practical choice, the Japanese conducted this exchange by means of this same Type B machine.

The truly horrified recipients of Baron Oshima's news were, of course, the cryptanalysts of the Signal Intelligence Service and its navy counterpart, no longer the Research Desk but now known as Op-20-G. Leaks were a constant problem in the intelligence business, ranging from minor indiscretions to outright treason. The strain imposed by the effort to keep oneself compartmentalized and on guard could be enormous (it might have been, for instance, that such a continual demand had pushed William Friedman into breakdown, exerting the kind of pressure that finds the weak spot in a metal bar and snaps it). Leaks of one kind or another, the specter of Herbert Yardley's performance perhaps chief among them, constituted the great continuing British fear when it came to turning secrets over to the Americans—as the latter by now had ample reason to know. But if the greatest of all U.S. intelligence secrets had somehow been handed over to the Japanese, this was potentially the most fateful leak in which Americans had been involved since that September morning in 1862 when a Union soldier lounging in a Maryland meadow discovered a fistful of cigars wrapped in a paper that proved to contain the entire disposition and operational plans of Robert E. Lee's army. The Union commander had muffed this miraculous chance to end the Civil War in a few days. Now, what use would the Japanese make of the report from the Germans?

After spending two weeks looking into the charges, the Japanese ambassador reported to Tokyo on May 20 that yes, the United States had, in fact, been reading some of the Japanese code messages.[35] Maddeningly, he failed to say how he knew, or which messages he meant. He would not trust that information to a cipher; he would send it by courier. This was appalling.

Meanwhile, the SIS, Op-20-G, and the FBI had been asking themselves, and each other, the same kinds of questions as were being put in
the Japanese embassy. Aside from the action of a traitor, the most likely
means of disclosure of the American secret was a carelessly handled
decrypted message, or the unwise use of the information within such a
message—with the content in one way or another catching the attention of the Germans. A piece of paper could itself have gone astray, or a
diplomat could have made a statement based on information that
could have come only from a Magic decrypt, and, depending upon who
his listener was, the news could have made some sort of circuit to the
ears of Baron Oshima in Berlin. The paper trail seemed to lead more to
the State Department than anywhere else; at least, a number of persons
there had access to Magic decrypts—more, it turned out, than were
supposed to—and, besides, weren't they the people who dealt with
foreigners all the time?

AT THE BEGINNING of 1941, the enterprising American commercial
attaché at the Berlin embassy, a Texan named Sam E. Woods, sent a
report to Washington outlining, with considerable precision, the
German plan of attack on Russia; he had learned it from a trustworthy
anti-Nazi German source. After weighing the matter, the U.S. government, through Undersecretary of State Sumner Welles,[36] had turned
Woods's information over to the Soviet ambassador. Anything to stop
Hitler, was the American thought; but the Russians, seeing what they
most wanted to see, deemed the American move a provocation, an act
designed to sow live enmity where they prayed to God none existed,
between Nazi Germany and Red Russia. There is every reason to
believe that they reported this American act to their German friends—
who could only have been stunned by the news (Hitler had emphasized in his original directive that "it is of decisive importance that our
intention to attack should not be known"). How had the Americans
found out the truth? One obvious possibility was that they had been
reading somebody's secret telegrams.

Or the course of disclosure was perhaps simpler. Undersecretary
Welles simply warned the Russians by showing Ambassador Constan-
tin Oumansky some relevant Magic material,[37] including Oshima telegrams from Berlin to Tokyo, and the ambassador proceeded to blow
the whistle, alerting the Germans—and thereby Oshima. If Welles
actually committed such a breach of security, it was—however pure
his motive—a supercolossal and inexcusable lapse on his part. From
the written record it is impossible to know for certain whether he was

indeed the security leak. (The record does show, however, that Joseph
Stalin had startling deficiencies as an evaluator of intelligence. In spite
of this American warning and the eighty-three others he received from
a remarkable variety of sources,[38] he was taken by surprise when the
Wehrmacht advanced into Russia on June 22.)

Friedman, who had returned to duty part-time, and Safford and their
cryptanalytic teams spent two fretful weeks waiting to see what the
Japanese were deciding. "*Some* of the secret codes": what on earth was
the ambassador talking about? Unhelpfully, Nomura offered no further
explanation. Earlier a message had come from the foreign minister,
containing strict orders for the admiral. He must "have only one man
use the special government code for the enciphering of important
dispatches. No telegraph clerks were to be called in to assist this
individual, no matter how overwhelming was the volume of traffic nor
how urgent the necessity for speed."[39] Was this to be all? As days
passed, it began to appear that it was. It was marvelous, incredible, too
good to be true. The Japanese were settling for Mercurochrome and
Band-Aids; they were tightening procedures, restricting access to the
ciphers, making sure that some obscure little clerk did not, through
accident or design, betray them. But they were doing nothing about
the real culprit, the Purple machine itself. They would go right on
using it. The sense of relief at SIS and Op-20-G was profound. The
Japanese could only have decided, and it would not be the first time in
the history of war that such a belief had been held, that their device was
perfect, impregnable, unsolvable. Whatever fault there was would be
found in a person, not in the machine. After all, they were using Purple
to discuss and analyze the whole security problem.

The American triumph was preserved—and a measure of American
credibility with it.

IT WAS CLASSICAL army doctrine that the process of intelligence consisted of three steps: collection, evaluation, dissemination. As regards
the collecting of information, the American cryptanalysts had shown
themselves to be unparalleled suppliers of secrets. But what about the
rest of the chain? What else did the Americans need to learn?

Certainly the happy outcome of the Oshima horror story did not
mean that everybody in Washington was satisfied with the handling of
Magic intelligence. The hunt for possible American leaks had turned
up some shockers. President Roosevelt's military aide and confidante,
Maj. Gen. Edwin M. Watson—although not the amiable bumbler his
nickname, "Pa," suggested—nevertheless had dropped a Magic sum-

mary into his office wastebasket as heedlessly as if it were yesterday's *Post,* and he had managed to lose another one entirely. At the State Department, violations of the agreed-upon procedures had themselves become standard procedure. To make sure that all his senior staff members had access to Magic decrypts and the summaries based on them, Secretary of State Cordell Hull had gone so far as to allow stencils to be cut so that mimeographed copies could be run off. (These senior officials, of course, included Sumner Welles.) Other lapses were equally unsettling.

After the alarms of May, particularly the revealed untidiness of Pa Watson, the army, remarkably, decided to handle this security problem by simply cutting off the already thin flow of Magic to the White House, on the alleged reasoning that since Magic involved diplomatic traffic, the whole thing was really not the president's business anyway but belonged to the Secretary of State.[40] Of all the conceivable tightening-up procedures, this was not only the strangest, but the worst: in the name of security, the professional military men were going to treat the president as just another civilian, with no right to inside information, thereby depriving him of any opportunity to develop a fingertip feel for what the Japanese were up to by listening to them talk. The navy, however, refused to go that far; it would still inform the White House, at least in a limited way, through the president's naval aide.

When, by radio, teletype, or airmail, the raw intercepts picked up by the listening ears of the army and navy arrived in Washington, they were decrypted by the SIS and Op-20-G, according to the odd/even-day formula (although this system was flexible enough to respond to special circumstances). After deciphering, decoding, and translating had produced an English-language version, the message was delivered by hand to army and navy intelligence officers, who first sorted out what they considered to be significant information and then themselves usually acted as couriers; these were not low-level duty officers, but specialists in Japanese language and affairs. On an army day, for example, Col. Rufus Bratton, the chief of the Far Eastern section of G-2 and "the War Department's authority on all Japanese matters,"[41] read all of the material, screened it, and burned the discards. As the traffic increased in late 1941, he began to require help. He and his aides then arranged the surviving material in separate piles, one for each of the recipients on the Magic list. Each pile was put into an individual cardboard folder, which was inserted into a leather briefcase that was then locked. The colonel himself now became a messenger, making the rounds of the recipients's offices with his bagful of Magic. Where possible, the security-conscious intelligence officers liked the client to read the message on the spot, ask any questions that occurred to him, and then hand the dispatch back; it was an almost foolproof way of ensuring that the telegrams did not wind up in somebody's wastebasket.

After the trauma of the Oshima revelation, security—strict physical security—clearly obsessed the handlers of Magic. A limited number of copies of messages, spending as little time as possible out of the hands of the intelligence officers, burned as quickly as they were reclaimed: this would keep the "great secret" safe. But the most effective evaluation and exploitation of the evidence could be made by persons who could read it and reread it, doing some ear-tugging here and some gazing out of the window there, riffling through last week's or last month's decrypts, calling up something from the files when an idea struck them, analyzing, comparing, sharing reactions with other recipients.

It was impossible to do any of this when you had to whip through a telegram and hand it right back to the officer standing there, breathing, waiting, clutching his briefcase with its dangling padlock. It was really impossible, as well, to do any of it even when you had the message in your possession for twenty-four whole hours, particularly when you had only a hazy idea of the other names on the list of recipients. But so precious was the secret deemed to be that its preservation was what received all the explicit attention; the users had to make do with the restrictions as best they could.

ON OCTOBER 9, 1941, Magic recipients were shown a request (made on September 24) from Tokyo to the Japanese consul in Honolulu.[42] Would he keep them informed about what ships were in Pearl Harbor and where and how they were moored? Other telegrams followed on the same subject. On November 19, Tokyo sent the first of a series of messages establishing a code (which became known as the Winds code), for use in daily Japanese-language shortwave broadcasts to alert overseas personnel in case of emergency.[43]

November 5 had seen the beginning of a curious series of "deadline" messages, relating to the current Japanese-U.S. negotiations being conducted in Washington and containing phrases like "it is absolutely necessary that all arrangements for the signing of this agreement be completed by the twenty-fifth of this month" and "the date set forth in my message . . . is an absolutely immovable one." When, nevertheless, the deadline was later extended four days, at the urgent request of Nomura and Kurusu, Tokyo told its ambassadors that "this time we mean it . . . the deadline absolutely cannot be changed. After that things are automatically going to happen."[44]

On November 28, the Japanese Foreign Minister pulled the plug: the negotiations had failed, the American proposal being regarded as humiliating. The message from Tokyo was ". . . however, I do not wish you to give the impression that the negotiations are broken off. Merely say to them that you are awaiting instructions . . ."[45] In other words, the meetings with Secretary Hull were to go right on, but they would be only a sham. On December 1 the U.S. translators produced a message,[46] intercepted the previous day, from Tokyo to Oshima in Berlin. The ambassador was to tell Hitler and Foreign Minister Joachim von Ribbentrop that negotiations between Japan and the United States "now stand ruptured" and that, in view of the break, "there is extreme danger that war may suddenly break out between the Anglo-Saxon nations and Japan through some clash of arms," and add that "the time of the breaking out of this war may come quicker than anyone dreams."

All of these messages, and scores more, had been decrypted, translated, put into the special briefcases with their padlocks, and taken from office to office to the recipients on the Magic list. "Quicker than anyone dreams" . . . "things are automatically going to happen" . . . "absolutely immovable" . . . *higashi no kazeame*: east wind rain—what did all this mean? Certainly this was talk among politicians and not the language of military planners (though most of the participants had military backgrounds), but "clash of arms" and other phrases were clear enough in their military implications. These expressions, though coming from only a fraction of the messages that were distributed, stood out from the mass. What did they imply? And what about the questions concerning the berthing of the Pacific fleet in Pearl Harbor? Other intercepts had shown that the Japanese were curious about other naval installations, too[47]—the Canal Zone, Manila, even Seattle and San Diego. Did the highly detailed questions about Pearl Harbor have any special significance?

Clearly, it was of the first importance for the army and the navy, as well as the civilians, to exchange views, share ideas, and develop a picture of the situation, no matter what the "clash of arms" might prove to be and which "Anglo-Saxon nations" should be involved. On July 16, well before the beginning of the crescendo of telegrams building to a crisis, the army's G-2, Brig. Gen. Sherman Miles, and the current chief of the Office of Naval Intelligence, Capt. Alan G. Kirk (who was one of three men to head ONI during 1941, a shuttling in and out of directors indicative of the low esteem in which naval intelligence was held by the admirals), had proposed to the country's highest military coordinating agency, the joint Army and Navy Board, that steps be taken to integrate intelligence into the deliberations of that body. In consequence, it was agreed that a joint intelligence committee be formed. Obviously not feeling the hot breath of disaster on his neck, the secretary of war got around to approving the plan two-and-a-half months later, on September 29; the secretary of the navy followed on October 1, just about a week before the receipt of Tokyo's query to the consul in Hawaii concerning the berthing of the fleet in Pearl Harbor.

The Joint Intelligence Committee (JIC), which was to consist of Miles and Kirk, or of subordinates designated by them, met for the first time on October 31, but the proceedings were so inconsequential that no one even bothered to keep minutes. It became clear that the respective army and navy heads of the War Plans Divisions, Brig. Gen. Leonard T. Gerow and Rear Adm. Richmond K. Turner, had differing ideas about the role of the committee;[48] this was a key point because the committee had to work through them. Gerow wanted it to "collate, analyze, and interpret information with its implications, to estimate hostile capabilities and probable intentions." Turner did not buy that—the committee had no business invading what he regarded as his turf; he wished "to limit it to presentation of such factual evidence as might be available, but to make no estimate or other form of prediction." Gazing into the politico-military crystal ball was apparently a task he wanted to reserve for himself.

There was another hitch as well. Like any other standing committee, the new JIC was supposed to have a staff to do the detail work. Nothing would really happen until people were delegated by the chiefs to compose and type up the memos, keep track of information, and perform all the other specific duties that make up the life of a committee, but there could not be any such people until office space had been acquired in which to lodge them. For some reason, it had been agreed that the navy was to supply the offices; however, "the head of the foreign branch office of Naval Intelligence was unable to obtain agreement within the Navy Department as to the office space to be provided."[49] Did this lack of urgency represent typical bureaucratic indifference to any undertaking outside the well-worn grooves, or was it deliberate foot-dragging inspired by Turner? It was not that General Miles never talked with his navy counterpart,[50] a role that on October 15 had been assumed by Rear Adm. Theodore S. Wilkinson, an officer with no background in intelligence. The two men met frequently, in fact, but they had no place to do so *as the committee*. Accordingly, as the committee they did not meet. Such was the effort the U.S. Army and Navy made to coordinate intelligence operations in the latter part of 1941, as crisis boiled up in the Pacific.

IN THE WEE hours of December 7, a few minutes after three o'clock, a Navy intercept station picked up the fourteenth and last part of a long Japanese memorandum eagerly awaited by American listeners in Washington.[51] It had been decrypted and typed up by 8:00 A.M., and the naval aide Capt. John R. Beardall took it to the president's room about ten o'clock. Roosevelt read through it, including the concluding words:

> The Japanese Government regrets to have to notify hereby the American Government that in view of the attitude of the American Government it cannot but consider that it is impossible to reach an agreement through further negotiations."[52]

The president observed that it looked as though the Japanese were going to break off negotiations, but nothing in his manner suggested that he was expecting an attack anywhere on the United States; "there was no alarm, or no mention of this, mention of war . . ."[53]

Two more telegrams from Tokyo were captured early Sunday morning by listening American ears, and both had been processed by midmorning. One message ordered the Japanese embassy to destroy the remaining cipher machine, all machine codes, and all secret documents.[54] The other was unusual in its own way:

> Will the ambassador please submit to the United States Government (if possible to the Secretary of State) our reply to the United States at 1:00 P.M. on the 7th, your time.[55]

This stirred up some excitement, especially with Bratton and Kramer. It was hardly customary for a precise hour to be specified for the delivery of a diplomatic communication. What could it mean? The message was rushed to the State Department and the White House, and General Marshall was urgently summoned from his morning horseback ride at Fort Myer. When the Chief of Staff reached his desk, he found a folder with the fourteen parts and the "one o'clock delivery" message. The latter struck the general forcibly, far more than had the lengthy argument of the fourteen parts; he was moved to action by this telegram, "which, unfortunately, they put on the bottom of the pile."[56] Unfortunately, too, Colonel Bratton and General Gerow, after making one or two attempts, did not run the risk of angering General Marshall by insisting that he skip ahead to the delivery message. When he had read it, it was agreed that U.S. outposts ought to receive a fresh warning: "Just what significance the hour set may have we do not know, but be on alert accordingly."[57]

The head of the army message center, Col. Edward T. French, failed to inform General Marshall that because of atmospheric problems he was having trouble raising Hawaii by radio that morning. The navy had a more powerful transmitter, but the colonel thought he could see all kinds of difficulty in getting the message to the navy (let the *navy* handle an army message?) and getting it delivered. A dandy idea suggested itself: he would send General Marshall's warning by Western Union! The message was filed at the army signal center at 12:01 P.M. and the teletyping to the Western Union office was completed at 12:17. The transmission was received by RCA in Honolulu at 1:03 P.M. Washington time—7:33 A.M. in Hawaii. Colonel French had thought that RCA would teletype the message to army headquarters at Fort Shafter, but, in fact, the wire link was not in operation. The warning dispatch from the Chief of Staff would therefore have to be delivered like any telegram from one private citizen to another.

JUST BEFORE TWO o'clock in the afternoon of December 7—it had been fifteen months now since the American Purple machine had begun cranking out its Magic—the news reached Washington that Japanese aircraft had attacked the U.S. fleet and facilities at Pearl Harbor on Oahu. It appeared that the intruders had achieved total surprise; this was not the fault of the cryptanalysts. It was clear, however, that the material the code-breakers had consistently made available to the intelligence services of the army and the navy had begun to lose its magical qualities as soon as it left their hands. Evaluation had been arbitrary and limited, dissemination had been haphazard. Security, exploitation, and the relationship between them—these were areas in which the Americans were still in the crawling stage.

General Marshall's telegram was delivered to the message center at Fort Shafter about three-thirty Washington time. The messenger boy on the motorcycle was conscientious, but he had trouble finding a way to get to Fort Shafter, since all the main roads had been closed to traffic after the Japanese bombs began falling. In any case, Colonel French had not bothered to mark the message as urgent. For all the telegraph people could know, it might have contained nothing more important than birthday greetings to General Short from his brother-in-law.[58]

Those Japanese bombs sounded the sudden end of the Anglo-American courtship. Like the shotgun traditionally flourished by an angry father, they left no room for further doubts and questions. For better or worse, a marriage had been forcibly arranged.

4

The Purloined Pindar

I

THE LADIES WERE becoming quite puzzled. It was not that they objected to the visits of the colonels and the majors and the captains—Fort Myer was not far away, after all, and officers would sometimes come over and ride with the girls when the school's riding academy was having a show—but these men were appearing in groups and just standing around. What could they possibly want? The president, Miss Carrie Sutherlin, and the dean, Miss Frances Jennings, couldn't imagine.

The two women, one a Virginian, one a Kentuckian, were devoted to their school; indeed, they loved it. Although it was a young institution, only fifteen years old, its sister school, Sullins College in Bristol, Virginia, had enjoyed a reputation for seventy years as a fine finishing school for well-bred young southern women. Miss Jennings had taught one year at Sullins, 1926-1927, before accepting the invitation to help launch the new junior college up in northern Virginia, out in a hundred acres of thickly wooded country, reachable from Alexandria by a muddy path called Glebe Road. When she had arrived at the unfinished building, stepping carefully through the front door, past bags of plaster and over piles of boards, she was met by a chaperone in a long dress, picking her way down the cluttered staircase. It was a Thursday evening, and at Sullins you always dressed up for dinner on Thursdays; it was going to be the same way here, whether or not the building was finished.

Arlington Hall became a worthy sister to Sullins. The building itself was impressive: yellow brick, three stories with dormer windows lining the peaked roof, with six big white more-or-less Ionic columns along the great porch in front. Through the 1930s and into the forties it was home during the school year to about 250 girls, and it had quickly added a dining room wing and then a separate yellow-brick building

77

for the swimming pool and gymnasium. A log-cabin tea house was built in the woods, and winding bridle paths were laid out among the trees, making it all, as one of the ladies said, "a beautiful place for recreation."

But now it was the spring of 1942, and the army officers, it turned out, were gazing on the building itself with lustful eyes, sizing the place up. One day Miss Sutherlin was given the ghastly news that the army had instituted condemnation proceedings. They wanted to turn the girls out of Arlington Hall, close it down as a school, and take possession of it for "the intelligence corps" (the army representatives made no attempt to conceal the nature of the would-be occupying force). The Arlington Hall trustees fumed when they heard the news. Let the army find some other building, somewhere else, for its intelligence people, and leave Arlington Hall alone! A girls' junior college was important, too. Arlington Hall was not for sale!

The board members contacted what senators they knew, but all this was happening just a few months after Pearl Harbor, and the outcome was foreordained. Miss Sutherlin and Miss Jennings called the members of the faculty together on the Saturday evening before commencement on Monday, the first of June, and told them the melancholy story. "It was to be absolutely secret"; the girls were not to be disturbed until the ceremonies were over, because the ladies "didn't want to have a funeral" instead of a graduation exercise. Commencement was held Monday morning; by late afternoon all the members of the faculty except the president and the dean had moved out, and "by six o'clock that night they had soldiers marching up and down the halls." It was the end of Arlington Hall as a school.[1]

The "intelligence corps" had struck swiftly.

BUT THE NEED to expand operations was increasingly urgent. During the 1930s the Signal Corps—which was, in fact, the "intelligence corps" that had moved in on the territory of Miss Sutherlin and Miss Jennings—had, like the army as a whole, been forced to subsist on the thin diet. This was the inevitable result, not only of the Great Depression, but of the national "never again" impulse with regard to armed conflict, symbolized by the various pieces of neutrality legislation passed by Congress. "The Army between the wars was not a big business," as an official history points out, "but an enterprise conserved for bigness, its agents trustees for a critical and universal public."[2] As for the Signal Intelligence Service, "it was not until 1939 that any considerable increase in funds . . . was provided,"[3] according to Friedman, and though by December 7, 1941, the total strength was 181 officers, enlisted men, and civilians in Washington and 150 more

persons in the field[4]—impressive by comparison with earlier years—
"there was much more to do than hands to do it with."[5]

In the aftermath of Pearl Harbor, the Signal Intelligence Service, like
everything else military and naval, entered a great new world of
increased demands and increased dimensions. By an agreement
reached in June 1942, the SIS took over the navy's Magic files, and with
them total responsibility for handling Japanese diplomatic traffic,[6]
leaving the navy free to grapple with its long-preferred adversary—
Japanese naval codes and ciphers. These, as an understated account
dryly puts it, "then required its undivided attention."[7] The army had
also decided to establish a signal intelligence school, which would be
separate from the other Signal Corps training carried on at Fort Monmouth, New Jersey. The SIS would have charge of this school, and in
view of the stepped-up traffic it would be handling and its increased
overall duties, the service began looking for more room than was
available in the old Munitions Building, where, several years earlier,
the state of overcrowding had been used by the budgeteers as an
excuse to keep the SIS lean. In surveying the Washington area, the
responsible officers paused briefly at Fort Hunt, Virginia, "virtually
abandoned to the weeds after World War I,"[8] but they quickly moved
on to the fancy girls' school that was sitting three miles out in Arlington, with its sweep of manicured green lawn. The decision was made,
the lawyers were unleashed, and very shortly Arlington Hall became
Arlington Hall Station.

Then, just as a house, by its draperies, chairs, books, and pictures,
will tell a great deal about the people who live in it, the new SIS home
began to reflect the tastes and needs of its occupants. It began, in fact,
to follow the universal course of military-installation development, in
which a preempted core building chosen, at least to some extent,
because of its size and its appointments, progressively acquires a
system of barrackslike wooden satellites in which more and more of
the actual work is done. The central building, meanwhile, becomes
merely the administrative center, as more and more administrators
appear on the scene. The handsome grounds (such institutions naturally have handsome grounds) are encircled by heavy steel fencing,
embellished with bristles of barbed wire, and presently the distinctive
character of the original establishment has vanished entirely. It has
become an army post. Such was the direction events took at Miss
Sutherlin's and Miss Jennings's beloved school.

The navy was facing similar space problems. Life in the Navy
Department building on Constitution Avenue, another of the World
War I temporaries like the Munitions Building, was remembered by a

naval historian as a melee in which "flag officers en route to vital conferences collided with whistling messengers delivering mail by tricycle, ensigns' wives bringing babies to the dispensary, plumbers with tools, civil servants in search of a cup of coffee, and laborers engaged in the perennial task of shifting somebody's desk and filing case from one place to another."[9] Enough of this, the navy chiefs decided—especially when, five miles away, out in northwest Washington at Massachusetts and Nebraska Avenues, lay one of the answers to their problem: Mount Vernon Academy, a girls' school, of all things—a big ivy-covered brick building sitting on large grounds. The requisitioning process was put in hand with the usual successful results, and to what now became the Naval Communications Annex moved the staff of Op-20-G, numbering in July 720 men and women—officers, enlisted personnel, and civilians; in December 1942, the total reached 1,188, a complement swollen by graduates of the Navy Language School at Boulder, Colorado, and also by specialists who came directly from civilian life. In the plans of the Allied strategists, Germany might be the number one target, but for the Americans during most of 1942, the Pacific was where the action was, and the cryptanalysts' assault on the Japanese naval ciphers was now producing a stream of intelligence. This made possible the almost miraculous American victory at Midway and provided information details of Japanese activities and plans concerning the remote island of Guadalcanal.

The grounds of Mount Vernon Academy began to undergo some of the standard changes, notably the erecting of a drab office building behind the original school. Housing had to be provided for the marine guards, and a series of barracks were run up for the Waves assigned to the annex, ultimately furnishing quarters for three thousand women. The academy had its drawbacks as a place to work (one young officer complained that it was hard "to concentrate on the IBM runs as bugs flew in from the nearby woods and hit [him] in the face"),[11] but in both the army and the navy, the coming of hot war had finally made cryptology into a growth industry.

II

ONE OF THE heaviest pressures pushing the Signal Intelligence Service into its expansion came not from the impersonal force of events, powerful as that was, but from the determination of one man, a slim, almost visibly hard-driving Signal Corps veteran, Col. Carter W. Clarke. This linguistically colorful Kentuckian had been one of the officers standing about the grounds of Arlington Hall, sizing the place up, and he was, in fact, the man who made the decision that brought such grief to Miss Sutherlin and Miss Jennings.[12]

His involvement with the SIS was the result of actions taken by Secretary of War Stimson. After the Japanese had scored their total surprise in the assault on the U.S. fleet and shore facilities at Oahu, Stimson, along with others in high places, felt that the Japanese diplomatic traffic made abundantly available by the decrypters with their Purple machine must surely have contained foreshadowings of the sneak attack and indications of its object—foreshadowings and indications that the existing methods of evaluating and exploiting the Magic intelligence had failed to perceive. Suddenly, procedures that had been viewed with some complacency only days earlier appeared tragically inadequate. The individual work of Friedman's and Safford's people was marvelous, to be sure. But analysis showed the deficiencies all along the line: "intercept facilities were extremely limited; arrangements for transmitting material from the point of intercept to the cryptanalytic center were hit or miss; cryptanalysis had been carried on successfully only in certain narrow fields."[13] When it came to personnel, translators were in critically short supply (a point of which the SIS was fully aware), and "there were neither sufficient personnel nor adequate procedures for studying and checking the translated product to squeeze out of it all useful intelligence obtainable." Such intelligence as was squeezed out was inadequately handled in Washington, and arrangements for getting it promptly to commanders in the field were practically nonexistent.

Now, looked at objectively, after the fact, it was all quite clear: those busy officers with their locked bags, delivering and picking up intercepts in ones and twos and threes; those Signal Corps cryptanalysts working in isolation from G-2; those persistent Japanese queries about the ships in harbor; those puzzled commanders out in Hawaii, unresponsive to messages they received containing unannotated phrases like "war warning"; those army and navy intelligence coordinators who could not even manage to find a room to meet in—the system was not a system at all, but chaos, with nobody or no group at any level having knowledge of the whole picture or responsibility for it, from interception through evaluation to dissemination. Reading the enemy's mail was clearly just the first step, nothing more.

It was too late to prevent Pearl Harbor; but the war was only beginning. What to do about intelligence? In the next weeks Stimson conferred with his special assistant, John J. McCloy, "the man who handled everything that no one else happened to be handling."[14] Like Stimson, McCloy had come from Wall Street, and the two agreed that the whole matter ought to be studied by somebody outside the structure of government, a lawyer "having a special type of competence and training, such as may be acquired in the handling and presentation of large cases involving complicated facts."[15] The facts were certainly complicated enough; by unwittingly planting incomplete and even false ideas in the minds of American leaders, Magic—seemingly a triumph—had on balance proved to be a negative factor for the United States. Only the future would show whether this paradox would be matched by the paradox of Pearl Harbor, a tactical clean sweep for the Japanese that might yet reveal itself itself as a strategic defeat.

McCloy thought he knew just the man for the job, a partner in his own former firm, known at the time as Cravath, de Gersdorff, Swaine, and Wood. A forty-one-year-old graduate of Princeton and head of his class at the Columbia Law School, Alfred McCormack was summed up by a later associate as "very quick, very perceptive, hard-working."[16] If it was McCloy's intention to bring in somebody who would not hesitate to slap the intelligence establishment in the face, he had picked his man. McCormack was indeed able; beyond that, impatient to get ahead with whatever the job was, he did not suffer fools gladly and did not mind saying so. A round-faced, rather studious-looking fellow, tending to plumpness, he was not only industrious but also believed in enjoying life (in his Greenwich home he kept a jug of martinis at-the-ready in a downstairs refrigerator);[17] and as a somewhat precocious ornament of the Establishment, he stood in no awe of generals or anybody else. McCormack agreed to take the assignment and six weeks after Pearl Harbor began work as a special assistant to the secretary. He was being assigned the overall task of diagnosing the ills of military intelligence and drawing up a plan to cure them. The speed of his appointment contrasted favorably with the somnolent pace of army–navy efforts at liaison during all of 1941. A shooting war had made a difference.

Two months later, during which time he had worked closely with Colonel Clarke, McCormack returned to Stimson with a report that began, not surprisingly, by saying that "there was a very large job to be done all along the line."[18] Accustomed to a civilian sphere of crisp decisions and effective follow-up, all based on knowledge of the subject at hand, McCormack had undergone a sort of cultural shock on confronting the routinized sluggishness of G-2. In Military Intelligence, personnel served only with great reluctance "because of its reputation as a graveyard for Regular Army careers."[19]

In his report, McCormack proceeded to outline the task ahead. In the first place, the radio intelligence operations of the Signal Corps must be expanded, and, in fact, since "the whole radio intelligence process, from the intercept operation down through the issuance of a finished intelligence report, presented so many interrelated problems," he recommended that it be "considered as an intelligence operation throughout and placed under the operational control of G-2."[20] This, to be sure, would have to be a different G-2 from the lackluster enterprise he had just been scrutinizing.

As for the content of the intercepts, "the individual messages arriving at G-2 were far from finished intelligence," and "to exploit the source properly it was necessary to consider the individual messages together with related messages and all available information from other sources, to run down clues appearing in the messages in order to dig out information which was not apparent on first reading, to check back on obscure points with the Signal Corps, to determine then whether the item added anything of real significance . . ."

No more impatient couriers, then, eager to press on in their rounds, concerned with iron security at the expense of practical application, but order, breathing space, time for reflection, and material to reflect with. McCormack also observed that solid intelligence derived from a message ought to be reported in "clear, simple English and in a manner which would bring out its significance, together with any necessary evaluation . . ." Finally, the task of transforming the intercepted messages into real intelligence "could be done effectively only by imaginative persons of absolutely first-class ability and suitable training, and not simply by any reserve officer or college graduate who happened to be available."[22] It could be done, that is, only by persons not now assigned to G-2.

To carry out McCormack's recommendations, which in general called for the development and exploitation of a great many new attitudes in the intelligence establishment of the army, an already existing section of the Military Intelligence Service was made into what was called the Special Branch, with Colonel Clarke named to be its chief. Not long afterward, McCloy "seduced McCormack into climbing into a colonel's uniform"[23] and becoming deputy chief; helping overcome McCormack's reluctance was the new Assistant Chief of Staff, G-2—Maj. Gen. George Strong. McCormack's first big job was to seek out and try to attract his "imaginative persons of absolutely first-class ability and suitable training."

During his first months in his new command, Colonel Clarke concerned himself with the McCormack recommendations having to do with stepping up the activities of the Signal Corps side of things—interception, decryption, and translation. In spite of McCormack's suggestion, however, these activities (and therefore the Signal Intelligence Service) would remain under the control of the Signal Corps; a transfer of power of this magnitude was something that could not lightly be brought about but could only happen, if at all, after what would practically amount to a shooting war between the chief signal officer and the assistant chief of staff, G-2. Any general's empire was supposed to grow, not shrink. Clarke, now identified with G-2, therefore had to work with the Signal Corps without line authority; nevertheless, he pushed for a much broader approach to the signal intelligence problem, leading the SIS to set up new intercept stations and to acquire as the new headquarters the building and grounds of Arlington Hall. He also urged the acquisition and training of new people in large numbers, but this, as the Signal Corps was finding at Fort Monmouth, was easier said than done.

McCormack was finding that it was easier said than done at Special Branch headquarters as well, particularly since the terms of his own report meant that he had to start practically from scratch. To carry out the first assignment of the Special Branch, the establishment and production of a daily intelligence report, the chiefs drew up a plan calling for a three-part organization consisting of a small headquarters section; area sections to deal with the traffic on a geographical basis; and a small reports section to act as a "traffic cop" for the incoming messages, assigning them to area sections, as well as to produce reports.

On May 27, 1942, the Special Branch told General Marshall that it needed a staff of fifty-nine officers and eighty-five civilians.[24] Seeming in no way excessive to McCormack, this request led to manpower problems of bureaucratic complexity, including a clash with orders that limited the total number of army officers who could be kept on duty in the Military District of Washington. These orders no doubt represented a sound concept—otherwise the capital would have been an even greater hive of queens, workers, and drones than it was—but they sometimes produced unhappiness in their application. McCormack found such arbitrariness and rigidity maddening.

The Wall Street lawyer's real bête noire was the Civil Service, "which could not understand why the war should interfere with its time-worn procedures." If he wanted to do something so seemingly simple as hiring an indexer, he had to prove not only that the person was qualified for the job but that an indexer was really needed; quite often the Civil Service examiners, "many of whom were incapable of understanding what G-2 was doing or what its problems were,"[25] simply turned him down. The Civil Service Commission, with its "artificial standards and negative approach to every problem," was unable "to understand the principal standard being used in selecting personnel, i.e., ability . . ."[26]

By the end of July 1942 the Special Branch had managed to build a staff of only twenty officers, one enlisted man (brought in the back door from the Counter Intelligence Corps, with its blessing), and eighteen civilians. Using "Cravath methods," McCormack had concentrated on lawyers (resulting in the creation of what was waggishly termed "the best law office in Washington"), but the group also included university professors, a student in theology, a newspaper editor, and the assistant curator of an art museum. One recruit, Telford Taylor, a graduate of Williams and the Harvard Law School, was general counsel of the Federal Communications Commission when he decided that, with a war on, his duty lay in the army. A mutual friend already in the Special Branch introduced him to McCormack, and the delighted deputy chief snapped him up.

By autumn, despite the thinness of the staff in comparison with what was called for by the table of organization, the Special Branch was expanding its activities. One way it could do this was through hard work and long hours on the job, reflecting the attitudes of Clarke and McCormack. By comparison, one fall afternoon, early in the North African campaign, McCormack found that he was still capable of shock when, seeking pertinent information from another G-2 office, he was told that it was too late in the day for that; he would have to wait till tomorrow.[27] It was a fixed rule of his branch, the colonel in charge said, that all personnel must start putting their papers away by 4:40 P.M. so that their desks might be clear and the files locked by 5:00. The situation had clearly improved from the beginning of the year when, in the words of Col. Truman Smith, a former military attaché in Berlin, G-2 was "the least efficient and the least regarded section of the General Staff,"[28] but one could not yet say that the importance of intelligence and the scope it might achieve had fully been recognized by its own practitioners.

There were exceptions, of course, among these practitioners— McCormack, the newcomer, prominent among them. With the Special Branch report system now functioning, the deputy director could look elsewhere, into other needs and opportunities. One of the directions he looked was eastward, toward Europe and the war against Hitler.

III

IN THE BITTER-COLD February and March of 1942, one of the forlorn GIs taking basic training at Fort Dix, New Jersey, was a former mathematician for the National Bureau of Standards, a slim six-foot New Yorker named Arthur Levenson.[29] Although the weather was terrible for everybody and presumably nobody was ecstatic about his own situation, Levenson was truly miserable. In addition to the usual problems plaguing draftees, he had somehow managed to run afoul of a certain sergeant, a fellow named Lydecker, who had a way of storming into the barracks shouting, "I want six volunteers—Levenson, and who are the other five?" Though he was gifted with a lively sense of humor, Levenson quickly found this routine anything but funny. He did, however, have something going for him. On a visit to Washington, shortly before he was inducted into the army, he had been introduced by a friend to Solomon Kullback, who was teaching a night class in statistics at George Washington University.

Levenson expressed some interest in the subject of cryptology, and he found that Kullback could make arrangements for him to take appropriate correspondence courses—some of which he completed while shivering at Fort Dix. After several weeks of basic, deciding that he had "better do something about these courses," he sent off a letter to the captain in charge; he was in the army now, he said, and as long as that was the case he would like to get involved in cryptological work. Back came a reply from the captain, now a major, who said that was fine, he was taking steps for Levenson to be assigned to an installation at Fort Monmouth.

Levenson reported to the cryptological school in April 1942. At the time, Fort Monmouth presented, at least to those in the know, a frantic picture. The crypt school taught cryptography, cryptanalysis, and crypt security. Before Pearl Harbor, the cryptanalysis course had been a year long; now, because of the pressure to get more and more men on the real job, students were being withdrawn from the course early, and its length was cut in half. The United States was paying the price for having ignored the principle that "actual or physical warfare is intermittent, but mental, that is, cryptanalytic, warfare is continuous," as William Friedman pointed out; cryptanalysts were truly never at peace. And, since "cryptanalytic activities have no counterpart in civil life," on the outbreak of war "there is no important source from which trained, experienced personnel can be drawn for immediate usefulness."[30] Yet some persons could learn fast. One of Levenson's teachers was a brand-new Signal Corps second lieutenant, a Monmouth graduate himself, a tall young Bostonian named William Bundy. Because Levenson had done some correspondence work, he was able to skip part of the training, and in July he found himself on orders for Arlington Hall Station.

There, Levenson was put to work, but not the sort of work he had expected. Along with a number of other enlisted men he was assigned to guard duty. Since these GIs had not had much experience with rifles, the army protected itself against mishaps by issuing no real ammunition to them, although they had blanks in case they found it desirable to make a little noise. One day, as Levenson was patrolling his beat, he was engaged in conversation by a tall, soft-spoken lieutenant, a friendly man in his thirties, who said his name was Frank Rowlett. Levenson remembered having heard the name.

"How're you doing?" Rowlett asked, and he went on to inquire about Levenson's background. Levenson was only too happy to answer the questions; two days later he was happy indeed to discover that he had not been wasting his time in idle talk. So effective was Rowlett by this point in his career that Levenson was transferred inside the hall and set to work on Japanese codes and ciphers. A little ritual developed. Rowlett would come by every day and say, "How're you doing? Do you like it?" and Levenson would answer simply and truthfully, "This is great!"

As Arlington Hall proceeded on its course of conversion to a military facility, barracks were put up, and even before they were completed the men were moved into them. The thick grass of the lawns having given way to the standard concomitant of construction, mud, the men tracked the covering sawdust everywhere. The latrines were small. In one, the "sergeant had one private mirror all to himself, and the rest of the men were jammed in front of the other; you never knew whose face you were shaving."

But the atmosphere in these enlisted men's barracks was heady nonetheless, since brains and education were the criteria for determining whether a man was chosen for duty at Arlington Hall. One fellow, a young B.A. from Columbia, had been told by well-meaning friends that after he was drafted he had better put his erudition in mothballs if he wanted to get along with the great cross section of America that his fellow GIs would represent. Following this advice, he discarded his scholarly books and pinned up pictures of Lefty Gomez and Lana Turner, a tactic that may have served him well in earlier phases of his army career but produced unexpected results after he arrived at Arlington Hall, where, it seemed, everybody spoke at least three languages and had at least three degrees. His barracks mates treated him gently, like a backward child.

Late one night, as the Columbia B.A. and Levenson and their fellows lay snug in their cots dreaming GI dreams, there erupted an uproar that—at least for such an unusual cause—had probably never before been heard at an army post. A fellow of classical bent, just back from a furlough, was fussing about in his small space, frantically looking for something and disturbing his neighbors in the process. Finally the barracks resounded to an enraged and memorable cry: *"Who has purloined my Pindar?"*

To a striking extent, and in a relatively short time, the army had managed to create a meritocracy.

From time to time William Friedman, still the "dapper figure with the Adolphe Menjou moustache, the characteristic bow tie, and the two-tone black-and-white shoes,"[31] would poke his head into the workrooms, just to see how things were going. One day somebody in one of the sections started a sort of challenge cryptogram moving through the offices; Friedman finally solved it and then said, "Now that you've all tried to break it, please go back to your jobs."[32] Friedman was also active as a recruiter, writing, for instance, to an old classmate from Cornell, William F. Edgerton, who had become director of the Oriental Institute at the University of Chicago. "I feel that we *should* have men of your calibre, training and experience on hand or at least on our lists,"[33] Friedman said in a February 1942 letter. By learning something about military cryptography and cryptanalysis, should the war last a long time, such persons could be available in case of need. (A year later, the need clearly being present, Edgerton was on board at Arlington Hall, employing his scholarly background to derive ideas from monographs on ancient Egyptian ciphers, such as "Cryptogrammes de la Reine Nefertari," from the French journal *Annales du Service des Antiquités de l'Egypte.*)

On the whole, Arlington Hall was not exactly a spit-and-polish, hierarchical military operation, in part simply because much of the staff was civilian. The work schedule was hard—seven days on and one day off, with two days off every seventh week—a more rigorous arrangement, to Alfred McCormack's disgust, than prevailed at the same time in the offices of G-2. Aside from the schedule, the routine for the officers was much like that of civilian workers. And they were not oblivious to the fact that Washington was a young bachelor's Elysium, there being, it was said, thirteen women for every man.

AT VINT HILL Farms, out in the Virginia hunt country on the Prince William-Fauquier line, the SIS opened a new station in the early autumn of 1942. Here, a big gambrel-roofed barn, rather than a girls' school, served as the core building; and on the grounds stood a large old brick house and Civil War-vintage outbuildings. The usual steel fence signified the farm's conversion to military purposes, as did a phalanx of radio towers. At Vint Hill, intercepted enemy messages were copied and recorded and fed to Arlington Hall for cryptanalysis; the station also became the SIS training center.

The saying at Vint Hill in its early days was that "Ph.D. in this outfit stands for Post-Hole Digger."[34] When the staff and students of the Fort Monmouth crypt school moved to Vint Hill after it came under the direction of the SIS*—the transfer, as one participant remembered it, taking place when the Cardinals beat the Yankees in the World Series—the new installation was still under construction. Thus, many of the men were put to work digging the holes for the posts supporting the intercept towers, as well as the needed latrines.

Among the arrivals was a well-known flute virtuoso, Labros Callimahos, who was Cairo born, of Greek parentage, but an American since childhood. During the 1930s, while performing in Europe, he had fallen under the spell of Friedman's writings and, as a consequence, cryptology became his hobby. Since 1941 he had been at Fort Monmouth, having arrived to volunteer looking the complete virtuoso— mustache and goatee, floppy black hat and black spats, ebony cane, "like something out of a Dumas novel." In spite of his appearance, he was accepted for service and promptly sent to the crypt school. Now at Vint Hill he had the chance to meet his idol, "the cryptologic giant who asked the most searching questions and understood our answers even before we had finished our explanations." (Later, working directly for Friedman, Callimahos developed a splendid insight: "Mr. Friedman had complete faith in his subordinates—otherwise, he felt, they wouldn't be working for him.")[35]

Another post-hole digger was 2d Lt. William Bundy, who had been drafted into the army in 1941 and placed in the Signal Corps, then assigned to the crypt school at Monmouth. (For cryptanalytic training, the selection was made primarily on the basis of one's performance on the Army General Classification Test, the preferred score being 140

---

*In the summer of 1942, the Signal Intelligence Service began to undergo a peculiarly frequent series of changes in name, ending up in 1943 as the Signal Security Agency. For the sake of simplicity, it will here be called the Signal Security Agency (SSA) from this point forward.

or better; Bundy was said to have done remarkably on the test.) After putting in about three months in the course he was chosen for the second Signal Corps Officer Candidate School (OCS) class; he reported in January and graduated in March as a second lieutenant, then promptly was assigned to the crypt school as a teacher. He spent the autumn of 1942 at Vint Hill. Then in January, two weeks before his wedding to Mary Acheson, daughter of Assistant Secretary of State Dean Acheson, he was called to Arlington Hall as a cryptanalyst, where he did "odds and bits of things." Owing to his intelligence and drive and a sort of native air of command, he was looked on by his superiors with great favor; this became evident one day in April when he was summoned to a briefing on something he had never heard of, something code-named Yellow.

IN JANUARY 1943, a New York lawyer and cryptological hobbyist named Walter Fried received a commission in the Signal Corps and joined the team at Arlington Hall,[36] where he reported to Captain Frank Rowlett, the chief of the branch in which he was to work. (Once Rowlett was moved from the Army Reserve to active duty, on February 16, 1942, his rise in rank was rapid; on January 22, 1943, he would become a major.) Fried also began to develop a friendship with Friedman, who, though recovered now from his breakdown, appeared to nurse a feeling of bitterness. Having, with what seemed indecent speed, lost his commission early in 1941, at the time of the army-navy mission to Bletchley Park, he was a civilian without line authority in an operation now dominated by officers. Fried's wife, the daughter of the famous band leader Edwin Franko Goldman, accompanied him to Washington, and the couple sought—and were lucky enough to find—a small house reasonably close to Arlington Hall. In February, they acquired as a lodger one of Fried's newly arrived fellow officers, the quiet, deliberate-spoken, scholarly professor of German, Paul Whitaker.

TO GET INSIDE the fence with its barbed wire, you had to show your badge to the guard at the gate. Except for that detail, the routine at Arlington Hall seemed to Whitaker to have much in common with work in a factory; for him it lacked the kind of faculty-club atmosphere he had become accustomed to as a university teacher. One reason for that, of course, was that you simply did not talk about what you were doing except with persons in your own section, and the time even for that was limited. As a contentedly married man uninterested in the national capital's girl:boy ratio, Whitaker found it a quiet life. He labored over messages during the day, and wrote letters and read in the evenings, feeling himself one small part of the mass of people—the thousands and thousands of them—whom the war had uprooted and then set down in the Washington area. If anybody outside of Arlington Hall happened to ask you what your duties were, you were supposed to say that you worked in filing, Major Crawford's wartime successors apparently having decided that this was an eminently believable cover story in a national capital that had grown into a federation of great bureaucracies.

By the time Whitaker arrived at Arlington Hall, the grounds had acquired a number of big, two-story temporary buildings. Occupying the second floor of one of these was the German section, a huge space with rows of desks, like a schoolroom for perhaps a hundred students—except that the people at those desks were mathematicians, English graduates, archaeologists. "It was a strange assortment of people, but you learned to do this routine job. You didn't have to be a specialist to do most of the work."[37]

After living with the Frieds for a time, Whitaker managed to find a small apartment nearby, and his wife came to join him. But by now the spring of 1943 was well along.

5

To the Altar

I

"WE ARE GAINING knowledge and experience in many parts of the world, some of it rather expensively," Col. Alfred McCormack observed in April 1943, "but we still have a lot to learn. In the field of intercept intelligence we have at hand, in my opinion, one of the greatest potential sources of information; but we are not making the most of it. We need to raise our sights."[1]

Need to raise our sights. That had been McCormack's song since his arrival in Washington fifteen months earlier. It was not only the strict office hours kept and the limited amount of sweat exuded that had perturbed him about G-2; another of the bothersome characteristics was a "certain supine attitude toward intelligence." The "G-2 colonels . . . operated in the manner of soothsayers,"[2] he felt, with about the same respect for solid evidence. They seemed to have given little thought to the obvious fact that evaluation and dissemination are worthless, if the information that has been collected is worthless.

By the previous autumn it had become clear to McCormack and to Col. Carter Clarke that, three-quarters of a year after the declaration of war, U.S. Army intelligence actually knew little about the military situation in Europe; and some of the information that was in hand was not only wrong, but ridiculously so. At a time, for instance, when careful analysis showed that the German Luftwaffe had a total of some five thousand operational aircraft in service, "there were devout believers in G-2 in a rumor picked up by an attaché in Roumania that the Germans had ten thousand spare airplanes hidden in the Black Forest."[3]

Utterly different in background and training, Clarke and McCormack had quickly forged a close and effective working partnership. Things might not have turned out that way. McCormack was obviously a master at extracting the essence from a great pile of documents, rapidly and thoroughly, but when he arrived on the scene as a special assistant to Secretary of War Stimson, "he knew as much about the military"—observed Carter Clarke—"as I knew about revealed religion." As technical helpers, the New York lawyer was assigned a succession of Regular Army officers—a brigadier general and three colonels—and he fired all of them. Upset at this turnover, General Strong summoned Clarke to his office and uttered a terse command: "You go down there and get along with that goddamned man!"[4]

In carrying out this order, Clarke decided that the sensible move would be to see to it that McCormack left the privileged sanctuary of civilian status for a place in the military hierarchy, thereby becoming an officer junior to Clarke himself. Once the switch was made, however, no problem of seniority or status arose to disturb the relationship between the two. McCormack, as deputy chief of the Special Branch, took on the research and intelligence work and the agonizing task of recruiting personnel and training them, while Clarke, the chief of the branch, devoted himself to administration, security, relations with other branches and organizations, and, notably, to the building up of the Signal Security Agency. "We made a very good team," Clarke said, doing less than justice to himself: "He furnished the brains and I did the hatchet work. He was exactly the type of man for the job he was given to do, and he did it superbly."[5]

Gazing eastward in late 1942, Clarke and McCormack concluded that the United States was receiving no dependable current information about the war in Europe, and they saw just why this was the case. Although the military attaché in London and his sizable staff collected reams of paper from the various British intelligence agencies and duly forwarded the contents to Washington, the catch amounted to little more news than one could read in the *Times* or the *Guardian*. In the British view, it seemed, military attachés were not among the persons entitled to receive top-level information. What material did reach Washington "was solemnly studied in G-2, though there was in the organization an almost universal suspicion of the British and a tendency to disagree with British conclusions, simply because they were British conclusions."[6] But with its wild tales of 10,000 German planes hidden in the Black Forest, G-2 hardly appeared to McCormack to be in a position to criticize somebody else's intelligence analyses. In assessing matters in Europe, U.S. intelligence was, as Carter Clarke might have said, trying to attack a viper with a toothpick.

Yet the day was inevitably coming when, at the side of the British, American soldiers would take part in great land battles on the Continent. Already they were confronting the Germans elsewhere, having landed in North Africa on November 8 in what was proving not to be the cakewalk some observers had predicted.

In 1943 or 1944, the chiefs of U.S. intelligence knew, American forces would begin playing a great, and ultimately decisive, part in the Allied return to the Continent. Should U.S. armies, as was at present the case in North Africa, be wholly dependent on the British for signal intelligence—for the interception, decryption, translation, delivery, and interpretation of German intercepts? And should the War Department in Washington have no liaison with British intelligence at the working level, receive no transatlantic flow of raw material? Since the Atlantic Charter conference, off Argentia, Newfoundland, in August 1941, when "those seagoing twins Roosevelt and Churchill,"[7] as Clarke termed the leaders, had spoken of cooperation in cryptological intelligence, such relations had been carried on at high levels, but concerning generalities more than nuts-and-bolts details. The officers of the Special Branch and the Military Intelligence Service generally did not really know the workings of the British system—how signal intelligence was produced at Bletchley Park and disseminated to units in the field. This state of affairs was not satisfactory.

ALTHOUGH IN THEIR contacts of various kinds, U.S. and British intelligence officers seemed to one American to be "walking around and eyeing each other like two mongrels who have just met,"[8] the relationship on the signals side, between Arlington Hall and the British cryptanalytic people, was somewhat different. Still independent of G-2, though watched and prodded by Clarke, the Signal Security Agency had ties with Bletchley Park running back to the winter of 1941, when Abe Sinkov and Leo Rosen and the two young navy officers, Robert Weeks and Prescott Currier, had made the trip, as Clark put it, "just to go over there to sniff"[9]—and to escort the flower of the SIS effort, the Purple machine.

Commander Denniston, the head of Bletchley Park, had visited Washington later in 1941, inaugurating a firm friendship with Billy Friedman and, as a fervent golfer, demonstrating his mastery on the army-navy course. (Golf balls being in desperately short supply in wartime Britain, Friedman later sent the commander a package of them, earning heartfelt thanks for a gift that had "reduced my handicap by several strokes"; and "believe me," Denniston added, "no one loses a ball here these days. It may add an hour or so to the round but *balls must be found!*"[10])

In addition to the exchange of visits, arrangements were struck for the U.S. signal intelligence services, army and navy, to maintain a few technical liaison persons at Bletchley Park (BP). This cooperation, generally believed to have been brought about because of Churchill's pronounced interest in signal intelligence as well as his belief in close relations with the United States, was concerned not with the content and handling of the intercepted German messages but with cryptana- lytic devices and techniques. Like a volunteer worker collecting for various good causes, each American representative made rounds of the British offices, picking up donations of technical information for transmission to Washington. The hosts, of course, were free to tell the liaison persons only what they chose to tell, but one of these repre- sentatives, John Seaman, in civilian life a lawyer in Lansing, Michigan, felt that the British were very open. The head of Bletchley Park, he said, "was very cordial and let me do whatever I wanted to."[11]

Yet, now that the war was developing on the German side of the world, such liaison was simply not good enough. Like Clarke and McCormack in the Special Branch, Frank Rowlett and his fellows at Arlington Hall wanted much more, for a number of reasons.[12] Since a German air attack on England was a continuing threat, Bletchley Park could in one blow be put out of commission; the United States ought to have full knowledge of the operation, in order to be able to establish a new nerve center, if that terrible need should arise. Another point— though certainly not one to be uttered in the wrong company—was that the Americans had to protect themselves against the possibility, however unlikely, of a British capitulation to the Germans as the result of some unforeseeable series of events. The men of the SSA believed, besides, that when American technicians had become thoroughly familiar with Bletchley Park procedures and devices, they might well be able to suggest and develop useful changes. And, to be sure, BP would provide an admirable training ground for U.S. cryptological personnel.

But perhaps the predominant reason was the same for the SSA as for the Special Branch: in the coming great Allied operations in Europe, the Americans ought not, in the realm of cryptanalytic intelligence, to be nothing more than clients of the British. The Americans ought to have a finger in the pie at each stage, and thus some say in determining what went into it, how it should be baked, and to whom it should be served. Accordingly, both the Special Branch and the SSA felt that Americans should be integrated into the British signal intelligence operation, from the decrypting of the enemy intercepts all the way through the last stage in the process—the use of the material in the field. As an alternative, G-2 and Arlington Hall could combine their forces and create an American Bletchley Park.

Neither of these options was initially beguiling to the British, who felt, hardly to anyone's surprise, that Bletchley Park was doing a damn fine job as it was. Why rock the boat? And with Americans this much in the picture, with their numbers, riches, and resources, would not British influence be bound to decline in the sphere of signal intelligence, as it was inevitably going to in others?[13] One had better hold on to what trump cards one had. Certainly the infusion of a number of Americans could provide some new blood, fresh talent, to a war-strained British intelligence establishment. But, with some exceptions, this establishment showed few signs of having acquired an uncharacteristic appreciation of American ideas and intellectual achievements and of their potential worth in war. In any case, such a pooling—not a collaboration, but a blending—of the intelligence forces of allied nations could hardly be expected; it would represent something new in history, although the creation of the Anglo-American Combined Chiefs of Staff, who gave orders to U.S. and British commanders alike, and the setting up of General Eisenhower's integrated North African headquarters were both evidence that the relationship of these allies, for all their differences and disagreements, was close beyond precedent.

Then there was the old, haunting, perpetual question of security. In the United States, the British student of politics and practical politician Harold J. Laski observed, "something always escapes the net which is thrown about the people."[14] And the net itself often seemed more hole, less cord, as a ghastly breach of security had freshly demonstrated in the summer of 1942. Within a few days of the Battle of Midway, that epochal U.S. victory had been tarnished by a *Chicago Tribune* story making it plain to the most dim-witted reader that the American triumph owed much to signal intelligence. Yet nobody had been punished, no padlock had been snapped on the offices of the newspaper. The government, in horrible fact, had no means of redress except through a public trial, which would only spread the news further and hence was not to be thought of. No writer or editor need fear being tried *in camera* and dragged off to some Yankee counterpart of the Tower of London. Most disquieting!

But an American Bletchley Park? Yanks on their own, not satisfied with watching the Japanese, trampling this carefully tended German turf? That was simply unthinkable.

All these questions, certainly far from easy to resolve, were the subject of "difficult and protracted"[15] negotiations in April and May of 1943, carried on, without any touch of hostility, between Colonel Clarke and Royal Navy Capt. Edward Hastings, who was the Washington liaison person for Brig. Stewart Menzies, now the head of British intelligence. The two men met often, sometimes talking in Clarke's Pentagon office twice a day, with proposals being forwarded to Menzies in London. On May 17, the negotiators initialed a complex agreement, formalizing the primary responsibility of the United States for the reading of Japanese military and air codes and ciphers and of the British for German and Italian codes and ciphers, detailing with elaborate care the procedures for the handling of intelligence, and carrying in an appendix the provisions that opened the doors of Bletchley Park to the Americans.[16] All desired intelligence from German machine ciphers would be made available to the War Department. U.S. officers would be stationed at Bletchley Park to select messages for transmittal to Washington or to theater commanders. The "Special Intelligence" would be passed to American commanders-in-chief in the field through the existing British units, but a U.S. officer would be attached to each unit "to advise and act as liaison officer to overcome difficulties that may arise in regard to differences in language." This agreement, amiably arrived at and laying the ghost of a separate, competing American Bletchley Park with all the rivalry, inefficiency, and tendency to hoard information that would have resulted, was the vital step forward for the United States with respect to Ultra. It was perhaps not a complete triumph; the American officer in the field was envisioned only as a sort of translator, in case any regrettable necessity should arise for translating British English into the American idiom. But it was the needed beginning—and much more.

WHILE CLARKE AND Hastings were engaged in their daily sessions in the Pentagon, Alfred McCormack was involved in a parallel series of discussions, and in a setting that to the Americans was far more inviting. Shortly after issuing his observation that U.S. intelligence needed "to raise our sights," McCormack, Lt. Col. Telford Taylor of the Special Branch, and William Friedman, representing the Signal Security Agency (and at last getting the outing he had missed in 1941), sailed for England to see the Government Code and Cipher School for themselves and to discuss at that end the kinds of arrangements that would ensure a full flow of British intelligence to U.S. field commands and to the War Department in Washington.

In preparation for the trip, Taylor, who had been specializing in the complex and crucial area of intercept priorities—since only a fraction of the world's radio traffic could be listened to, what should be selected and when and by whom?—had spent three months at Arlington Hall acquainting himself, "as far as a layman could, with the rudiments"[17] of cryptanalysis. The inclusion of Friedman in the mission was a sound idea, not only for technical reasons, but from the public relations point of view: he was indeed William Friedman, not only a universally respected name in the trade, but a person to whom the British would feel some sense of indebtedness, because of Purple, and to whom they would be bound to listen.

Arriving on April 25, 1943, the American representatives were received in London by Brigadier Menzies at his splendid office, with its view of Whitehall—a legendary citadel of cloak-and-daggerism, complete with a secret staircase for use when the chief wished to conceal his connection with the Secret Service. Mainly, however, the Americans dealt in the capital with Commander Denniston, who had been removed as head of Bletchley Park and now directed a branch of GC & CS based in the city. British intelligence operations in London were scattered about in various anonymous offices in innocuous-looking buildings; Denniston's headquarters was located in what purported to be Peggy Carter's Hat Shop, No. 8 Berkeley Street, off Piccadilly.

Most of the visiting group's time was spent at Bletchley Park itself, where Cmdr. Edward Travis, who had succeeded Denniston, saw to it that they were introduced to every side of the operation. As is typical of the world of intelligence, BP was highly compartmentalized, its secrets kept as close as possible by the working of the need-to-know principle. Now, for two months, the American intelligence officers had the opportunity to transcend normal restrictions and become "fully aware of the amazing successes achieved by the British in exploiting German military traffic."[18]

This detailed exposure to the British system for developing and handling the information was an eye-opener. McCormack, enormously impressed both by the process and by the people who made it work, was ruefully aware that he was being given a glimpse of a personnel heaven. While he had been forced to battle War Department rules and Civil Service incomprehension to acquire his lawyers and file clerks, "British intelligence had a first call on military and civilian personnel."[19] With his sights now fixed on the goal of integrating Americans into the entire operation at Bletchley Park, he knew that the U.S. Military Intelligence Service faced a new and sizable recruiting challenge. He would have much to do when he got back to Washington.

II

THE YELLOW BRIEFING to which Bill Bundy and a handful of other officers at Arlington Hall had been summoned was conducted by Frank Rowlett,[20] who began the proceedings on a note of high seriousness: "No one will leave this room a free man. You will never talk about this to anybody who isn't cleared, and you will never hereafter go anywhere where you can be captured." Then Rowlett went on to unveil and describe Yellow—the secret of Bletchley Park. The British, he told his listeners, were enjoying great success in the reading of German military communications enciphered by means of the Enigma machine.

Not that day, but shortly afterward, Bundy was informed that he was to be the commanding officer of a detachment to be integrated into the British operation "as part of the overall deal we've worked out with them," and he was given, in effect, "the pick of the litter," since as a teacher in the crypt school he "knew who the crack students were." Working with Rowlett, he managed to secure a high proportion of the top people—"it seemed important from every standpoint that we put our best foot forward."

The choice of Bundy to head the group was interesting. Even though he was no career signal intelligence person, having entered the army as a draftee in 1941, his demonstrated ability and his quietly effective personality, with its touch of Bostonian starch, were obvious qualifications for the job. Such traits in nonprofessionals had not always led to due recognition by the armed services, but the field of intelligence was somewhat different from the norm.

IN JULY THE chosen men, one by one, were told that they were going to be shipped overseas—and not much else. Paul Whitaker was not particularly pleased at the news. He was over-age in grade, he pointed out to his superiors, and therefore could not, under the regulations, be posted overseas unless he received a promotion. Was that their intention? The superiors had at their command a repertory of terse army phrases for responding to such comments, and they answered Whitaker with some of the choicer ones.

Whitaker was not disturbed at the rebuff. He was endowed with a quiet, even temperament—very much, indeed, like a layman's idea of a scholarly personality—and he was not given to worry.

The orders for Bill Bundy's group, Shipment No. 0192-A, were cut on July 28. They said only that the officers concerned were "relieved from present assignment" and would "proceed to New York Port of Embarkation."[21] On reaching New York, the signal intelligence officers reported to Fort Hamilton in Brooklyn for processing, and they soon found themselves part of a preembarkation scene that resembled nothing imaginable in peacetime.

Thousands and thousands of enlisted men waited for the order to begin boarding a great ocean liner, her name and identifying markings buried under a heavy layer of wartime camouflage gray. In long lines the GIs sat on their equipment on the dock, with little talking. Then gangways were opened up and the men, bored and tired from the old army game of hurry-up-and-wait, got to their feet and shuffled along, leaning forward to balance the weight of the equipment they carried.

"As you stand on deck watching those long lines of brown, bent figures come aboard," said Edward R. Murrow, who made such a crossing, "it's like watching one of those old movies where twenty men emerge from a single taxicab; it seems that the ship must burst her sides, or the men spill into the harbor. Even to one who has done some traveling on crowded cruise ships the thing seems impossible; someone must have made a mistake, forgot to give the order to stop that long twisting line of boys coming aboard . . ."[22]

Half the men would sleep on the decks, the other half inside in ballrooms, dining rooms, passageways, on triple-decker bunks, on hammocks, on floors. Each night the two groups would switch; the men would not be out of their clothes until they were on dry land again. They would spend a good part of each day waiting in line for the two meals that were served into their mess kits; this was, indeed, not a pleasure cruise. They were the population of a good-sized town, and those below-decks would share what one writer characterized as "the stale air, the snoring and the vulgar jokes, the smells—sweat and dirty socks, farts and vomit."[23]

For the officers, Bundy and his group soon discovered, the circumstances were somewhat different; the arrangements had an oddly combined prewar and wartime flavor. The officers were not packed in like the enlisted men, although with eight of them on double-decker bunks in a first-class cabin they had no room to spare. They were, however, "very carefully attended by Cunard stewards, and [they] went into the dining saloon at mealtime and sat at tables with white tablecloths and were waited on by Cunard waiters."[24] They had three meals a day, and the food was excellent. The waiters were in the Cunard service because, as the men learned after they were at sea, they were aboard the British liner *Aquitania.* But the food, however good it was, posed a problem for at least one member of Bill Bundy's group: Lieutenant Selmer Norland, from Iowa, had trouble facing kippers and kidneys at breakfast time.

NORLAND, A SOLIDLY built man of five-eleven, born on a farm in northern Iowa, was a graduate of Luther College, a small and venerable school in Decorah, Iowa. He had majored in history and English, with a minor in German, and after graduating he had for three years taught history and German in high school. At the time of Pearl Harbor, having taken a leave from teaching to work on a master's in history at the University of Iowa, he was granted a draft deferment to enable him to collect the degree. In August 1942 he entered the army and was assigned to the Signal Corps, which meant that he was sent for basic training to Camp Crowder, Missouri, a new and raw Midwestern version of Fort Monmouth. His stay was memorable for "the red clay and the heat and the soaking thunderstorms,"[25] and also for the fact that he moved straight from basic training into officer candidate prep school. In November he transferred to Monmouth for OCS itself.

Three or four weeks prior to being commissioned, at the customary interview to discuss possible assignments, Norland expressed a preferance for signal intelligence; the gratifying result was that his first orders as an officer called for him to report to Arlington Hall Station on March 1, 1943. It was actually quite a personal tribute to him that with an academic background in German hardly comparable to Whitaker's, he nevertheless had been given the military occupational specialty number of a crypto officer linguist.

Norland had been at Arlington Hall not quite five months when he was assigned to Shipment No. 0192-A. Bill Bundy was the only one of the group who knew that these men were the advance guard of an utterly new American involvement in the Allied war effort. In reality, if not officially, they were guinea pigs, and much attention would be paid to them, by the British, by Friedman and Rowlett, and by the whole U.S. intelligence establishment. In this new milieu, until now inhabited largely by the pick of Cambridge dons and by other Britons of similar talent and education, the American authorities would certainly not desire anyone who performed at a level even a half-step down from excellence. Hence, the choice of Norland, with his limited credentials, was interesting; his abilities had definitely impressed somebody.

UNTIL THE APPEARANCE of the great "Queens," the *Mary* and the *Elizabeth,* the *Aquitania* had been the pride of the Cunard Line. A few years younger than the ill-fated and controversial *Lusitania,* she had been laid down in 1913 and came into service in time to serve for a spell as a British auxiliary cruiser in the first war, before the admiralty decided that the big passenger ships were unsuitable for such use. And the *Aquitania* was big enough—45,647 tons, 902 feet in length. Now, like many of the older, higher-ranking officers, she was serving in her second war.

Because of the speed of which they were capable, the big liners sailed singly, not in convoy, and they had no armed escorts. They could easily outrun the fastest submarine, the only danger on that score being that the *Aquitania* or one of her sisters might chance upon a lurking U-boat that happened to have everything in readiness for a quick wing shot. Thus, no matter how casual the men might seem as they stood in the eternal lines, or sat at their white-clothed tables being served by waiters, or knelt in their crap games, or lay stretched out reading paperbacks, the underwater menace was never far from their minds, and the ship periodically seethed with rumors.

Not everything was GI scuttlebutt. "One night a sub sank a tanker about fifteen miles to the left of us," Whitaker wrote in his journal. And just the day before the *Aquitania* reached port, "some of us felt some concussions while we were eating dinner and thought possibly they were firing some practice shots from the deck guns. Then someone happened to look out a porthole and saw some destroyers a few miles away laying depth charges while huge geysers of white water rose into the air as each exploded."[26]

The *Aquitania*'s destination was Gourock, Scotland, near the head of the Firth of Clyde, and she was met at sea by land-based RAF fighters—Spitfires—when she came within range. As she proceeded closer and closer to land and the lines of her approach became narrow, she was actually in greater peril than she had been in the open sea. She turned and twisted constantly. But the crossing ended as peacefully as it had begun in New York harbor. Norland, for whom the first encounter with the ocean had been a greater worry than the duties he would encounter on the other side, had not suffered even a touch of seasickness; the ocean had been glassy smooth all the way.

After spending several days at a "repple depple"—replacement depot—the signal intelligence officers moved on to London, where they were assigned to Headquarters, European Theater of Operations, United States Army (ETOUSA) in Grosvenor Square. This did not mean that any of them were to serve at the headquarters but was simply an administrative device for moving them along. Bundy and two other officers were installed in a flat just around the corner from the office. Norland and the rest were billeted in what appeared to have been a club or small hotel on South Audley Street, a short walk from ETOUSA HQ. These quarters were intended for the housing of short-term transients, officers who would be around for only two or three days, but as no word came for the signal intelligence group, they had to keep extending their stay. Every morning the men would go downstairs and register again, until they began to feel definitely unwanted. A few of the fellows even began looking for some other lodgings.

Since this was the first trip to England for most of the men, they spent much of their three weeks in London walking around, seeing the sights. Norland was particularly struck by the devastation in the midst of which sat St. Paul's Cathedral; there was something haunting in the sight of the great landmark surrounded by absolute emptiness. Whitaker noted that the Londoners seemed to have a favorite adjective; when they wished to speak of something in a negative way, they said it was "grim." But in August 1943 London was actually at a relatively fortunate point in the war; the Blitz that had wreaked the striking devastation was long past, and life was much less frantic. "There were theaters to see and girls to dance with," recorded an American staff officer. "There was beer in the pubs and Scotch from Harrod's if you had a receipt from the last bottle you had bought."[27] But everywhere you could look up and see fat little sausagelike barrage balloons floating at the ends of their cables, shielding the city from possible low-level air attack, and by night the blackout was still creating a mazy dimness.

In spite of the relative calm, the blackouts were still necessary, too. On one of their first nights in South Audley Street, the signal intelligence lodgers heard the massed wailing of hundreds of sirens across the city. It was their first exposure to air attack, but Whitaker, for one, felt little concern. The chances of being hit were pretty infinitesimal, it seemed to him; London was "an awfully big city, and a few planes going over aren't likely to drop a bomb right where you are."

III

ON AUGUST 28, a month to the day after the original overseas orders had been cut at Arlington Hall, a mimeograph machine at ETOUSA headquarters cranked out explicit but remarkably brief instructions. Second Lts. Arthur J. Levenson, Selmer S. Norland, and Paul K. Whitaker "will proceed on or about Aug. 30, 1943 from this headquarters to Bletchley, England on detached service for approximately three (3) months, for the purpose of carrying out the instructions of the Commanding General . . ."[28] The officers were authorized a per diem of six dollars while traveling and four dollars while on the assigned duty. No outfit—company, regiment, detachment, anything—was named, but the three were told that they would be met at the Bletchley railway station. And they would be followed right away by the rest of the signal intelligence group.

Bletchley being a railway-junction town about fifty miles northwest of London, the three officers had little opportunity to squander their six-dollar travel per diem. Around midday, musette bags over their shoulders, and bending under the weight of their duffel bags, the Americans stepped out of the train and onto the platform at Bletchley. They were indeed met, by a transportation officer, who led them to his little car, telling them that he would drive them to their destination, "the Park," just a short way from the station.

It was obvious that Bletchley had not been chosen for its scenic charm. It was a dingy town in what had once been a brick-manufacturing region, as was suggested by the names of the nearby villages—Little Brickhill, Big Brickhill, Bow Brickhill. In a few minutes the overloaded car had climbed the slight rise northwest of the railway junction and stopped at the gates of the Park. After scrutinizing the papers of the three Americans, the guard returned them, the gate swung back, and the little black car carried the newcomers forward into a secret world.

This first visit was brief. Once inside, the Americans were told that they would shortly be put on a bus and be taken to their billets, where they could settle in. Tomorrow some of the mysteries would be unveiled.

IN THE AFTERNOON, they were driven from Bletchley Park to Bedford, a city of some fifty thousand about twenty miles away. Whitaker's hosts were to be Mr. and Mrs. George Whyte, who lived in middle-class respectability in a detached brick one-family house—65 Beverly Crescent—with their two teenage daughters. The scene was a bit different for Norland; he "wound up assigned to an old maid named Winnie Judge,"[29] who, he was told right away, had once been the secret love of the poet Rupert Brooke—or so Miss Judge asserted. She lived in an ordinary row house a quarter of a mile or so from the Whytes' home, and "as part of the war effort she took in a Yank as a roomer." The arrangement was that the lodgers would have breakfast and the evening meal at their billets and lunch at the Bletchley Park canteen. For Norland, this would prove to involve a certain amount of daily suspense; Miss Judge was fond of playing the ponies, and "if she won, which wasn't very often, we would have a very nice joint for dinner. But if she didn't win, which was most of the time, we ate an awful lot of rabbit." Levenson was assigned to a larger house along with two others from the *Aquitania,* Bill Bijur and Art Prengel—the latter from Wisconsin, not a translator, though he had a heavy linguistic background. Also in residence were two Englishmen and a kilt-wearing Scot.

Bill Bundy, the boss, was installed in the Hunt, which was described by one U.S. officer as "a charming and venerable inn with a first-class pub";[30] it was located in the town of Leighton Buzzard—the Americans were amused by the name—about seven miles from Bletchley. A fellow lodger was John Seaman, at that time the Arlington Hall liaison person at BP. Although a lawyer, Seaman had graduated from Michigan State in modern languages ("just the usual—French, German, Spanish and some others"), with an ROTC commission.[31] Later, after studying cryptanalysis in the correspondence courses, he worked at Arlington Hall until the higher-ups chose him (another nonprofessional, like Bill Bundy) for the important liaison mission in England.

The men billeted at Leighton Buzzard and other villages would be picked up daily and taken to Bletchley Park by bus. For the officers lodging in Bedford, the routine would be different. In the mornings, they would have a fifteen- or twenty-minute walk to the railway station, where—like civilian commuters—they would board a train of the London, Midland, and Scottish railway for the trip to the office.

Bundy's group, consisting in this spearhead phase of nineteen persons (nine officers and ten enlisted men) was designated the 6813th Signal Service Detachment. Along with it was the 6812th, whose personnel were to help the British in the operation of the high-speed decrypting equipment—the Bletchley Park version of Marian Rejewski's *bomba*; the commander of the 6812th was to be a Captain Stewart who had come over on the *Aquitania* with the Bundy group. A third Signal Corps outfit was also to be in the picture, the 6811th, which would be concerned with radio interception. Americans were thus to be phased into all parts of the intelligence-producing operation, at Bletchley Park and at other stations as well.

The 6813th itself, Bundy's group, was made up of two types of officers—seven cryptanalysts, including Levenson and Bundy—and the two men who had come as translators, Whitaker and Norland. When all the members of the team had arrived at BP and been settled in their billets, the next step was indoctrination. The men now learned that each of the two main phases of the Enigma-reading operation was designated by the term "hut." The combined army and air force section consisted of Hut 6, which produced the decrypts, and Hut 3, which translated these messages from military German into English; the navy, which had its own special problems and which dealt with a different form of the Enigma, had its Hut 8 and Hut 4. But these huts, although separate in the past, turned out to be all in the same building now, a new one-story brick structure.

Entering the gates of the Park, the men were taken along the drive, past the oval with the old Tudor Gothic mansion sprawling on the left and the duck pond on the right, past scattered white temporary buildings that were the original huts, to the new building, which sat in what clearly had been, a few months earlier, a meadow. This building, which faced the drive, had several wings, each perhaps sixty feet long, projecting from either side of its axis. These wings, as the Americans would learn, housed the huts, as well as offices for supervisors. Although all the huts were together now, separated only by partitions, opening off a common corridor, this proximity did not mean that the need-to-know principle did not prevail here. Hut 6 was to the left of a short entrance hall running at right angles to the main corridor, and Hut 3 to the right, but the two remained quite independent entities; and it would soon become evident that a thick, if invisible, wall divided the naval section from the rest of the building.

As the Americans approached, all of them except Bundy still in the dark about what parts they would be playing, they felt, as Norland put it, "a mixture of excitement, anticipation, and wonderment."[32] It seemed obvious that the cryptanalytic members of the group would carry on here the trade they had learned at Fort Monmouth and Vint Hill and Arlington Hall; and the men who had come as translators, Whitaker and Norland, would presumably be applying their linguistic knowledge to the rendering of German messages into English. But in what circumstances, with whom, and—above all—on what level, none of the men could know. What kinds of German messages were being read, and in what volume, were questions that were still mysteries. Now the Americans would find out what the work that was "something special" really was.

North Africa had been cleared of German forces during the spring, the campaign in Sicily had ended just about the time the Americans had arrived in England, and an Allied leap onto the Italian mainland was expected any day. In the brick building ahead lay the answers concerning the part the U.S. team would play in relation to the coming events on the Continent of Europe.

In the entrance hall of the building the Americans came to a parting of the ways. Whitaker and Norland were taken to the right, into Hut 3, to the office of the chief, Wing Cmdr. Eric Jones, a meticulously groomed officer with a neat thin mustache. With Jones was the deputy chief, Bill Marchant. Although Jones appeared decisive and crisp (which, as a successful manufacturer of biscuits, he appropriately was), most of the talking was done by Marchant, who before the war had been a master at Harrow. The former schoolmaster's words began to reveal to the Americans the incredible dimensions of the British operation.

The other Americans, Bill Bundy and his fellow cryptanalysts, had been taken to a small office at the end of the entrance hall, facing the main door of the building. There they were introduced to a smooth-faced, dark-haired English civilian, with a classically ruddy face, a man bearing a resemblance to the movie actor Arthur Treacher. This was Gordon Welchman, the head of Hut 6.

Although, as new arrivals, the Americans did not know what to expect, they could have no inkling that this man who was about to brief them was a little nervous. Just what sorts of attitudes had these Americans brought with them? Welchman had launched into a little speech of welcome when one of his listeners, Lieutenant Bill Bijur, a Manhattan advertising man, broke in to ask, "Do you mind if we smoke?" and then introduced the largest cigar Welchman had ever seen and proceeded to light it. "From there on, the party was easy," Welchman said; he began chatting in a casual fashion. As for the attitude of the Americans, it "was just delightful. They simply wanted to know what they could do to help. They were such a damn good group of people." But at the beginning, Welchman had "felt somewhat ill at ease as I started to tell them the Hut 6 story."[33] Yet, like Bill Marchant, he had a stupendous tale to tell.

6

"A Complete Meritocracy"

AS THE THREE American newcomers had observed, Bletchley was not a pretty town. Commander Denniston had chosen it, however, not for its looks but for its location—reasonably close to London and about halfway between Oxford and Cambridge, with good rail connections to both university towns. In selecting "the otherwise blameless environs of Bletchley" as the site of Station X, as it was called with surprising provocativeness, Denniston had the most likely source of brain power in mind. The area might already have boasted an intellectual citadel if, as the writer Michael Innes remarked, "those Oxford clerks who centuries ago attempted a secession had gone to Bletchley."[1]

The principle of using university dons as code-breakers had become established in the first war, under the famous Adm. "Blinker" Hall, the czar of the even more famous Room 40. The results—notably the decrypting of the Zimmermann telegram, which had given Woodrow Wilson the final push into calling for an American declaration of war on Germany—had been highly satisfactory. But in the years following 1918, cryptological intelligence had not proved to be much more popular in Britain than it had in the United States. The generals and the admirals, like their American counterparts, were at best bored by their colleagues in intelligence, and at worst actively hostile to them. Intelligence—spying—was a sneaky business, the dishonorable underside of war, and it was suitable only for a man whom destiny, in the form of a selection board, seemed unlikely ever to place at the head of a regiment or on the bridge of a battleship. Worse, it had, or was thought potentially to have, intellectual content. Bad! Such attitudes hardly encouraged promising officers to seek out the intelligence branches.

Yet the British did not completely close up the old cryptology shop.

109

In 1919 about twenty-five officers who had served in naval or military cryptology were assigned to a new entity called the Government Code and Cipher School,[2] which was placed under the control of the admiralty; in 1922 it was transferred to the Foreign Office empire, and in the following year, though maintaining its own identity, it came under the overall supervision of the head of the Special Intelligence Service.

GC&CS was housed in Broadway Buildings, near Victoria Station and St. James's Park. It was a gloomy building, "more dingy than sinister,"[3] with the kind of elevator that rose with a slow clatter; the corridors were painted dark brown from the floor to a height of about four feet. It was an anonymous spot in the midst of the city, suitable enough for peacetime, but Denniston, who had nursed GC&CS through the 1920s, and during the 1930s was facing the problems the now-foreseeable war was likely to bring, knew that the outbreak of hostilities would call for other arrangements. At the time, practically everybody believed that in the first stages of a war with Germany, London would be obliterated by Luftwaffe bombs. Denniston's answer was Bletchley Park.

At the time of the Munich crisis in 1938, when the prime minister, Neville Chamberlain, was crying "how horrible, fantastic, incredible it is that we should be digging trenches and trying on gas masks here"[4] because of that quarrel involving those faraway Czech chaps, Commander Denniston, wishing to be ready for what might come, put on a dry-run move of GC&CS to Bletchley Park. But the signing of the Munich agreement meant that the time had not yet arrived for the cryptological establishment to remain outside of London.

During this same period Denniston sent notes to a number of lecturers at Oxford and Cambridge, asking whether, in the event of war, they would be willing to serve their country. One of these men was Gordon Welchman, a thirtyish lecturer in mathematics at Sidney Sussex College, Cambridge; shortly afterward, he took part in some days of informal indoctrination, being "introduced to the established manual methods of cryptography and cryptanalysis, and also to the various types of cipher machines that were in use at that time."[5] Welchman was particularly impressed by the commander's incisive way of speaking. As for the German problem, he came away from the sessions with the impression that Denniston's group did not think their chances of success were any better than minimal, unless somehow one of the Enigma machines could be acquired. "The Germans do not mean us to read their signals,"[6] Denniston would say; solving the problem seemed beyond the powers of unaided cryptanalysis.

FOR ALL HIS remarkable dedication to the cause, year in and year out since the Room 40 days, Denniston had not understood some of the most important implications of machine encipherment. Unlike William Friedman and his superiors in the U.S. Signal Intelligence Service, the commander had not sought out mathematicians to turn into code-breakers. Even Dilly Knox, the veteran of Room 40, was, as Welchman said, "neither an organization man nor a technical man. He was, essentially, an idea-struck man."[7] A typical member of GC&CS during the 1930s tended to be literary rather than mathematical, more at home with Plautus than with probability distributions. And it was to this group that the Enigma with all its current refinements appeared increasingly unbreakable.[8] The group of about sixty men "of the professor type"[9] to whom Denniston wrote his letters of invitation in 1938 included mathematicians, but they were not to come on board unless war broke out.

IN AUGUST 1939, with the full glare of Hitler's fury turned on Poland and war seeming only days or weeks away, a group of some fifty men and women, code-named "Captain Ridley's Hunting Party," arrived from London to take up working residence at Bletchley Park. The Tudor Gothic mansion, with its stone fancifulness outside and its crocketed inside paneling, suggestive to one observer of a 1920s movie palace, sat in grounds of several acres.[10] It had been the seat of a local magnate, but in coming to house the imaginative and mysterious activities involved in code breaking, it seemed at last to have acquired tenants to match its architecture. Behind the house was a block of stables and, farther along, a small building called "the School."

On September 4, in accordance with his promise, Gordon Welchman made his adieus at Cambridge and drove the fifty-four miles to Bletchley. Welchman had for ten years been a college lecturer in mathematics at Cambridge, but only in the brief training sessions had he been involved with GC&CS. After being received by Commander Denniston in his ground-floor office, which looked out across a wide lawn to a pond, with attractively landscaped banks, he was turned over to Dilly Knox, who was working with a group of about ten persons in "the Cottage," a small building in the stableyard. Knox, never the easiest of men, was suffering from his chronic stomach trouble, and he did not appear delighted to have Welchman on his team.

Also reporting on the fourth was a fellow Cantabrigian, Alan Turing, "a very extraordinary chap."[11] During the previous year Turing had been in closer contact with GC&CS than Welchman had, and he was immediately integrated into a four-man team assigned to attack the Enigma; this team, of course, could work with the prize new acquisition, the Polish machine delivered in August by Gustave Bertrand.

Knox banished Welchman to a large bare office in the School, where he was supposed to study intercepted Enigma messages for call signs and discriminants, or message keys. What Welchman had to work on was a collection of signals that had lain undecrypted—and undecryptable—since being delivered to GC&CS from British interception stations. Presently, he also received the only Enigma decrypts in British hands, two or three days' worth that had been turned over by Bertrand at the beginning of the year. Welchman was not trying to read the encrypted messages (having no method by which to do it) but was studying them like a landscape for distinguishing features and characteristics—analyzing, dividing, and classifying.

He soon began to identify three different keys,[12] underlining the appropriate entries on his charts in different colors—red, blue, green. With the aid of intercepts sent over from France, where Bertrand and the Rejewski team were working together, Welchman ascertained that the Green key was used by the administrative network of the German army. (These networks consisted of any number of stations that communicated among themselves, all using the same frequency. The employment of such nets was a vital part of the German concept of mobile war; in fact, as much as tanks and dive bombers, it made the blitzkrieg possible, as the Wehrmacht was demonstrating in its rush into Poland. But listening for German signals was nothing like tuning in to a large metropolitan station; the transmitters were weak and distant and the frequencies tended to drift, all this making great demands on the ears and the devotion of the intercept operators.) Before long Red, Blue, and Green were joined on Welchman's charts by Brown and Orange.

But Welchman's mind was not content to concern itself solely with traffic analysis—that is, with the gleaning of information from messages by all means except actually reading them. One thing that caught his eye in the intercepts was the use of the six-letter message key, doubly enciphered; it was the feature that, seven years earlier, Marian Rejewski had seen as a partly open door into the German Enigma secret. What this led Welchman to, by a chain of mathematical reasoning and, again, on the Polish example, was the idea of perforated sheets to be stacked on a light table—Zygalski sheets, as the Poles called them. But no one had told Welchman about Zygalski's invention. On his own, Welchman had created the idea of "a thoroughly practical method of breaking some of the German Enigma traffic . . . When the correct combination, giving the key for the day, was discovered, the stackings would be discontinued and decoding of the day's traffic could begin."[13]

Dilly Knox was not thrilled. When Welchman reported his idea, Knox, who of course had been told about the sheets as well as the other Polish discoveries, informed him that such sheets were already being made under the direction of John Jeffreys, one of the two mathematicians on Knox's four-man team. Why had Knox failed to mention such a development? "Dilly was notorious for not telling anyone anything, though he often thought he had done so."

Welchman managed to take the news philosophically, reasoning that the important thing was that such a good idea was being put into practice. And he went on to think about the implications of it. If Bletchley Park developed the ability to crack the Enigma regularly and substantially, what would be needed to exploit this breakthrough? More people, certainly—more people to compile traffic-analysis charts, more people to know when to mount the sheet-stacking operation, more people to handle the sheets themselves. And a deciphering room, to decrypt the messages in a broken key and get them into the hands of consumers—intelligence staffs—in time for full advantage to be taken of them. The Germans were quiescent now, after the destruction of Poland, but no one, unless motivated by hope and ignorance, could doubt that the "phony" war would not last forever, and that it would be succeeded by a very hot war indeed. BP must be ready for the heat. Welchman drew up a plan and won quick and unbureaucratic approval from Cmdr. Edward Travis, Denniston's deputy. A new, interservice (army and RAF) section would be created to work systematically on cracking Enigma ciphers.

Immediately after the move of GC&CS from London to Bletchley Park a local contractor had begun putting up a series of small wooden buildings, or huts, of various shapes and sizes, here and there in the grounds of the Park. Inside, they had movable partitions, so that they could be adapted to changing requirements. One of these buildings, some sixty feet long by thirty feet wide, was designated in the plans as Hut 6. Early in the new year the interservice section proposed by Welchman became the tenant of the hut, and Welchman himself, who just a few months before had been a Cambridge lecturer with only an incidental acquaintance with GC&CS, became its head.

UNTIL THEIR EXPOSURE to the Polish *bomba,* the members of Denniston's team appear to have given little thought to the possibility of using high-speed machinery in the decrypting effort. But after the trip to Poland and a later visit to BP by members of the Polish group who had escaped to France, Knox gave the assignment of creating a British *bomba*—to be rechristened Bombe—to Alan Turing. Whatever Knox's deficiencies as a manager of men, no one could have looked on this as an inappropriate assignment. Although Turing was only twenty-seven, he had already published a landmark paper, "On Computable Numbers," which proved that "there are classes of mathematical problems which cannot be solved by any fixed and definite process."[15] His definition of "definite process" was certainly of interest: "something that could be done by an automatic machine." In a time when "computer" referred to a person and not a device, Turing maintained that whatever could be done by a human computer could be done by a machine, and he "imagined machines."[16] The term "Turing machine" had entered the talk of those in the rarefied know. Even prior to the appearance of his paper, he had been notable enough to be greeted by a personal message from Bertrand Russell before a lecture he was about to give.

Turing was tall and strongly built, with bright blue eyes in a face so youthful that he was often taken for an undergraduate; his dress and bearing certainly proclaimed him a denizen of academe at some level. "He tended to be slovenly," as his mother conceded. "His hair was usually too long, with an overhanging lock which he would toss back with a jerk of his head." But "when he did take the trouble to comb it, five minutes later he would run his fingers through it so that once more it would be standing on end." Nevertheless, "considering how little his appearance indicated his academic stature and how little he did to advance his own interests, it was a matter of wonder to me that wherever he went he was quickly recognized as a remarkable person." It is perhaps superfluous to add that he was notably absent-minded—"abstracted and dreamy,"[17] as his mother put it.

WHILE TURING WAS working on the British exploitation of the Polish *bomba* idea, he had a visit from Welchman, whom he had not known before the war. Welchman, at that time still officially in his traffic-analysis phase, although he had at this point devised his plan for the equivalent of the Zygalski sheets, had just been delivered of a fresh idea—a new way of connecting the scramblers of the Bombe that "could increase the effectiveness of the automatic test by a very large factor."[18] Turing, although disbelieving at first, listened carefully. Welchman had noticed, with respect to Turing, that "to people who could understand what he was talking about, or at least register a little intelligence, he was very nice, but he wasn't good with people who were rather stupid, and sometimes he wasn't good with administrative people."[19] But he was good that day with Welchman, a fellow mathematician, studying Welchman's diagram, grasping the idea of this efficiency-enhancing "diagonal board," becoming as excited as Welchman was. Once again, Commander Travis was presented with a brand-new plan, and once again he acted quickly, putting Welchman in touch with the company that was already designing the actual machine.

This did not mean that the problem of the Enigma was solved. It only meant that a far better beginning was possible than had seemed likely only a short time earlier. The traffic was complex, and surely would become much more so. But without the Bombe, there would have been no hope of success. And no Americans would have come to hear the story.

II

IN THE SUMMER of 1943 an American staff officer arrived in London for his third wartime tour in England. The people, he quickly decided, had changed since his earlier visits; they were "so visibly tired as to seem close to total exhaustion." The war effort was still thorough and absorbing, but "it had simply slowed down to a pace that seemed almost lethargic to one recently arrived from a country that was only just beginning to take on the load."[20]

The officer, a journalist in civilian life, was one of the few nonregulars assigned to the joint Anglo-American staff that was called COSSAC (the acronym stood for Chief of Staff to the Supreme Allied Commander) and that was supposed to be planning the great invasion of northwest Europe. But this staff, dominated as was perhaps inevitable at that point by Britons, seemed infected by the prevailing torpor; the newly arrived group of eager Americans, who acquired from the old hands the label Johnnies-come-lately, found themselves in "a world of interminable politeness in high places—and inaction."[21] Literally nothing seemed to be happening. It was true that COSSAC (the title referred to both the person who was Chief of Staff and to the organization under him) was a man without a boss as well as a staff without a head, since no Supreme Allied Commander had yet been appointed.

But there seemed to this restless American officer to be more to the whole problem than could be explained either by British war-weariness or by the lack of a designated supreme commander. The British, he decided, simply did not believe in the invasion but did not wish to say so. Nor did they need to; they had other and highly effective ways of achieving their hidden purpose. A mighty operation was demanded against "the still undefeated German Army . . . across the

Channel," but "to meet the urgency there seemed only interminable talk—and always talk of obstacles, never talk of how anything could be done. Striking out into its inertia was like driving your fist into a punching bag of wet manure: it gave a little, it swayed gently—but when your fist came away, its shape filled out again and it was as if it had not been touched. Only you felt soiled."[22] Since Great Britain was clearly a well-run country, even in wartime, and the British obviously made sense when they wished, "when they made no sense it could only be because they didn't choose to."[23] Their tactics were shrewd and effective. They would extract every conversational advantage from the fact that they had been at war for almost four years now, whereas the American planners had come direct from the States without even the benefit of participation in the North African campaign, which at the time was still the only action in which U.S. forces had been engaged on the German side of the world.

If possible, and it often was, the British would anglicize the American newcomer, sending him to a London tailor, supplying him with "a pretty British girl driver,"[24] giving him cards to nightclubs. If the anglicization process failed to work and the marked man proved to be not only neutral but actually anglophobic, the British had subtle methods for getting rid of him. Or if the man was not an anglophobe but still disagreed with British views, he would find himself transferred to some theater far from the center of things—"and he would never know why."[25]

The Allied courtship had long been officially over, and the marriage was now well along in its second year. American and British forces had combined to sweep Africa clean of Germans. Allied armies were leaping from Tunisia across to Sicily, and from Sicily to the mainland of Italy. Names like Eisenhower and Patton had moved into the headlines, sharing space with Alexander and Montgomery.

But there was this dismaying scene in London, as it seemed to the Johnnies-come-lately: Was it marital discord or a deeper rift? Could the British really not be trusted?

III

PERHAPS FORTUNATELY, BLETCHLEY Park was a center for the extracting and processing of information; it did not make policy. Neither its Indians nor its chiefs had to concern themselves with such questions as the respective merits of the Pas de Calais and the coast of Normandy as sites for the proposed invasion landings or, more deeply, with the wisdom of putting greater weight into Allied operations in the Mediterranean as against building up strength in England for the cross-Channel operation. BP was a servant, not a master.

If, as has been asserted, some persons at Bletchley Park at first resented the arrival of Bill Bundy's group because of "the extra effort that would be required from a weary staff in training them,"[26] these BP veterans succeeded admirably in keeping their feelings to themselves. Welchman had felt no particular need for reinforcements from overseas, but after that first day, he had no misgivings. He hadn't known that he needed them, but he was glad they were there. These were the attitudes that would have existed in an ideal world; they were an actual fact at Bletchley Park in August 1943.

Art Levenson felt that everybody at BP made quite a fuss over these newly arrived Americans and "once they got over the shock of having foreigners, we were just like the British."[27] Bill Bundy, who as a cryptanalyst was headed for Hut 6, participated in the "memorable first briefing"[28] with Welchman, and then, as the head of the U.S. group, went into placement talks with Stuart Milner-Barry, the British chess champion who was just taking over as head of Hut 6, and with Eric Jones and Bill Marchant of Hut 3.

The British, Bundy realized, were "very goosy" about one possibility. What would happen if they thought it necessary to reject an American? Fortunately, Rowlett and Bundy had had the Americans "pretty well taped" when the group was put together at Arlington Hall; they were sure they knew what their men could do. But Bletchley Park was not Arlington Hall, of course. It was differently organized and, in spite of the relative commonality of language, was a foreign operation.

The British put the Americans through an introductory scrutiny, sorting them out "pretty much the way we did in terms of their capacities." Because of the complexity of the entire signal-intelligence operation, various kinds of slots existed into which any newcomers, British or American, could be inserted. It was agreed at the outset that "each man was to be judged on his merits, regardless of rank, no matter what this did to the structure"; the Americans could see that this was what the British were doing, with "a major working for a civilian or alongside a sergeant who was the smarter of the two." These various kinds of slots were available because there was simply more to the procedure than one person or hut cracking a cipher, and the other person or hut translating the results.

As the Americans saw immediately, Hut 6, in spite of its modest name, was an enormously complex affair,[29] filling up several rooms and areas, each of these representing a particular aspect of the operation. What the newcomers could not at first know was that this going concern, like many a corporation, had grown from humble one-man beginnings, the original entrepreneur here having been Welchman in one small office with his bundles of undecrypted intercepts. Now there was a registration room, to which were brought—by motorcycle and increasingly by teleprinter—German messages that had been snatched from the air by young women of what was called the Y Service, who sat with earphones at intercept stations at Beaumanor in Leicestershire and elsewhere. An area called the intercept control room kept in around-the-clock telephone communication with the intercept stations. Interception was not merely random; an operator did not simply turn on her set and, like an amateur shortwave enthusiast, tune around to see what she could pick up. The control room was continually in touch with the duty officers at the intercept stations, telling them, on the basis of traffic analysis and of previous decrypts, what frequencies needed special attention. Early in the game, specific items requested by Hut 6 had acquired the nickname "Welchman's Specials."

Associated with Hut 6—although working in quarters outside the brick building, in an actual white hut—was the Central Party in Hut 5,[30] consisting of a number of servicemen and -women who studied German radio nets, links between headquarters and subordinate units. Because of the tendency of the radio transmitters of the time to drift in frequency and to fade out, the controller of a German net was constantly in the position of a grade-school teacher taking a class on a field trip, issuing bursts of short messages ordering his charges to behave and stay in line—so that his net would remain in working order. The "chitchat" by which he did this was recorded in logs by the intercept operators, giving rise to "log reading"—the basic, painfully detailed intelligence technique of the Central Party, or Hut 5.

The heart of Hut 6 was the "watch"—a group of twelve or fourteen men sitting at plain wooden tables in a large, bare room, which tended to be cold and damp. Behind and alongside them, "like a hockey coach walking up and down behind his players," as one American put it, paced the head of the watch, "usually pretty much of a genius," ready to deal with problems. Even the lighting, very dim, conformed to the Spartan mode—but the men were "all young and had good eyes."[31] Adding to the atmosphere was the fact that, since the room was in continuous use, twenty-four hours a day, seven days a week, it apparently was never cleaned; it was "cluttered with teapots and coffeepots and dirty mugs, papers and trash—all kinds of wonderful memorabilia all over the place."[32]

The members of the watch were a mixture of service personnel and civilians, and matters were conducted with no military protocol or punctilio whatsoever. A cryptanalyst reporting for work simply took off his coat ("unless," as one said, "it was wintertime"), sat down at his table, and began attacking a bundle of intercepts that had been received, registered, and sorted by the traffic analysts. These intercepts were assigned to the cryptanalysts by frequency, each person being responsible for the traffic on a particular wave length. The aim was to solve the daily key for each cipher used by the German army and the Luftwaffe. By this time Hut 6 had reached a level of performance marked by consistent successes, particularly with air force keys.

The Hut 6 team was divided into three shifts—the day shift from 9:00 in the morning to 4:00 P.M., the evening shift from 4:00 P.M. to midnight, and the graveyard from midnight to 9:00 A.M. The graveyard shift included an extra hour because, it seemed, those who designed such arrangements felt that the night workers would not object to working a little longer, whereas those who worked days could have more time for recreation. Since one changed shifts every two weeks, the scheme was thoroughly egalitarian.

"The fun of being on the night shift," one American said, "was that the first code of the day came in about three o'clock in the morning." The fatal flaw of the Germans—at least with regard to codes—was exactly what every commentator had pointed to since the First World War—their undeviating precision and regularity of procedure. Here the myth was true: every day at the same time came the message about the same kind of subject matter. This was the weather report, transmitted in the Luftwaffe general-purpose key. "We all tried to get it because it was the first code of the day, which was fun, and because getting the weather was important. It was usually easy to break not only because of the timing, which told you what key it was, but because if it was going to be cloudy, rainy, or fair, they would start off with the standard phrase for it. Of course, sitting in Bletchley Park, you didn't know what the weather was in Heidelberg, but you knew it was going to be rainy or snowy or whatever."[33] This fact gave the cryptanalyst a good chance of getting a kind of peek through the ciphertext into a bit of the plaintext—a crib, it was called, almost as though the Germans were university examiners creating a test for the Allies to pass or flunk. The code-breakers depended on human errors by the Germans, and the use of standard phrases was one of the enemy's most helpful ones.

Another kind of regular crib had long been provided by a German officer who had sat out in the North African desert faithfully reporting to his superiors, every day, that he had nothing to report. In such cases, Welchman wished he could "ask the British commanders to be sure to leave our helper alone." If a crib proved out, the cryptanalyst could then produce a menu to be fed to one of the Bombes. The Bombe was not a creator, but a tester of hypotheses given it by human beings. The cryptoanalyst would offer it his best guess at what a piece of cipher-text said in German; the machines would click away and either con-firm or deny the hypothesis.

So complex was the work of the watch that it was divided on functional lines. Besides the persons engaged in straight cryptanalysis, one group was engaged in a search for "kisses"—the same message transmitted on different radio nets and hence enciphered on different keys (the name came from the fact that the Registration Room recorded the key of each message with an X in the color of that key). And then "you had people studying the decodes just before they went into Hut 3 to make note of messages that had crib value"—for example, that contained phrases likely to be used again. "And you had people watching the traffic register, looking for what was important to them."[35] Sometimes persons especially gifted in cryptanalysis would work in back rooms on particularly difficult keys. There was also a special team whose efforts were devoted to research, so that when the Germans would introduce a new element or a new procedure, this group could prepare a counterattack.

When the Wrens who operated the Bombes reported that the key was broken, the cryptanalyst's work on those particular intercepts was finished. As a high-level specialist, he did not proceed to decipher the whole message; the head of the watch turned the key and the inter-cepts over to the "magnificent crowd of girls"[36] who made up the Decoding Room, rendering the intercept from ciphertext into military German. As it happened, however, messages would sometimes not come out at the first try. Hence, "They were not only doing straight decoding. Those girls became sort of cryptologists, in order to try and guess what had gone wrong. Very often they decoded a message that the Germans themselves had failed to decode"[37] (as could be learned when the legitimate recipient was forced to ask for a repeat).

With personnel constantly increasing, as the Germans became engaged on more and more fronts, setting up more nets, using more keys, sending more messages, Hut 6 with all its complexity offered the Americans a variety of job possibilities—the watch, intercept control, traffic analysis—everything except the opportunity to join the young women operating their Typex machines in the decoding room. That privilege was not available.

All of the parts of Hut 6 were in a constant flow of purposeful movement, keeping in close contact with each other. The people in the watch would be going in and out of the registration room to watch the traffic, and the people in the control room would continually be buzzing into the registration room to see what was happening, so that they could compare notes with the duty officers at the intercept stations. It all worked, Welchman felt, like a fine machine.

In Bundy's view, "there never was a more complete meritocracy than Hut 6."[38] Levenson went into the watch, and in what would appear to be a good example of the working of the merit principle, Bundy himself, though only twenty-six, was "in fairly short order" assigned as one of the five rotating heads of watch. When, modestly, he protested, he was simply told, "We want you." A later member of the American group at Bletchley Park had a similar assessment of the U.S. chief: "Technically, Bundy was probably the best mind we had over there."[39] One thing Bundy, and all of the Americans, quickly learned: Although Hut 6 was next to the navy's Hut 8, separated from it only by a partition, you "never, never" paid a visit to your navy counterpart. It was a matter of two separate worlds. To an American, of course, a gulf between army and navy hardly seemed strange.

THE MEMBERS OF the American team had been in place only a week or so when they were summoned to a large reception room in the Tudor Gothic mansion. Amid a scene of military formality, presided over by Commander Travis, they were presented to a visiting U.S. two-star general, tall and stern-looking. George Strong, the head of military intelligence, was honoring, with a personal greeting, the American newcomers to the signal-intelligence nerve center of the war against Hitler.[40] The Americans lined up and filed past the general, shaking his hand, and "he said to each of us: 'How long have you been here?' And each of us said to him, 'About a week, sir.' Then he said, 'Well, you're going to like it. This is a great assignment.' And we said, 'Thank you, sir,' and moved on." But at the tail end of the line was a short fellow, a U.S. captain, whom no one appeared to know. Not a member of Bill Bundy's group, he had stood by himself, speaking to nobody, and to Levenson he seemed "like a character out of Dostoyevsky." As this captain reached the general and the two were shaking hands, Strong asked his question: "How long have you been here, son?"

"Two years, sir," said the captain.

Strong was startled. "Two years! By God, we'll have to send you home and get the tea wrung out of you!"

This little scene became Levenson's favorite memory of his first days at Bletchley Park.

7

Inside Hut 3

ONCE THE decoding room had turned a message from ciphertext into German, it went onto a conveyer belt, like luggage at an airport, and was trundled the short distance into the Hut 3 watch room. Up to this point it had been only raw material, of great interest as a technical phenomenon to the persons in Hut 6, but essentially without content; now it was about to become actual intelligence. Here was where Paul Whitaker and Selmer Norland, the only two translators in the initial American group, were to make their contribution. Although not code-breakers, they would have an advantage over their friends in Hut 6—they would know what the messages actually said.

It was possible in theory for a cryptanalyst to labor for years on Enigma traffic and never know the meaning of even one intercept. His function was to produce enough words that looked like German for the Bombe to do its work, and he himself might well know no German at all; "in fact," said one cryptanalyst, "very few if any of us did."[1] The Hut 6 operation was mathematical and mechanical, not linguistic. This applied as well to the women operating the Typex machines, which did the decoding, so that it was not until a message reached Hut 3 that it began to be treated as a piece of information about real people and events.

At the time the Americans came, Bletchley Park had grown into a sizable community, with a population of about five thousand[2]—men and women performing all sorts of functions relating to signal intelligence, at various levels. Very few of them, however—no more than four or five hundred—were associated with Hut 6 and Hut 3, or even knew of the existence and work of these key operations. Of this group some fifty or sixty, now including Whitaker and Norland, were German specialists.

123

Like Hut 6, Hut 3 was a complex operation[3]—much more than a few men sitting with scratch pads, translating neat German into nice English. Its heart was also a watch, which sat in a room no larger than about twenty-five feet square. The main feature of the room was a plain wooden semicircular table, perhaps fifteen feet long and two-and-a-half feet wide, with a brown fiberboard top. Around the table, in eight or ten equally plain wooden chairs that looked as though they had been rather hastily run up by some local craftsman, sat the members of the watch, their work illuminated by a single fluorescent light hanging from the ceiling; the room's one window was blacked out. In the center of the semicircle, behind a low partition, was the chair of the head of the watch. The head would receive the material that came in from Hut 6, scan it to decide its degree of urgency—whether it should be translated immediately or put aside for the moment. If it was to be worked on right away, he would place it on the little shelf atop the partition, very much in the manner of a short-order cook setting out dishes for waiters to pick up.

Whitaker and Norland were told, however, that they would not immediately join this watch. Instead, they were shown into an adjacent room, which for some time now had been the seat of what was called the back-room, or sometimes training, watch. This watch served the very practical purpose of handling the sort of intercepts the head of the main watch might set aside, either because of the type of subject matter or because they were less time-sensitive than many of the other messages; essentially, these signals served as background material. Many of them had to do with railways, questions of supply, and the like—all matters that could, in particular contexts, take on considerable importance. In addition, as the Americans were to find, some of the back-room messages had reached that particular destination because they were very corrupt texts that required painstaking emendation.

Whitaker and Norland were told that they would be assigned to the back room until they had become fully familiar with the procedures, with the resources of Hut 3, and with all the peculiarities of the Enigma traffic; and then, in due course, they would be worked into regular watches. This period of time would also allow the newcomers to become familiar with the kinds of achievements and problems associated with Ultra since it became operational early in the war. There was no formal training course, no prescribed indoctrination into the glories of Hut 3, but through handling a variety of messages and—more important, actually—through informal conversation on the back watch and during meal and tea breaks, Whitaker and Norland would hear stories about the moments when Ultra had figured prominently in earlier events—the "perhaps apocryphal story of Churchill and Coventry,"[4] the desert fighting in North Africa, and other notable times— going back to the beginning of the war.

II

DURING THE SEVEN months of the "phony war"—September 1939 to April 1940—while French and German soldiers gazed at each other across the border but carefully refrained from attempts to do each other harm, the cryptanalytic teams at Bletchley Park, using the Polish-built Enigma, eagerly attacked enemy ciphers. Since no British Bombe had yet been produced, this was hand work, but it was conducted with encouraging news from across the Channel. Although Colonel Bertrand's Polish cryptological stars, installed in a chateau about twenty-five miles northeast of Paris, had been forced to start almost from scratch, having arrived in France with little in the way of documents and other material, late in the autumn they succeeded in breaking a German army Enigma key for October 28.[5] Similar success with this same key, the Green, followed in England, and in January 1940 came "the first great cryptanalytic advance of the war":[6] Bletchley Park cracked the important German Red key (as Welchman's team called it), which was used for operational instructions and air-ground liaison.

At this point, however, with Poland having been crushed months before and deep, if utterly artificial, tranquillity prevailing in the West, the Germans had no operational secrets for the British listeners to steal. But in April the "Sitzkrieg," as sarcastic commentators termed the strange war, came to an end with surprising and swift German landings in Norway. Not only did this invasion present the Bletchley Park code-breakers with their first operational challenge, it demonstrated with disconcerting clarity the grave inadequacies of the British system for collecting, collating, and exploiting intelligence.[7]

During the night of April 8-9, the duty officer at the War Office received a telephone call from a *Daily Express* reporter. Was the War Office aware that the Germans had landed in Norway?

"No," the duty officer said, politely thanking the caller "for the tip."[8]

Norway was the British Pearl Harbor; the Germans had given no single unmistakable indication of their intention, but bits of evidence were offered in abundance—clues to which the British government, preoccupied with its own dithering about Norway (to land there? not to land there?) was incapable of responding. And no intelligence organization had the mission of dispassionately collecting and ordering the facts and presenting them to the commanders and the Cabinet. The sluggishness, the bewilderment, and the surprise all went to create a prototype for Washington, autumn 1941—one which the Americans unfortunately followed to the letter.

Yet, even before this debacle, one person had devoted a great deal of attention to the problems likely to be presented by a swelling flow of information. At the beginning of the war, Group Captain Fred Winterbotham was the senior representative of the Air Staff with the Secret (Special) Intelligence Service. A handsome, worldly officer, who had spent much time in Nazi Germany, Winterbotham was attuned to advances in science, such as radar, and from conversations with Commander Denniston he had come to appreciate the possibilities offered by cryptanalysis. Early in 1940 he was summoned to the presence of Brigadier Menzies,[9] who handed him "four little slips of paper, each with a short Luftwaffe message dealing with personnel postings to units." Unimportant in themselves, these messages had been produced by Bletchley Park from German intercepts; to Winterbotham this was a tremendous event, the promise of a new age in British intelligence. If BP had read these signals, it would surely go on to read a great many more. How should this vitally important new material be handled? Obviously a plan was needed, and by the next morning, after a sleepless night, Winterbotham had created one.

Returning to Menzies's sanctum, he drew for the chief a convincing picture of the chaos that was likely to prevail if a new signal-intelligence plan were not adopted. If normal customs prevailed, the Enigma intelligence would be directly distributed to the directors of intelligence of the army, the navy, and the RAF, who could make any further distribution they chose—leading to the awful probability that during one single day, hundreds of intercepts would be handled separately by each service, with its own translation, its own evaluation, and the transmission of the information in its own cipher to field commanders. Besides the obvious inefficiency of such duplication of effort, a ghastly security problem would be posed. Who, for instance, could know what a general in the field might take it into his head to do with a piece of information that gave him the chance to make a quick but telltale *coup*?

Winterbotham proposed to bring order to this scene of potential disaster by setting forth three distinct procedures. The first of these would require the establishment of a translation service, which could be lodged in Hut 3 at Bletchley Park, close to Hut 6. The second step would involve processing the message after it was translated to give it a priority and determine who ought to receive it. The third step would ensure security in distribution, since wide dissemination of this priceless material obviously had its dangers. Winterbotham proposed that each overseas field command have attached to it a unit consisting of radio and cryptological personnel, to whom the SIS would transmit, in its own cipher, messages originating in Hut 3. The members of this unit would serve as Bletchley Park contact points to the field command, and their commanding officer would be charged with enforcing security provisions, keeping the information to a restricted circle, explaining to the commanders the dangers of making any move that could cause the enemy to have doubts about the security of the Enigma. Such units, Winterbotham suggested, should be called Special Liaison Units.

Winterbotham made one other notable contribution. The admiralty had long employed a special code phrase for the transmission of signals from intercepted enemy messages—"Ultra Secret," outranking even "Most Secret," a term used by all the services. "I got the Director of Naval Intelligence to agree to let me use the simple word 'Ultra' and persuaded the Director of Military Intelligence and the Director of Air Intelligence to agree."[10]

Thus, the new intelligence now had its name—although, in a jocular tribute to the author of the plan, the Air Ministry chose to call it "Fred." Nobody yet knew how many intercepts there would be, how many keys Hut 6 would break, or how long the process would take. But it was clear that the Germans, when they made a major move, would have to abandon land lines for the air waves. Brigadier Menzies approved the plan, provided Winterbotham could sell it to the directors of intelligence of the services, and within a short time the army and the air force were on board. The navy, although lodged at Bletchley Park, too, decided that it would operate its own equivalents of Huts 6 and 3.

On April 10, the day after the German landings in Norway, Hut 6 received intercepts in a new key. Dubbed Yellow, it was cracked in five days; its messages proved to be concerned with Luftwaffe operations, and it was broken continuously as long as the Norwegian operation lasted. But this triumph was of little account: Ultra was too new, its practitioners too few and too inexperienced, the information received too complex and too abundant, the German air-land communications too efficient, British efforts at operational coordination too inept. At this point in the war, the Germans were simply playing in a much higher league than their opponents; even a far more refined Ultra operation could not have changed the dismal outcome.

On May 10, a month after the Norwegian invasion, when the cold war in the West turned hot, the infant operation at Bletchley Park had a fresh opportunity to try to walk. The plans for the German operation, called *Sichelschnitt* (Cut of the Sickle), were not the kind of thing the enemy would put on the air, because they were observing strict security and because, prior to the beginning of active operations, land lines could perform the work of communication; Ultra, accordingly, had no opportunity to be of service here. Worse still, for two weeks after the attack began Hut 6 was unable to supply any operational intelligence; as one of the many fine details of its preparations, the German command had introduced modifications into the Enigma; the Red key suddenly went black.

What had happened was that the Enigma operators had stopped the double encipherment of the message setting—the feature that had helped Marian Rejewski to his early success. This meant that the British version of the Zygalski perforated sheets, known after their deviser as Jeffreys sheets, became useless. But, as ever, the Germans made vital human procedural errors (one set of which was known in Hut 6 as "sillies"), enabling the cryptanalytic team to break the Red key again by the last week of May. A torrent of messages (as many as a thousand a day)[11] poured out of Bletchley Park to the army and air staffs and thence to the generals in the field, still not without difficulty and delay, but far more efficiently than had been the case in Norway.

By the last week in May the issue had already been settled—had been settled, in fact, only three days after the campaign began, when General der Panzertruppen Heinz Guderian's assault troops paddled their rubber boats across the Meuse, attacking and putting out of commission the French pillboxes on the west bank, preparing the way for engineers with pontoon bridges. Across these bridges rolled columns of panzers that, a bare week later, found themselves triumphant on the Channel coast, behind the Anglo-French forces that had moved into Belgium. This was a victory that amazed the civilized world and also the Nazi leaders themselves. It wasn't supposed to be this easy. As had been the case in Norway, the greatest signal intelligence in the world could not have changed the outcome.

Even though Ultra had played only a minor part in these first great collisions between the Allies and the Wehrmacht, Norway and France had served as training schools for Bletchley Park and for the consumers of BP's product. Consistent signal intelligence on this level was something so new that both producers and intelligence staffs had to learn how to evaluate it, distribute it, and put it to good use. During the ensuing summer months, it became clear that one of the greatest contributions Ultra would make in the war was not the dramatic revelation of some great Hitlerian operational plan but, more mundanely, the supplying of pieces of evidence, hundreds to thousands of them, that could painstakingly be fitted together to produce a picture of the enemy's organization and dispositions. Facing the possibility of invasion, the British could not allow themselves to proceed on the assumption that the enemy was as surprised as his victims had been by his rapid triumph in France. Ultra therefore was closely watched for signs of German activity that might be related to plans for a cross-Channel operation. The suggestions might be minor and unexplicit, so they therefore called for close attention; for instance, on August 11 an air commander was informed that thirty men with a perfect knowledge of English were being transferred to him.[12] The intelligence officers were beginning to learn how to create meaningful mosaics from such bits of fact.

As it happened, the Luftwaffe and its commander, Reichsmarschall Göring, had no doubt that if invasion was to take place, air supremacy must first be secured. They knew, as the rest of the world did not, that Hitler and his generals had no plan at all beyond *Sichelschnitt*. Who would have thought the whole thing would go so stunningly well? What quickly came to be called the Battle of Britain therefore had to be fought. This contest in the air began in earnest in August. *Adlertag* (Eagle Day) was originally set for August 10 but, owing to bad weather, was postponed to August 13. By this time Bletchley Park had, through its collation of situation reports and other signals from air units, built up an order of battle for the Luftwaffe. This was truly an epochal development, both in itself and because high-level strategic conversations between Berlin and the commanders at their headquarters in France were conducted by land lines rather than radio, giving Ultra no chance to capture such secrets. To the surprise of the British, the Germans used Enigma for tactical as well as higher purposes, but this short-run intelligence was difficult to use in air battle for several reasons—timing, changes in enemy plans caused by weather and other factors, and the lack of any system for rapid exploitation of such information.

But the signals were, nevertheless, matters of fascination for Winston Churchill. At the outset of the battle the prime minister informed the SIS that he wished to see any important decrypts, each to be accompanied by a note about its significance. Menzies assigned the job of selecting, annotating, and overseeing the delivery of the messages to Winterbotham. It had to be done carefully—"there was no room for mistakes in this business."[13] Churchill read the signals with the avidity one might expect; not only was the material fascinating stuff in itself, it was most useful to receive the same information as was given the generals and the air marshals, and at the same time.

The code name applied to the Ultra material at the prime minister's level was Boniface,[14] the implication to the staff being that this was the pseudonym of some phenomenally industrious and resourceful spy at Hitler's elbow; but Churchill's pet name for the intercept material was "my eggs"—eggs laid by the indubitably golden goose of Bletchley Park. According to one of the prime minister's secretaries, Boniface was the "sole form of intelligence, or indeed of spying, in which Churchill was constantly interested."[15] And what an interest he showed! Here was a source of fresh information, unfiltered and unadulterated by staffs and committees, from which he relished drawing specific facts with which to bombard his advisers in London and to hector commanders in the field. The chiefs of staff were not thrilled. But the benefits for Bletchley Park were obvious.

After the Luftwaffe failed to win the day against the RAF fighter force, thus relieving Hitler's generals of the need to pursue their halfhearted plans for amphibious invasion of the island, the Germans turned to the sustained night-bombing attack on cities, which the British called the blitz. On November 14, 1940, came Operation Moonlight Sonata,[16] when the Luftwaffe sent 449 bombers, carrying 503 tons of high explosives and 881 incendiary canisters, over the midlands industrial city of Coventry—the raid that gave rise to what Selmer Norland called the "possibly apocryphal" story involving Winston Churchill. The story was that one of the Boniface boxes had contained decrypts making it plain that Coventry was to be the first target in this wave of assaults on industrial centers, but that, in order to safeguard the precious source of the intelligence, Churchill ordered that no use be made of it, no special air defenses assigned to the city, no evacuation of the population undertaken; and Coventry was therefore left to its fate, with its gutted cathedral destined to become a symbol of the Blitz.

The fact was that BP had produced relevant Enigma decrypts in the days before the attack on Coventry—the Hut 3 veterans were certainly right—but, curiously, the accurate information about the attack and its target was gained from other sources.[17] It came from a prisoner of war's revelations to a stool pigeon in his barracks and, on the afternoon of the attack, from the setting of the radio beams that were to guide the German bombers to their destination.

Unfortunately, the POW's remarks were largely disregarded because (and here, as often, entered the curse of the intelligence profession—expectation) the British air intelligence staff was, for other reasons, looking for a German attack on the London area. By the time the beams were read, it was midafternoon and, though countermeasures were taken, they were ineffective; of the 449 Luftwaffe bombers arriving over the target, only one was shot down. Winston Churchill appears to have had no part in the whole affair.

ON FEBRUARY 12, 1941, came a notable event in the war—the arrival in North Africa of Lt. Gen. Erwin Rommel, who was to command the Afrika Korps, a German force sent to sustain the Italians in Libya. From then on, throughout his remarkable career in the desert, Rommel waged war not only against the tangible British troops and tanks in front of him but against the invisible forces of Ultra. One of BP's first contributions in this theater was to inform the War Office of the identity of the new commander,[18] but no one was prepared (or probably could have been) for the independence, resourcefulness, and skill at improvisation of this general, who, despite the fact that Ultra showed that he did not yet have a substantial enough force for a major attack, proceeded to launch one within ten days of his arrival. By April 28, in the first of the great ebb-and-flow dramas in which he was to engage, Rommel had led the Afrika Korps to the frontier of Egypt.

As time went on, Ultra began making a vital contribution to the British effort in North Africa. Paul Whitaker was told about a striking Ultra accomplishment: it "reported all ships supplying Rommel. . . . In Egypt there were six weeks when not a single supply vessel got through to Rommel. Italian dock workers, suspected of reporting ship movements to the Allies, were shot by the hundreds, protesting their innocence."[19]

In early 1941, while Ultra was sketching its picture of the Afrika Korps, it was also providing Whitehall with information about a matter of much larger scale and greater complexity—the German shift of concentration from west to east, into the Balkans in the direction of Greece, and into eastern Europe opposite the Soviet Union. When it came to weighing the significance of the increasing German buildup against Russia, British intelligence officers had trouble convincing themselves that it meant what one might hope it would mean. Why should Hitler, with Great Britain undefeated at his rear, hurl his forces into the great expanses of the Soviet Union, a country that was faithfully honoring its agreements to keep him supplied with all sorts of vital materials? No English statesman would make such a gamble; why, therefore, would Hitler? At this point the British intelligence staffs might well have been the Americans a few months later, looking across the Pacific and allowing for every possibility except the one actually chosen by the Japanese, who did not know that they were supposed to think and act the way Americans would. And Hitler was certainly neither English nor even marginally a gentleman.

The unleashing of Operation Barbarossa on June 22 transformed the war and, not quite six months later, the entry of the United States meant that there was now arrayed against Hitler a "grand alliance," as Churchill called the great but uneasy coalition. In November 1942, with the Anglo-American landings in French Northwest Africa under the overall command of General Eisenhower, the American ground forces for the first time became direct beneficiaries of the work of Hut 6 and Hut 3 at Bletchley Park. Eisenhower's Allied Force Headquarters had an integrated—but of necessity mostly British—intelligence staff, headed by Brig. Eric Mockler-Ferryman.

Two months earlier, some twenty-two hundred miles across North Africa, the British effort against the Afrika Korps had acquired a new director when Lt. Gen. B. L. Montgomery took command of the Eighth Army. Monty quickly showed himself a general who could arouse comment and hostility not only in the field and in the press but behind the scenes at Bletchley Park. What Whitaker's and Norland's informants on the ways and wonders of Hut 3 knew—and the newspaper readers outside Bletchley Park did not know—was that the "intuition" of which Monty spoke, his feel for what his opponent was likely to do next, owed little to any crystal ball on the general's desk and much to Enigma intelligence flashed to North Africa from BP. (Just how avid a consumer of Ultra Montgomery really was was described by Brigadier E. T. Williams, the senior intelligence officer of the Eighth Army; speaking of an Ultra briefing, Williams observed that "Monty had completely seized every point which one had made—immediately."[20] Before the battle of Alam Halfa in August 1942, "believing that the confidence of his men was the prerequisite of victory, he told them with remarkable assurance how the enemy was going to be defeated. . . . A day or two later everything happened according to plan.")[21]

After the British victory at El Alamein, the Allied forces in North Africa were converging on Tunisia from opposite ends of the continent. When in his retreat Rommel reached the Mareth Line, an old French defensive position on the Libyan-Tunisian border, he stopped and, a true Desert Fox at bay, turned on his foe; Montgomery's pursuit, never pressed with urgency, came to a halt. Meanwhile, the Germans poured reinforcements from Sicily into northern Tunisia. Col. Gen. Jürgen von Arnim, a grim-faced veteran of the Russian front and no admirer of Rommel, was sent along as commander. Thus, there were two Axis chiefs in what had now shrunk to one theater. Rommel's

German-Italian Panzer Army, as his forces had been designated, lay between the British Eighth Army to the southeast and the Allied forces west and north; north of Rommel's position stood Arnim's army.

In February 1943, Arnim decided to move against the Allies through passes in the mountain chain called the Eastern Dorsal; Rommel, at the same time, determined to strike northwest in a flanking attempt to cut the Allied forces off from their bases of supply and thus force the British First Army to pull out of Tunisia.[22] The Allied forces at this time were neither well led nor well organized, and they were spread over a front too long to be held everywhere in strength. Lt. Gen. Sir Kenneth Anderson, the commander of the British First Army, charged by Eisenhower with coordinating Allied operations, expected the enemy thrust to come through the Fondouk Pass; a U.S. brigadier general, Paul Robinett, reported however that patrols of his Combat Command B, 1st Armored Division, had scouted far to the eastward in the area and spotted no German buildup. Robinett's report was made personally to the visiting General Eisenhower, who was "satisfying myself that everything was in good order to receive the expected attack."[23]

Robinett's news had been brushed off by his superiors, including General Anderson and the commander of the U.S. II Corps, Maj. Gen. Lloyd R. Fredendall. Eisenhower proved to be a more responsive audience, telling Robinett he would take the matter up next day, February 14, with the corps and army commanders. But when he arrived at Fredendall's headquarters the following morning, he found that the Germans had already struck—through the Faid Pass, some thirty-five miles south of Fondouk.

At first nobody at headquarters realized the weight of the advance, General Anderson holding to his view that the main attack would still come through the Fondouk Pass. For their part, the Americans on the spot were slow to understand what was happening and to ask for sizable reinforcements; and the accounts of the Axis strength they did submit to Anderson and to Allied Force Headquarters back in Algiers were discounted as the exaggerations of untried troops in their first real battle. But the Axis forces drove on, Arnim's troops across the Sbeitla Plain toward Kasserine, Rommel's coming up from Gafsa toward the Kasserine Pass;[24] the only troops the Allies had available to defend the pass were a U.S. infantry battalion, a field artillery battalion, and an engineer combat regiment, the latter being utterly untrained in such fighting; Fredendall ordered the American infantry commander, Col. Alexander N. Stark, Jr., to "pull a Stonewall Jackson."[25] It was Stark's force that had to stand up against an assault by Afrika Korps veterans led by their renowned commander, who was bent on pushing through in a major strategic move all the way to Tebessa in Algeria.

At daybreak on February 19 the Desert Fox sent forward a reconnaissance battalion with the mission of seizing the pass by surprise, but the defenders of Stark's mixed force were on the alert. In fact Stark and his men, though not winning the battle to save the pass during the next two days, fought the kind of vital delaying action that changes the outcome of campaigns. Time was Rommel's greatest foe: he had to make his breakthrough and win his victory before the far more numerous Allies could amass strength against him. This he did not do. He won the pass but lost the greater battle. The Allies—amid much doubt, confusion, and recrimination—had refused to be trapped or outflanked.

General Eisenhower was greatly disturbed by a number of aspects of this battle—the conduct of General Fredendall, who seemed remote from the fighting almost in the long-derided fashion of the First World War generals lolling miles behind the trenches in their comfortable chateaux; the disposition of the American troops and their morale and lack of training; and the working of the overall command arrangements. But nothing upset him more than the discounting by the intelligence divisions of the "very accurate reports . . . submitted by the American troops to General Anderson concerning the strength and direction of the German attack."[26] What was the matter with intelligence at First Army headquarters and with G-2 back in Algiers?

It was a difficult business to sort out (and, in fact, Eisenhower took some actions without waiting for much sorting-out to take place), but the true root cause of the trouble was the divided German command, a scene of confusion almost as great as that of the Allies and compounded by the personal and reciprocal detestation between Arnim and Rommel. Here is where Ultra made its entrance onto the stage. If a single, unified Axis command had prevailed, with instructions coming properly along the line to the field generals from *Comando Supremo* (it was Hitler's fancy to act as if the Italians were in charge in North Africa), orders might have been clear, timely, and acted on. As it was, the situation was almost the opposite; Arnim and Rommel disagreed over the purposes of the operation and the allocation of troops and matériel for it. As an official historian conservatively observed, "the enemy's plans were being developed with frequent changes of mind and with a large element of improvisation within an uncertain structure of command."[27] Hence, though BP was decrypting German signals between Rome and Tunisia in the Chaffinch key (the names of birds being used as designations for army keys) and sending the results to

Allied headquarters, these messages were not as authoritative and conclusive as they might have been under other circumstances. And there was another factor: the messages partly concerned Erwin Rommel; the British might have remembered that this general had confounded their expectations and intelligence "appreciations" almost from the moment of his arrival in Africa.

Brigadier Mockler-Ferryman, the Allied G-2, had for more than two years found the oracle of Bletchley Park a faithful and reliable source of information about the enemy. But now his distant partner had turned on him; it had not kept up with the changes in Axis plans or with the tug of war between Arnim and Rommel. One detail had been of special importance to Mockler-Ferryman: The 10th Panzer Division,[28] Arnim's best, had been kept close to the Fondouk area; therefore, the brigadier reasoned, this was the spot to watch.

What Ultra did not tell Mockler-Ferryman was that Rommel had won his case with Field Marshal Kesselring in Rome for greater support to his southern thrust but that Arnim, more concerned with his own limited offensive plans than with Rommel's grander ideas, was nevertheless keeping the panzer division in his own grasp as long as possible. Arnim appeared to like few people, and Rommel less than most; why help him out at one's own expense, merely because those were the orders? It was all quite un-Germanic, and Allied intelligence, of course, made no allowance for that.

Nor did Eisenhower make allowances for Mockler-Ferryman, on account of the unpredictability of Rommel, or anything else. On February 20 Ike asked the British for a new intelligence officer, one "who has a broader insight into German mentality and method"[29]—one who "is never satisfied with his information, who procures it with spies, reconnaissance, and any means available."[30] In the opinion of General Montgomery, who knew him, Mockler-Ferryman was "a pure theorist"[31] with no practical experience. He had made the mistake of relying too much on a single source, a source that had already proved to be without peer but, in this first great test for Americans, had shown itself not to be perfect. Had a lasting lesson been learned by the Allied command?

It had been a peculiar stroke of fate for Rommel, of whom it has been observed that "no leader of World War II had more reason to complain about the tricks played him in the guise of Ultra . . . No other commander over so prolonged a period was affected so outrageously by the ability of his opponents to look into his cards."[32] Yet this time, in a great paradox, Ultra—or its agent—had come to the aid of the Desert Fox, giving him a greater chance of success than he would have had with the help of the ready 10th Panzer Division, on which Mockler-Ferryman's eyes were focused.

Overall, however, it seems fair to say that Ultra was the most important factor in the Allied success in the Mediterranean. Without it, victory there would at best have taken much longer and been far harder to come by. The rest of the war, however it had gone, would have been quite different. No U.S. and British armies would have been concluding a thirty-eight-day sweep through Sicily as Americans from Arlington Hall arrived to join the team at Bletchley Park.

III

WING CMDR. ERIC Jones and his deputy, Bill Marchant, did not automatically accept either Whitaker or Norland into Hut 3. No one looking at Whitaker's credentials could question the breadth or depth of his knowledge, but service on a watch was a grueling, relentless task for which fresh young men in their twenties were deemed most suitable. There was also the question of Whitaker's calm and deliberate personal style. Did he have the temperament and the endurance to hold his own in this demanding context? Would he be quick enough in catching on to the very specialized terms and abbreviations that constituted military German (a language that had confounded British interpreters in the early campaigns of the war in Norway and France)? But "very quickly," Bill Bundy said, Whitaker "showed that he'd come at it slowly but he'd get it right. He was a total scholar."[33]

Norland, of course, had a background in German hardly comparable with Whitaker's; "he was the one about whom the real doubt was raised."[34] Bundy himself, in fact, was not sure why someone with more impressive credentials had not been chosen as one of the first two Americans to be showcased in Hut 3. But he asked the British to "give it every try you possibly can"; Norland, he told them, was a "very able and certainly conscientious and energetic fellow." And, after a month or so on the back watch, Norland, as well as Whitaker, was receiving approving nods from the chiefs.

Whitaker, as might have been expected, was the first to move from the back watch into a seat at the big table in the main room. The members of the watch were divided into groups,[35] each of which took one of the three shifts, with another group having the day off. The day watch (each shift was also called a watch) reported at nine in the morning and worked until six; the second shift came in at four, worked for two hours on messages in the back room, then sat on the main watch, and the same routine was followed for the night shift. You were permanently assigned to one group, which would rotate shifts, so that in time everybody worked at every hour of the day. The head of Whitaker's watch was Harold Knight, a Cambridge don who had been one of the first persons to come to Hut 3 in 1940; aside from a casual, widely traveled fellow named Robbins, who served on this watch, it was actually a highly academic group. It also included Humphrey Trevelyan, the son of the Cambridge historian G. M. Trevelyan.

When Whitaker picked up a message from Knight's little shelf, it was rarely in the kind of neat form the idea of telegram might suggest; Hut 6 did not produce nicely edited German. Most of the messages were "pretty corrupt," so that emendation was the first order of business. The message would appear in the standard five-letter groups, making up German words now instead of the original meaningless-looking encryption. But some of the letters might be incorrect or be missing altogether; radio interception could not be perfect. The translator would mark off the German words and then set about correcting the text. PANDER might appear, for instance, and it would be an easy matter to emend it to PANZER. A word might be lacking only one letter, but sometimes there might be a gap of ten or a dozen letters; the translator would then provide what presumably belonged in the space, on the basis of what the rest of the sentence or the message said. The shorter omissions caused few problems; "they were usually something that anybody who knew German would be able to supply."[36] For a longer gap, the translator would work out the meaning as well as he could, then turn the message back to Knight, who might agree or disagree, or check with another member of the watch.

Whitaker was also introduced to tricks of the trade. Ultra being the precious secret it was, "you would do funny things to conceal the nature of the message." Where something was not decipherable, "you would have the message say, 'The following three or four words obscured by a grease spot,' or maybe a bloodstain."[37] No violence would be done to the message by any cover device, but at the end it might be tagged as coming from some such supplier as the French Resistance—just to disguise the source. Cryptically enough, the intelligence generally was said to come from "source."[35] Occasionally, a message was said to have been seen in some German headquarters file.

When the capitulation of Italy was announced, shortly after Whitaker and Norland had arrived, a current of apprehension swept through Hut 3; it became known that "zealous cops had captured some Enigma machines and cryptographic instructions, causing the Germans to issue new keys which had to be broken."[39] Veterans of Hut 3 were reminded of the time in North Africa when the Germans lost a truck carrying Enigmas. The prayer in the hut had been that the enemy would recover the truck before Allied forces found it.

During his early days on the watch, Whitaker found himself spending a great deal of his time at a cabinet holding filing cards. This was the preserve of a Cambridge lexicographer named Trevor Jones, who filled those cards with German military terms and abbreviations and their English equivalents; for instance, FESTPISTAB = FESTUNGSPIONIER- STAB, which meant "staff of fortification engineers." It sometimes seemed to Whitaker that half of a message was abbreviations. Jones was not a member of the watch but would come in and out, from time to time adding another card to his hoard.

Files, in fact, were one of the secrets of Hut 3's success. Adjacent to the watch room was a veritable treasure house—lines of cabinets like inverted Vs, with pockets holding thousands and thousands of cards. Staffed by dozens of young women, this constituted an unrivaled archive on the German army and the Luftwaffe, providing a scholarly context for the interpretation of messages—a literal Wehrmacht encyclopedia. Persons, military and air units, devices, code names— everything that appeared in the intercepts had its card.

Besides performing as a translating and emending machine, turning rough German texts into complete and edited messages in English, Hut 3 had to do another job as well. The hut contained, in addition to the main desk, another table at which sat four men—two military advisers and two air advisers. All jobs in Hut 3, and in Hut 6 as well, were important, but the advisers in exercising their function summed up the purpose of the overall enterprise. They had to decide on the importance of each piece of information and, if it was deemed to have immediate value, get it into the hands of commanders who needed it or could make good use of it.

Their contribution often began even before a translator had finished his part of the job. "If we got something whose significance we weren't exactly certain about," Norland said, "we talked to the advisers before putting the message into final form. That had two purposes, really—to alert them to something that was coming along, and to take advantage of their specialized knowledge of the potential significance of an item. There was very close interplay."[40]

After a message was passed on to the advisers, who were all young army and RAF officers, they not only had to decide whether the material it contained should go anywhere except to London headquarters and into the files, they also had to decide to whom it should be sent and how urgent it was. But it was not the translated intercept itself that was dispatched to the headquarters of Alexander or Eisenhower or

Mark Clark, and here entered one of the special contributions made by Hut 3 to the process of intelligence. To send out the bare intercept itself would have been to repeat the mistake made by the Americans before Pearl Harbor in their handling of the Magic decrypts. A commander in the field might, or might not, grasp the import of a particular fact—a change in a unit strength report, say, or the movement of a regiment from one place to another. The adviser, from his close knowledge of Enigma traffic, gave the commander a helping hand, pointing out how the information compared with that in previous messages concerning the particular unit. The fact supplied by the adviser was labeled "comment," the strict rule being that all the information in the message was supposed to be straight from the German original, unless otherwise identified—as in this 1944 message about action in the Mediterranean: "Comment, ship not stated but previous reference was to Seeraeuber convoy."[41] In addition, the advisers would sometimes supply facts they thought important but which did not appear in the particular message. They would have to introduce these with qualifying phrases. Even an emendation in a text, if it was very heavy, had to be given with qualification, for the recipient was supposed to read the message in the assurance that everything that was presented as fact *was* fact to the Germans.

In any case, even if the adviser did not include comment and supplementary information, he had to draft a message saying the same thing as the enemy original but in different words; from the point of view of security, it was not considered proper to put the same text back into circulation, although this rule was relaxed as the war went on. On finishing, the adviser turned the message over to the duty officer, who approved it and then sent it on for typing. The limit to the advisers' role was suggested by one veteran of Hut 3: "our function was to elucidate each item, not to assess the broad significance of them all or to issue periodical commentaries upon the intelligence as a whole."[42] Within this ample limit, the military and air advisers performed their vital task.

Overall, the intercept trundling from Hut 6 into Hut 3 had undergone quite an experience—having its importance judged twice, being translated, discussed and emended, approved, redrafted, commented on, supplemented with other facts, and, finally, approved again, then marked with Z or ZZ—up to five Zs—indicating its degree of priority. After being typed, it was sent by teleprinter to intelligence and service headquarters in England and over the SIS network to the Special Liaison Units at field commands.

Doing its best to see that nothing was overlooked, Hut 3 even made room for liaison persons from the navy, who were on hand in case naval expertise was needed, or an item came in that was of potential interest to the navy. This recognition that the work of the army and air force intelligence teams might have value was almost out of character for the Royal Navy. In the early days the admirals had grudgingly allowed a naval contingent to set up shop at Bletchley Park, but only with the strictest segregation. And, in the best tradition of navies, in the United States as well as Britain, separate it had remained.

8

Dolphin, Shark, Frankfurt

THE AVERAGE Miami hotel proprietor or nightclub operator was probably as patriotic as the next American, but in the first weeks and months after Pearl Harbor such businessmen had not been willing to accept the fact that in the balance sheet of war, life and death demanded a higher priority than profit and loss. And nobody in Washington had made the Miami businessmen aware of that fact. Until well into 1942 the city and its suburbs continued, for six miles along the ocean edge, to light up the night sky with a neon glow that formed the backdrop for a sinister drama.

The same attitude prevailed northward along the East Coast, at Charleston, at smaller cities along the shore, at Atlantic City. Anybody who had lights, it seemed, left them on. The government was guilty, too: lighthouses blazed, the buoys marking channels continued to twinkle. The East Coast of the United States was as bright during war as it had been in peacetime. It was all an invitation to disaster, and the disaster was quick to come.

THIS AMERICAN RELUCTANCE to turn off the coastal lights surprised and delighted Lt. Comdr. Reinhard Hardegen, skipper of *U-123*.[1] Arriving at the approaches to New York, he and his men saw all the fantastic array of colorful city lights, all the harbor lights, all the lights from cars on coast roads they would have seen had they paid a call before the war broke out. Even more surprising, the ships—endless numbers of them, it seemed—were lit up as well.

"It's absolutely unbelievable," Hardegen said to the second officer. "I have the feeling the Americans are going to be very surprised when they find out where we are."[2]

But U-boats on the American Atlantic seaboard, all the way across the ocean from their bases? They didn't have a long-enough range, did they? The captain of an oil tanker was apparently of that opinion. With his vessel ripped by two torpedoes from the submarine, he said in his distress signal that the ship had struck a mine. The message was sent *en clair*.

"You're certain they're saying mine?" Hardegen shouted to his radio-man. "A mine! What assholes!"[3]

It was the opening of *Paukenschlag* (Drum Roll), the first move in Adm. Karl Dönitz's U-boat offensive against the unprepared and untried Americans. In spite of Japanese hints (the outbreak of war "may come sooner than anyone dreams"), the attack on Pearl Harbor had surprised the Germans as much as it had the Americans; the Axis was not a coalition that ran to such refinements as a combined chiefs of staff organization. Consequently Dönitz, the commander of the Kriegsmarine U-boat arm, was caught with no submarines in American waters to follow up the German declaration of war on December 11. But the admiral, a thoroughly seasoned and resourceful professional, knew a ripe opportunity when he saw it. Asking for twelve U-boats for operations off the American coast, he "confidently expected great things of these twelve boats. American waters had hitherto remained untouched by war."[4] Coastal merchant ships sailed independently, not in convoy, and even if the Americans had developed some degree of antisubmarine defense, it would be untried and inefficient. Looking back to the glorious days of 1940, when his U-boats had gathered such rich pickings in British waters that the men called it "the happy time," Dönitz foresaw another such spell off the coast of the raw British ally. But the harvest season would not last long. Experience would be gained, defenses would be strengthened, convoys would be instituted. He must move fast.

For what Dönitz regarded as misguided reasons, Hitler and his naval commander in chief, Grand Adm. Erich Raeder (the admiral possessed the notable distinction of being the last naval officer anywhere to wear the formal wing collar with his day uniform), granted him only six submarines for the operation, of which five proved to be ready for service in time for the quick blow the U-boat chief wished to strike. He therefore decided to concentrate the operation on the area between the St. Lawrence and Cape Hatteras; the first day of *Paukenschlag* was to be January 13.

But when *U-123* encountered the British steamer *Cyclops* about three hundred miles east of Cape Cod, Lieutenant Commander Harde-gen could not bring himself to allow this prize to escape, even though the date was only January 12. Asking himself what the admiral would do in such a situation, he decided that the answer was obvious, and he proceeded to put two torpedoes into *Cyclops*, sending her stern-first to the bottom.[5] *Paukenschlag* was launched. Working his way south, Hardegen on January 18 found himself off Cape Hatteras, the southern boundary of the *Paukenschlag* zone. Confronted by the unbelievable abundance, he and his fellow skippers had quickly worked out a highly effective method of plucking the fruit. During the day they lay on the bottom, a few hundred feet below the surface and a few miles off the shipping lanes. At dusk they moved submerged toward the coast, and when night fell they rose to the surface, decks awash, ready for action, in the midst of what seemed a caravan of ships. On the night of January 18-19, Hardegen commented in his war diary that there were targets "enough to keep ten or twenty U-boats busy."[6] During the night *U-123* sank three large ships and blew a hole in a fourth.

The results of this first offensive were all that Dönitz could have asked for: *U-123* netted nine ships totaling 53,173 tons (besides the one damaged); *U-130* (Commander Kals), six ships, 36,993 tons, and one damaged; *U-66* (the well-named Commander Zapp), five ships, 33,456 tons; *U-109* (Lieutenant Commander Bleichrodt), five ships, 33,733 tons. *U-125,* skippered by Lieutenant Commander Folkers, was the sole disappointment, sinking only one ship, of 5,666 tons. But the grand total of 163,021 tons, for only half a month's work, was remarkable when compared with the monthly totals for November and December, for all sinkings by U-boats, of 100,000 tons.[7]

The destruction of the Allied shipping capacity was of prime importance; but, besides that, there was nothing abstract about this lost tonnage. A U.S. Navy training manual pointed out the general effect of a U-boat's work. "If a submarine sinks two 6,000-ton ships and one 3,000-ton tanker, here is a typical account of what we have totally lost: 42 tanks, 8 six-inch howitzers, 88 twenty-five-pound guns, 40 two-pound guns, 24 armored cars, 50 Bren carriers, 5,210 tons of ammunition, 600 rifles, 428 tons of tank supplies, 2,000 tons of stores, and 1,000 tanks of gasoline. . . . In order to knock out the same amount of equipment by air bombing [if all this matériel were on land and normally dispersed] the enemy would have to make three thousand successful bombing sorties."[8] Besides this kind of transatlantic cargo, American coastal shipping carried iron and steel, oil, bauxite, cotton, and sugar.

The onslaught of the German U-boats had not taken the U.S. Navy totally by surprise. Before Pearl Harbor, foreseeing the possibility if not the power of such an attack, the navy had collected small craft—coast guard cutters, trawlers, civilian yachts—along the East Coast and provided them with small arms, to serve on antisubmarine patrol together with the few aircraft that were available. For all her size and wealth and talk of preparedness, the United States had not come to the war with armed services of commensurate size, training, and equipment. As Alfred McCormack observed in February 1942, "at least since the European war started, our diplomacy has far outrun our military ability to back it up," and "the same condition continues to prevail."[9] One reason for this, to be sure, was that for two years much of the matériel produced by defense plants had been shipped to Britain; and since the summer of 1941, aid to Russia had been given a high priority. But the American effort had nevertheless fallen far short of the need, and the outlook—the psychology—remained amateurish and even downright pacific. "Single destroyers, for example, sailed up and down the traffic lanes with such regularity that the U-boats were quickly able to work out the timetable being followed," Admiral Dönitz observed later. "They knew exactly when the destroyers would return, and the knowledge only added to their sense of security during the intervening period."[10] Merchant skippers used their radio freely, just as if no deadly enemy lurked in the sea lanes; they frequently signaled their positions, helping the U-boats build up a detailed picture of shipping in the area.

Although still not able to send as many submarines as he wished into American waters, and consequently burning with frustration at what seemed to him Hitler's obtuseness (what could be more effective than strangling the enemy by sending his shipping to the bottom of the sea?), Dönitz followed *Paukenschlag* with an extension of his attack from Halifax to the Caribbean. During the winter and spring the second "happy time" continued as frolicsome as it had begun. After sinking nine ships, Jochen Mohr, skipper of *U-124*, reported by radio to Dönitz:

> The new-moon night is black as ink.
> Off Hatteras the tankers sink.
> While sadly Roosevelt counts the score—
> Some fifty thousand tons—by
>
>   MOHR[11]

At night, as tankers and freighters sailed past the six miles of Miami, their shapes were outlined against the glow of the city; skippers like Hardegen and Mohr could hardly have asked for greater assistance. But put out the lights? A cry went up: "The tourist season would be ruined!"[12] Resistance was not confined just to Miami but was heard all along the coast, and the political will to take such a desperately needed step as ordering waterfront lights turned off was slow in asserting itself. It was, said the *New Republic*, "criminal negligence"[13] on the part of city administrations, highway departments, and every boardwalk operator. The federal government, relying on cajolery instead of issuing orders, was perhaps even guiltier. On March 14 a sailor hauled from the sea off a New Jersey resort town told the press that some twenty of his shipmates had been lost because "it was lit up like daylight all along the beach. That submarine was right there, waiting for the first boat to come along."[14]

Crewmen of silhouetted freighters and tankers sometimes had to swim for their lives in oil scum an inch thick, which spread faster than a man could move, struggling to avoid swallowing it or taking it into their lungs, ducking beneath it when the waves turned into patches of fire, gasping cries that sometimes might be heard on shore, if anybody was listening. On a Florida night, the funeral pyre of a torpedoed tanker could often be seen by anybody who, bored with the click of the castanets, stepped outside a honky-tonk for a breath of fresh air.

Even after the imposition of dimout regulations along the coast, the slaughter continued; daylight operations, of course, were unaffected, and the dimout was far from a sufficient answer to the night attacks of U-boats. Ships were ordered to stop for the night in protected anchorages, and a limited convoy system began to appear. But the public continued to witness a strange spectacle, as on June 15, when thousands of sunners and swimmers at Virginia Beach saw two large freighters struck by U-boats. Feeling good about the whole thing, Dönitz told a German war correspondent that "bathers and sometimes entire coastal cities are witnesses to that drama of war whose visual climaxes are constituted by the red glorioles of blazing tankers."[15]

In the first seven months of 1942, U-boats overall sank 681 ships of 3,556,999 gross tons, for a monthly average of slightly more than half a million tons; in June the tonnage destroyed actually reached 700,235. The arresting point about these figures was that Dönitz reckoned 700,000 to be the monthly tonnage that had to be sunk from all causes[16]—air attack, mines, and surface raiders as well as U-boats— if Britain was to be brought to her knees and the Allies defeated. The prize seemed to be within Germany's grasp.

II

THE BRITISH REACTED with horror to reports of the carnage in what they called the "far west." They themselves had begun the war in 1939 ill prepared to combat submarine attacks, but in two years they had learned a great deal. Would the Americans, like a younger brother, insist on making their own mistakes and learning their own lessons, or could they be brought to listen to the voice of British experience? The island needed those endangered supplies in order to survive (the British estimate of the monthly tonnage loss that could be endured was 600,000, that is, 100,000 less than Dönitz's figure). But even more was at stake. Many of the weakly protected ships swelling the U-boats' bag in the Caribbean, the Gulf, and the western Atlantic were British, with British crews. Aside from any other considerations, did not that fact give the British the right to some control over, or at least involvement in, operations in those waters?

On February 6 Winston Churchill wrote quietly to Harry Hopkins, asking the president's confidant to see that FDR's "attention has been drawn to the very heavy sinkings by U-boats in the Western North Atlantic."[17] Four days later an arrangement was concluded whereby Britain sent the U.S. Navy twenty-four antisubmarine trawlers and ten corvettes with experienced crews, but at the same time the RAF refused to release some American-built bombers that were ready for delivery. In March, becoming more forthright, Churchill told Hopkins that "I am most deeply concerned at the immense sinkings of tankers west of the fortieth meridian and in the Caribbean Sea. . . . The situation is so serious that drastic action of some kind is necessary." After offering several suggestions, the prime minister said bluntly, "I should like these alternatives to be discussed on the highest naval level at once." Then, reverting to the care and caution with which he invariably approached Roosevelt, he added, "Please let me know whether you think it well to bring all this before the President straightaway."[18]

A few days later Roosevelt replied rather sheepishly that "my Navy has been definitely slack in preparing for this submarine war off our coast,"[19] but on March 20, with what Churchill felt "was a touch of strain," he suggested that the British might do well to bomb bases and repair yards, "thus checking submarine activities at their source . . ." The prime minister did not appreciate this bit of advice; the admiralty and the RAF were, he said, already devoting attention to the problem.

Clearly, the Americans were the ones who needed advice. It was not enough to send, in a sort of reverse lend-lease, vessels like trawlers and corvettes across the Atlantic. A man must go, one who could convince the Americans of the importance of a coordinated naval intelligence system and explain to them that keeping track of enemy submarines and predicting their movements was not simply a baffling proposition—there were a theory and an approach that worked. Admiral Godfrey, the director of naval intelligence, felt that only one man could do the job he wanted done.

Rodger Winn had come to the admiralty in 1939, just before the outbreak of war, and been assigned to a relatively new entity called the Operational Intelligence Centre; within the center was a brand-new section called the U-boat Tracking Room, in which, by great good fortune, Winn was placed. A polio victim—the disease had left him hunchbacked and with a limp—Winn had been precluded from the naval career he had dreamed of and had, instead, become a barrister, and a very successful one. Being fully aware of Winn's skill as an advocate, Admiral Godfrey felt that he was the very man to put into the ring against Adm. Ernest J. King and other Americans who, though they were officially asking for the doctor's help, might well be less than eager to follow his prescription.

But there was much more to Winn than his effectiveness as a lawyer. In his early days in the U-boat Tracking Room he had come to believe that, despite the views of his superiors—solid traditional navy types— it would indeed prove to be possible to forecast the movements of U-boats, not in a hit-or-miss fashion, but systematically. So sound had this idea proved—it amounted almost to an obsession—that Winn in little more than a year was rushed into uniform as a commander in the naval reserve and put in charge of the tracking room. As the veritable creator of the system, as well as a skillful pleader of causes, Winn was the ideal messenger for British naval intelligence to send to America, even though he was essentially a civilian being flung into as fierce a pride of naval lions as roared anywhere in the world.

The raw material of Winn's system was supplied in profound unawareness by Admiral Dönitz himself. An innovative thinker with respect to submarine strategy, the admiral had believed that the U-boat could be the decisive weapon in a war with Britain; "with very modest means, very considerable successes can be scored."[20] Before the beginning of hostilities, he had designed and tested his own new principles of attack. It was his rather unorthodox view that the U-boat ought to be looked at as a surface ship with the convenient ability to dive, rather than as an underwater vessel that could rise to the top as it chose. It therefore should normally make its attacks on the surface, taking advantage of the fact that, with its small profile, it was almost invisible in the darkness, and of the second fact that it was considerably faster than the freighters and tankers that were its prey. These tactics would render British sonar gear useless.

The other part of Dönitz's theory called for an end to the idea of the submarine as a lone wolf prowling the wilds in search of victims. He had begun the war with only forty-five serviceable U-boats and the number increased only slowly; "if only we had a hundred boats," he said one day in 1940, "what might we accomplish then!"[21] When a sufficient number did become available, he was able to put into effect his new approach, which called for the assembling of enough boats around a convoy to overwhelm the escort. Submarines on patrol were placed ten or twelve miles apart across routes on which convoys were expected. A sighting was immediately reported to the admiral, who ordered the U-boat not to attack but to shadow the convoy while the other submarines were called together; no shot was to be fired, no torpedo launched, until the wolf pack was assembled ahead of the convoy. Then, as darkness fell, they would move in on the surface, undetectable by sonar, creating the havoc associated with wild animals falling upon helpless prey.

This approach cast Dönitz in a new role for a naval commander in chief. Far from being limited to the traditional duties of a shore-based executive, he was, as he sat in his operational headquarters hundreds of miles from the scene of battle, in specific tactical command, like Frederick the Great issuing his orders from horseback, although his information arrived and his decisions were relayed not by messengers braving the fire of enemy musketry, but by means of radio. The wolf-pack principle demanded streams of messages from the U-boats, reports on the size, course, and speed of the convoy, on the weather, and on the condition of the submarines themselves. These reports not only furnished the admiral with the information he needed to make command decisions; they also, through direction-finding, told the British where the U-boats were. All these data, together with facts from other sources such as airplane sightings, poured into the U-boat Tracking Room and the hands of Rodger Winn.

But there was more. During the second half of 1941, the British had done more with the U-boat traffic than use it for purposes of direction-finding. For that half-year these messages, enciphered on the German naval Enigma, had been read at Bletchley Park; the Operational Intelligence Centre had thus been in the happy position of sitting at Dönitz's elbow as he received his reports and issued his orders. But when Rodger Winn made his journey to Washington, the picture had changed. Ultra had ceased to speak in the Atlantic.

III

SOMEWHAT AGAINST ITS inclinations, the admiralty had agreed at the beginning of the war that its cryptanalytic section might remain at Bletchley Park, but there was to be no nonsense about integrating it with the combined army-air force operation. Many critics felt that this aloofness on the part of the Royal Navy was simply another symptom of its encrusted belief that, as the senior service, it was measurably superior to its two little sisters. But the admirals could adduce strong practical reasons for it as well. Conveniently, the naval Enigma was different from the standard Wehrmacht model; and unlike the War Office and the Air Ministry, the admiralty was not only a high command but an operational headquarters, frequently flashing direct orders to ships at sea, some of which were likely to be based on information sent by teleprinter direct from Bletchley Park to the Operational Intelligence Centre—provided the cryptanalysts succeeded in breaking naval Enigma. Certainly no young men in an interservice intelligence hut at BP had a place in such a specialized operation!

Hence, it was in perfect accordance with the desires of the navy that early in 1940, as Gordon Welchman was taking charge of Hut 6, for work on army and air force Enigma, Alan Turing was assigned to the separate Hut 8, for naval Enigma. Hut 6 made rapid progress with Luftwaffe Enigma; the air commanders were chatty as hens and appeared to have absolute confidence in their cipher machine and their way of using it. But the Kriegsmarine, separatist like the Royal Navy, not only employed its own version of the Enigma but used it with greater care, committing no such blunders as the double encipherment of the message key.

Though endowed with only traces of executive ability, Turing was a commandingly original thinker who when he attacked a problem, as a colleague said, "liked to start from first principles, and he was hardly influenced by received opinion. This attitude gave depth and originality to his thinking, and also it helped him to choose important problems."[22] But naval Enigma presented a continuing smooth surface, with no projections offering possible handholds to the group in Hut 8; and Frank Birch, a veteran of the navy's famous Room 40 of the First World War, accordingly had no intercepts to toss to his team in the new Hut 4, the intelligence part of the navy chain at Bletchley Park, analogous to Hut 3 in the army-air force arrangement. The only real answer, BP told the admiralty, was for the sailors to capture a German vessel and seize the enciphering equipment.

Then, in April 1940, during the disastrous Norwegian campaign, the Royal Navy contributed a heartbreaking disaster of its own devising.[23] A German patrol boat bound for Narvik was captured (not as the result of any intelligence plan) and was looted by the British crew that boarded her before responsible officers could make a careful search. Although all such craft carried cipher machines, the most that could be recovered was papers listing some settings for encipherment. These provided glimpses into the workings of the naval Enigma—notably, they showed that the German navy had one primarily important key, the *Heimisch* (Home), used for all ships in the Atlantic and for U-boats—but the first real break into the system did not come until March 1941, when a special operation was mounted to seize a German ship and succeeded in netting rotors and code books. Other planned raids followed, and during this same spring a submarine (the *U-110*, commanded by the famous Fritz-Julius Lemp, who had won interna-tional notoriety in the first days of the war by torpedoing the passenger liner *Athenia*), was captured by chance, apparently with its Enigma intact, and in circumstances that made it highly probable that Dönitz and his staff would believe it to have been sunk—thus leaving the cipher equipment uncompromised.

The result of all these events was that by the beginning of August BP was reading the *Heimisch* settings normally within three days and often within a few hours;[24] the British gave this first naval cryptanalytic success the amiable designation "Dolphin" (the Germans later changed their own name for it to Hydra). With the cracking of Dol-phin, as an official historian observed, "the situation was profoundly altered."[25] Turing and his team had made a vital contribution to the struggle against the U-boats, and this naval Ultra had also played a part in the locating of the great battleship *Bismarck* when she had set out in May on a commerce-raiding expedition; thus both submarines and surface raiders had been held in check. In October the U-boat Com-mand caused temporary problems by making changes in the Dolphin settings. This was a curious move, since the Germans, puzzled at the efficiency of Royal Navy efforts against the U-boats, could not bring themselves to believe that the Enigma was at fault, but they neverthe-less went on to introduce the changes. Bletchley Park lost only a few days as the result; then the picture was bright again, and if the Ameri-cans could just get straightened out on their side of the ocean, every-thing looked promising for 1942.

But on February 1, 1942, the enemy changed sea creatures. Naval Ultra fell silent. The friendly Dolphin had been replaced by the deadly new Shark.

IV

RODGER WINN SCORED a great success in Washington, in part, he felt, because he dared to be candid. When Admiral King's deputy chief of staff, Rear Adm. Richard S. Edwards, said something to the effect that the Americans wished to learn their own lessons, Winn, acting on the simplistic belief that Americans respond well to blunt speaking, fired back: "The trouble is, Admiral, it's not only your bloody ships you are losing. A lot of them are ours!"[26] Luckily, Winn had judged his man correctly. After a moment's pause, Edwards laughed and admitted that his visitor might have a point there, and he proceeded to smooth the way for an audience with Admiral King.

This admiral was clearly the most formidable of the American naval lions, and not only because of his rank and position. Commander of the Atlantic fleet at the time of Pearl Harbor, the sixty-three-year-old King was within a few days appointed commander in chief of the U.S. fleet by President Roosevelt, who was notable for placing men of strong and independent character in high command positions; he was perhaps attracted by King's previously stated belief that "we must do all that we can with what we have."[27] Remarkably, the admiral had risen to the top of the navy in spite of an early reputation as an excessive drinker and a womanizer; one of his first struggles had been to win control of himself. More feared than loved, as Samuel Eliot Morison observed, the new commander in chief was "endowed with a superior intellect" and when anyone tried to argue with him beyond a certain point, "a characteristic bleak look came over his countenance as a signal that his mind was made up and further discussion useless."[28]

Overall, the climate in which Rodger Winn arrived in Washington for his performance as super salesman was mixed. The Americans, though remarkably ill-equipped considering how long the Axis handwriting had been disfiguring the walls, were making attempts to meet the challenge, and they seemed aware of some of the possibilities antisubmarine warfare could offer. But tactically, in their reluctance to concede that even a weakly protected convoy was better than none, they were in the Dark Ages.

No one, so far as is known, had told Winn about one of King's salient peculiarities—a pronounced dislike for the British and all their works; it was an inconvenient way to feel about an ally, though history as recent as that of World War I offered endless examples of the same kind of prejudice (who could forget the mutual distaste and distrust between various French and British generals?), and it was no doubt made worse by the embarrassment King felt at the feeble American response to Admiral Dönitz's U-boat offensive.

Admiral Edwards, however, seemed to have been an effective intermediary. Winn emerged from the lion's den completely unscarred,[29] having received a thoughtful hearing, whatever King's feelings about

his British allies. The commander in chief issued orders for the immediate establishment of a submarine tracking room on the admiralty
model, and, as Patrick Beesly, a British veteran of the Operational
Intelligence Centre, observed, "once convinced, the Americans
moved with a speed and efficiency that was surprising to anyone
accustomed to the ways of the admiralty. Before Winn left Washington
. . . the necessary accommodation had been found and the additional
staff required were being selected."[30] Had Beesly been privy during the
previous year to the fumbling and faltering of the U.S. army-navy
intelligence liaison officers as they were supposedly looking for a table
around which to meet, his amazement at the change would no doubt
have been boundless.

To set up and direct the new tracking room, the navy chiefs summoned a tall, slim officer from Maryland, Comdr. Kenneth A. Knowles, a
1927 Naval Academy graduate who had been retired in 1938 because
of nearsightedness. "The Navy was very particular in those days,"
Knowles said. "We didn't have radar, and in a destroyer going thirty-
five knots you had to be pretty alert. We didn't have contact lenses
then, and glasses would fog up."[31] The Navy had kept its eye on the
serious-minded man, finding uses for him as an editor and a naval
ROTC officer, and in early 1942 came a call from Admiral King's chief
of staff, Rear Adm. Russell Willson, asking Knowles whether he would
be interested in taking on a "very important job." "By all means,"[32]
Knowles responded, and he came to Washington with the title Head,
Atlantic Section, Combat Intelligence, Cominch; the section itself was
designated F-21.

Knowles came aboard in June and the next month was off to London
for meetings with Rodger Winn, the master of the tracking trade,
whom Knowles found to be "utterly brilliant." He hoped, Knowles
said, "that some of that brilliance would brush off on me, because he
had things so beautifully laid out over there." Winn's operation was
located in the Citadel, a "concrete ship" adjacent to the admiralty; the
most secret part of the British naval operation, it was protected against
attack by an array of machine guns and could on brief notice be
flooded. Its inhabitants "worked themselves to death," Knowles said.
"They were poorly fed, and they didn't see the light of the sun for years.
They were just like moles down there."[33]

After Knowles returned to Washington, he and Winn worked very
closely together. "We would exchange messages every day, and frequently, with his brilliant wit, he would try to push me around a bit,
and I would come back at him. We had a nice working relationship."[34]

This relationship and the Anglo-American cooperation that grew out of it came to represent an Allied model—"probably closer," Beesly said, "than that between any other British and American organizations in any Service and any theatre."[35] Knowles in his situation room and Winn in his tracking room were able to keep in full and free communication with each other over a cable that was exclusively reserved for their use; "the two of us," Knowles said, "had pretty much an independent operation."[36]

But for all that, Knowles was not entering on his task at the most propitious time, because of the great bite that Shark had taken out of Atlantic intelligence, although the loss of Ultra did not mean the loss of all information about Dönitz's moves and methods. During the six months of 1941 when Dolphin had been read more or less currently, the British had enjoyed a thorough and continuing look into Dönitz's brain and the organization he had created. In addition, a great deal of information had been built up about the characteristics and habits of the U-boats and the kinds of messages they sent off; without reading the signals, the tracking room knew which ones told of ship sightings and which were weather or position reports. Besides, the Germans continued to use Dolphin for some purposes, as well as another minor key that BP was able to read. These decrypts made contributions to the stream of information; but even putting the best face on the situation, the British, and now the Americans, knew that the breaking of Shark was an urgent matter, demanding the highest priority.

At least, it seems clear, the British ought to have known it. During 1941 they had received hints and indications that for U-boat Enigma a fourth rotor was on the way; when this dismal event came about, the messages thereby transmitted would have to be attacked by a high-speed Bombe designed to match the four rotors now used by the enemy, or else they would take up to twenty-six times as long to be solved, once a crib—a bit of plaintext—had been obtained. (In other words, to the original 26x26x26 positions of the three rotors had been added a new factor of 26.)

Certainly British resources were now both scanty and strained, but one could nevertheless have felt with reason that the question of the high-speed Bombe was not pursued with the kind of urgency that protection of the Atlantic lifeline demanded. Perhaps, even in those critical times, Bletchley Park provided some justification for the picture drawn of it by Malcolm Muggeridge, who spent a brief time there when he entered the Secret Service: "It might have been taken to be a Fabian summer-school, or—a more ancient model—one of those reading parties Victorians were so fond of organising in the long vacation, in the Lake District, or further afield, in Switzerland or Italy, when they all grew bored together over unreadable books, instead of separately."[37]

Just a few months earlier, in October 1941, frustrated at trying to do their job without the people they needed, Turing and Welchman and two others had slashed the administrative Gordian knot by writing directly to Churchill to ask for help. On hearing that he would have to supply more geese in order to get more of his beloved golden eggs, Churchill that same day ordered his military factotum, General Ismay, to "make sure they have all they want on extreme priority . . ."[38] Muggeridge, on a few days' further acquaintance, had upgraded BP from a Victorian reading party to the languid Cambridge of his youth: he "thought how long the afternoon was bound to be, how interminable the wait for tea."[39] Such a flavor, such an absence of driving power, was not what was demanded by the times, and its existence, as well as Alistair Denniston's illness, was surely behind the deposing of that scholarly man, and his replacement by Commander Travis, less of an intellectual but more of a table thumper, to Jack Good of Hut 8, "a strong bulldog of a man."[40] Welchman, though a profound admirer of Denniston, said of the red-faced, tough, and brisk Travis that "we wouldn't have done so well without him."[41]

In any case, after the second German "happy time" came to its end early in the summer, as the Americans managed to put the coastal traffic under the protection of convoy, Dönitz flung his U-boats into a new onslaught on the Atlantic convoys. Now, with production reaching thirty boats a month, he was able to bring sizable packs together, concentrating them especially in the "Black Pit" area—the wide stretch of the central North Atlantic (also called the Greenland air gap), out of range of any land-based Allied aircraft. Here, more than anywhere else, was the opportunity for the decisive U-boat victory he dreamed of, and the figures began to bear him out, the November losses mounting to the figure of 807,754 tons.

During this period, U.S. and British authorities engaged in various visits and negotiations about the parts each would play in the cipher war against the Axis, now that they had become full-fledged allies. The British desired strongly that the Americans concentrate on the Japanese and leave the Germans to Bletchley Park. But the U.S. Navy, concerned at the losing battle in the Atlantic and at what appeared to be British foot-dragging on the promise to deliver a Bombe to Washington, informed their allies not only that they had developed an

American Bombe with which they intended to mount their own attack on the U-boat Enigma, but that they would produce an enormous number of them and crack ciphers in a hurry. A bargain was struck under which the two sides would swap intercepts (U.S. Japanese intercepts for British German),[42] with the Americans agreeing to build only 100 Bombes instead of the 360 originally announced. This was a figure that to some of the British may have seemed to represent American bragging (a trait for which they were always on the look-out), but that also meant a kind of "thinking big" to which the Government Code and Cipher School came only by slow stages. The U.S. Navy thus won its primary point—work on decrypting German naval messages would take place at Op-20-G, as well as at Bletchley Park.

In November 1942, as its representative in the conferences required to work out the coordination called for by the agreement, GC&CS dispatched Alan Turing to Washington. This was a shrewd move, inasmuch as it took advantage of Turing's technical knowledge (rivaled, perhaps, only by Welchman's) and confirmed the fact that he was no longer exercising executive responsibilities (Hut 8 had been taken over by Hugh Alexander, another of the many chess whizzes recruited by BP, and a man who, in profound contrast to Turing, had a flair for administration).

As a person who seemed notably eccentric, even to his fellow countrymen at Bletchley Park, Turing could be expected to pose some questions for Americans; yet, as the holder of a Ph.D. from Princeton, he was no stranger to the United States. In Washington, young navy mathematician-cryptologists were assigned to show him about and keep him happy. One of them, Joe Eachus, was a Middle Westerner, born in Indiana and brought up in Ohio.[43] Actually a physics major, he was a graduate of Miami University in Ohio and held a doctorate from the University of Illinois; at the time of Pearl Harbor he was teaching at Purdue and as a sort of hobby he took a navy correspondence course in cryptanalysis. The result was that "they shortened the academic year by wiping out all vacations" and Eachus went straight into the navy. Thus, at the time of Turing's visit, though a lieutenant (jg), he had been in the service only a few months.

If there were ever a time and a field in which naval reservists flourished, this was it. As was the case in the army, regular officers coveted command assignments; here, too, the intelligence branch was an open city waiting to be occupied. So it was that a greater assignment than escorting a visiting Briton around Washington was awaiting

Eachus. Despite the brevity of his service, he was shortly sent on his way to England as the navy's first officer to be assigned more than temporarily to the naval section at Bletchley Park. Thereby, in the autumn of 1942 some eight months before Bill Bundy and his team arrived to begin formal, organized American partnership, he became the first American of any service to go to BP not as a visitor or as a liaison officer but as a working cryptanalyst.

Eachus went at a promising time. While Turing was in Washington working with navy signal intelligence officers to knit together a fabric of Anglo-American cryptological cooperation, great events were occurring in Hut 8 at Bletchley Park. They were coming not an instant too soon. For the year now drawing to an end, the U-boat haul would be colossal: Dönitz's raiders would sink 1,160 ships, of 6,266,215 tons.[44] The total Allied shipping losses from all causes would amount to 1,664 ships, of 7,790,691 tons—more than a million tons above the tonnage of new ships built annually throughout the non-Nazi world. For all the efforts of American shipbuilders, all the ingenuity devoted to applying mass-production techniques in this long-established field, the Allies were losing cargo ships and tankers substantially faster than they were being built. And the crews of the merchant ships had to sail into battle knowing that their defense depended on others; they could only await the coming of their own fate. With each single ship perished men who died obscurely, in anguish and without glory—the latter a concept that still had some standing at the time.

Britain lived and died by the flow of supplies from overseas. But beyond that, as 1943 approached, the Atlantic highway had to be open for the great buildup, for the concentration in the island of men and equipment that would one day take the offensive in Europe against the Axis. The Atlantic battle, in Churchill's view, "was the dominating factor all through the war. Never for one moment could we forget that everything happening elsewhere, on land, at sea, or in the air, depended ultimately on its outcome."[45] And the U-boats held the key to the battle.

Now on October 30, 1942, actually just a few days before Turing left for Washington, the Royal Navy set an ultimately decisive course of events in motion by capturing a German submarine in the Mediterranean and recovering its code book used for transmitting weather reports. This prize acquisition, together with short-sighted carelessness by the Germans in the use of the fourth rotor, gave the game away. By December, BP was decoding Shark with regularity—curiously, without the use of high-speed Bombes. The Atlantic battle appeared won when Joe Eachus arrived on the scene. But in this great oceanic game of cloak and dagger, the other side still held an unsuspected deadly weapon that would cause the Allies tremendous losses.

V

IN HARBOR, THE ships of a convoy exhibited what one observer called "sham confusion"[46]—sham because each ship actually knew exactly what it was doing. Before sailing, the captains of each vessel attended a conference in which every detail of the forthcoming voyage was discussed; there was, literally, no room for careless moves. After steaming out of the anchorage in a straight line, ships would begin creeping up to take their allotted places. Each flew flags indicating its place; green and yellow flags reading "seven-one," for instance, meant that the ship was the first one in the seventh line; the relative position was to be maintained regardless of weather conditions or anything else, though under clear skies the whole great formation—often fifty ships or more—could maintain a tighter pattern than when the weather turned foul. To prevent a rear-end collision on the ocean highway, each ship except those in the last rank trailed a fog buoy, which was a cable stretched four hundred feet astern, towing a funnellike device that created an artificial wake for the ship. As aids to the lookouts, the fog buoys were perhaps more valuable on dark nights than during actual foggy spells. If a ship strayed from its position, a destroyer or destroyer escort would appear and with horn or blinker sternly order it to resume its place. This maintenance of station was one of the cardinal principles of convoy—stragglers were easy prey for lurking U-boats. The assignments were also conceived with care and according to a fixed design: troop ships in the inner circle, then tankers, then freighters, and outside them all the vessels of the escort, behaving in their own fashion. As the long gray rows of ships advanced at their slow and steady pace, the destroyers and smaller escort vessels were continuously active, now loafing along at convoy speed only to spring forward suddenly as if unleashed, circling the slow merchant ships, behaving for all the world like lively guard dogs with sheep of even greater than normal orthodoxy. If heavy weather scattered the ships, the guards had to range afar to call them back from the jaws of the wolf pack that presumably was aware that succulent victims might be in the vicinity.

As the crewmen went about their work—four hours on, eight hours off, seven days a week—life was quiet, even boring. The leisure-time pursuits were card-playing, shooting the bull, and reading; and if it was a troopship, shooting craps with the GIs, who to the sailors were transient figures with plenty of money to spare. But the boredom would give way to quiet tension if there was evidence, such as a distress signal or an aerial spotting, that the Germans could be presumed to know where the convoy was. Then you could expect General Quarters to sound at any time. If you were a member of the black gang down in the engine room, you were in the worst spot—"you don't know if you'll get out. All the time, you're expecting . . ."[47]

In March 1943 the growing numbers of troops and swelling quantities of material being shipped across the Atlantic to Britain were reflected in the doubling of the number of ships convoyed. Early in the month two convoys sailed from New York within a few days of each other—SC-122 on March 5, with sixty ships, and HX-229, which was faster, on March 8, with forty. It was not the season of the year when the tightest patterns could be maintained by convoy commodores. March gales, snow and hail squalls, and the concomitant poor visibility made all operations difficult; the escorts were not lacking in problems—it was hard even to signal their charges. Nor was it ideal weather for U-boats.

The North Atlantic during these weeks was a sea of convoys.[48] Besides SC-122 and HX-229, the U-boats had as potential targets the westbound ONS-169 and ON-170 and two earlier eastbound convoys, SC-121 and HX-228. The ocean was also, by comparison with Dönitz's earlier days, a sea of U-boats; the admiral could now keep more than a hundred on patrol at a time. In response to the mass of convoys, Dönitz formed various ad hoc wolf packs to meet the challenge. On March 14, in order to evade the Raubgraf pack, which it knew from Ultra was shadowing ON-170, the admiralty shifted SC-122 and HX-229 to a more southerly route. But Dönitz was playing the same game; he ordered the ON-170 U-boats moved to the expected track of SC-122. A March gale delayed the arrival of some of the U-boats, however, which allowed SC-122 to slip unsighted through the gap in Dönitz's trip line. Then, on the morning of March 16, along came the speedier HX-229, and in came the wolf packs; gradually, in the ensuing action, the two convoys, each disrupted by the violent weather, blended into one great overall fleet of merchant ships. On March 18 Dönitz realized that what he thought was SC-122 was actually two separate convoys—an incredible potential bag of 100 ships—and he assigned eighteen U-boats to HX-229 and thirteen to SC-122.

The great streams of message traffic generated between the admiral and all these U-boats was dramatic evidence to the trackers in London and Washington that an enormous number of ships were facing death out in the Atlantic. A huge battle was raging, and through direction-finding the U-boat Tracking Room knew just which ships they were, and it also knew that available escorts were at the moment in short supply; HX-229 was shepherded by only four destroyers and one corvette. Scanning the sea for reinforcements, the admiralty could find only three destroyers, two American and one British, in Iceland, and in a necessary but futile gesture, these were ordered to the scene: U-boat after U-boat—*U-603, U-758, U-91, U-600*—slashed through the lines of freighters and tankers, performing in spite of the foul weather exactly like the wolves Admiral Dönitz had seen in his mind when he was developing his tactical ideas. The thin convoy defenders were overwhelmed; seamen from torpedoed vessels had to be left to freeze in the icy water. Long-range reconnaissance aircraft were sent out, but snow showers blinded them. The slaughter went on until the morning of March 19, when the two convoys came within six hundred miles of Northern Ireland and thus within range of land-based antisubmarine planes. The next day, settling for his profits, Dönitz decreed the operation concluded: to the admiral it was "the biggest success so far in a convoy battle."[49] It had been profitable indeed, this greatest convoy battle of the war—twenty-one ships of 140,842 tons had been sent to the bottom by the wolf packs. March had proved to be Black March; during the first ten days forty-one ships had been lost, and the next ten days saw forty-four more go down; the total amounted to more than half a million tons. And many hundreds of seamen, roistering veterans and rookies fresh from school, had perished with those ships. Fears were expressed in the admiralty that "we should not be able to continue convoy as an effective system of defence."[50]

Behind Admiral Dönitz and his wolf-pack tactics, and the bad weather, and the dozens of U-boats now available, and the greatly increased volume of Allied shipping, there loomed a great question: How did the admiral so often seem to know where to send his U-boats? What kind of probing eyes did he have?

ONE DAY IN mid-October 1943, Comdr. Laurance Safford had a caller. Brig. John Tiltman, who had welcomed Abraham Sinkov and his fellow U.S. cryptological officers to Britain in 1941 and had won not only the respect but the affection of most Americans who had come to know him, was now serving in Washington as cipher expert for the British military representatives. Safford, who was no longer in cryptanalysis but since 1942 had been assistant director of naval communications for cryptographic research, was interested in Tiltman's news and angered by it, but hardly surprised.

"You were right about Naval Cipher No. 3," Tiltman said. "It is no good, and the Germans have been reading it all along just as you predicted. Our faces are very red and your stock is very high in London."[51]

The American had been concerned about the security of this cipher since Admiral Ghormley, who seems to have been something of a bête noire for him, had agreed with the British that it would be suitable for use in combined Anglo-American operations. The cipher was one a series of hand—nonmachine—systems developed by the Royal Navy, which at the outset of the war had rejected the idea of employing cipher machines aboard ship. (In a triumph of class-consciousness, the navy had managed to create its own definitions of code and cipher, relating the concepts to rank instead of working principle; in its definition, a cipher was what officers used; a code was for ratings, or enlisted personnel, and hence for secrets of lesser import.) The German naval cryptological branch, called the B-dienst (Beobachtungsdienst), had begun reading the standard British naval code before the war, and it proceeded to pierce the wartime successor, called Naval Code No. 1.[52] This experience gave it a good start toward reading Naval Cipher No. 1 (in America, each of these codes and ciphers would have been regarded as a code, since it consisted of groups of figures with assigned meanings). By the time of the operation in Norway—April 1940—the B-dienst had cracked Cipher No. 1, and in September 1941 its successor, No. 2, had yielded; a later cipher, No. 4, was to prove secure.

That left No. 3, which the British, United States, and Canadian navies began using in June 1941 in the Atlantic. After the United States entered the war, realizing the increasing importance of the cipher, the B-dienst's English section, under its veteran and very capable chief, Wilhelm Tranow[53]—who was famous within his restricted circle for never forgetting the movements of a ship, even years after the fact—concentrated its efforts on reconstructing the book of No. 3. Success came within a month, and except for a setback around the beginning of 1943 lasted until the following June. With relish the B-dienst cryptologists called No. 3 the "convoy cipher"; following their practice of naming British ciphers after German cities, they gave it the official designation "Frankfurt." Not only did the breaking of Frankfurt give the Germans direct information about convoy sailing, it told them—with great accuracy—where the British believed the U-boats to be and thus what areas the convoys would be likely to avoid. So it was Shark telling the British about the German plans and dispositions, and Frankfurt telling the Germans what the British knew. But how did the British get their information? It could not come from the Enigma or its operators, the Germans decided. It had to be a matter of spies, direction finding, radar—anything but the machine.

But in 1943, after the great convoy convulsions of the winter and spring months, the back-and-forth shadow game came to its end. The Government Code and Cipher School—which was officially responsible for signal security as well as for code breaking—realized, as the result of Shark decrypts, that the Germans had information that could only have come from cryptanalysis; clearly, Cipher No. 3 was not secure. Actually, the admiralty had long had questions about the safety of this cipher,[54] but it had not moved with the force and efficiency demanded by the situation. It is hard to understand why—just as it had been hard for the American clerical personnel at the Argentia "Atlantic Charter" conference in August 1941 to understand how it was that the battleship *Prince of Wales*, bringing Churchill and his generals and admirals to the meeting, had not a single typewriter on board. The age of the quill pen, the Americans thought, had vanished with the age of sail.

Particularly poignant for men like Safford, the cipher-machine specialist, was the fact that the U.S. Navy was using and thus had available a machine of whose security it was sure. Their confidence was well-founded; the B-dienst never found a chink in it.

During the late spring and the summer of 1943—with the Allied cipher victories, improved organization, the introduction of escort carriers, better air cover, improved radar—the Battle of the Atlantic swung against Admiral Dönitz and his wolf packs. The American Bombes at Nebraska Avenue were now contributing their share to the Allied attack on naval Enigma; their output was whisked to Commander Knowles's situation room by pneumatic tube as well as teleprinter. It was finally an across-the-board victory for the Allies, ending quietly two years later in "bubbles, blown tanks, a sulky yielding."[55]

The Atlantic toll in human life was enormous, perhaps one seaman in five. On the other side the price was the highest paid by the members of any service for any country: of the 39,000 men who sailed in Dönitz's U-boats, 28,000 perished at sea.

Since Commander Safford was not directly involved in the Battle of the Atlantic, there was one thing he did not know. Bletchley Park had divined early in the year that the B-dienst was reading the convoy cipher, but Tiltman paid his little courtesy call on the American expert only in October. Faces in London were still "very red."

9

"I Don't Believe It"

DURING THE WINTER of 1943-1944, the British Ministry of Works completed the transformation of a girls' school into a residence for the officers and enlisted men of the 6813th Signal Service Detachment, whose number was now approaching fifty. The quarters were not elegant, but the school was converted into a dormitory with dining room, library, and other facilities.

This was to be Selmer Norland's third lodging since coming to Bletchley Park; around New Year's, finally acknowledging that his complicated sometimes-day, sometimes-night schedule was disruptive of Miss Winnie Judge's maidenly routine, he had moved to the Swan Hotel in the village of Woburn Sands, three miles from Bletchley, where he shared a room with a U.S. sergeant, a brilliant young cryptanalyst named George Vergine, who was assigned to Hut 6; now Norland could bicycle to work when he felt like it. Within a few weeks came his move to the new residence at Little Brickhill, on the southeast fringe of Bletchley, also about three miles from the Park.

Whitaker, who with his remarkable equanimity could justly have represented the phlegmatic temperament in a Ben Jonson comedy of humors, changed quarters at the same time, the Little Brickhill residence now becoming home for all of Bill Bundy's flock. Whitaker left his previous billet with regret, however. Not only was his room at the Whytes, large and clean and blessed with a refreshing view over green fields and gardens, the Whytes themselves were exemplary landlords. He had found "little by little" that he had been extremely fortunate in the billet selected for him. His hosts and their two daughters, both in their early twenties, were friendly and went out of their way to make things pleasant, and the food was "unbelievably good for wartime"— all this for a charge of $10 a week for lodging and two meals (the other

163

meal was taken at the BP cafeteria, at a cost of $4 a month): Thus, as Whitaker noted agreeably one day, his total expenses for the month amounted to about $50. His only complaint about the Whytes, in fact, was that sitting and chatting with them in the dining room after dinner was so pleasant that on such evenings he never managed to get anything done.[1]

Bundy moved from the Hunt at the same time, acquiring several roommates, including Art Levenson, Bob Nunn from the University of Chicago, and a new arrival for Hut 6, Lou Smadbeck, a short, red-haired product of Brown. Smadbeck's indoctrination was admirably simple.[2] He and other newcomers were taken straight to Hut 6, and they were told at that time what Hut 6 was doing and how each of the three shifts would be responsible for breaking as many of the codes of the day as possible. But help was present: the head of the watch, Smadbeck discovered, functioned as a sort of combination mother and father and teacher. The newcomer was assigned to a watch presided over by Howard Smith, a man from Gordon Welchman's college, though not a mathematician, and he found that it really did resemble school. "Howard," he might say, "I've got stuck here. What do you think about this?" And Smith would look a the problem or perhaps say "I haven't time for that. Come back in fifteen minutes." The Red key, in which the early-morning messages were always enciphered, was broken almost every day. "The others were sent at different times, but you could tell by the call signs pretty well what code or what cipher it was. And it was a thrill for me to break any one other than Red because they were more difficult. It was like shooting par on a golf course."

A routine quickly grew up at Little Brickhill. If you were on the swing shift, which Whitaker preferred because he felt it enabled him to live a more normal life than the others did, you would get up about nine and have breakfast—the cooks were first-rate, most of the men felt, but they were forced to serve what Whitaker called "these damned powdered eggs." If you were on another shift, your breakfast might be dinner to most of your companions. The mess was, at Bundy's direction, combined; "he was a superb commanding officer," Smadbeck decided, and "extremely democratic; there was no such thing as an officers' mess." After breakfast you could lounge around the day room, talk or read, play Ping-Pong, or go outside for volleyball; and BP offered a lone tennis court, available on a first-come, first-served basis. Play on this court had its own peculiarites. There being no rubber for balls or tennis shoes, owing to wartime restrictions, the balls were totally lacking in fuzz, and sneakers were often worn on the wrong feet so as to even the wear on the soles. A little before four o'clock, the twelve or fifteen men who were due to work in one job or another on the swing shift would pile into the back of a truck and be driven the few miles to BP; you could walk it, if you chose, as Bundy usually did. After dinner, for many of those off duty it was cards—much bridge, much poker.

If you wished, you could go back "inside the Park" in the evenings for entertainment. The off-duty attraction for the cryptanalysts and the other intelligence specialists was a large brick building, resembling the combination assembly hall and basketball gym one often sees on the campus of an American college, which housed a stage, projection booth, and screen, and also was the scene of dances, which were held with some frequency.

The creation of the Little Brickhill establishment meant that Bundy took on increased executive duties, because he was now the commanding officer of an American post—and one that was just off the main north-south road. "We had a lot of visitors," he said. "Here was this American outfit thirty miles from the nearest base. When people went by at mealtime, they'd say 'Let me get some chow here.' We'd have colonels and brigadiers and God knows who coming and sharing our meals." In spite of his democratic style as a commander and the informality on the job in Hut 6 and Hut 3, the 6813th "was a very remarkable outfit, because we were spit-and-polish military. We were running a three-shift base, and you couldn't turn everybody out at any time, but when they were around they knew they had to behave as if they were military. We had to look shipshape or we'd get reported."[3]

Being reported was, on the other hand, one possibility that did not concern Commander Travis, who as commanding officer of Bletchley Park presided over a mixture of men and women from all services, as well as hundreds of civilians. Of the latter group, not a single one had been chosen because of any military qualities. As one American observed, "some of the Bletchleyites were, it must be confessed, a queer lot."[4]

Alan Turing stories were limitless, partly because in his conduct Turing was inner-directed to an extraordinary degree, moving in a world that only occasionally resembled the one dwelt in by the persons around him. Given to bicycling in the neighborhood of Bletchley, Turing fought the pollen that stirred up his hay fever by wearing his gas mask—on the simple principle that this was the logical thing to do in the situation: there is no reason to suppose that he gave any thought to how he would look to the natives. Endlessly inquisitive, he would wander about the countryside peering through hedges and into ditches, once exciting the suspicions of a local spy hunter who summoned the police; his identity card was unpersuasive, since he had not signed it—not because he had forgotten to do it but because he claimed to have been told never to write anything on the card; one of his means of battling any bureaucracy was to take its strictures with childlike literalness. It was not surprising that at BP he was better known as "the Prof" than by his name.

Turing's method of dealing with a chronically ailing bicycle chain was not to repair or replace it but to count the number of revolutions the wheel could make between breakdowns, stop just in time, render first aid, and proceed on. His classic adventure was probably his flier in silver. Deciding, early in the war, that if Britain were invaded and occupied by Germany, his bank account would be valueless, he converted it into two silver ingots and buried them in different spots, his confident plan being to recover them when the Germans should be expelled. He drew a rather cryptic map of the burial areas, but when he went to recover the bullion he was unable to decipher his drawing and never saw his money again. "He used to tell this story rather shamefacedly," said his mother, "though it was quite a sensible proceeding, had it been efficiently carried out."[5]

A kindred spirit to Turing was Josh Cooper, a mathematician-cryptanalyst from Denniston's prewar stable who specialized in Luftwaffe ciphers. Looking every bit the absent-minded professor with his long black hair and Coke-bottle glasses, he was reported to have been seen walking through the gates of Bletchley Park with his hat in his hand and an open briefcase covering his head. But Cooper had another side, terse and direct, as exemplified in his maxim "any report that contains the word 'vital' is balls."[6] Group Captain Winterbotham found such types endearing but formidable: "It was rather frightening playing one's evening bridge with these men. It all came easily to them . . . "[7]

Other characters were present in abundance. There was one linguist who always proclaimed his current area of research by his clothing. When he appeared wearing a long black coat and a broad-brimmed felt hat and sporting a heavy beard, he was telling everybody that he was working on Rumanian. Another scholar, a mathematician, felt an occasional need to run around the duck pond, removing items of clothing like a frenzied striptease artist until he had achieved nudity, while Wrens and WAAFs trailed after him to pick up his discards. One day this same remarkable fellow concluded a quarrel with a young woman by threatening to throw her out of a second-story window.

"Nonsense," she said. "You couldn't throw anyone out of the window."

"Is that so? I'll show you"—and he promptly hurled himself out.

It took the attainment of a truly bizarre standard of deportment to be fired from BP, but this mathematician managed the feat several times, being summoned back after each dismissal because some vital process was suffering in his absence.[8]

As Churchill's response to the letter from Turing, Welchman, and their colleagues suggests, Bletchley Park was not only close to his heart as the supplier of his precious "eggs," he was always ready to take practical steps to see that its needs were met. It was said, in fact, and with considerable truth, that BP was his favorite establishment and that he had ordered that no stone be left unturned to get it equipment and staff. On a visit one day, according to a characteristic—if perhaps apocryphal—story, after watching the donnish types streaming by on their way to lunch, the prime minister turned to the commandant, saying, "I told you to leave no stone unturned to get the people you wanted. But I did not think you would take me so literally."[9]

If the doings inside the Park often seemed odd to outsiders, Bletchleyites had their retaliatory stories about visitors. Norland recalled the tale told of an intelligence officer from a field army. Shown some of the workings of Hut 3, this officer expressed astonishment: "What? You mean to say that these intercepted signals are in *German?*"[10]

All in all, as one American concluded, "it was a bad place in which to play chess for money." And, he added, "you could occasionally hear snatches of conversation at lunchtime on the grounds which indicated that the speakers were playing blindfold, three-dimensional tic-tac-toe as a relaxation from the daily grind."[11] In the same vein, Levenson one day stopped by the U.S. enlisted men's dayroom at Little Brickhill and, glancing through the books and magazines, was amazed to come across a Turkish-Latin dictionary—"something I never knew existed."[12]

Bundy's 6813th Signal Service Detachment also included people notably senior to its commander in age and experience. One such who had arrived was Bill Edgerton, the Chicago Orientalist recruited by Friedman early in 1943. Edgerton "cheated to the nth degree on the physical"[13] in order to get overseas; at BP he was assigned to arcane duties related to Hut 3. Bundy himself did not know what Edgerton worked on, but he "was a truly magnificent fellow—so wise, so learned, and so obviously impressive that I am sure they used him properly."

Social patterns, to some extent, tended to follow work patterns; you spent your leisure time with the persons whose interests you shared; thus Edgerton and other notable American literary and linguistic scholars, such as Gwynne Evans from Harvard, Howard Porter from

Columbia, and Charles Donohue from Yale, developed strong friendships in Hut 3. This was true to a degree of Whitaker and Norland as
well. For some time, as the only U.S. representatives in Hut 3, working
apart from the bulk of Bundy's group, they had been "deliberately or
accidentally left out of activities," because they were "just the tail of
the American dog."[14] But this situation had its bright side. Bundy gave
assignments to the officers for conducting early-morning calisthenics,
but the rotating watch schedule of Hut 3 did not mesh with the routine
followed by the others and, as Norland said, "somehow I managed to
escape the entire time I was there."

II

"ON JANUARY TWENTY," Whitaker noted in his secret cipher, "the Allies'
Mediterranean command sent us details of the projected landing at
Anzio to be made before daylight on January twenty-three."[15] Hut 3
was to take special note of German units in the area and to be on the
alert for intercepts relating to enemy plans and reactions to the Allied
blow from the sea—the attempt to get the frustrating Italian campaign
moving. Churchill, the leading proponent, saw the landing, code-
named Shingle, as opening the road to Rome and cutting off Kesselring's forces south of the city, in an aim to wind up the fight in Italy
before the beginning of the great operations contemplated for the
summer. For a number of reasons Shingle was a failure, but none of
these had to do with Ultra, which faithfully reported the German side
of the story. The fault lay with the planners and the commanders, and
credit was also due Kesselring for the speed and resourcefulness with
which he faced the situation; here this general proved the accuracy of a
British intelligence assessment of him as a soldier of "strong mind in
assessing tactical facts, a deep understanding of tactical detail, an
unfaltering spirit and a stern hold on his troops."[16]
     Lt. Gen. Mark Clark, who seems to have possessed the Montgomery-
like flaw of being unable to admit error, attempted to cite signal-
intelligence (not necessarily Ultra) evidence of a German defensive
buildup as the reason for the failure of the landed troops to move
rapidly inland, as had been expected. But Clark's explanation was not
convincing. What was true, however, was that Clark himself had, for
some reason, always been skeptical of the value of signal intelligence.
The official history notes that it was a BP decrypt of January 28, laying
out Kesselring's plan for a counteroffensive against the beachhead, that
finally converted Clark into a believer in Ultra.[17] But by this time the

"wildcat" that Churchill had hoped to hurl ashore was well along in its metamorphosis into a "stranded whale."

Whitaker concluded his January cipher note about the furnishing of the details of Anzio with a provocative forward-looking comment: "We have requested two weeks' notice on the invasion of the Continent." But the fiasco at Anzio, on a lightly held shore, with the swift German reaction, could not be encouraging to those working for a landing in France.

EARLY IN DECEMBER 1943, on his way back to Washington from the Teheran "Big Three" conference, President Roosevelt had paused at Tunis where he was met at the airfield by the theater commander, General Eisenhower.[18] Scarcely had the president been seated in the general's car when he turned to his host and uttered a sentence that ended months of speculation. In his characteristically informal way, Roosevelt said: "Well, Ike, you are going to command Overlord."

Thus the projected invasion of the Continent acquired what it had lacked during all the months of desultory planning that had upset the Johnny-come-latelies in London. It had been widely believed both in the United States and in Britain that the job of commander would go to General Marshall as the crowning assignment for a man whom Churchill called the "American Carnot," the great raiser of citizen armies. It was deemed the president's plum to give because, in what was to be not only the greatest amphibious invasion in history but the most complex of all military operations, American forces would ultimately comprise three times the British number. But by the irony of rank the appointment of General Marshall proved politically impossible. It was the greatest prize a soldier could hope for, but the idea that Marshall might step down as Chief of Staff to become a theater commander, no matter how glorified, stirred up a brew of rumor and noisy opposition in Washington. Besides, the president had told the general in a memorable explanation, "I didn't feel I could sleep at ease with you out of the country."[19]

Eisenhower's response to Roosevelt's announcement was to say, "I hope you will not be disappointed."[20]

If this hope was to borne out, much work awaited Eisenhower himself, the commanders who would serve under him, the COSSAC planners, and the signal-intelligence teams. In mid-January Ike arrived in London "to undertake the organization of the mightiest fighting force that the two Western Allies could muster."[21] As the British army commander and overall ground commander for the assault, he had hoped to get General Alexander, who in the capacity of deputy Allied commander had taken over the land battles in both North Africa and Italy; a *beau sabreur*, Alex was dashing and charismatic without being overwhelming, winning through his charm and modesty the respect and affection of everybody who dealt with him, British and American alike. Eisenhower looked on him as a friend and thought it significant that "Americans instinctively liked him."[22]

The British instead gave the Overlord assignment to Montgomery, who was strongly sponsored by Gen. Alan Brooke, the Chief of the Imperial General Staff. Eisenhower was not thrilled, later observing stiffly that Montgomery was "a choice acceptable to me."[23] Alexander would have been easy to get along with, and Montgomery was not going to be—Ike had few illusions about that. Perhaps he would have felt better about the decision had he had some way of knowing the judgment of Alexander that would one day be made by Lord Mountbatten: "He had almost every quality you could wish to have, except that he had the average brain of an average English gentleman."[24] The Allied force already had its charming, honest, popular presiding officer in Ike himself; it most likely did not need another. And in Montgomery it certainly did not get one.

The invasion plan presented by Lt. Gen. F. E. Morgan was produced under shipping limits imposed by the Combined Chiefs of Staff. Governed by these strictures, COSSAC proposed an initial landing of three divisions; the location, as the result of COSSAC and various earlier studies, was to be the Bay of the Seine, on the Normandy coast. Having seen a general outline of the plan some weeks earlier, Eisenhower was doubtful that an assault limited to a three-division front could succeed in sticking in France. And Montgomery reacted to a draft of the plan by declaring it "impracticable."[25] These criticisms all concerned the size of the assault. "This will not do," Montgomery said to Churchill. "I must have more in the initial punch."[26] And there must be more than one beach involved to avoid the kind of congestion that would make it impossible to keep the scene, as Monty liked to say, "tidy."

The weight and width of the assault now had to be rethought and reargued by the generals and the planners, producing, as Ralph Ingersoll of the Johnny-come-latelies said, "the strengthening of the attack for which so many Americans had fought so long and so vainly."[27] But although other landing areas besides Normandy were looked at again, none henceforth received serious consideration. The early rival candidate had been the Pas de Calais region, the area just across the Strait of Dover, which offered obvious advantages based on the fact that it is much closer to England than is Normandy; the troops would have a shorter trip in their landing craft, with less exposure to hazard; turnaround would be faster; and fighter planes could fly more sorties. In addition, an invasion force landed in the Pas de Calais would be in a position to move directly eastward, which would take it toward the ultimate objectives in Germany and also offer the possibility of cutting off the Germans to the south. That the Germans saw all these points too was confirmed by their actions—the Calais area was the most strongly defended part of the French coast.

"In the winter of 1944, everything across the Channel was mysterious and, by and large, full of dread," Ingersoll observed. "What we were doing had no precedent."[28] Men who had survived earlier landings in the war emphasized the chancy nature of amphibious operations. Anzio had been a shocking disappointment, and before it the landing at Salerno, near Naples, had almost ended in the withdrawal of the Allied assaulting force. Even Sicily had offered its share of inadequacy and confusion. And none of these previous operations had faced anything comparable to the resistance the Germans could offer to the Overlord forces.

Observing a landing rehearsal, Ingersoll decided that "it was an awful thing to stand on a cliff, imagining one was a German commander, and to watch the assault waves spew forth, tangle on the beach and make obvious targets of themselves."[29] Vehicles flooded out or stalled in the sand or sank into marshy ground—and this confusion was taking place in a practice attempt without the harassment of enemy fire. What would happen when these troops flung themselves against the most strongly fortified coast in the world? Had the pessimists been right all along?

Not only was Overlord an operation of unprecedented scope, complexity, and difficulty, it absolutely had to succeed.[30] Failure at Salerno or Anzio, though unpalatable, could have been accepted and overcome. If the landing troops had been driven off, the war would have gone on, and the overall strategy would have remained the same. But if Overlord failed, resulting in withdrawal, that would be the end of any Allied attempt to land in Western Europe for at least the better part of a year. The Germans could concentrate on Russia, knowing that the Allies could not mount another attack until late spring weather arrived in 1945. No one could be sure how Stalin would react. Many in the West had, since 1941, lived in the continuing fear that the Russians and the Germans, who had surprised the world by striking a bargain in 1939, might do it again. If the great invasion proved a fiasco, would Stalin conclude that the British and the Americans were not willing to make supreme efforts against Germany—that they had not really tried?

There was also a counterpossibility. With no Anglo-American forces on the Continent except those mucking about in Italy, the Red Army would, if it continued its successful advance into Europe, have a free hand wherever it chose to deal itself in. Still another worry at SHAEF (Supreme Headquarters, Allied Expeditionary Force) was the presumed German progress in secret weapons.

So the invasion must not fail. The men of the Allied force must get ashore and stay ashore, and everything that was organizationally and technically possible must be done to ensure success. "We are putting the whole works on one number," Eisenhower wrote to a friend.[31]

The Germans did not know where the Allied assault would strike, but they obviously would look and listen eagerly for clues. The Allies must help them in that search, take them by the hand and make it unmistakably clear to them. Here was a vital role for all intelligence, certainly for Ultra.

AS THE SUPREME Anglo-American operation of the war, Overlord was able to draw on a wide range of brains and talent. Colonel Noel Wild, an officer with a particularly interesting specialty, arrived at SHAEF from exploits in the Middle East, which, befitting its centuries-old and well-earned reputation as a land of subtlety and intrigue, had served early in the war as the delivery room and nursery for British deception practices. The father of these practices, with the blessing of Field Marshal Wavell, the theater commander, was Brigadier Dudley Clarke, who created an outfit called "A" Force and who was himself the sort of character of whom legends are made. Seeming congenitally inclined to cloak and dagger, the brigadier was wonderingly and perhaps pettishly described by an air marshal as "forever buzzing about Istanbul in mufti."[32] Clarke ordered and peopled what one disciple called "his fantasy world" that did, in fact, "grow and prosper until it had become one of the major aids to victory." His right-hand man in this endeavor was Colonel Wild, who came to this shadowy world from service in an elite regiment.

Clarke's profession was making the enemy believe things that were not so. They might be partly true, or similar to the truth, or suggestive of the truth, but they were themselves false. And they might have no substance at all. Key words in Clarke's operating lexicon were *notional* and *bogus*, and his aim in every case was to put into effect a cover plan that would lead the enemy to concentrate his strength at a point or points other than where he was going to be attacked. It was Clarke's principle that, as one of his officers put it, "you can never, by deception, persuade an enemy of anything not according with his own expectations, which usually are not far removed from his hopes."[33] And this work was not ordinarily made up out of the flotsam and jetsam of momentary hunch and inspiration—as in "let's float a corpse into the Atlantic and fool the Krauts into believing it has real plans in its pockets"—but like other intelligence jobs was detailed and tedious, performed day in, day out.

The kind of deception practiced by Clarke and his "A" Force began with the "bogus" order of battle, which might include "notional" divisions, corps, and even armies, being marshaled for a notional attack on some objective against which no attack was, in fact, intended. These notional outfits normally contained an element of truth; they might actually be training schools, headquarters, and the like blown up and given designations as divisions or other large, active formations. Painstaking work by "A" Force over a long period of time, for instance, persuaded the enemy that the British were holding three whole armies in the Middle East with the likely purpose of invading southeastern Europe (and the presence of these notional armies predisposed the Germans to believe in the documents carried by "Major Martin," the celebrated corpse, which indicated that the Allies planned to hop from North Africa to Greece).

The second element in strategic deception, not separated from the bogus order of battle but supporting it, consisted of deception aids—dummy aircraft, tanks, and guns—and noise-making devices that could perform tricks like simulating small-arms fire. The third factor was the use of double agents who would confirm the enemy in his erroneous conclusions. At the time of the Overlord planning, British intelligence was running two stellar performers in this métier, known by the code names Garbo and Brutus, both of them highly trusted in Berlin.

But how could the deceivers know whether their cover plans were working? Actually, the confirmation would come through the very means by which the enemy had received much of his seemingly valid knowledge of the bogus order of battle—signal intelligence. One of the ironies of deception was that it fed the enemy cipher service false information—generating great amounts of phantom radio traffic in the process—while it benefited from the true information the enemy unwittingly put on the air. Ultra was the real check on the progress of deception; U.S. Magic would also have a part to play.

It was this background that Brigadier Clarke's friend and second in command, Colonel Wild, brought to SHAEF, where he took on the splendidly vague title of head of the Committee of Special Means. A huge and detailed variety of bogus plans and operations were weighed and drawn up, all with the purpose of keeping German forces scattered throughout Europe and away from the intended landing area. The operation designed to deceive the Germans into believing that the assault would not come on the beaches of Normandy was called Fortitude. Actually, Fortitude had even more ambitious goals than simply fooling the enemy in advance about the location of the landing. It also aimed at persuading the Germans that the operation would take place later than it actually would; and the crowning touch was the element designed to show, after Overlord had begun, that the assault in Normandy was merely the first blow and a mightier attack would soon fall on the Pas de Calais. The logical reason for choosing Normandy as the site of the invasion was simply that the Germans expected the blow to fall in the Calais area. A more subtle justification for the choice was that Normandy favored deception as Calais did not.[34] A real landing at Calais, where began the shortest road to Germany, would have brought German forces rushing from the Normandy area to try to beat back the Allied attack; in this case, deception would have been wasted. Why should the Germans keep divisions off to the west when they were needed at Calais?

The basis of the threat to the Pas de Calais was the creation of Allied forces, or what appeared to be Allied forces, in southeastern England. Two army groups were to be established, the actual 21st and the notional First United States Army Group, known as FUSAG. When the 21st, under General Montgomery, departed to cross the Channel, FUSAG would remain behind, presumably waiting for its turn to come. One element of this notional army group, the U.S. Third Army, would be real; it was due to go to Normandy some days after the assault, leaving behind two notional armies, the U.S. Fourteenth and the British Fourth, which would continue to pose threats to other areas. Every means of deception devised by Dudley Clarke was to be used to fix the bogus order of battle in the minds of the Germans—radio traffic, the reports of agents (since the British had "turned" all the enemy spies in Britain, every German agent was in fact a double agent), the creation of notional tanks, planes, guns, trucks . . . the entire panoply of trickery. One spring day Sydney Cripps, a farmer in one of the southeastern English counties, saw with surprise that several tanks had appeared in his meadow. His bull also noticed the tanks and, determined to drive them off, charged one broadside. After ferocious goring, the invader collapsed like a huge balloon—which was exactly what it was.[35]

One added detail gave unique verisimilitude to the FUSAG notion. As it happened, an outstanding American battlefield commander was at liberty. Ever since the public had heard the news that Lt. Gen. George S. Patton had slapped two GIs hospitalized for battle fatigue, this complex man had been in a limbo of disgrace. Nevertheless, Eisenhower had wanted the mercurial general for participation in the Normandy operation, though not in the initial assault—the U.S. command here being given to Omar Bradley. Ike seemed to regard Patton as a sort of fine but unusually temperamental Doberman given to harassing the postman and despoiling the neighbors' flower beds but unquestionably the star of the kennel when it came to tearing the pants off fleeing burglars. He should be disciplined but not discarded.

Shortly after he arrived in England, however, Patton made some remarks to the GIs of a U.S. division that "caused more than a ripple of astonishment and press comment," and some time later expressed to a British service club the opinion that "Britain and America would have to rule the world after the war." As Ike put it, the general "had a genius for explosive statements that rarely failed to startle his hearers."[36] Patton's last declaration, which resounded all over Britain and the United States despite the fact that the meeting at which Patton spoke was supposed to be private, with no reporters present, aroused fresh ire in America and strained Eisenhower's tolerance to the breaking point.

But one thing could certainly be said for the incident: the Germans could not have missed the news. If they had entertained any doubts about Patton's whereabouts, those remarks uttered in the town of Knutsford laid them to rest. Was the release of the story, as has been suggested, inspired by Colonel Wild's operatives? Certainly the Allied deceivers wished to be sure that the enemy knew from Allied sources as well as from double agents of the presence in England of the general whom Ike's confidant, Capt. Harry C. Butcher, called "the best ground gainer of the United Nations generals."[37] The Germans generally looked on the aggressive, thrusting Patton as the Allies viewed Erwin Rommel: if there was going to be an invasion, Patton would surely play a leading part; the Allies would, unfortunately, not be so stupid as to cashier this bold commander because of one or two hot-tempered incidents or a few verbal indiscretions.

Being thoroughly aware of the German opinion of Patton, which after all was perfectly sound, the deceivers had installed him as commanding general of FUSAG—a real general in command of a notional army. Double agents fed the story of Patton's command to their German controllers, who were ready to be convinced that FUSAG, in southeast England, was a force to be feared and carefully watched.

After what seemed the fiasco at Knutsford, which was followed by what had by now become the expected, ritual chewing out by Eisenhower, Patton wrote in his diary: "I feel like death, but I am not out yet.

If they will let me fight, I will . . ." And he added: "My final thought on the matter is that I am destined to achieve some great thing."[38] Though being commanding general of FUSAG might be useful to the Allied cause, it could hardly lead to greatness. But in due course, a month after the Normandy invasion, came the happy day when the Germans were told through agents that because of his indiscretions, Patton had been relieved as commander of FUSAG, stepping down to being merely the commander of Third Army. The enemy still did not know that Third Army was real but FUSAG only notional. Even more remarkably, in August, a month later still, the German staff section specializing in the western front was wondering who would be the new commander of FUSAG, "which apart from its airborne formations comprises around thirty-two large formations"[39] and still threatened the Pas de Calais.

The notional First U.S. Army Group had done all, and more than all, that could have been hoped for from any phantom. A fringe benefit of the operation had been the involvement of George Patton in the workings of intelligence.

BEFORE THE LAUNCHING of the invasion, the Allied commanders depended on intelligence to supply them with information about the strength and the disposition of the forces opposing them across the Channel. Intelligence would also give them the opportunity of seeing in advance whether the Germans were swallowing the deception bait. Here was a clear-cut role for Ultra.

On January 9, 1944, while Eisenhower was still in Washington meeting with General Marshall and others prior to taking up his appointment at SHAEF in London, an Enigma message decrypted in Hut 6 and translated in Hut 3 made reference to FUSAG, just as though it were as real as any other Allied formation.[40] Operation Fortitude was in business.

III

THIS SEASON OF plans and preparations for the main event on the Continent saw a wave of new faces in Hut 3, some passing through, some coming to stay.

During the previous June, Alfred McCormack and William Friedman had concluded their profoundly fruitful two-month visit to the Government Code and Cipher School and returned to Washington, leaving Telford Taylor behind as the Special Branch representative in England. McCormack went back to carry on the war in which he was most deeply engaged—the struggle against the rest of the Military Intelligence Service, against the Army personnel bureaucracy, and against Washington officialdom in general, much of which even a year and a half after Pearl Harbor seemed unable to grasp the fact that when you asked people to be willing to give their lives, you owed it to them to do your utmost to preserve those lives. But even now the General Staff seemed unaware of the personnel needs of intelligence and even that intelligence itself was a valuable resource;[41] despite the high personal qualifications required for effective work in intelligence, the service had been granted few priorities. The difference between this situation and what McCormack had seen at Bletchley Park was galling—but inspiring, as well. And inspiration was sometimes sorely needed. Once McCormack was moved to reflect: "What G-2 would be today if I had not been a personal appointee of the Secretary and a law partner of the Assistant Secretary, I do not know . . . Every move forward was hampered and sabotaged by the military authorities."[42]

What McCormack now had to accomplish, with respect to the German side of the war, was to find the people who could give life to the arrangements made with the British for ensuring that "American field commands would be furnished promptly with all relevant British intelligence and that the War Department would have access to British intelligence in all its aspects."[43] This agreement called for the establishment of a unit of the Special Branch in England, of which Colonel Taylor would be the head; for the integration into Hut 3 of Special Branch officers; and for the creation of a system of getting operational intelligence from Bletchley Park into the hands of U.S. commanders in the field. This new range of activities would clearly require men of education, perception, and tact. Run-of-the-mill officers would hardly do, but at a time when the Special Branch still numbered barely more than thirty officers, its deputy chief was faced with the need to find some forty more.

Because, by Allied agreement as well as by the nature of the beast, the war against Japan claimed the major portion of American intelligence efforts, McCormack could not devote all his time to a talent search; but he knew where to turn for assistance. As would anyone in such a limited-time pressure situation, he sought help from his own "old boy" world, Wall Street. The job of recruitment was taken on by the two-man team of Maj. Porter Chandler, formerly of the eminent Davis Polk law firm, and Lt. Col. Francis C. Reed, known as "Bus," of Hughes, Hubbard & Ewing.

With a few exceptions, it was too late now to hunt for qualified civilians to lure into the Special Branch; the kinds of people wanted now would already be serving officers. Chandler "combed the Army for officers of the caliber required, and Reed found ways to get them assigned to G-2."[44] Chandler, who had served in Africa as an air intelligence officer, had come to the Special Branch to do actual intelligence work, but he assumed the recruiting job as a vitally necessary chore, putting into it "the energy of a dynamo"; he "proved himself to have an extraordinary capacity for finding well-qualified intelligence personnel." Certainly the search through the ranks of the Army was thorough and unflagging, and it soon proved that there were quite a few old boys out there.

IN 1940 THE Davis Polk firm had acquired as an associate an urbane and cultivated young New Yorker named Langdon Van Norden, a graduate of Princeton who had just received his LL.B. from Yale.[45] Facing the draft in early 1942, Van Norden, a trim fellow of five-foot-eight, was casting about for a more promising avenue for his inevitable entry into the armed forces when he heard from two friends, the brothers Bill and McGeorge Bundy, that the thing to do was to come down to Fort Monmouth, enlist in the Signal Corps, and learn to be a cryptanalyst. Van Norden appeared at Fort Monmouth in May 1942, was assigned to the crypt school, and, emerging as a second lieutenant in November, was sent to Arlington Hall, where he was put to work on a German diplomatic code. In June 1943 he went overseas with a radio intelligence company whose "job was eavesdropping on German low-grade radio traffic—tank to tank, or tank to spotter aircraft or fighter-bomber, or tank back to headquarters." As far as he knew at the time, this would be his permanent assignment.

IN 1941 WALL Street, like much of the rest of America, was looking to the day when war would come. One of the activities of the most dedicatedly interventionist corporation lawyers was participation in a training camp upstate at Plattsburgh. One day a general arrived at the front gate of the camp and announced that he was in search of a Mr. Robert Patterson, who, when located, was found to be busily engaged in KP.

"You're being appointed Undersecretary of War," the general said.

"All right," Patterson said. "But you'll have to wait till I finish peeling these potatoes."

Another of the participants in the training camp was Edmund Kellogg, like Langdon Van Norden a Princeton graduate and Davis Polk associate (with an LL.B. from Harvard rather than Yale). In September 1941, Kellogg resigned from the law firm and went off to Washington to play a part in the diplomacy of the day, becoming an assistant to

Assistant Secretary of State Adolf Berle and later going into the Army as an intelligence officer.[46]

SOMEWHAT OLDER THAN either Van Norden or Kellogg—enough so that he would not have known either of them at Princeton, where he graduated in the class of 1927—was Adolph Rosengarten, an emphatically Main Line Philadelphian, a lawyer and a nephew of the president of the Pennsylvania Railroad. Somewhat military minded, Binx, as he was known at Princeton, joined the ROTC in college and also was a member of the famous and socially prominent First Troop, Philadelphia Cavalry. In March 1941 he entered active military service with a National Guard division, the 28th. The greater part of the next three years was spent in the coast artillery, until in December 1943 his outfit was disbanded. Rosengarten went off to Washington to look for a new job, and while touring the corridors of the Pentagon he encountered one of Alfred McCormack's ace recruiters, Lt. Col. Bus Reed.[47] His employment problem was quickly solved.

SOMEONE ELSE HAD a different sort of encounter with Colonel Reed. Beverly Kitchen, a lively woman from Long Island, a Junior League member and boarding-school graduate, had passed up college in order to get directly involved in work as a medical secretary.[48] When the war came along, she wanted to do something for the war effort, and she got a job with the Red Cross in Washington. Her great hope was to go overseas, but she found that she "was sitting in a room sort of typing things, not in any way interesting." There was just no challenge about the job. Naturally enough, family members heard of her discontent, and one day her uncle said, "Look, if you're serious about being so bored with your job, would you like to work in the Pentagon?" It seemed that the Special Branch of G-2 needed a secretary, and Uncle Bus was their ace recruiter.

LEWIS POWELL WAS a neat, precise, compactly built young man, a truly courtly but unassuming Virginian who had been first in his class at Washington and Lee (1929) and had acquired an LL.B. from the same school two years later and an LL.M. from Harvard in 1939.[49] Although he was beyond draft age in 1942, he wanted to fly, but his weak eyes ruled out any fulfillment of that desire; his next choice was air intelligence. Graduating in the second class produced by the new Air Force intelligence school, he was assigned to a medium bomber group. In October 1942, having been shipped to England, he was issued Arctic equipment and put aboard a troopship at Bristol. After a circuitous voyage the vessel passed through the Straits of Gibraltar and landed its passengers at the Gulf of Arzew in Algeria, some twenty miles east of the port of Oran. Operation Torch, the Allied move into Northwest Africa, was under way. Powell would be one of the first U.S. air intelligence officers to put his training to work.

DON BUSSEY WAS neither a lawyer nor an Easterner.[50] He attended first Antioch College and then the University of Chicago, getting his degree in 1937 and going on to graduate work in political science. Then came a Princeton connection: he was offered, and accepted, an instructor's job, and then two years later he went into the pre-Pearl Harbor army by way of the draft. He was sent to OCS after finishing basic training, but—most unusually—was released during the cycle for a project with the eminent public opinion pollster Elmo Roper, for whom he had worked during his Antioch days; the Army had decided it wanted to know what the public thought about the war and had given the assignment of finding out to Roper's organization.

On completing this task, Bussey returned to OCS, and then went to work in an enterprise called the American Intelligence Service, keeping an eye on Latin America. In August 1943 he was ordered to the Command and General Staff School at Fort Leavenworth and soon after was sent to the Special Branch in Washington.

The Special Branch occupied a series of offices on the ground floor of the outside of the Pentagon's E Ring, with a prized view of the lawn. In a row were the room with the officers at their specialized desks— Balkan, Russian front, German order of battle, and so on; next the secretaries' room; then Alfred McCormack's office; and finally Carter Clarke's. In these rooms Bussey came to know McCormack, who concentrated on producing the working intelligence while Clarke continued to perform his administrative and diplomatic chores; McCormack was not only "a very brilliant man" and "a giant" but "a magnificent editor." The daily intelligence reports—the "Magic Summary" and the Military and Naval Supplement—produced for the edification of the Chief of Staff and other higher-ups were edited personally by McCormack; "it was gone over with a very fine-tooth comb by him." The demands on his time and energy finally became too great, and the deputy chief brought in Ben Shute, an associate in his old Wall Street law firm, to take over the job. Before Shute had been on board very long, Bussey was off for the next phase of his Army career. He had been ordered to London, where he was to report to Lt. Col.

Telford Taylor at the U.S. embassy in Grosvenor Square. Shute himself was to come along later. It was always happening to McCormack: he would find a person to work with him, train him, and then see him lost to the imperious call of his new overseas branch—the Military Intelligence Service, London.

IV

TELFORD TAYLOR WAS one of those men who seem to have everything: background, brains, a strong personality, education, and, as one associate put it, "he was as handsome as Tyrone Power." Both men and women admired him. During June and July 1943, following the return to America of his traveling companions Alfred McCormack and William Friedman, Taylor had devoted himself to working as the U.S. liaison officer with Commander Denniston's diplomatic intelligence operation in London. This was a considerably different sort of role from that played by liaison persons from Arlington Hall, such as John Seaman and Walter Fried, whose preoccupations were technical. Bletchley Park and the U.S. Signal Intelligence Agency were sharing practical knowledge about machines, devices, and procedures involved in the cracking of enemy codes and ciphers. Taylor, on the other hand, was performing a substantive intelligence function, collecting information about enemy activities and plans, thus representing the first harvest for the Special Branch of the new Anglo-American cooperation agreement.[51] Having now discovered the truly great scope of the British intelligence operation vis-à-vis Germany, the War Department was eager to deal itself in.

But Taylor's portfolio was to be by no means limited to the Denniston diplomatic operation in London. In late July he moved on to Bletchley Park, where he spent an intensive month absorbing the mysteries of the entire process but particularly those of Hut 3, at the same time keeping his contact with Denniston's diplomatic intercepts and picking out items for transmission to the Special Branch in the Pentagon. Finally, on August 23, he received his first staff person, Maj. Samuel McKee, who in civilian life had been a history professor at Columbia. It was now time for Taylor, from his new base at Bletchley Park, to begin putting into practical effect, on a regular basis, the words of the Anglo-American agreement with respect to German machine ciphers that "all desired intelligence from this source will be made available to the War Department in Washington."[52] Military Ultra messages from BP to all customers were labeled with the arcane designation CX/MSS, and the first of these to be transmitted to Washington was dispatched on August 27, 1943. It told the Pentagon the interesting news that Army Group B under Field Marshal Erwin Rommel was taking control of German forces in northern Italy.[53]

What followed was a period of confusion rather than harmony. Who should send what to Washington? Was the staff of the Special Branch now large enough to handle a sizable volume of traffic? Some Britons at the War Office, which handled order of battle information, felt there really was very little point to the whole procedure. Transmit the material across the Atlantic? Whatever for? It was just at this point, early in September, that there arrived from Washington the Assistant Chief of Staff, G-2, Maj. Gen. George Strong. But the general had more to do than visit the American signal intelligence team newly arrived at BP. He and Taylor held muddled conferences with the British, which concluded, surprisingly, in Strong's expressing his agreement with General Menzies's view that no CX/MSS ought to be sent from BP to Washington.

This news was received in the Pentagon with astonishment. The Special Branch had set up a section to be devoted to German military traffic, and it had been the American belief that "intelligence of more than momentary significance which is important enough to send to commands abroad is also important enough to send to responsible staff officers in Washington."[54] The Americans also felt that information considered important enough to be given to the War Office and the Air Ministry in London was by the same token information that the War Department should receive, and the selection should be made not by British officials at the ministries but at the source, BP, by Americans familiar with the needs of G-2.

On returning home, General Strong, after conversation with Carter Clarke, realized that he had blundered and so informed Taylor, who then had to go back to the drawing board with Menzies, Group Capt. Eric Jones of Hut 3, and others. Finally, on September 25, this procedural wrangling was concluded by a new agreement, simple in essence: Taylor was to be responsible for choosing what was to go to Washington but was to keep the War Office and the Air Ministry informed about what he was sending. This was indeed procedural wrangling, but it also appears to have been something more—the clash between the American desire to hold a full hand in every respect, or at least to have the opportunity to do so if the U.S. representatives wished, and a still-strong desire on the part of the British service ministries (as distinct from Bletchley Park) to protect what they fancied to be their preserve.

And, no doubt, not all of the old hands in the ministries had yet been persuaded of the efficacy of U.S. Army security procedures. It was only by agreeing to adopt British methods of handling and disseminating the intelligence and of employing it in the field that the army was being granted access to this supply of secrets; and, in fact, it was only after these methods were put into practice that the U.S. Navy consented to share its traffic with the Army.[55] Skepticism began at home.

Yet the British skeptics, as well as Allied officers and politicians in general, had much to gain from intimate cooperation with the Special Branch, not only with respect to the war against Japan but also in relation to Germany. This was so because the Purple pipeline between Berlin and Tokyo was still in operation; from Italy and Spain, as well, Japanese diplomats and attachés kept in close touch with the Foreign Ministry at home. The Americans at Arlington Hall read all this diplomatic radio correspondence. Baron Oshima, who had reported to Tokyo in 1941 on the possibility that the Americans were reading the Japanese ciphers, was the ambassador in Berlin and fittingly so; described by a German diarist as "slick and smooth as an eel,"[56] the baron was, except for skin color and eye fold, as thorough a Nazi as Dr. Goebbels or Heinrich Himmler—a man who had admired Adolf Hitler to an almost incredible degree since arriving in Germany in 1934 and regarded the Führer's creation of the Third Reich as a feat unrivaled "in the history of all people and all times;"[57] much of the development of German-Japanese friendship and alliance was due to his tireless efforts. Hence it was hardly surprising that all the high-level doors in Berlin were open to him and that he and his attachés were freely given information not only about German policies but about military matters as well. As the war went on, Oshima became the chief Japanese diplomatic representative in Europe and the de facto head of his country's intelligence agencies in the West. He was, all in all, a very well-informed correspondent.

This diplomatic material—instructions and questions sent to Berlin from Tokyo as well as reports by the envoys to the Foreign Office—was carefully studied by the Special Branch. In July 1942 one of the early triumphs of Clarke's and McCormack's analysts had come when they decided, against the tide of supposedly informed Allied opinion, that Japan had no intention of attacking the Soviet Union but wanted above all things to stay out of war with her giant neighbor.[58] (When the Magic intercepts on which this conclusion was based were shown to other intelligence officers, they declared that the messages were surely a plant devised by some wily Oriental mind and ought to be disregarded.) Similar study of messages from Madrid at the time of the Torch landings in North Africa in November 1942 left the analysts of the Special Branch with the assurance that Spain would continue to talk a good Fascist game but would not take any steps to hinder the Allied operations.

In a striking example of the kind of military intelligence supplied by Magic intercepts, one of Baron Oshima's attachés, a Colonel Ito, reported in the autumn of 1943 on a tour he had been given of German anti-invasion defenses on the French Atlantic coast. The colonel observed, for example, that "defenses of places other than those with cliffs and precipices have all been fortified for more than 1,000 meters from the shore line." Troops, he said, "are held in reserve in the rear and can be immediately sent in as reinforcements." He described the protection of the highly important submarine bases, pointing out that the Germans not only had constructed defenses against sea attack but had built powerful defenses on the landward sides, consisting of "defensive positions which connect nests of resistance and strong points."[59] He even listed the depth of the defenses for each of the cities, almost as though it were the Japanese who needed such data for the purpose of planning an attack: La Rochelle, 10 to 15 kilometers; Le Havre, 6 to 8 kilometers, and so on. He described the armament of the harbor defenses; Le Havre, at the mouth of the Seine, was protected by four 300 mm. naval guns, and Cherbourg, the key port on the Cotentin peninsula, had four huge 380 mm. field pieces. Detailed descriptions followed of the strong points—their guns, mines, flame throwers. A devotedly specific and thorough note taker, Colonel Ito was an equally thorough informant of the Allies.

These were some of the gems produced by American Magic, and there would be more. Hence the Special Branch representatives had little reason to come hat in hand to General Menzies and the orthodox officers at the War Office and the Air Ministry. The most puzzling part of all the September debates was the surprising position taken by General Strong that CX/MSS ought not to be sent to Washington, but at least the general was willing to admit a mistake and change his mind; no doubt, firm and precise argument on the part of Colonel Clarke convinced him of his error. Two days after the signing of September 25 agreement, the CX/MSS traffic from Bletchley Park to the Pentagon was resumed. This traffic was, of course, only part of Colonel Taylor's responsibility. It was now time to take steps looking toward the participation of U.S. officers in the intelligence work of Hut 3—that is, as military and air advisers side by side with British officers—and toward the setting up of channels and arrangements by which, after the great invasion, Ultra intelligence would be handled in the field by American officers advising American commanders.

V

COLONEL HAYES OF the Allied Force Headquarters, Algiers, was absolutely furious.[60]

"Lieutenant," he said sternly, "you've been pulling wires behind my back. *And I don't like that sort of thing.*"

The lieutenant was dumbfounded but not so completely that he could not say, "Colonel, what do you mean?" He had no idea what fate had plucked him from the mud of Monte Cassino, in Italy, where his radio company was part of Mark Clark's Fifth Army, and brought him to the Maison Blanche in Algiers and the presence of this angry colonel.

"You have orders here to report to the United States embassy in London. You've been pulling wires."

"Colonel, I have not been doing that," the lieutenant said. "I love the outfit I'm in, sir. I ask nothing more than to be returned to duty." And it was perfectly true, the lieutenant thought. They were a great bunch of fellows; there wasn't any point in going to another outfit in the Army. The grass wasn't going to be any greener anywhere else. "I want to be returned."

"No," the colonel said, restrained but visibly furious, "I have orders from the Secretary of War."

The lieutenant was hardly displeased when the interview was over. But although he had high-level orders, he had not been given a comparable transportation priority, and this omission, combined with the foul winter weather, meant that it took him three weeks of short plane hops to make it to London. He had one consolation on the trip, however; he was given as companions two Luftwaffe fliers who had been shot down in a new version of the Messerschmitt Me-109 fighter; Allied air intelligence was "anxious to get these lads to England to interrogate them." They "were so glad to be captured," the lieutenant recalled. "They would be out of the war. They couldn't have been nicer. I would put the two of them in front of me on the plane, and I'd sit behind them. They would carry my bags . . . *Guten Morgen, Herr Leutnant!*" As he inched across the map toward London from one U.S. camp to another, each night the lieutenant would put the Germans in a prisoner-of-war cage, and every morning "I'd go down with a pack of cigarettes for each of them. 'How are you getting along?' 'Oh, fine!'"

The traveling party finally arrived in London where the lieutenant turned his prisoners over to the proper authorities. No force at all had been required to keep the fliers in line. The lieutenant had been serving as a code-breaker on the company level, but he had never fired a shot in anger. "I had a side arm," he said, "but they could have grabbed it and turned it on me." The prisoners, of course, knew their ultimate destination was Canada and three square meals a day.

The lieutenant then hied himself off to the United States embassy, where he was directed to Telford Taylor's office.

"Lieutenant Van Norden reporting, sir."

Although none of the other officers summoned to Bletchley Park followed a path quite like Van Norden's, none of them had known any more about what their orders portended.

Lewis Powell had had adventures of his own.[61] After the Allies ran the Germans out of North Africa, Powell was transferred to the headquarters of Jimmy Doolittle's Twelfth Air Force near Constantine, a period of service marked by miserable accommodations in a former French barracks, with the whole staff crammed into four rooms, no bottled water, and a toilet out in the open and elevated as if intended to be the seat of some great temporal or spiritual dignitary—though when it was in use the Arab women strolling by seemed unimpressed.

When the Twelfth was combined with RAF units to form the Northwest African Air Forces, Powell came under the command of Maj. Gen. Carl ("Tooey") Spaatz, a friendly, low-key commander, shy, seeming as untypical a West Pointer as Powell had ever met. As an intelligence officer, Powell had briefed air crews for missions over the Mediterranean, and at Spaatz's headquarters he worked on staff studies. But something puzzled him: What was the source of some of the intelligence that was received? He knew that messages were brought to headquarters by men from something called the Special Liaison Unit, housed in a trailer standing amid a grove of trees. But the future Supreme Court justice and the officers with whom he worked could only speculate about the origin of this information, and they were not pleased at being excluded from the circle of those in the know.

In September 1943, after the Germans had been driven out of Sicily, Powell was ordered home to share his experience with new officers. Around New Year's he had a fateful interview with Alfred McCormack, and soon thereafter he was aboard a C-54 transport plane bound for Prestwick, Scotland. One of a dozen persons on an aircraft built to carry fifty, he settled in for the expected all-night flight, to be awakened in darkness and told to start using oxygen. Caught in a violent storm, the C-54 descended to a level a few hundred feet above the waves, twisting and tossing. It appeared that they were lost—which was confirmed in the morning when the navigator determined that they were over the Bay of Biscay. Turning north, the skipper informed his passengers that they must prepare to ditch; the aircraft could run out of fuel before finding a place to land.

This news, bad enough in itself, brought with it a special problem for Powell; he carried a locked canvas pouch that he had been ordered to deliver to General Eisenhower in London. Taking out his .45, he tied it through the trigger guard to the bag, hoping to ensure its sinking to the bottom of the sea in the event of a crash landing. Off to the north appeared the coast of Ireland; any port in a storm, perhaps—but as a neutral country Ireland was not the most desirable landing spot. Fortunately, the fuel held out long enough to enable the C-54 to limp into Northern Ireland, thus allowing its military passengers to escape internment; and in due course, having removed his .45 from its intimate contact with the pouch, Powell was able to deliver his charge to General Eisenhower's office in Grosvenor Square. Then he reported to Colonel Taylor.

In this same January, when "a large number of inexperienced Americans were first groping down the dark corridors of Hut 3,"[62] Colonel Taylor's section was deemed sizable enough and distinctive enough to appear on the distribution list for Hut 3 periodicals under its own designation. On the model of 3A (for the air section of Hut 3) or 3M (for the army, or military, section), the new operation became 3-US. The stream of arriving Americans included more lawyers, a college professor or two, journalists, very largely but not exclusively Easterners, with a surprising proportion of Alfred McCormack's fellow Princeton Tigers. Besides Langdon Van Norden, Edmund Kellogg, Adolph Rosengarten, Lewis Powell, and Don Bussey, to 3-US came Bancroft Littlefield, Ted Hilles, William Calfee, James Fellers, David Blair, Lucius Buck, Alfred Friendly, Edward K. Thompson, Charles Haskins, Loftus Becker, Harry Groves, Yorke Allen, Edward Hitchcock, Robert Whitlow, Josiah Macy, Jr., Curt Zimansky, and Charles Murnane. These men, and all the others, would either perform liaison functions with the British, stay on with 3-US to work on the care and feeding of G-2 in Washington, be trained as advisers by the British officers of 3M and 3A, or learn the principles and methods of Hut 3 and then tour operational commands to see the working of Ultra in the field and to prepare themselves for becoming SSOs—special security officers—for American units.

The Americans approaching BP on the train from London never knew what lay ahead. Invariably, they were only told where to report,

not what they would be doing. One of them, Landis Gores, a Princeto-
nian with a degree in architecture from Harvard, perhaps put it best:
"Led into the very heart of the system that afternoon, I could only
repeat to myself 'I don't believe it.'"[63]

This picture, the only photo ever made of the U.S. Signal Intelligence Service staff, was taken about 1935. Included are (front row) Abraham Sinkov at center and Frank Rowlett at right. (Back row) Solomon Kullback at left and William Friedman, indicated by arrow. *(National Security Agency)*

(above) Close-up view showing how the rotor ring is set. Note that numbers are used instead of the letters of the alphabet. *(Louis Kruh Collection)*

(left) Spare rotor rings in their container. *(Louis Kruh Collection)*

(facing page) The German military Enigma enciphering machine with three rotors and plugboard. *(Louis Kruh Collection)*

Lt. Paul K. Whitaker *(Paul K. Whitaker)*

Capt. Bill Bundy, commanding officer of the U.S. 6813th Signal Service Detachment at Bletchley Park. *(William P. Bundy)*

(left) The Bombe—the high-speed electrome-chanical marvel that attacked the Enigma ci-phers. This U.S. Navy model was at the Nebraska Avenue station in Washington. *(National Security Agency)*

(below) Navy Bombes in mass formation at Ne-braska Avenue. The machines were built by the National Cash Register Company. After the war, Navy maintenance personnel demolished them with crowbars and sledgehammers. *(National Security Agency)*

(left) Lt. Selmer S. Norland *(Paul K. Whitaker)*

(below) The people who worked at Bletchley Park were billeted in inns like the White Hart in Buckingham.

Col. Telford Taylor, commander of 3-US, in his BP office. *(Beverly Kitchen Almond Collection)*

(above) Americans and Britons at the christening of Bill Marchant's son Timothy include Ted Hilles (front row, left), Beverly Kitchen (front row, second from right), Telford Taylor (rear, center), and Marchant (right of Taylor). *(Beverly Kitchen Almond Collection)*

(below) U.S. baseball players at BP include, in the front row, Warrack Wallace (left), Ed Kellogg (third from left), Ted Hilles (front), Bill Bundy (second from right), and, in the back row, Alfred Friendly (left), Langdon Van Norden (third from left), and Landis Gores (second from right). *Beverly Kitchen Almond Collection)*

(above) Capt. Bob Slusser of 3-US with his English bride, June 27, 1944. *(Beverly Kitchen Almond Collection)*

(below) This girls' school, once a manor house, was taken over as a residence by Bill Bundy's command. *(Paul K. Whitaker)*

(left) Ultra in the field: Maj. Melvin Helfers briefs General Patton and the Third Army chief of staff, Maj. Gen. Hugh J. Gaffey. (*Citadel Archives*)

(above) Air intelligence officer Jim Rose standing in civilian clothes with friends from 3-US. *(Beverly Kitchen Almond Collection)*

(below) Thanksgiving at the 3-US residence, Potterspury, 1944. Those around the table include Jim Fellers (seated, second from left), Beverly Kitchen (fourth), Bob Slusser (eighth), and Ted Hilles (ninth). *(Beverly Kitchen Almond Collection)*

Lt. Col. Lewis F. Powell (right) at U.S. Strategic Air Force headquarters, Bushy Park, near London. With the future U.S. Supreme Court justice is fellow intelligence officer Lt. Col. William W. Haines who later wrote the famous war novel *Command Decision. (Lewis F. Powell)*

Bundy's men: The American Signal Corps group on the lawn of their residence at Little Brickhill. Paul Whitaker is second from left in the front row, Arthur Levenson (capless) peers over Whitaker's left shoulder, and to the right of Levenson is Selmer Norland. Bundy stands at the extreme right, front row. *(William P. Bundy)*

(left) Ultra officer Adolph Rosengarten found this cap in an office hastily abandoned by the Germans, grew a mustache to go with it, and produced this photo for the amusement of 3-US friends back at Bletchley Park. *(Beverly Kitchen Almond Collection)*

(below) German prisoners unearth part of the "Russian Fish" equipment. *(Paul K. Whitaker)*

(above) German prisoners prepare the "Russian Fish" for loading and shipment to England. These are the only pictures of this highly secret equipment ever published. *(Paul K. Whitaker)*

(below) The "Russian Fish" receiver set-up, showing the multichannel receptor. *(Paul K. Whitaker)*

10

"The Largest Undertaking"

ON MARCH 15, 1944, in a letter addressed in his characteristic style to "Dear Eisenhower," General Marshall made unmistakably clear how much importance he attached to the proper use of Ultra in the field, and he proceeded to outline the steps in the process. Now that the time was approaching for American special security advisers to begin performing the parts for which they had been trained, the Chief of Staff wanted no slipups, no confusion in lines of authority, no such bungling by commanders and intelligence officers as had marked the handling of Magic in the weeks before Pearl Harbor, and emphatically no inadvertent revealing of the Ultra secret. "Please give this matter your personal attention," General Marshall said, "and take all necessary steps to insure that the security regulations governing the dissemination of 'Ultra' intelligence are meticulously observed."[1]

No slot for "special security officer" appeared in the tables of organization of American formations, those bibles that lay out the functions and ranks of all the members of a command. The notion of a special officer interposed between the cipher people receiving the intelligence from Bletchley Park and the commander who was to make use of it was newly conceived in Washington to fit American circumstances (the British had no such position), and it was being made crystal clear to Eisenhower so that he could pass the word to Omar Bradley and Courtney Hodges and George Patton and other field generals. These Ultra representatives would be young men of low rank, almost all of them civilians at heart, and relatively new to the army. But the generals must not, for such reasons, brush them off. What these men would have that was possessed by no one else in any of the commands was training, often beginning in the Special Branch but always polished at Bletchley Park, in the handling of items of signal intelligence not in isolation but in a stream of intercepts against a background of related facts; and they would have no duties or loyalties that clashed with the objective weighing of the intelligence.

"In order to safeguard the continued availability of this enormously important source of intelligence," General Marshall said—i.e., to keep the British goose that produced the golden eggs satisfied with American precautions—"it is vital that these security regulations be meticulously observed," and he went on to discuss the procedures in detail. But the generals had to be told not only how they must keep the secret but what to make of these young men who were going to appear at their headquarters. Marshall made it plain:

> Their primary responsibility will be to evaluate Ultra intelligence, present it in useable form to the Commanding Officer and to such of his senior staff officers as are authorized Ultra recipients, assist in fusing Ultra intelligence with intelligence derived from other sources, and give advice in connection with making operational use of Ultra intelligence in such fashion that the security of the source is not endangered.

A powerful charter for the young Ultra representatives who were to deal in an advisory way on a level with veteran, high-ranking officers—telling them what the information meant and then watching them to make sure they did not misuse it and thus give the game away. It was no wonder that General Marshall felt the need to put his authority squarely behind them. American ground and air generals, many of them about to exercise combat command for the first time, might not readily assent to the assumption of so much authority by some young fellow called a special security officer.

An austere man and thoroughly army, and certainly not one to approve of idleness, General Marshall could not resist ending his letter to Eisenhower with the thought that "if at any time the flow of Ultra intelligence is not sufficient to occupy fully the time of these officers, they may be used for other related intelligence assignments." It was a standard sort of closing, to be sure, and may well have been drafted by some assistant. But if the overall document could be described as the charter of the American Ultra representatives, this final point was to serve at least one officer as a loophole.

REGARDLESS OF WHAT their previous duties might have been, the Americans of 3-US acquired the status of students at Bletchley Park. Since the most regularly broken keys were those employed by the Luftwaffe, the officers destined to be air advisers or Ultra representatives at an air force headquarters perhaps had the greatest amount of material to absorb. Lecturers (British air advisers) told them, as Maj. Lewis Powell noted, about Benito, a device used to enable Luftwaffe ground controllers to identify and plot their own fighters. "The system can't be used to plot Allied aircraft as it involves sending a radio signal to an aircraft equipped with a device that re-radiates the signal to ground control. It is used at night to vector NJGs [night fighter groups] into a stream of bombers."[2]

On March 1, 1944, Powell took extensive notes on a detailed account of the estimated effect of Allied attacks on German aircraft plants. Raids in February were said to have reduced the output of single-engine fighters by 60 percent to 260 a month; of twin-engine fighters by 75 percent to 85 a month; of long-range bombers by 30 percent to 225 a month (the figures were later revised, since German production was higher than had been supposed). Squadron Leader Jim Rose, air intelligence chief of Hut 3, described the German bomber force order of battle in the Mediterranean and in the west *Kampfgruppe* by *Kampfgruppe*. On March 22 Flight Lieutenant Peter Calvocoressi, a senior air adviser, lectured on the organization and disposition of day-fighter units on the western front—*Jagdkorps* and *Jagddivisionen*. It was as though the essence of the wonderfully detailed files of 3A were being poured into the ears of the listeners. Certainly those who, like Powell or Van Norden, were going to the headquarters of a command would arrive not as new boys who had to start from scratch but as both technicians and officers with contextual knowledge.

The depth of knowledge an air adviser would ideally possess was demonstrated to Ed Kellogg one morning somewhat later when, as he sat by Jim Rose's desk, the scrambler phone rang. It was the Air Ministry, asking where Bomber Command should strike that night in order to cut down on German mining of the Scheldt estuary leading to Antwerp. Although Rose was not expecting such a call, he was able to answer immediately without referring to even a single note. What he said sounded something like this:

That mining is done by three *Geschwader* of the German Air Force. *Geschwader 1* is located at Airfield A [giving map coordinates]. The *Geschwader* has three *Staffeln*. The first *Staffel* has been having engine trouble and morale is down. The second had had some losses and it's on rest and refit. The third is the one you should go for. It is at the northwest corner of Airfield A. They have about twenty serviceable aircraft, and you should be able to knock out quite a few of them if you approach from the east.

As to *Geschwader 2*, it is located at Airfield B [coordinates again]. They have recently been transferred to mining work and are not yet very efficient.

As to *Geschwader 3* at Airfield C [coordinates], you might want to give them a few bombing runs. The three *Staffeln* are grouped along the west side of the field, and there are some hangars there you might wish to knock out. But mind the ack-ack on the north side of the field. They have just received new ammunition.[3]

So, Kellogg thought, that's how it's done!

FOR SOME SIX months Beverly Kitchen, as the only woman and *a fortiori* the only secretarial person in 3-US, was incessantly busy taking dictation and producing translations, letters, and reports, none of which interested her in the slightest. "There were Luftwaffes, SS's, and all this kind of stuff I typed up by the yard," but "I was so uninterested in it."[4] She was at Bletchley Park to be useful and to be part of an adventure, but in the most traditional fashion she thought of war as a man's game. She worked for everybody in the office, though first of all she was Telford Taylor's secretary, and the volume of work, the flood of endless specific details about German military organizations, no doubt had a numbing effect on a mind that was sprightly but hardly military.

Taylor was often away, either in London or studying the Ultra operation at British field commands, leaving as the boss Sam McKee, who to Miss Kitchen was a "very warm-heated, jovial, easygoing character, a very lovable soul," round and rosy-faced like an ideal Santa Claus; and when for a time Taylor and McKee both had to devote most of their efforts to establishing ties with American commands that were going to be customers of BP once Overlord was launched, 3-US was presided over by Ted Hilles, who had been an English professor at Yale.

The members of Colonel Taylor's flock were billeted in inns and houses throughout the area. Miss Kitchen was assigned to an establishment in Buckingham called the White Hart, about ten miles from the Park. Ed Kellogg, who had been granted his wish for overseas duty, and Adolph Rosengarten were at the Hunt, in Leighton Buzzard, where Bill Bundy and a number of the other members of the signal-intelligence group had lived before the creation of the manor at Little Brickhill.

Heating one's room posed problems. "We had a very parsimonious ration of coal," one officer recalled. "We could burn three lumps a day, and we did that right after dinner. We sat around the fire till they burned out, and then we went to bed to keep warm."[5] But, as Ed Kellogg saw it, life at BP was on a higher than normal plane, where the "lack of things" was of little account. They were all involved in a common endeavor, and they were winning. That was what really mattered.

Kellogg deeply admired his British hosts, who "had been through bombing, deprivation, losses of family members, nervous pressures which must have been stifling. The constant irritation of very sparse rationing had been on their nerves for years. Suddenly in came a bunch of Americans who had been through nothing in the way of deprivation even mildly comparable to that which the British had undergone. Yet never was any word said which showed envy, jealousy, or resentment." For Kellogg and most of the others, work acted as a tonic. "Each person took it for granted that his colleagues would be very intelligent, and this acted as an automatic, built-in stimulant"; everyone therefore "did better work than he or she would otherwise have done, and there was a genuine cross-fertilization of ideas." Each person assumed that each colleague, with few exceptions, would have an excellent sense of humor; "the result was electric—and delightful,"[6] with such touches as, from time to time, sending down orders (what few there were) in Latin and some days in Greek; bureaucratese was rare, except to the Britons who were subject to the rules of Wing Commander Eric Jones. Even the navy got into the game. In its section the large map on which Hut 4 kept track, by means of Ultra, of the movements of the Greek caiques used by the Germans for their communications in the Aegean bore the heading: "You can't sink your caique and have it too." And in off moments some of the Hut 4 team devoted themselves to the translation of Lewis Carroll's "Jabberwocky" into French.

To Malcolm Muggeridge, this donnishness had suggested a Victorian reading party or a chromo of long-gone university days. But Muggeridge, though sensing the need for more driving power at the top, was present only briefly. To those who spent long periods at BP, by such whimsies were pressures "both lightened and brightened" and the atmosphere rendered ideal.

Characteristically, the prime minister joined in the verbal byplay. Known to be reading Ultra material with great regularity, he would demonstrate the fact—and give the workers in the huts a lift—by sometimes returning a message with such marginal comments as "I think I should have used the subjunctive in that clause."[7]

Kellogg genuinely hated to leave Hut 3 at the end of his daily shift, and he developed the habit of coming in early—which gave rise to what he called "a true Anglo-American scene." Arriving at 6:30 one morning, he found all the windows open and the temperature in the office "a sprightly 48 degrees—a good British springlike atmosphere." He closed the windows and, without removing overcoat, scarf, or gloves, huddled over his work. An hour later an English colleague buzzed in and threw up all the windows, exclaiming, by way of explanation: "Frightful smell of drains!" This man then departed— "secure," Kellogg said, "in the knowledge that I would be a healthier man in body and spirit."

For those who did not happen to have a railroad line handy, Bletchley Park had created an elaborate transportation system, consisting of buses (for larger groups) and station wagons (known as "brakes") for persons coming from more isolated billets, the vehicles being driven by WAAFs—"lovely ladies," as Al Friendly saw them, "mostly from the London stage." In the evening, at least for the men, going home took on a sort of romantic connotation. As the darkness made it impossible to see the signs on the buses and brakes, the drivers would stand by them, calling out the destinations in clear, pleasant English voices: Potterspury, Wolverton, Stony Stratford, Leighton Buzzard, Buckingham . . .

Oftentimes there was reason to stay around BP even if you were off duty, not only on account of the dances, which were held with some regularity, but because of the other diversions such as concerts, theatricals, and chess matches.

Art Levenson became secretary of the Bletchley Park chess club, an involvement that put him in rarefied company; as might be expected, BP was a citadel of chess mastery, including Hugh Alexander, the perennial British chess champion; Stuart Milner-Barry, a former British boy champion and the president of the British Chess Federation; Harry Golombek, editor of the *British Chess Review*; Alexander Aitken, the Scottish champion; and Jack Good, the champion of Cambridge University. Acting as club secretary, Levenson sent off a challenge to Oxford. Notable among those not on the competitive team was Alan Turing, whom Levenson found to be "not a very good chess player, brilliant as he was. In everything else, he was fantastic."[8] The Oxford chess club combed the university for the best players, but they were simply overmatched; the victorious BP club was a truly world-class group.

Entertainment and social contacts were also to be found in the dance halls and pubs of Bedford, Wolverton, and the other towns in the area. Major Glenn Miller and his phenomenally popular air force big band would appear at public places like the Corn Exchange in Bedford, attracting a heterogeneous English and American crowd, all dancing to "American Patrol," the big favorite. At the Science and Arts Institute in Wolverton, dances were held in what was normally the lecture hall, with the band playing on the stage and a rotating mirrored ball hanging from the ceiling. "The forces came for light relief and anything else that was going, if you get my meaning,"[9] said a woman who was then a young working-class girl from London, spending her days patching up damaged airplanes. Americans joined in on all these occasions, and this girl noted that the U.S. officers "had jackets of a bracken brown colour with trousers of light beige. I noticed what good-quality material their uniforms were made of."[10]

This young woman liked the Americans, but some of the people who regularly attended the dances aroused her resentment. "One group in the corner looked immaculate and very standoffish. *Their* nails were like an advert for 'Cutex.' These girls worked at Bletchley Park. What they did over there at the Park no one knew; it was very hush-hush. They kept to the Secrets Act as they were supposed to, for as the posters said—'Careless talk costs lives' and 'Walls have ears.'" But it was clear that these immaculate and stylish young women were not making their contribution to the war effort through the use of hammers and rivet guns. They seemed to carry with them the elite tone that characterized the whole BP operation. They went to all the dances, but "they did not mix much, and while we attracted the ordinary ranks, these girls seemed better suited to the officers. We factory girls could see that they came from good backgrounds, while we were what was sometimes termed as 'born on the wrong doorstep.'"[11]

Because of the shift arrangements and the working of the transportation network, the two American groups at BP led essentially separate existences. "You went to lunch or whatever meal was appropriate to your shift with your own hut," Bundy observed, "and so you tended to form your friendships that way."[12] Even though he and Van Norden were old friends, for instance, they had little chance to get together. In fact, some members of 3-US were only vaguely aware that Bletchley Park was also host to an entirely different contingent of Americans who worked on the production of the intelligence; and, for their part, the Hut 6 crew knew that other Americans were around—"Taylor's group," as they thought of them—but they were uncertain about their function.

Although Bundy himself was at home in both worlds, one spring day in a joking observation he pointed out a difference between the two that had nothing to do with assignments or schedules. Bob Slusser, a captain who had been the first officer to join Taylor and McKee, back in

November, was something of an artist and was commissioned to create a poster announcing an American dance being held, as one person recalled, "in honor of everyone." Slusser produced a picture that, he said, represented spring at BP as it would have been painted by Titian: a man running along a path in pursuit of a nude girl who was wearing glasses. On being shown the proposed poster, Bundy shook his head. His people, he said, were all Bible Belt. They would be offended.[13]

Bundy's signal-intelligence people, of course, were by no means Bible Belt fundamentalist types, but they were in reality a far more varied group of Americans—ethnically and geographically—than the largely Eastern, Ivy League, Wall Street group of Old Boys assembled by Alfred McCormack, Porter Chandler, and Bus Reed. The signal-intelligence line traced straight back to William Friedman and his original 1930 Civil Service recruits, all three of them men looking for jobs, none of them the type to be blessed with connections in the moneyed world (and few persons with connections would have sought such jobs, at such pay). After 1940, persons of all backgrounds were taken into the Signal Intelligence Service, being picked from the draftee ranks on the basis of test scores; thus Bundy, who seemed to have arrived neither on account of nor despite his connections (including the fact that his father was adviser and assistant to the Secretary of War), was the precise kind of person that McCormack's recruiters dreamed of. He surely would have been plucked for the Special Branch had he not already found his top-secret niche.

But the Special Branch recruiters were not simply motivated by Eastern snobbery. The problem facing McCormack on his return from England was not merely that he had to find a number of officers who could do more or less well in some kind of intelligence capacity. He had to recruit extremely able men for the most secret duty in the war, on a par with the work on the atomic bomb, and he had to accomplish it in a hurry; these men had to be selected, cleared with respect to security, and on their way within a few months' time. The way to do it, it was therefore decided, was to seek people you knew or your friends knew. It was a time when nepotism and its extension from kinship to friendship seemed the logical answer to a colossal recruiting challenge. The method, actually quite in the British style, tended to produce surprises for its recipients, as when Van Norden suddenly found himself summoned from the mud of the Cassino front to the Maison Blanche in Algiers. Little or no "positive vetting" was involved; no investigator had come around to ask Van Norden whether he had ever read *Mein Kampf* or whether he liked girls.

The unintended result of these procedures was to create two contrasting American subcultures at Bletchley Park. Amusingly, however, the members of neither group knew enough about the other to be aware of their differences—except for Bill Bundy, who didn't miss much.

II

THE INTELLIGENCE OFFICERS at the Special Branch in the Pentagon always found Baron Oshima an interesting correspondent, even though the ambassador did not dream that the Americans were on his mailing list. Intercepts from Oshima, his fellow ambassadors in Europe, and his attachés reported on interviews with Hitler (and, earlier, with Benito Mussolini, before the Italian dictator's fall); described scenes the Allies could hardly see for themselves, such as the results of Allied bombing; and produced various kinds of military and political intelligence.

On May 27, 1944, the talkative baron enjoyed a stimulating conversation with the Führer;[14] the Magic team at Arlington Hall supplied G-2 with a decrypt of Oshima's account of it on June 1. The talk covered the Allied advance in Italy ("In my opinion," Hitler said, "the main object of this new drive is to lure German military strength to that theater, and we are therefore not making too great an effort to prevent the loss of territory") and moved on to consider matters on the Russian front. Then Oshima asked a broad and leading question: "What is your feeling about the second front?" Hitler's answer was enlightening, less perhaps to Oshima than to the Allied commanders when it was transmitted to them (the baron did not know when, or even whether, the allies planned to invade). "I believe," Hitler said, "that sooner or later an invasion of Europe will be attempted." In a moment Oshima chimed his agreement: yes, "sooner or later" the Anglo-Americans were going to do it. This hazy analysis was being read by U.S. intelligence on June 1, less than a week before the Overlord assault.

Pressing on, Oshima said provocatively to his hero: "I wonder what ideas you have as to how the second front will be carried out." As he quickly learned, Hitler had plenty of thoughts. It would be an elaborate process, the Führer believed, beginning with diversionary actions against "Norway, Denmark, the southern part of western France, and the French Mediterranean coast. After that—when they have established bridgeheads in Normandy and Brittany and have sized up their prospects—they will then come forward with an all-out second front across the Straits of Dover"—the Pas de Calais. Wonderful news for the Allied commanders and flattering for the deception artists. The Fortitude plan might not be entitled to take all the credit—for one thing, independent German strategic judgment was involved—but Hitler was certainly following its principles, even to the idea of diversionary actions in Norway (a notional force had been created in Scotland to make such a possibility seem likely).

In forecasting the main Allied assault for the Pas de Calais, Hitler was actually agreeing with the view of his advisers in Berlin and of the veteran Field Marshal Gerd von Rundstedt, Commander in Chief West, and to some extent that of Field Marshal Erwin Rommel, whom the Führer had dispatched to France to command the anti-invasion forces in the field. But here again, deception played a part in the development of this German view because the Allies had led the Germans to believe that their strength in England was far greater than it actually was. "I understand," Hitler said, "that the enemy has already assembled about eighty divisions in the British Isles"; the real figure was half that. Yet, in spite of the opinions of his generals and of the "evidence," the Führer toyed with the thought—one of his celebrated intuitions—that the main Allied blow would fall upon Normandy. But he did not believe in it so strongly that he made his commanders act on it. Without Fortitude and all its trappings . . . who knows? Since the Germans could call on more forces in western Europe that the Anglo-Americans had available for the invasion, the right German force at the right place might well have kept the Allies from getting ashore or driven them back into the sea.

"We ourselves would like nothing better than to strike one great blow as soon as possible," Hitler told Oshima. "But that will not be feasible if the enemy does what I anticipate; their men will be dispersed"—in Norway, the south of France, and Brittany. "In that event"—deprived of one great Allied assault to focus on—"we intend to finish off the enemy's troops at the several bridgeheads."

It was easy to visualize Oshima's nod. "There is," the baron said, "much to think about."

III

THE TOWN OF Bletchley was ringed by a number of airfields, and for some weeks Paul Whitaker had watched with interest as planes practiced picking up gliders, each aircraft with its hook swooping low and seizing the long cable. You could look up and see planes circling BP with gliders trailing.

Beginning early one morning—it was little more than a week after Baron Oshima's chat with Hitler—Whitaker saw that practice was over. Not only planes towing gliders but aircraft of all sorts—he noted particularly the twin-tailed P-38 Lightnings—were moving out in a steady stream, heading south. The wings were marked with special dark identification bars that in the distance looked blue.

During the week of June 4, Bill Bundy was head of watch on the Hut 6 night shift, which began at midnight. On Monday evening, June 5, [15] one of the big all-Park dances was scheduled for the recreation center, and a number of people, including Bundy, gathered at one of the nearby inns for a little cheer before moving on to the party. Bundy recalled that it was the first time he had ever sampled a martini with sherry doing the work of vermouth . . . "It's not a bad drink, really." Afterward, everybody proceeded to enjoy "a most vigorous dance" and thanks "to the exuberance and strength of youth, I think were were operationally OK." Those on the Hut 6 night shift left the recreation hall and checked in by 12:00. To his surprise, Bundy saw Milner-Barry, in a dinner jacket, coming from one of the back rooms. This was surprising. Why was the chief of the hut on the job after midnight? He "was sort of around," as if waiting for something, and along about one-thirty in the morning there came a great hurrah from the room where the messages came in, followed by a buzz of excited talk running through the offices. Hut 6 was getting cleartext messages from the Germans that Allied parachutists were landing in France. (As Bundy and the others soon learned, these were not airborne troops but straw dummies, armed with sputtering firecrackers, dropped to distract the defenders from the real glider and parachute landings, which had the vital mission of seizing bridges and causeways and cutting roads, sealing off the landing area.) But the messages made one thing clear: "This was it!" In spite of the request Whitaker had noted in his diary, the workers in the Bletchley huts had received no advance word of the invasion.

On this same evening, pubs in Wiltshire that had for months been crowded with noisy, boisterous Americans were strangely quiet, with only the old regulars on hand. The whisky, usually drunk up in a hurry, stayed on the shelves. Where, everybody wondered, had the Americans gone? They were really rather missed. After closing time, the answer came—planes overhead by the hundreds, forming up, heading south. Standing outside, watching the mighty spectacle, the landlord of the Stag's Head in the village of Chilton Foliat called to his wife to come and look: "This is it!"[16]

Over London, the roar of the air armada coming from bases to the north sounded for hour after hour. Nothing like it had ever been heard and, wonderfully, no bombs fell from this array of aircraft above the clouds. On the south coast, those who had seen the marshaling of the fleets—landing craft, troop transports, cargo ships, coasters, and minesweepers, as well as warships ranging up to battleships themselves—knew the answer too. The number of airplanes was enormous, almost 13,000 American bombers and fighters alone. The ships altogether numbered 5.000. This was it!

On the other side of the Channel, just after first light, Bob Goold, a machine gunner in the U.S. 1st Division, stepped onto Omaha Beach in ankle-deep water, "waved farewell to the young kid at the helm of the landing barge, and saw it suddenly blown apart by a direct hit from the 88 in the pillbox on the cliff."[17] Seven hours later his company was still pinned down at the edge of the water, dominated by fire from the bluff. Hours later still, the position was taken by U.S. Rangers, who scaled the height with ropes and also worked around from the rear. "The cliff looked like a tree full of grapevines," one of the Rangers recalled, "and there was blood everywhere."[18]

The whole thing "was awfully confusing," said a GI from the follow-up 9th Division, which went into Utah Beach. "Shells were flying every which way. I sure was glad the higher-ups knew what was going on"[19]—an ironic thought: once the assault was launched, the higher-ups back across the Channel knew only what they were told. They had to wait for news. And as for their plan of campaign, that was another story still. The Combined Chiefs of Staff had ordered the Supreme Commander to "enter the Continent of Europe, and, in conjunction with the other United Nations, undertake operations aimed at the heart of Germany and the destruction of her armed forces."[20] They had not said what these "operations" were to be; that decision lay with Ike and Montgomery and their subordinates—the men in charge of Overlord. But, to be sure, they had agreed on a plan. Had they not?

AT BLETCHLEY PARK on the morning of June 6, there was no fuss, no special orders, but word spread that the king would speak on the radio at nine o'clock. The only set that was at all public was a small one in the drawing room of the mansion. People came from all areas of BP, and the windows were opened so that the broadcast could be heard outside. No one in the crowd was saying much. Finally the king spoke. His voice was low—most listeners could barely hear him—and he stuttered. Yet Ed Kellogg thought that nobody who was there would ever forget the experience. He saw not a single dry eye.

During that day Paul Whitaker noted in his diary that "the start of the final phase of the European war has been made," adding that "the landing itself was the largest undertaking of its kind in the history of the world." Then he said: "The air landings, consisting of parachute and glider-borne troops, began in the early hours of the morning and by the time the other troops began landing on the beach 3 or 4 battalions, 15-18,000 men, were already in Normandy going after their objectives." These airborne operations were in fact daring and risky moves. At the eastern end of the anticipated beachhead, the men of the British Sixth Airborne Division, consisting of the 5th and 3rd brigades, had the assignment of seizing a strip of land east of the city of Caen, eight miles from the coast, and if necessary beating off German armored counterattacks on the British ground troops as they landed during the ensuing day. The other end of the bridgehead would be the field of action of the two American airborne divisions, the 82nd and 101st, totaling six regiments—amounting, with supporting units, to more than 13,000 men. They were to land in the eastern half of the Cotentin peninsula, south of Cherbourg, between the village of Sainte-Mère-Eglise and the larger town of Carentan. Reinforcements in gliders were to be flown in at dawn on landing zones from which the paratroops were supposed to have ejected the enemy.

The plan for the use of the American divisions was deeply upsetting to Air Marshal Sir Trafford Leigh-Mallory, Allied air chief for the invasion.[21] The Cotentin held too many German troops, he thought; it was unwise to land airborne troops in areas where they would face immediate opposition, before they had the chance to consolidate. American casualties might run as high as 80 percent. No tactical objectives could be worth such a cost. What Leigh-Mallory feared was the immediate presence on the scene of two German static divisions, of questionable quality, that had long been deemed by the German command sufficient for the defense of this backwater far from the Pas de Calais.

Originally, the plan had called for dropping the 82nd Airborne near the village of Saint Sauveur-le Vicomte, to prevent reinforcement of the peninsula from the south. As the result of a meeting held on May 27, the mission of the 82nd was changed. Now it would land just west of Sainte-Mère-Eglise, in partly marshy ground on both sides of the Merderet River. The new plan meant that it would be operating some seven or eight miles east of its originally planned drop zone. What had caused the change? Switching in his diary from plaintext to cipher, Whitaker added this note to his remarks about D-Day: "Our eight-two para div was slated to land at a given place when Paris jellyfish reported that to be exactly in middle of one four Panzer Gren Div. We sent out a signal and were credited with saving eight two from annihilation." This note, though unmistakably right in essence, is puzzling. If "Paris jellyfish" was speaking of the German dispositions before the landings, as the decrypted wording suggests, then it was correct in saying that a new division had moved into the vicinity of Saint Saveur-le Vicomte but wrong in calling it the 14th Panzer Grenadier (there was no such division, but there was in reserve south of the Loire the 17th SS Panzer Grenadier Division).[22] The division that was moved into the Cotentin in May was the 91st, an outfit of much higher quality than the two static divisions previously present. The 91st was transferred on the suggestion of Hitler's chief operations officer, Col. Gen. Alfred Jodl, who pointed out to Rundstedt that the army had really better not overlook Normandy completely; in spite of expert opinion to the contrary, the Führer had some notion that it actually could be important.

It is also true, however, that on June 8 the 17th Panzer Grenadier Division was ordered by Field Marshal Rommel to the defense of Carentan; this important center must be held to keep General Bradley's forces from cutting across the neck of the peninsula, isolating Cherbourg and its German defenders. The 17th, though not a veteran formation, was, like all the SS divisions, considerably stronger than an army division of the same type. Numbering about 17,000 men, it was essentially an infantry division, with a complement of antitank and other field guns. Allied air attacks delayed the movement of the 17th to Carentan, and before it reached the area the town had fallen to the Allies. Taking up a position to the southwest, after its guns had arrived on June 12, the newly arrived division, early in the morning of June 13, counterattacked two parachute regiments of the 101st Airborne, but at 10:30 an armored task force came rushing to the aid of the paratroopers, and the Germans were thrown back with the estimated loss of 500 men. The Americans, freed from the threat, could now drive on Cherbourg.

How did General Bradley know that he should order Maj. Gen. Leonard T. Gerow, the V Corps commander, to send the tanks and armored infantry to Carentan? Messages from Hut 3—not one but a series—shadowed the panzer grenadier force as if the men at BP were detectives paid to dog its footsteps. Intercepts revealed the orders to other German forces in the area, making it clear on June 11 that a counterattack with the 17th division was to take place the next day (the delay in the arrival of the guns held it over to June 13). And when it came, the American reinforcements were rushing to meet it.

Thus, at crucial moments on the Cotentin, both U.S. airborne divisions were beneficiaries of the codebreakers and intelligence officers at Bletchley Park. Oddly, Whitaker's encrypted note, which was undated, seemed to address both actions—the 82nd Airborne and a panzer grenadier division—but the phrase "slated to land" would appear to refer to the preinvasion change of plan rather than to a later ground action.

The codebreakers of Hut 6 were rarely told much about the practical effect of their labors—occasionally, word would come along from Hut 3 that a particular message had been a good piece of work, or something of that sort—but one day Stuart Milner-Barry broke the pattern. Coming in to the watch room, the head of the hut called for attention. "Ladies and gentlemen, may I interrupt you, please. I wish to congratulate you, because you have just saved fifteen thousand American lives."[23] The presumption is that he was speaking of the change in plans brought about by the Germans' posting of the 91st Division to the Cotentin. The 82nd had indeed suffered casualties, for a variety of reasons—the operation was amply hazardous without the presence of the 91st—but the overall airborne losses were about 2,500, nothing remotely like Leigh-Mallory's 80 percent, and the bridgehead was secure. But with equal justice Milner-Barry could have meant the attack of the panzer grenadier division with its thirty-seven 75-mm. assault guns (an assault gun was a bargain-basement version of a tank, with a light hull and no turret) and its battalion of the versatile antiaircraft 88s. Either way, the praise was surely earned. Lou Smadbeck did not know exactly which message Milner-Barry was referring to, but he had never seen his British boss so excited.

IV

IT WAS AN exciting time back in the Pentagon as well. Col. Alfred McCormack, one of the world's more continuingly frustrated men, had spent much of the spring in a fresh series of battles with the army bureaucracy, which always seemed to find a new way to upset a carefully built and urgently needed but nontraditional structure. In his dealings with the rest of the War Department, McCormack often resembled a man in a hurry who, to his consternation, has come upon a village peopled by tradition-minded natives heedlessly continuing to perform their ancient rituals even though the forest is blazing just outside the comfortable circle of their huts. Now reorganization was in the air, for some reason having to do with ceilings on G-2 personnel in Washington. General Strong, whose health had been poor for some time, retired, being replaced as Assistant Chief of Staff, G-2—and hence the top U.S. intelligence officer—by Maj. Gen. Clayton Bissell, a World War I flying ace who earlier in the second war commanded the Tenth Air Force in the China-Burma-India Theater.

On taking over in April, Bissell "promptly departed for a trip abroad," leaving the development of the reorganization plan in the hands of a committee made up of "either old-line G-2 officers or officers whom General Bissell brought in from the outside, most of them having had no experience in intelligence."[24] It was a prime objective of these planners, McCormack felt, "to insure that the Special Branch would be broken up—'and good.'" This was, indeed, the plan the committe produced; under it the personnel and functions of the Special Branch were to be distributed among fifty-three separate branches, sections, and subsections; literally followed, McCormack knew, this scheme would not only eliminate the branch but destroy its work—work that he and Col. Carter Clarke knew to be vital, even if many traditional officers could not seem to see it.

The key position in the new G-2 organization was that of director of intelligence, and "a strenuous attempt was made to find a suitable regular officer for the post."[25] Fortunately, Clarke was able to thwart this move, and he even succeeded in getting McCormack appointed to the job; as a Pentagon infighter, Clarke seems to have had few peers; his forthrightness and the respect he had earned at the very top levels of the military hierarchy could not have been minor factors (during the summer of 1944 he was to carry out a confidential and uniquely sensitive mission for General Marshall to Governor Thomas E. Dewey, then running for president on the Republican ticket). Clarke himself was appointed deputy chief of the Military Intelligence Service; since the new regime could not see any reason to name an intelligence officer to the No. 1 position, a new chief was brought in from the Quartermaster Corps.

Even though Clarke had managed to secure the job of director of intelligence for McCormack, the shifting and shuffling of roles and branches went on under the direction of the reorganization committee. It is not necessary to suppose that the members of this committee were either unpatriotic or stupid. They were doubtless the kinds of officers who rise and flourish in a peacetime army, where such traits as obedience, orderliness, need for approval, and fear of failure can combine to push one into high rank[26]—traits that carry with them hostility to the exercise of daring and innovation. Nor are these rigid characteristics confined to armies; a military bureaucrat, as McCormack found, was simply a bureaucrat in olive drab or sun-tans. The Civil Service Commission was just as bad.

But even if the members of the committee were not ignobly motivated, they "put into key positions a number of officers without a shadow of qualifications. All McCormack's subordinates, down to the

Branch Chiefs, were chosen for him and without consultation with him."[27] He refused to let this unhappy state of affairs put him out of action, however. Counterattacking on his first day in office as director of intelligence, he demanded the dismissal of the officer who was supposed to become acting supervisor of reports, on the ground that he was "incompetent and dangerous." To win his point and to protest other features of the reorganization, McCormack resorted to a Bismarckian maneuver. "In the end, having knocked my head for weeks against a monumental structure of stupidity, I filed a request for relief and return to civilian life, and in this manner brought about a result that should have taken no more than 5 minutes to accomplish." Here again, the continuing support of Clarke was highly important.

Nevertheless, it was farewell to McCormack's baby, the Special Branch, as a separate entity (the designation survived as that of a smaller office that included among its duties the maintenance of the tie with Bletchley Park). It had not been perfect, any more than any other baby was perfect; for example, despite all its efforts, it had not been able to bring about a consistently complete processing of material in a number of fields, so that the facts contained in diplomatic intercepts, say, were always checked against those in army intercepts. But the Special Branch had amply fulfilled Secretary Stimson's hope for a new standard of intellect and competence in military intelligence.   G-2's new order arrived in a blaze of ignominy. At the behest of the reorganization committee, which appears to have been singularly absorbed in its work, there was much moving of offices and equipment. If you had been the President, or the secretary of war, or the Chief of Staff, and you decided to call military intelligence on D-Day, June 6, to hear what was happening with the invasion, you would not have learned much. It was moving day for the section doing German intelligence. There were no telephones.

D-DAY HAD FOUND Frank Rowlett, now holding the rank of major, visiting Bletchley Park. As Arlington Hall's chief cipher-machine expert, he had come to Britain to establish his own official contact with his counterparts at BP. That evening, he, Selmer Norland, and Alex Prengel, another member of the signal-intelligence group, went to a pub in Little Brickhill for a bit of refreshment. But, even thirstier for information, they did not tarry, making it a point to hurry back to the American manor in order not to miss the nine o'clock news on the BBC.

11

"We Are Advancing Constantly"

I

ON D+4—JUNE 10—Lt. Gen. Omar Bradley, commander of the U.S. First Army and thus the leader of the American invasion force, arrived in France to stay. He had made earlier visits to the beachhead; on D+1, when he had come over to see for himself what was happening on Omaha and had hitched a ride back on a landing craft, the return trip had been particularly memorable. "On the wet, open bottom of the tiny craft a dozen litters had been loaded. And on those litters a dozen wounded young Americans lay wrapped in blankets already soggy from the spray. All in their raw twenties, they lay quiet, uncomplaining, awaiting their transfer to a hospital ship. I was aware that there in the pitching bottom of a landing craft lay the fragments of a generation rashly condemned for being 'corrupted' by the ease of democracy and 'debased' by the luxury of freedom."[1] General Bradley's new headquarters was simple, consisting of a group of tents set up in an apple orchard at Grandcamps-les Bains. But his headquarters commandant "insisted on one amenity: a portable enclosed one-man latrine, about the size of a telephone booth."[2]

That traveling john was not the only piece of unusual equipment coming ashore from the cruiser *Augusta,* which had served as Bradley's floating headquarters during the Overlord assault. Also landing were the personnel of the Special Liaison Unit, with their radio gear and their cipher machines in a huge green vehicle that appeared to be a plywood box mounted on a truck body. These men, as the assistant G-2 of First Army put it, "went over to the far side of the field all by themselves and, as far as I could see, never talked to anybody."[3] The assistant, not privy to Ultra, wondered what these British officers and enlisted men were engaged in: probably, he decided, it was some form of signal intelligence.

General Marshall's rules for Ultra representatives, as laid out in his letter to Eisenhower of March 15, were about to be tested; the guinea pig—the first American special security officer to set up shop on the Continent—was Adolph Rosengarten, the Philadelphia lawyer. It was a test for Group Captain Winterbotham's powers of indoctrination, too; he had expanded his Special Liaison Unit organization to take care of the new American customers, and he had impressed on them all, SLU sergeants and American generals alike, the vital need to follow undeviatingly the established security procedures.

When Rosengarten had bumped into Bus Reed in the Pentagon, he had been asked whether he knew German. He could read it, Rosengarten said, but he couldn't speak it well enough to carry on a conversation at a dinner table. Persisting, Reed induced Rosengarten to take a reading test, on which the Philadelphian performed satisfactorily, and the Special Branch thus had acquired a new recruit. After two weeks or so of instruction in McCormack's operation, Rosengarten was sent across to Bletchley Park, where he was introduced to the work and wonders of Hut 3. Then Telford Taylor shepherded a high-powered legal group—Rosengarten, Lewis Powell, and Jim Fellers from Oklahoma, all of them lawyers, like Taylor himself—on a tour of the Italian front so that they "could see what Ultra means to an army in the field."[4] The other two were to become air Ultra representatives; Rosengarten was down for First Army. Returning, he reported to General Bradley at Clifton College in Bristol, England, on May 15. When the general went across to France, Rosengarten would follow him there.

Reporting to General Bradley meant in practice reporting to the First Army G-2, the chief intelligence officer, Colonel Benjamin Dickson, known as "Monk." Dickson, in his sphere, was rather like Montgomery or Patton—the kind of person who evoked strong feelings, positive or negative, from others. He had a stiff leg, acquired in a midnight escapade in North Africa, when he and some friends had run into a little enemy gunfire, which had led to a freak accident; the colonel was hit by a stone chip that took out a healthy nick as if it were a ricocheting bullet. But otherwise he was the picture of an officer, well-built, standing a shade under six-feet-three, with a thick but neat black mustache. His whole personality "leapt out at you." Monk "was so colorful," said his assistant G-2, Major Bernard Brungs, "that I always thought some others felt that they were in the shadow. He would use these crazy expressions." Brungs credited Dickson, for instance, with coining the term "poop sheet"[5] to describe any of the endless Army documents that were turned out by the mimeograph machines like so much toilet paper. Interviewing Dickson once, the much-loved war correspondent Ernie Pyle had been amused by his using the phrase "toss in the towel."[6] That was how his wife, reading the story back home, had known which colonel Pyle was talking about: Monk had always been fond of alliteration. He was not fond, however, of Bradley's chief of staff, Maj. Gen. William B. Kean, a man who in fact inspired little love in his associates; in the office he was known as Captain Bligh. And according to a story told at headquarters, Kean for his part had once told Bradley: "General, my principal value to you is protecting you from Monk Dickson."[7]

It quickly became clear to Rosengarten that Monk did not appreciate orders from on high telling him how to run his intelligence operation; it was also obvious that whatever General Marshall might have written to Eisenhower, he had not written a letter to Monk Dickson. Any briefing of generals was going to be conducted by the Army G-2, not by some newly assigned special security officer. Dickson himself was not a career officer, though he was a graduate of West Point. That had been in the World War I era, but afterward, considering the business world more promising than the army, Dickson acquired an engineering degree from MIT and went into the warehouse business in Philadelphia. Having returned to active duty in 1940, he had been with Bradley as an intelligence officer since the campaign in Tunisia. He was said to have foreseen the German attack at Kasserine, only to have his warning brushed aside.[8]

Although General Marshall had told General Eisenhower that the Ultra representative was to deal directly with the commanding officer, presenting the intelligence "in useable form," Monk Dickson did not see it that way, nor did he seem to believe that the SSO should "assist in fusing Ultra intelligence with intelligence derived from other sources." General Marshall had envisioned a separate, independent intellectual existence for the Ultra representative, but as a veteran of four decades in the army he had felt it right to say that the representatives would "be subject to the administration and discipline of the command to which they were detailed" and would "work under the control of G-2 or A-2 of the Command as part of his staff." There was nothing surprising about the "administration and discipline" proviso—you could not expect Colonel Taylor, back in England, to exercise on-the-ground supervision of his men—but whether or not Dickson had read the Marshall letter, he acted as if he had thoroughly embraced the Chief of Staff's latter point. General Marshall had even gone on to enlarge the loophole he had made, with his sentence saying that "if at any time the flow of Ultra intelligence is not sufficient to occupy fully the time of these officers, they may be used for other related intelligence assignments."[9] The result was, it seemed to Rosengarten, that the First Army G-2 said to himself that this special security officer was simply another body to be integrated into his section; Rosengarten, in other words, would simply be required to perform like any other officer on Dickson's staff.

But there was no way Dickson could prevent Rosengarten's receiving the CX/MSS material from the SLU. As the army moved, this unit, with its two officers and five or six "other ranks," would set up its operation fifty or sixty yards from the headquarters tents. Three times a day Rosengarten would walk across the field to the SLU and go through the signals, noting especially in the early phase what troops the Germans were sending to try to contain the Allied beachheads and where they were likely to commit them. If an important message came in between scheduled visits to the SLU, one of the British sergeants or corporals would walk it over to the First Army intelligence tent and give it to Rosengarten, the authorized recipient. Rosengarten would put his information together in his own head and then relay it to Dickson, whose procedure was to pool these facts with the more traditional kinds of intelligence—interrogation of prisoners of war, photo reconnaissance, reports of agents, and captured documents. And, though Dickson could not change Rosengarten's status as the official recipient of the Ultra material, he saw to it that Rosengarten did not go into the command post to talk to the general; this contact Dickson reserved exclusively for himself. Rosengarten was simply made a member of the G-2 staff, and he was told that special security officer or no, he would serve eight hours a day on the duty desk, and perform other chores like writing the weekly periodic report and a number of after-action reports. Dickson also made it plain that he would be sent on various kinds of errands. He was going to be Monk's boy, that was clear enough. Before long, Rosengarten was beginning to feel that Telford Taylor had dropped him in Dickson's lap and left him there. As he said a little later, "I got no help from 'home.'"[10]

Something else that bothered Rosengarten was the lack of a cover story. People at headquarters were curious about him and what seemed to be his special information. And those SLU vans with their British officers and enlisted men . . . what about them? "Initially there was much curiosity as to the nature of SLU's work and my connection with it, particularly as two of the assigned members of G-2 Section had the inevitable curiosity of all professional newspapermen."[11] Even so, Dickson did not think it necessary to say anything at all to the former reporters or to any other curious observer; "he tried to pretend the whole thing wasn't there."[12] But, fortunately for First Army, it was.

II

BEFORE THE LAUNCHING of the invasion, Ultra had performed wonderfully as a source of information about the German order of battle in France (although not everybody was aware of it; some intelligence officers in Montgomery's headquarters sneered at Ultra as "BBR"—Burn Before Reading[13]). Following the landings, Ultra kept a close eye on the movement of enemy reinforcements, including the already referred-to transfer of the 17th SS Panzer Grenadier Division to Carentan during the first week. The initial American objective in Normandy was to unite the Omaha and Utah landing areas into a single beachhead. Next the Cotentin peninsula had to be cleared of Germans, to make room for the kind of American buildup that would lead to future operations—whatever these operations might turn out to be. Capture of the port of Cherbourg was a matter of early and high priority.

The Americans already knew the order of battle of the German Seventh Army in Normandy, and after the assault Ultra confirmed the location of many German units that otherwise would not have been identified until prisoners of war were taken and interrogated. In addition, it often supplied "the composition of larger formations, their boundaries, the chain of command, and, particularly significant, any change in the location of the headquarters of divisions and corps."[14] All this work by Ultra during the critical early phase of Overlord was summed up by Rosengarten as "an invaluable contribution to our intelligence."

On June 12 Omaha and Utah beachheads were consolidated, and on the 18th U.S. forces completed the cutting of the Cotentin peninsula. In this fighting, the GIs had been introduced to the hedgerow. This innocuous word, sounding like the name of something you might have enclosing your front yard at home, in actuality described a dense line of bushes and trees growing in a thick mound of earth four or five feet high, the whole affair sometimes reaching a height of twenty-five feet and forming an impenetrable wall. In the Norman countryside these earthen dikes marked off farm fields and orchards, few of them as large as a football field. The barriers were made even more formidable by trenches and foxholes and were often connected by tunnels. In the flat land of the beachhead, spotting for artillery fire was thus extremely limited. The June fighting was largely a battle of rifle and grenade.

On June 17 Hitler, in response to Rundstedt's entreaties, had journeyed to France for a talk with his commanders, who had now decided that Normandy was the big show; the Allies would stage no second landing in the Calais area. Therefore divisions from General von Salmuth's Fifteenth Army should be switched to Normandy, where they were urgently needed. The old Rundstedt, who had previously treated Rommel like an upstart from the desert, and the younger man now found themselves in perfect agreement. But the Führer did not make a third; Salmuth must stay where he was. Further, the generals were to make no tactical withdrawals or anything of the kind in Normandy ("you must stay where you are"[15]) and "fortress Cherbourg must be held at any cost."[16] But on June 27, organized resistance in the fortress came to an end. With the surrender of Cherbourg, General Bradley's First Army had achieved its primary objective of the Overlord assault.

MEANWHILE, AT THE other end of the Allied beachhead, strange things were happening. Or so it appeared to some of the Allied commanders and intelligence officers. A controversy was blowing up, one whose first winds stirred even before the great Channel storm of June 19 and one that not only would long outlast any gale ever recorded but would increase in force as years and decades passed.

On the three British and Canadian invasion beaches—Gold, June, and Sword, stretching eastward to the Orne River—the Second Army under Lt. Gen. Sir Miles Dempsey had landed on D-Day with the benefit of a half-hour's longer naval bombardment than the Americans had enjoyed and onto beaches that nowhere were overlooked by towering bluffs like those at Omaha. The assault went well.

Like the U.S. First Army, the British Second was operating under the direction of General Sir Bernard Montgomery, the land-force commander for the first period of Allied operations in France (at a later date, after the establishment of separate British and American army groups, General Eisenhower was to assume the land command). General Bradley's program for the first phase of Overlord seemed clear enough, and his army was following it: consolidate the beachheads, secure the Cotentin, take Cherbourg so that the invasion force would have the large port it was believed to require. In late May, prior to the landings, General Bradley had thought that Cherbourg ought to be taken by D+15; it fell in fact on D+21. What with all the hazards and unknowns that had confronted the cross-Channel assault, this performance had to be deemed quite satisfactory.

Now, on the Allied eastern flank, what was General Dempsey's Second Army supposed to be doing? There was a plan, was there not?

In a general sense, no one questioned the strategic role the Second Army was to perform. Clearly, it was to keep the Germans busy in the east so that the U.S. First Army in the west could go about its assigned task of capturing Cherbourg. The Mulberries—the artificial harbors—were unknown quantities before the assault, and no one could say how much tonnage could be landed directly on the beaches, though estimates were not high; but everybody knew what a seaport like Cherbourg could do. Even though it was obvious that the Germans would do their expert best to make a mess of it, capturing it was still the first great Allied objective.

But how was Second Army supposed to play its part? Was there a master plan? General Montgomery certainly said so. On May 15, pointer in hand like a schoolmaster, he had presided over the second of two high-level meetings devoted to Overlord; this preinvasion meeting was, as the offical historian of SHAEF said, "one of the great military gatherings of the war."[17] The king, the prime minister, members of the War Cabinet, the chiefs of staff of the services, the Allied invasion commanders—all were present. Since one of Montgomery's most effective means of sharpening his armies for battle was to lay out before them, officers and other ranks alike, his detailed plan of operations (this approach had worked brilliantly with the Eighth Army in North Africa), no one could have been surprised that, as ground-force commander, he thought it fitting at these two meetings to present a highly specific blueprint for Overlord as well as to demonstrate to his audiences his confidence in the soundness of the operation. A master of exposition, Monty presumably made sense to his listeners, no naive group but colleagues, fellow professionals. Yet, several weeks after the May meeting, it would have been difficult to find more than two or three persons who agreed on what this meticulous planner had said. The controversy had begun, and the storm clouds blew from the direction of the Norman city of Caen.

This old stone city, a favorite home of William the Conqueror, stood some eight miles inland from the Sword Beach assault area, on the Orne River, at the edge of flat open country that, unobstructed by hedgerows, stretched away to the south and east, offering fine terrain for airfields and a highway to Paris. Had Montgomery envisioned an early capture of Caen or had he not? Pointing with his stick to the flat country to the south of the city, as shown on a large-scale model of the coast of Normandy, Monty, as General Bradley remembered it, said that he hoped to "'knock about' down there with his tanks on D-Day."[18] Armored columns "must thrust aggressively southwards, if possible on

D-Day."[19] British armored units should seek out enemy panzer divisions "in terrain suitable for armored warfare"[20]—i.e., on the plains south of Caen.

But three weeks after the landings, as Cherbourg fell, Caen was still in German hands. Under Montgomery, General Dempsey mounted attacks on the Germans—Operations Epsom and Goodwood—but Caen continued to resist like a medieval citadel beating off besiegers. Ordered by the Führer to stand and fight, the German commanders had no choice but to try to hold this strategically important city—and hold it they did.

Well, that was all right, Montgomery said. It made little difference whether Caen fell or did not fall. The important thing was that he was keeping German armored divisions busy, drawing them to the British front so that Bradley and his corps commanders could pursue their tasks in the Cherbourg peninsula. What confused the issue was not only the failure to take Caen but the less substantive yet significant point that Montgomery insisted to all comers that everything was going according to plan. Anybody who thought otherwise simply hadn't been paying attention. Nevertheless, as the first week of July came and went, Caen and the area to which it was key were still held by the Germans.

Much of the storm about his strategy in general and his aim at Caen seems almost to have been stirred up deliberately by Monty. In describing him, others would often liken him to some small animal, a monkey (in his boyhood), later a ferret—not only because of his size but, it seemed, because of a wariness he projected, a readiness to hear unpleasant sounds in the distance. Like some religious figures and politicians, he was born to controversy but seemed always surprised by it. And in the matter of Caen, he may not have known that General Dempsey's notes for the May 15 dress parade at St. Paul's contained this unequivocal sentence: *"I must have CAEN."*

In any case, the fact remains that the GI landing at Utah Beach and grateful that the high-ups knew what it was all about had it wrong. His generals knew they wanted to land in France and hold on, but beyond that there was nothing you could point to and say, "There is the plan." As soon as you did, somebody would contradict you.

BLETCHLEY PARK HAD done its share to help the embattled Second Army, keeping Dempsey apprised of the movement of panzer divisions in the area—though, prior to the landings, its record had borne a blemish. In April the 21st Panzer had been transferred from Rennes in Brittany to Caen, where it took up its positions on each side of the Orne, but Ultra had missed this move. The transfer did not increase the German forces in the area, because the 21st replaced an infantry division that had previously been in place at Caen, but it represented a considerable qualitative improvement. Dempsey's men would face the counterattack of an unsuspected tank force.

As the battle wore on at Caen, the men of Hut 3 began to form their own opinions about Montgomery's proclaimed strategy,[21] and it was the British who led the way. The more they heard Montgomery's talk of "holding the pivot," Whitaker said, the more they would laugh. Lewis Powell, now on his field assignment at General Spaatz's strategic air headquarters, saw a different scene, one with a nice bit of deference to inter-Allied amity: "We used to cuss Montgomery when the British were not around."[22] GIs in the field who knew or had picked up some sexy French ridiculed Monty by saying that he was pivoting not on Caen but on *le con.*

REPORTERS LOVED OMAR Bradley, the quiet-spoken Missourian with the heavy black eyebrows and the bony, homely face. He wore an old stained trenchcoat, and beneath it his whole uniform was straight out of the supply room—combat jacket, shirt, tie, helmet or impossible GI cap, and all. He looked as uncomfortable as a draftee. The Savile Row tailors hadn't made a shilling off his time in England. In his seeming simplicity he was called "Lincolnesque."[23]

To Bradley, however, it seemed that his present superior, General Montgomery, viewed his simplicity in a different way: "He left me with the feeling that I was a poor country cousin whom he had to tolerate."[24] Bradley might have drawn comfort from the realization that to Monty the world was peopled with poor country cousins; he thought nothing of condescending to General Alexander, the son of an earl. Perhaps the American, who was literally born in a log cabin, was sensitive to the kinds of slights that Montgomery, though no aristocrat himself, could throw off without even being aware of it. It seemed that between Monty and each U.S. commander there had to grow up some particular area of dissension.

Bradley's deliverance was to come after the Third Army was activated ashore in France and he was elevated to commander of the 12th Army Group, thereby becoming Montgomery's equal under Eisenhower's overall command. Meanwhile, some of the Allied commanders, including Bradley, began to see looming up a ghastly possibility. The British seemed frozen at Caen; Bradley's own forces, in their southward offensive toward Avranches, were bogged down in the *bocage,* the hedgerow country. Was it possible that the Allies could drift into a stalemate, their forces locked in place as the armies of World War I had been for four of the worst years in modern history? That was a nightmare that must be swiftly banished.

Whether or not he expected to fight a great battle in the hedgerow country—"this goddam country," as the GIs quickly came to call it—Bradley now found himself in the position of planning one and presiding over it, helped by Sgt. Curtis G. Culin's invention of the "hedgerow cutter," a multipronged earth-moving attachment for tanks. Frustrated by the stalemate, the U.S. commander determined to try something new. Instead of typical broad-front attacks, he would "breach the German defenses with a massive blow by VII Corps on a narrow front in the center of the army zone" and "unhinge the German defenses opposing VII Corps by then making a powerful armored thrust to Coutances."[25] During the planning period of this Operation Cobra, Adolph Rosengarten said, "Ultra penetrated the fog of war, and the accuracy of its identification of the enemy formations was invaluable information from which to develop true intelligence."[26] The principal source was Luftwaffe Enigma intercepts, which presented a picture of depression and gloom on the other side of the hill, such as the message transmitted on July 15 by II Parachute Corps in which its losses in the steady hedgerow fighting were declared to be so great that the corps would not be capable of resisting an American thrust to St. Lô. Other signals paid tribute to the power of the American artillery and its devastating effects. German unit commanders were clearly anything but optimistic at this point, days before the launching of Cobra. Order of battle information of particular importance was the news on July 8 from BP that the powerful Panzer Lehr division had been ordered *away* from Caen *to* the St. Lô area—presumably to counterattack the Americans. This news, according to Ralph Bennett,[27] was available thirty-six hours before the first tank arrived. As Rosengarten observed, "Ultra, when we got it, was timely."[28]

Before the Cobra attack could be launched, the weather intervened with a series of July rains, forcing the U.S. commander to postpone the operation from day to day. Finally, at eleven o'clock in the morning on July 25, following ferocious Allied saturation-bombing attacks on the Panzer Lehr and 5th Parachute Divisions, both on that morning and the day before, the men of Lightning Joe Collins's VII Corps jumped off on the attack. What General Bradley was attempting to accomplish was his part of the strategic plan as he understood it. Acting rather like a great bulldozer, his forces were to push the Germans back and to the east, so that the First Army, facing east on a north-south line, could form a dike to protect the movement behind it of the soon-to-be-activated Third Army, under George Patton—a movement into Brittany and on to the Brittany ports. First Army would act toward Third Army as the British Second Army had acted in general up till now; it was to be shield and defender. Then, with Breton ports secured, the Allies, British in the north, Americans to the south, could begin the slow, methodical shoving of the Germans eastward across France. That was the intention and the plan, but nobody knew that the war in western Europe was about to be transformed. What the coach was calling for in Cobra was a line plunge by the fullback. Nobody was expecting an end run, nor did anybody have a dream in which the play magically turned into a quarterback throwing the long bomb.

III

A MILITARY CAREER was what Melvin Helfers had wanted from childhood on.[29] His family had little money ("my father tried a few things—things that went bust for some reason"), but with $350 he had saved from caddying at the nearby country club west of Chicago, he enrolled himself in 1928 in a Lutheran prep school that was both military and designed to start one on a course toward the ministry; on graduation, however, Helfers turned not toward the pulpit but toward the Citadel, in Charleston, South Carolina. He stayed this course and graduated in 1937 with a commission in the army reserve. A new law allowed a thousand reserve officers to go on active duty; at the end of a year fifty of these men were to be offered regular commissions, and thus Helfers became an officer in the U.S. Army.

Pearl Harbor found him in Hawaii as a captain training Nisei, who apparently were considered loyal up until the attack, but afterward he and a number of other regular officers were ordered back to the mainland to be spread around among units of the expanding army. Helfers, who had learned German thoroughly at his Lutheran school, applied for military intelligence, but he did not receive the kind of rapid and favorable response that characterized the army's dealings with Paul Whitaker. Instead of being given an intelligence assignment, Helfers was ordered to a bizarre fledgling enterprise called the Austrian Battalion, which was supposed to draw to it the many Austrians by whom America presumably was populated. The hoped-for flood proved to be the thinnest trickle, and fresh trouble arose when the New York newspaper *PM* managed to twist the fact that language courses were being given into the assertion that German was the official language of the battalion. Secretary Stimson did not need headaches of this absurd variety, and the 101st Battalion, as it was called, was officially dissolved.

Mercifully, after misadventures with "another joke"—a so-called mountain infantry regiment—Helfers finally received orders to report to Camp Ritchie, Maryland, for the intelligence course, which was followed by the Command and General Staff course at Fort Leavenworth. "Now," he said, "I report back to Camp Ritchie in April 1944, wondering what will happen to me."[30] As he found, his orders were already there; he was to report to a Col. Carter Clarke in the Pentagon. Clarke was cordial, saying, "We've got you in mind for a kind of special job. I can't tell you what it is, but you'll do all right."[31] Helfers was told that he was not to "talk to anybody about anything connected with it"[32] until he reported to a Lt. Col. Telford Taylor at the United States embassy in London.

And so the old-boy club of U.S. Ultra representatives acquired its maverick member, who apparently had been recommended to Clarke on the basis of his work in the army schools he attended. There was nothing eastern about him; he was not a lawyer, Establishment or otherwise, and he was the only Regular Army officer chosen to be an Ultra representative.

Taylor, who as a person impressed Helfers highly, did not tell the newcomer a great deal except that he was to go by train to Knutsford, in north-central England near Chester, and report to the commanding general of the U.S. Third Army. Helfers arrived at Knutsford the evening of that same day, spent the night at an inn near the station, and the next morning walked to Peover Hall (*pea*-ver), the black-and-white timbered manor house a few miles from town that served as the headquarters of Third Army and the residence of the commanding general.

On a raw early spring day not long before, this general had summoned the officers and enlisted men of his newly arrived staff together on the terrace in front of the house; he stood on the stone steps facing them. It was a scene such as the First Army commander, Omar Bradley, could never have produced.[33] Where Bradley, with his quiet style and supply-room uniform, was Mr. Humility, the Third Army commanding general consciously and deliberately chose to be Mr. Theater. He wore a tailored, form-fitting battle jacket ornate with brass buttons and twinkling with four rows of campaign ribbons and decorations; pink whipcord riding breeches; and lustrous high-topped cavalry boots with spurs. His wide, hand-tooled leather belt was fastened by an embossed brass buckle. The stars on his shoulders, shirt collar, and helmet totaled fifteen. As he spoke he gestured with a long riding crop.

"I am here because of the confidence of two men," he told his audience, "the President of the United States and the theater commander. They have confidence in me because they don't believe a lot of goddamned lies that have been printed about me and also because they know I mean business when I fight. I don't fight for fun and I won't tolerate anyone on my staff who does." He stressed the point that the staff as well as the men on the line were in fact there to fight. "You can't afford to be a goddamned fool, because in battle fools mean dead men. It is inevitable for men to be killed and wounded in battle. But there is no reason why such losses should be increased because of the incompetence and carelessness of some stupid son of a bitch. I don't tolerate such men on my staff."

Those who had served with the general before, and those who were new to him, could have few doubts about what was expected of them, and it was more than simple fighting reflexes. "You've got to have more than guts to lick the enemy. You must also have brains. It takes brains and guts to win wars."

To the newly arrived Major Helfers, the tone of Third Army seemed much as one would imagine the headquarters of "an old-fashioned cavalry troop, with General Patton as the troop commander and the four Gs as the platoon commanders."[34] Helfers reported to the G-2, Col. Oscar W. Koch (*kotch*), who had made arrangements for him to eat and sleep in the headquarters complex, but—unlike Monk Dickson with Adolph Rosengarten—assigned him to no duties. For the time being, he was simply to sit tight. Helfers took that as permission to sightsee and wandered off to places he had always wanted to see— Salisbury cathedral, Sandhurst, Oxford, Cambridge. After ten days or so of these pleasant pursuits, he was informed by the British captain of the special liaison unit, with whom Helfers had thus far had no dealings, that all the officers connected with special intelligence were to attend a short orientation course at Bletchley.

Helfers's reaction to BP was unique among the Americans who spent time there—a blunter version of Malcolm Muggeridge's judgment made earlier in the war. "The course itself was a British joke, I am sure. The main item of equipment used was a mug for drinking tea, the dirtier the better. I don't remember learning anything important during the ten-day or two-week course. We were to see an Enigma machine and learn something about how it worked," but they were not encouraged to press the matter, being told that if there was any possibility of their ending up in combat, it was best if they knew nothing about the machine. So, Helfers said, "I played it safe and didn't even bother to see it."[35] Not only was he not Ivy League and establishment, he lacked the Anglophile touch common among the easterners. The British, like anybody else, would have to show him.

Shortly after returning from Bletchley to Knutsford, Helfers began encountering the kind of problem created by his in-between status; he was with Third Army but not in it, and when orders came to prepare to move to France and become operational, he and the cipher group were in the position of having personal gear and the decoding equipment but nothing more—no transportation, no tents, no field gear. Turning maddeningly but predictably GI, Third Army headquarters refused to issue what was needed because Helfers and the cryptanalytic group were not on the table of organization. In a remarkable joke of fate, supplies for the Third Army G-2 section were in the hands of Lt. Col. Robert S. Allen, the former colleague in the production of the "Washington Merry-Go-Round" column of Drew Pearson, who had broken the story about Patton's slapping the soldiers with battle fatigue. Allen was not in the circle of those cleared for Ultra (Winterbotham would surely have taken to his bed if prior to the invasion the Americans had imparted the Ultra secret to a nationally syndicated Washington scandal columnist), but he indicated that he could not even talk to Helfers unless he was told what this was all about. Colonel Koch saw the need but felt unable to do anything toward meeting it.

There was only one thing to do. Getting a list of requirements from Captain Hutchinson, the British officer in charge of the SLU, Helfers added it to the list of his own needs and went to London to see Telford Taylor. The timing was neat; he met Taylor at his office the morning of D-Day. Adding a few items to Helfers's list, Taylor assured him that the matter would be taken care of by the time he got back to Knutsford. That proved to be an understatement. The special intelligence section, Helfers found on his return, was authorized to draw twice what it had requested, even including a jeep for the special security officer. Hutchinson wondered what sort of tricks the American had pulled in London.

FOR A MONTH after D-Day, General Patton had been eager, impatient, sometimes despondent, waiting to get into the battle and perhaps fearing that it all might end before he could play the kind of part to which he had devoted a lifetime of preparation. At last, on the morning of July 6, a month after D-Day, he took off from an air strip near Salisbury, flew over the Channel and over what looked to be the colossal junkyard of Omaha Beach, littered with the remains of landing craft and beach obstacles, touched down, and was driven to General Bradley's headquarters.

His staff journeyed to Normandy in less style, coming over from Southampton in convoy. "The vehicles drove directly from the ship to the shore," Helfers recounted, "and we didn't even get our feet wet. After all vehicles of the G-2 section were ashore, we formed a motor convoy and moved directly to an apple orchard in the vicinity of Nehou and set up a camouflaged camp. If we had had horses and wagons instead of trucks and jeeps, it might have been an army of Napoleon's camping just prior to an active campaign."[36] A few days later, during the interlude before Third Army became operational, a different historical parallel suggested itself to Helfers. One morning, looking at Patton and his chief of staff, Maj. Gen. Hugh J. Gaffey, as they sat on camp stools under an apple tree near the mess tent, Helfers felt that "only the beards were missing to make it an authentic Civil War scene—Southern, that is, since the North had little of the romantic connected with it."

But if, seen through the haze of history, the Confederates were endowed with romance, they had not possessed any tanks. George Patton would not have changed places with them.

IV

THE ABBEY CHURCH stands on a peak of solid granite, 240 feet above the sea that almost totally surrounds it. Only a curving neck of land like a pier or a breakwater connects the site with the mainland. In the eleventh century, when the church was begun, the place was called, fittingly, the "mount in peril of the sea." It was a shrine to the most potent of the archangels, Michael, "the conqueror of Satan, the mightiest of all created spirits." As long as the world held pagans calling for conversion, Michael would be the patron saint of France, and "his place was where the danger was greatest."[37]

In the twentieth century the archangel or earthly visitor looking east from the spiky tower that tops the church would see, across some seven miles of water at the head of the bay, a rock-bound coast and the medieval hilltop-fortress town of Avranches, the hinge at which Normandy swings into Brittany. During the days following the striking of Cobra on July 25, a farseeing visitor to Mont-St.-Michel would have enjoyed a gallery seat at the pivotal drama of the war in western Europe; and had it been the Archangel Michael himself, militant symbol of church and state, protector of France, he would have been in the position to which his duty called him.

By the evening of July 27, it was obvious to General Bradley that Cobra's strike was deadly—though, as Adolph Rosengarten observed, "we were not ready to erase the red symbols indicating bits and pieces of Seventh Army from our maps."[38] The German defenses had been penetrated, and enemy units were fleeing down the wet coast of the Contentin. It was a breakthrough, and it must now be exploited. By the following evening, Maj. Gen. Troy Middleton's VIII Corps had taken the town of Coutances, toward which for a month it had strained through the hedgerows. "Trees along a 200-yard line in Coutances had been notched for felling across the highway, but were still standing when American troops arrived, clear evidence of the haste of the German withdrawal."[39]

Something else had occurred at the same time. First Army now had four corps, with fifteen divisions, in the line; two divisions in reserve; and another one on the way from England. General Bradley had under his command in France more than 900,000 American soldiers—far too many to be efficiently controlled by one army headquarters. Now that Cobra had transformed American operations into something more than a slugging match in the *bocage*, it was time for 12th Army Group to be established, with Third Army taking its place beside First. On July 28, even before this development became official, Bradley placed General Hodges in a supervisory role over U.S. forces on the left and General Patton over those on the right, while for the moment retaining direct command responsibility. Bradley may have had several reasons for adopting this arrangement, among them a desire to determine the precise shape of the Cobra exploitation before removing himself from the forefront of the operational picture. In the view of the historian Russell Weigley, he had probably not wanted the activation of Third Army to take place prior to this because he "distrusted Patton's impetuosity too much to risk giving him leadership in the critical effort to escape the deadlock in the *bocage*."[40] In fact, Bradley had not wanted Patton in Overlord at all: "I did not look forward to having him in my command."[41] Bradley felt that his former superior's legendary reputation was "the product of an uncritical media buildup." In his criticisms of Patton, Bradley sometimes took on the tone of a nice maiden lady shocked by the riotous activities of the swinging bachelor next door.

Nevertheless, Patton was now in the battle, supervising the advance of VIII Corps to the south, eager to swing open at the Avranches hinge the door into Brittany. On the evening of July 30 troops of the 4th Armored Division—commanded by Maj. Gen. John S. Wood, if possible an even more driving commander than Patton—entered Avranches. For a day there was confused fighting around the town, but Patton pushed his men on southward. At this point he was still not in official command of these units but, though he remained in the background to the best of his ability, "his presence was unmistakable, and his imprint on the operations developed was as visible as his shadow on the wall of the operations tent."[42] The first thing he had done was to put two armored divisions in the van: that was what armor was for.

At noon on August 1, Third Army became operational. Headquarters had now moved from Nehou to a new command post close to the fighting, but before leaving the old spot in the apple orchard, the commanding general told his staff what he expected of his army: "I don't want to get any messages saying, 'I am holding my position.' We're not holding anything. Let the Hun do that. We are advancing constantly and are not interested in holding anything, except onto the enemy. We're going to hold onto him and kick the hell out of him all the time."[43]

Through the Avranches corridor and the swinging door, the road into Brittany was now open. There were also other roads out of the Avranches area, leading not west into the Breton peninsula but eastward, into the heart of France.

DURING THE EVENING of August 6, Major Melvin Helfers was taking it easy in his tent when a visitor announced himself—Captain Hutchinson, the commander of the SLU and not one of Helfers's favorite people. He had a message that Helfers must read immediately.

Up until this time, Helfers's arrangement with Colonel Koch had been surprisingly casual, when one considers the importance of the information that Ultra could convey. Having scrounged up a good map, some acetate film, and a collection of colored grease pencils—still with no help from the inquisitive Lt. Col. Robert S. Allen—Helfers "was beginning to fight the war" himself. He had shown his intelligence reports and map to Koch, who told him to prepare a daily one-page typewritten sheet "giving such intelligence of the Germans as the G-2 of Third Army might be interested in," and afterward Koch would from time to time come by Helfers's tent and look through some of the Ultra messages. At this point, clearly, Ultra was not being greeted with the eagerness that might have been imagined at Bletchley Park. Nor was Helfers's operation deemed worthy of such conveniences as lights or a phone. But Koch, who was unfailingly pleasant, was suffering from ulcers and, Helfers felt, "was glad when nobody bothered him." Captain Hutchinson, however, expressed strong disapproval of the arrangement; these Ultra messages should be seen by the army commander. Helfers would reply that he could not go over Koch's head. "Usually then Captain Hutchinson would turn around, fart, and walk back to his signals section."[44]

During the afternoon of August 6, Helfers had obtained a brand-new map from a friend in the engineers and, transferring his intelligence data to it, had produced what he regarded as an up-to-date master-piece. Now, in the evening, here was Hutchinson with a message from Bletchley Park[45]—and what a message! Five German armored divisions had somehow been transferred to the vicinity of the town of Mortain, in hilly country twenty miles east of Avranches; Mortain, in the First Army area of operation, had been taken on August 3. The armored divisions were to smash through the American lines, seize Mortain, and roll on westward. If they were successful, they could cut the thin corridor through which Third Army was maintained both in Brittany and to the south of First Army; the two U.S. armies would be split.

"That," as Helfers said, "was getting close to home." After transfer-ring the contents of the Ultra message to his map, he decided that if General Patton didn't get the intelligence, and immediately, the result would be a court-martial for Major Helfers. But, so low was the status of the special security officer at Third Army, he had never even met the general. Picking up his map, his notes, and his flashlight, Helfers set off for Colonel Koch's tent. He found the army G-2 dozing fully dressed on his cot. After he had looked at Helfers's map and heard the details of the message, Koch agreed that Patton should get the news at once. Button-ing his shirt collar, pushing up his tie, and settling his helmet on his head, the colonel led the way to General Patton's trailer.

They caught the general just as he was coming in from visiting front-line troops, and Koch introduced Helfers as a major who had some special intelligence of importance. Helfers spread out his map on the floor, and the three men squatted around it, while the Ultra representative told his tale. What did Colonel Koch think of it? Patton asked. He believed it to be genuine, Koch said; it fit with the rest of the German situation. Patton immediately went to the phone and called the command post of Maj. Gen. Walton H. Walker, commander of XX Corps, ordering him to halt the southeastward advance of the 35th Division and hold it in place to meet an expected German drive to the north, on Mortain.

After making the call, Patton turned to Helfers and asked how long he had been with Third Army headquarters. And this intelligence he was receiving from his special source—how valuable did he think it was? Helfers answered simply that he had usually known twenty-four hours in advance what the Germans in front of Third Army units would try to do. Well then, Patton said, turning to Colonel Koch, why hadn't he been told about this major and what he was doing at Third Army? Koch's answer was not exactly a piece of unassailable logic. They'd had such trouble with the British signal-intelligence people attached to them in Africa and Sicily, the G-2 said, that he had thought it best not to tell the general that there was a similar operation in connection with Third Army. Helfers was perhaps not utterly surprised at Koch's reasoning, since in his own view the conduct of the SLU contingent was bound to be upsetting to the spit-and-polish Patton, who would have no control over them; "they wore their uniforms as they pleased, they came and went as they pleased, they kept their quarters as they pleased, and they cooked and ate as they pleased."[46] They lived "like gypsies."[47]

In any case, however lacking in intellectual rigor Koch's explanation was, Patton seemed to accept it. But he also told Helfers that beginning the next morning at seven he was to come every day directly to the command trailer and present a short briefing on the Ultra intelligence that had been received in the past twenty-four hours and that if any single piece of important intelligence came in Helfers was to get it to the commanding general or the chief of staff at once.

The next morning the Third Army Ultra show had its first performance, with Patton and several officers "in the picture" making up the audience. Helfers's chronological approach seemed to please Patton, who, Helfers decided, "preferred to be his own intelligence analyst"; he "was perfectly satisfied with the when, where, how, who, and what." As time went on, the method was refined. Helfers would spread the Ultra map over the regular war map and present the information from notes, with frequent references to the map—which itself presented physical problems, being large and awkward for "trundling around through rain and brambles";[48] one reason for the size was that Patton wished to follow all operations, not just those in the Third Army area. "When the traffic was heavy, the preparation of the statement and the map frequently required a nearly all-night vigil . . . but it was worth every possible effort as it made the intelligence shout out loud as no mere reading of messages or desultory pencil sketch could have done."[49]

The routine that grew up was for a general conference attended by about forty officers to be followed by the "special briefing," attended by the small group on the Ultra list. At the conclusion of this briefing, Patton would discuss particular situations, ask for enemy strength estimates and other information, and issue his orders. Patton was keenly interested in the Ultra material, and Helfers found that despite the general's colorful and profane image, working with him was very much like sitting in a seminar being conducted by a college professor—"with the exception of a bit of hazing now and then."[50] Patton's officers were respectful, "but that did not keep them from speaking their minds to him and joking with him."[51] One joke, however, was Patton's; the briefings had quickly moved to the war tent, and one morning Helfers had leaned one of his lovingly crafted maps against a table. Into the tent and over to the map wandered Willie, the general's white bull pup, who sniffed for a moment and then raised his leg and proceeded to stake a territorial claim to a large part of Third Army's operational area.

Patton burst out laughing. "Look, major, see what Willie thinks of your map!"

Less amused, Helfers felt a flash of gratitude to the inventor of acetate.[52]

ON THE EVENING of August 1 there had been a flare of excitement in Hut 3 at Bletchley Park. Intercepts were arriving in which mention was made of fighting in the area of Rennes. Where exactly was this city? Selmer Norland and others hastily consulted a map of France: Rennes was about forty miles southwest of Avranches. Armored units of Patton's Third Army, activated only that day, were inside Brittany, approaching the ancient Breton capital. It was the first news in Hut 3 that the Cobra breakthrough had turned into a breakout.

The Overlord plan had called for a careful, methodical push through Brittany to clear the peninsula of Germans and claim the ports thought essential to support developing operations. But by August 7 the 6th Armored Division had sliced all the way to Brest, past the ports, which were fortified; the garrisons were under Hitler's orders to hold out to the end. Even earlier, by August 3, a new light had shone on the Allied plan. One corps, it became evident, could take care of Brittany. Here was a breakout, something not truly foreseen in the Overlord plan but a palpable fact. And here was an army to exploit it. Third Army in the Allied plan was supposed to serve as a flank guard for First Army and the British as they advanced to the east. But that was before the events of the last week in July. Now was the time for an end run around the Germans toward the Seine. Happily, Montgomery and Bradley agreed on the idea, and Patton was unleashed. It was time for his words to come true: "We are advancing constantly and are not interested in holding anything, except onto the enemy."[53]

The Mortain counterattack would constitute a desperate attempt by Hitler to reverse the American breakout. One afternoon, as the assistant G-2 of First Army was manning the operations tent, Monk Dickson came in. Motioning toward the big maps mounted on folding boards, with the German positions marked in red and the American in blue,

Dickson said, "Let's take a look, Bernie. What do you think the Germans are going to do?"

Brungs said he thought they would continue retreating, delaying enough to prevent their entire front from collapsing.

"I don't think so," Dickson said. "I think they're going to stage a major counterattack right here." He pointed to Mortain.

"I think they'd be crazy to do that,"[54] Brungs said.

The Führer first ordered the Mortain operation on August 2—by telephone in a conversation with his new Commander in Chief West, Field Marshal Günther von Kluge; hence the order was not heard at Bletchley Park. During the evening of August 6 several messages came, one of them being the first intercept that caused Captain Hutchinson to turn Helfers out of his tent. The German attack was set for 1830 (6:30 P.M.), well before the message was received, but it was delayed till the early hours of August 7—time enough for the American commanders to take countermeasures. The German push penetrated the U.S. line at the seam between XIX Corps and Collins's VII Corps, overrunning Mortain and rolling on several miles farther before being stopped by ground forces with powerful help from the dominant U.S. air. Heavy fighting was involved but the outcome was foreordained, and what Hitler had not chosen to see was that in thrusting his head forward at Mortain he had run his neck into a noose. "This is an opportunity that comes to a commander not more than once in a century," General Bradley told Secretary of the Treasury Henry Morgenthau who was visiting 12th Army Group headquarters. "We are about to destroy an entire German army."[55]

Sweeping around the rear of the Germans, Patton's Third Army pushed toward the town of Argentan while II Canadian Corps fought slowly south toward Falaise. If the two met, the life would be squeezed out of the German Seventh Army and Fifth Panzer Army. But here again, as often in the campaign in western Europe, entered the dispute-ridden figure of General Montgomery, and again it became clear that one's attitude toward him as a general was governed, much more than was usually the case, by one's feelings about him as a person. His failure to take Caen, and his subsequent denial that he had entertained any such intention, rankled U.S. commanders who thought he was trying to conserve British lives at American expense, or at least was unwilling to risk appearing unsuccessful because his reputation was what mattered most to him.

Amid a cloud of undying controversy, Patton's forces were halted at Argentan. Patton had ordered a force attached to Third Army, the 2nd

French Armored Division, to push north toward Falaise, but Montgomery—as reported by his own intelligence officer, Bill Williams—told his chief of staff that the French unit "ought to get back"[56] and Bradley should be so ordered. The chief of staff, Major General Francis de Guingand, remarked that "Monty is too tidy"[57]; Williams's conclusion was that "Monty missed closing the sack." The Allied fingers gripped the German throat but they did not squeeze it. A Canadian flying officer, to his deep frustration, watched "a column of every imaginable type of vehicle, a mixed bag of trucks, horsedrawn artillery, tanks, ambulances, anything that could move,"[58] escape to the east, the men and the matériel being saved to fight another day. It was a great Allied victory, but not a complete one.

Still, the war was transformed, Allied forces rolled eastward— Patton's Third Army gaining its fame in the process, turning an end run into a big-gain pass play—Paris was liberated in August, and September found the Anglo-Americans in the Low Countries; Antwerp fell to the British Second Army on September 4. It began to look to many in the Allied camp as if the Germans were beaten.

As Third Army advanced across France, it became clear that Colonel Koch had finally grasped the importance of Ultra. Helfers and his temporary assistant. Maj. Warrack Wallace, were given priority on electric-light and telephone installations at each new headquarters, transportation was always provided, and—of particular importance— the Ultra officers were never diverted from their own work (unlike Rosengarten's situation in First Army G-2) and were encouraged by Koch to present their information directly to General Patton and in their own way. Wallace felt that "the position of Ultra in Third Army intelligence could hardly be improved."[59]

What had made a believer of Koch was not only the warning on the night of the German counterattack at Mortain but the fact that "an army [had] never moved as fast and as far as the Third Army in its drive across France and Ultra was invaluable every mile of the way." For example, Wallace said, one day when the army headquarters was near Chalons-sur-Marne, a 5Z message from Bletchley Park arrived at 0100, containing information about an order for an attack in two hours, at 0300, by the 15th Panzer Grenadier Division and the 17th SS Panzer Division; "means were devised to warn the division concerned without jeopardizing security." It was vital information because the German attack was supposed to fall on an exposed flank at a time when the army was spread out, in General Patton's words, as "thin as the skin on an egg."[60] No other kind of intelligence could possibly have given such warnings.

V

AMONG SELMER NORLAND'S positive qualities that had not appeared in any personnel assessment was the fact that he was gifted with a fine fast-ball. Although he was a translator in Hut 3, for baseball purposes he was considered to be in Hut 6—a producer of intelligence rather than an exploiter, as the Special Branch people were called. In the periodic games between Hut 6 and Hut 3, with Norland on the mound for the Bundys and Ben Shute, who had now come over from the Pentagon, pitching for the Taylors, you would have been well advised to bet on the Bundys. "Selmer being a better pitcher," Bundy said, "we usually won the game."[61]

Efforts to teach baseball to the British were surprisingly successful. They adapted rather quickly to the "round bat," Whitaker thought, performing far better than did the Americans being taught cricket. To help the allies get started, Al Friendly composed a "child's guide to customs, conventions and polite uses of the game," containing such rules as "interfering with a fielder attempting to catch a ball by spiking, kicking, pinching or goosing him lays the interferer open to a slug on the kisser," and "in eye-gouging, only one thumb per eye is allowed."[62] Also, hitters were advised not to carry the bat to first base and they were warned not to hurl it at the catcher's head more than twice in one inning.

In attempting to extend the teaching into the realm of American football, Norland ran into a language problem. After assuring his listeners that blocking was a key element of the game, he and Whitaker were surprised to see the Englishmen looking at each other and laughing. The Americans soon learned that "blocking" had another sort of athletic meaning, it being a slang synonym for "copulation."

Accommodations for many of Taylor's group had improved considerably over those offered by such establishments as the Swan in Woburn Sands where Langdon Van Norden had been billeted. A rival establishment to Bill Bundy's was set up, though on a smaller scale, in a stone farmhouse standing on the single street of Potterspury, a village about ten miles from the Park. Run very efficiently by a widow with two teenage daughters, this residence housing ten Americans was recalled by Van Norden as being utterly delightful. "She served us all meals, each of us had a room, and we got double rations—and then we had the PX on top of that. We really lived high on the hog. Besides, we were on a farm, and we got eggs and milk."[63]

A friendly and fun-loving young man, Van Norden found his work as an air intelligence officer in the watch room of Hut 3 fascinating, and

he enjoyed such leisure-time diversions as bicycle excursions in the
countryside with Beverly Kitchen. But he had an adventurous side as
well, and, despite the fact that he knew he was performing satisfactorily in his work at BP, he wanted to see some action. Life was simply too
confining, he decided, and as the Allied armies were moving across
France and new commands were being established, he sought out
Taylor and McKee and told them: "You need somebody in the field. I'd
like to go."[64] Van Norden's superiors agreed. They could find plenty for
him to do on the Continent.

Although he did not leave Bletchley Park, Art Levenson experienced
two significant changes in his life during the year. Shortly after D-Day,
he and the sergeant cryptanalyst, George Vergine, were transferred
from Hut 6 to an enterprise nicknamed the Testery (after its director,
Major Ralph Tester), which was attacking intercepts from an even
higher-level German encrypting device than the Enigma. Dubbed the
"Fish" by the British, this machine, which they had never seen, was a
radio teletype, working on an entirely different principle from the
Enigma. Rather than Morse, it employed the Baudot 32-character
code, and it was on-line; that is, encrypting and decrypting were
automatic; plaintext was typed into the machine, transformed into
cipher and transmitted, and produced at the other end as plaintext.
The Fish was used by the Germans for the highest-level communications, such as those between the Führer and top commanders.
Although a breakthrough against it had been achieved at the end of
1943 (owing to the development of a huge high-speed machine with
1,500 vacuum tubes called the Colossus), the enemy introduced fresh
complications following the invasion of Normandy. More hands were
needed to attack it.

In his private life, Levenson dealt with the question of romance very
neatly by inducing his fiance, who worked for Wild Bill Donovan's OSS,
to arrange for a transfer to London. This move was followed just after
New Year's by a wedding and a honeymoon. The honeymoon was not
without its odd coincidence. Working at the next table to Levenson's
in the Testery was Roy Jenkins, a historian from Oxford who had been
recommended to Tester by the master of Balliol; and Jenkins and his
bride turned up at the same honeymoon inn, also on their wedding
trip. The circumstance enabled Levenson to have a little fun by telling
people that he and Jenkins had spent their honeymoon together.

The most delightful romance involving Bletchley Park was no doubt
the relationship that developed between an American enlisted man
whose last name was Blank and a British WAAF surnamed Plank. They
were said to have been sitting in the same room when the name of one

was called out and they both looked up and thus met; it was love at first syllable, in due course followed by marriage.[65]

VI

THE STIRRING SUMMER events on the Continent were followed in the Pentagon with what could justly be called excessive detail. At nine o'clock every weekday morning and 10:30 on Sundays, as had long been the custom, General Marshall met with his top staff members to be briefed on developments in the war. With the coming of General Bissell, the G-2 contribution to these meetings underwent a dramatic change.[66] Bissell, it seemed to Col. Alfred McCormack, "lived in deadly fear that somebody would arrive at General Marshall's office with an item of news that he, Bissell, had not heard about"; further, the new G-2 "loved to put on a show." Where Bissell's predecessor, General Strong, would "go to the Chief of Staff's meeting with a couple of small maps to illustrate G-2's idea of enemy dispositions and movements," Bissell's "appetite for visual aids was insatiable."[67] As much as possible, all figures had to be translated into graphs and charts, and every intelligence estimate (such as the weekly strength estimate of an enemy air force) required "an enormous map with all figures on it, handlettered at specified places along the margins by an ever increasing crew of draftsmen. If there was the faintest excuse for a picture, a series of pictures had to be obtained and pasted on a board, with suitable lettering."[68]

As time went on, the enterprise began suffering from gigantism. At first, two enlisted men carried the visual aids to General Marshall's office. Then as these became both more numerous and bigger, a special truck was required. In due (or undue) course, the aids outgrew this truck, necessitating the obtaining of a larger one. Because of the general's rules for the design of maps, special easels had to be constructed.

In order to make sure that he was master of his material before he was due to make his appearance in front of the Chief of Staff, General Bissell held his own meeting beginning an hour earlier. These gatherings consisted of a series of presentations by G-2 specialists, who had to get to work by six o'clock or so in order to prepare their material. Since the object of Bissell's meeting was to get through the maximum amount of information in the minimum amount of time, the proceedings were conducted at a frantic pace. At 7:55 the specialists and the chiefs of the Military Intelligence Service assembled in Bissell's outer office. On the dot of eight the general pressed his buzzer, and the specialist who was scheduled to speak first hurled himself through the door, dashed across the room to the spot where all speakers were required to stand, and uttered his first lines even before he had assumed the required position. No sloppiness was tolerated; not only did the speakers have to use memo paper of the right color (white, yellow, pink), depending on the type of report involved, they were governed in their preparation by an order regulating the size of the sheets, the typography, the margins, and the manner in which the sheets were clipped together. A man might be forgiven, McCormack observed sourly, for an intelligence summary containing some such fantastic conclusion as that "the Nazis were about to launch a gigantic counterattack that would throw the Reds back to the Volga," but "a man who clipped the summary sheets in the lower right-hand corner insted of the lower left-hand corner, was in a fair way of being sent to the Aleutians."[69]

Tinting took on great significance. Since it was deemed vitally important that the visual material be appealing to General Marshall's eye, maps were produced with delicate pastel shading; soothing color combinations were fervently sought. Each map or chart was covered with acetate, which caused a problem. Bissell noticed that some acetate produced more of a glare than other kinds, and occasionally the acetate would bulge, accentuating the glare. That caused General Marshall to have to shift his head. Unthinkable! G-2's best minds were unleashed on the acetate problem, and after numerous experiments a new kind of slightly pigmented acetate was found that solved the problem, except that it tended to render dull the map or chart that it covered. That problem was solved by a change in the tinting procedures.

The entire operation of the Military Intelligence Service seemed now to center in the morning meeting, or what Carter Clarke called "the daily rodent intercourse." McCormack, who had not had a military education and had not spent his formative years in the Army learning to accept with phlegm even the most bizarre whims of a commanding officer as simply a part of life—and temporary, at that, since one might be in Leavenworth this tour and the Philippines or Governor's Island the next—burned with frustration at the sight of the intelligence specialists being turned into "hacks that came to work at 5:30 or 6:30 and, in an atmosphere of rush and hysteria, put up yesterday's events in a graphically illustrated package."[70]

And McCormack was no mere bystander at this scene. To his mortification and disgust, General Bissell had put him in charge of the daily intercourse.

12

"A Bit of a Panic"

IT WAS SUPPOSED to be a milk run. It was not one of the deep missions into the teeth of the air defenses of the Reich; the target this time was the buzz-bomb storage area at St.-Martin-l'Hortier, in eastern France. Since the Allies had absolute control of the air over the Normandy beachhead where the armies had been ashore for three weeks now, no German fighters would offer a threat. Bearing on her nose the cryptic name *Nightjar n-Nan*,[1] the lead B-17 in the flight, flying at ten to fifteen thousand feet, would hop over the battle on the ground, deliver her deadly load, and return home. A late beginning—7:30 A.M. takeoff, over the target at 10:00—and an early ending. Much better than the way it was on the long flights into Germany.

The crew was all aboard, the engines were turning, and across the hardstand came a late arrival, a passenger—a brigadier general. "We didn't ask him why he was there and he didn't tell us," said the navigator, Lieutenant John W. Huston. "He was a general, a minor deity, and we were nineteen-year-old lieutenants."

The mission did not go as planned. Cloud cover completely obscured the area of the primary target. It was too much even for the Mickey, the H2X radar blind-bombing gear. The pilot, Lieutenant Clarence Jamison, ordered the attack switched to a secondary target, a line of locks along a canal. But over that target the Fort met a sky full of flak. She bucked as if she had been punched from below. Smoke began pouring from No. 4 engine.

The crew members up front with Jamison were ordered to bail out. But the men in back, the H2X operator and the gunners, did not hear the command. They stayed where they were, and after a struggle the pilot managed to steady the bomber and keep her on course.

But below the ship white parachutes belled out amid the clouds and

233

the puffs of flak. Through the murk, floating down into enemy-held territory, went the copilot, the regular bombardier, the navigator, and the engineer. And with them went the passenger, the man with a star on each shoulder, jumping from the B-17 not only into the hands of the Germans but into a sea of rumor, a legend that would be known only inside a limited group but that would still be alive to stir doubt and resentment more than four decades later.

ARTHUR VANAMAN WAS the kind of youngster that sportswriters love to describe with phrases like "born competitor." He grew up in the South Jersey town of Millville—"situated in the heart of the finest fruit and trucking section of New Jersey, every fruit and vegetable growing in profusion,"[2] according to the Municipal League's 1915 boast—and was an outstanding athlete, a muscular boy, a shade under six feet tall, barrel-chested but long-legged. "Anything he'd do, he was out to win, believe me," Vanaman's closest boyhood friend said. He was the quarterback of the high school football team; he was a "damned good left-handed pitcher—he could throw a good hard ball—and he played in all the sandlots around there"; he was an excellent tennis player. Boxing? "I remember many a bloody nose he gave me, boxing down in the basement." He was a "very aggressive guy, and anything he did was near perfection; he would do it completely and do it better than anyone else I knew." He was good-looking too, with piercing black eyes, "very attractive to the girls."[3]

Glass manufacturing was the predominant industry in the area, and Vanaman's father was a skilled artisan. Young Arthur grew up with no illusion that life was going to be easy; on his graduation from high school in 1910, his father arranged for him to enter apprenticeship in the Pennsylvania Railroad shops at Trenton, where his best friend had already gone. "We were learning to be boilermakers and to repair locomotives," the friend said. "We got six cents an hour for a sixty-hour week—$3.60 a week, paid monthly."

Building and patching up locomotives wasn't really young Art Vanaman's idea of the best way to spend his life, and after a year of this grind he arranged to enter the Drexel Institute of Technology in Philadelphia. After graduation in 1915, he went to work for Westinghouse. But, like many another male of that era, he had never been able to forget the thrilling sight of the first airplane he had seen in flight and in June 1917, shortly after the United States entered World War I, he went to a recruiting sergeant and said he wanted to learn to fly. He received his wings just a few days before the Armistice; to his regret, he had no opportunity to fly in combat.

Army air had now become Vanaman's career. Air Service Command headquarters at Dayton, where he was chief procurement officer in the early 1930s, was a bubbling center of experimentation. "We developed metal wings for greater strength; we were getting away from 'wood and canvas.'" The air was "that part of the Army that didn't stand still. We really went to town with the funds we could get."

In 1937, as an expert in aircraft design and construction, Vanaman was whirled into an entirely new world:[4] he was sent to Berlin to scrutinize the new German air force as assistant attaché for air to the U.S. embassy in Berlin. Here he was to have frequent contact with Nazi officials, notably Hermann Göring, the commander of the rapidly growing Luftwaffe, the new German air force that was beginning to cause some sleepless nights in London and Paris.

During Charles Lindbergh's tours of German air installations, Vanaman served as one of the escorts, sometimes flying the Lone Eagle in his own plane, a little Messerschmitt. "There were two different lines in Germany at the time," Vanaman said. "There were the military and the Nazis. The firmness of the education of the regular military was impressive. They were well schooled in what they had to do." But, certainly, he was impressed with the strength of Göring's Luftwaffe, considered the most Nazi-oriented of the services: "A great amount of labor had gone into it, and a great amount of money had been spent on it. Here was a competition that had to be met sometime." But the German air weapon had its weaknesses: "Hitler dictated that air was just an extension of artillery. It was long-range artillery and artillery was supposed to work with ground forces. They did not have airplanes of the nature of the B-17 or the B-24."[5] Vanaman was still in Berlin at the time of the Battle of Britain in 1940. "We just had to admire Britain's guts. They did a magnificent job." But "they would never have come out of it that way if the military in Germany had had their say"[6] about the choice of aircraft types.

Vanaman brought back a bagful of firsthand impressions and insights when he was recalled to the United States in 1941 just as the Germans were launching their great invasion of the Soviet Union. Surprisingly, at least to a layman, he spent the next three years—the bulk of the war—rotating into and out of various stateside jobs, only a few of which drew on his specialized knowledge of German air hardware. But in May 1944, now a brigadier general, he was summoned to England to fill a post in which, it seemed certain, he would be able to make highly effective use of his knowledge of Germany and German thinking. His new boss was to be an old friend from World War I days in the Air Corps, Maj. Gen. Jimmy Doolittle.

AS THE YEAR 1943 had unfolded, the faith reposed by American air commanders in daylight precision strategic bombing, though never dying, had been sorely tried by the realities of day-in, day-out war—by the contrast between practice bombing in the clear light of the southwestern United States and the problems presented by the cloud cover and frequent fogs of northern Europe; by the depredations of the German day fighters ("Flying Fortress," after all, was originally a newspaper accolade, not a technical description); by the lack of a truly satisfactory long-range fighter escort to destroy or chase away those enemy fighters; by the inevitable disparity between what strategic bombing could actually achieve and the excessive expectations of airmen who seemed to see in it a sole and self-sufficient weapon of victory. The greatest blow had been the second attack on German ball-bearing works at Schweinfurt, Bavaria, on October 14, 1943; eighty-two of 291 Fortresses were either lost or damaged beyond repair. The most costly air attack of the war, "it exploded the theory of the self-defending bomber formation, forcing the Americans to curtail their daylight bombing offensive until technical developments allowed the fighters to accompany them round trip."[7] What these technical developments consisted of, essentially, was the fitting of the P-51 Mustang fighter with a Packard-made version of the 1,600-horsepower Rolls-Royce Merlin engine and the adding of auxiliary fuel tanks.

Three men, all of them pioneer army aviators, had commanded the Eighth Air Force, but the chief most closely identified with it was a stocky, square-jawed Texan, Maj. Gen. Ira C. Eaker, who had come to England as an observer before the United States entered the war and in early 1942 had been put in charge of developing the force that was to be called VIII Bomber Command. Eaker was the senior U.S. air officer in Britain until June 1942, when General Spaatz arrived to take overall command of the now-official Eighth Air Force. A few years older than Eaker, Spaatz too had been a pioneer flier in the 1920s; in 1929, the two had been together aboard the trimotor Fokker that had set an 11,000-mile endurance record by spending more than six days in the air. Spaatz, who consistently held the highest U.S. overseas air commands, did not stay long at the Eighth; in November came the move to North Africa where he established the headquarters at which Lewis Powell first served overseas. Before leaving England, Spaatz had a confidential chat with his old friend Eaker, who was to succeed him in command of the Eighth. Eaker believed it important for the force's commanding general to fly on missions; Spaatz thought it important, too, but he had not been able to do it because he possessed knowledge of a certain kind of special intelligence, and the Anglo-American rules prohibited anyone with this knowledge from exposing himself to risk of capture by the enemy. Eisenhower himself had sworn to obey the rule, and the oath had been personally administered by Winston Churchill. Eaker would be well advised, accordingly, to turn deaf when the British briefing officer on Ultra arrived.

"I was required to brief all the Allied commanders and their principal staff officers on Ultra when they took up their commands, either in the United Kingdom or elsewhere on the European front," said Group Captain Winterbotham. "I had imagined that all generals were much alike, with perhaps slightly different training on how to fight their wars. In the event, I found a vastly different variety of men, so that my approach to each one was different in order to get the best results."[8] But Eaker was unyielding. "Winterbotham came over to see me, to explain it, and I told him I didn't want to know about it." Just being aware that special intelligence existed was enough, Eaker felt. "I didn't want to know the details. It would keep me from flying missions." It was that simple. As for Bletchley Park as the source of the special intelligence: "I didn't want to know any of that."[9] Eaker's decision, of course, did not mean that the Eighth Air Force under his direction turned its back on Ultra; the secret simply became the province of the A-2, the intelligence officer. Eaker remained free to share the adventures of his crews during the long, troubled developmental year of 1943, a year when anxious young men could take courage from the sight of the commanding general climbing into a warmed-up B-17.

The beginning of 1944 brought some controversial command changes; they were to have an unexpected result. General Eisenhower arrived in England from the Mediterranean to take up his formidable new duties as Supreme Commander, Allied Expeditionary Force, in preparation for the Normandy invasion; he brought with him a new commander for the Eighth Air Force—America's most famous flier, the leader of the carrier-borne air strike on Tokyo in April 1942, Maj. Gen. James H. Doolittle. When Eisenhower got the news that he would be going to England to command the invasion, he told Washington that he wished to bring Spaatz along as chief of the U.S. Strategic Air Forces in Europe, to consist of the Eighth Air Force and the Fifteenth, which was based in Italy; also from the Mediterranean would come the overall Allied air commander in the theater, Air Chief Marshal Sir Arthur Tedder, as Deputy Supreme Commander to Eisenhower. These moves would leave a very big empty seat in the Med; the man to fill it was surely Eaker. The game of aeronautical chairs could then be completed by the appointment of Doolittle to succeed Eaker at the Eighth Air Force.

Hence, as a result of complex forces, Jimmy Doolittle found himself in 1944 the commander of the mightiest American air organization of the war, sharing with RAF Bomber Command the mission of pulverizing the warmaking potential of Hitler's Reich. Earlier, in North Africa, Group Captain Winterbotham had appeared before him with his bag of Ultra tricks. Doolittle was the hard case *par excellence.* His whole career was built on getting into the air, testing the planes, seeing things with his own eyes, taking shrewdly calculated risks. On D-Day he flew a P-38 back and forth over the invasion beaches, watching as the Allied troops splashed ashore. He went on bombing missions: "I periodically flew over enemy lines but none of them deep."[10] He could not conceive of himself as fighting the war just by "flying a desk." Yet he knew the Ultra secret. Spaatz had not flown, and Eaker deliberately had not known, but "you must understand that Jimmy Doolittle was a rebel about Ultra," Winterbotham said. He "refused to bind himself not to go on air missions."[11]

IT WAS KNOWN that George Patton and some other U.S. and British commanders knowledgeable about Ultra sometimes found themselves up front in spots where capture by the enemy was conceivable. A measure of such risk was probably inevitable, given the mobile nature of much of the World War II fighting—and given, as well, the bitterness that had been created in World War I by the remoteness of the generals deep behind the lines in their chateaux, learning about the fighting from the reports of young officers who had driven or galloped back to headquarters, and studying the bands and markings on the maps that hung on their office walls, while miles away the men struggled in the reddened mud of the trenches. It was different this time; and even Ultra's guardians could not expect perfect security for their treasure. But for an Ultra-briefed air force general deliberately to tantalize fate, to place himself in positions in which he was far more likely to be seized by the enemy than any forward-venturing ground general would be, to play a game with such unfavorable odds—this was to give a good many hostages to fortune. Yet Doolittle gave them. Did he somehow feel that security provisions were designed for other men, that if he fell into enemy hands he would somehow be invulnerable to whatever interrogation techniques the enemy might use on an obviously well-informed officer, that he was immune to the danger of verbal slips? Doolittle's answer to the question was simply: "I carried a .45 with me, and I would not have fallen into enemy hands."[12]

No problem, therefore, would have arisen. Doolittle was patently sincere in saying this. But could so vital a person, a man who had lived with relish one of the most sparkling lives of the era, who had many times risked death in unproven airplanes in uncertain conditions and had sometimes felt its presence but had always triumphed over it—when the critical moment came, could such a man destroy himself in cold blood? Nothing else about him suggests a *kamikaze* mentality, a phenomenon that healthy westerners marvel at but rarely emulate. And what would the German intelligence services have made of an American general, a famous hero, dead by his own hand, shooting himself to keep from being captured? What was he afraid of? What was he hiding? They might not have known how he died, of course. But if they had found out . . .

As a part of the preparations for the invasion, Eisenhower's head-quarters put forth the "Transportation Plan," for the bombing of railway yards and facilities in the general area of the landings (but, in line with the Fortitude deception plan, more bombs were dropped on the Pas de Calais than on Normandy). Doolittle, now a lieutenant general, and his superior, Tooey Spaatz, like true strategic-bombing believers, were firmly opposed to the transportation plan; they wanted to concentrate on Reich industrial targets, notably oil refineries, but Eisenhower carried the day. The attacks began in May, and they roared like a tidal wave across the marshaling yards of northern France, whirling locomotives into the air, smashing freight cars to splinters, ripping up tracks, and gouging holes in the earth beneath them; bridges were swept away. By D-Day 76,200 tons of bombs had blasted some eighty targets, and the routes across the Seine downstream from Paris were closed for a month. Railroad traffic was slashed in half; the trains that were still running had to crawl through endless detours, and they dared move only at night.

Something else happened in May. Although Doolittle and other Eighth Air Force officers were already in the Ultra picture, receiving their information from the U.S. strategic air liaison at the Air Ministry, now an SLU was activated at Eighth Air Force headquarters, and Major Ansel Talbert, a newspaperman, was assigned as Ultra representative.[13] These moves were made "largely at the insistence of General Doolittle." But, even though the commanding general was a strong believer in the value of Ultra, he did not see to it that Major Talbert was given the most suitable quarters for his work. The SSO was stuck in a small office on the lowest level of the underground operations block, two levels away from the SLU. Nor was his billeting arrangement satisfactory; he was quartered with three other officers who were not privy to Ultra. If during the night he needed to discuss a message that had arrived, he had to dress and go to an adjoining building where he could have the use of a scrambler telephone. Unlike First Army, however, the Eighth Air Force provided its Ultra representative with a splendid title; he was styled "chief of the general liaison and special reports section of the directorate of intelligence."

The CX/MSS messages from Bletchley Park were kept either in the SLU or in Talbert's room in the depths of the operations block, each entrance to which was guarded. The key to the Ultra office was left each night at the SLU office, where a twenty-four-hour watch was kept. When Talbert took messages with him to the morning briefing session, they were carried in a ring binder from which they could not become detached. Except for the fact that his room was not soundproof, which meant that he frequently had to caution visitors to keep their voices low, Talbert had full confidence in the security procedures for Ultra at Eighth Air Force headquarters.

There was still another notable event in May. A vacancy occurred on the Eighth Air Force headquarters staff—a high-level, demanding, challenging post opened up, that of A-2, air intelligence officer. As it happened, an old acquaintance of Doolittle's was available, a friend from 1917, a tough go-getter, a man highly qualified; he knew Germany, knew the German leaders, and had expert knowledge of German aircraft: Brig. Gen. Arthur W. Vanaman.

Vanaman's arrival at High Wycombe in Buckinghamshire, about thirty miles northwest of London, where the Eighth Air Force was headquartered in what (of course) had been a girls' school, occurred on the eve of the Normandy invasion when Doolittle and his fliers were devoting much of their effort to attacking the railroad yards and bridges under SHAEF's Transportation Plan and to knocking out the launching sites of the German G-1 buzz bombs (Operation Crossbow). It was a busy and complex time for the new A-2, whose fundamental duty was defined as keeping the commander informed "as to the situation and capabilities of the enemy."[14] A particular part of this task called for close study of possible enemy targets; it was from the A-2's office that briefing officers acquired the information they passed on to the combat crew prior to missions. When Vanaman had been on the job for no more than two weeks—"I was really just breaking in,"[15] he said—a busy Jimmy Doolittle summoned him to a confidential meeting; the subject was Ultra. "Jimmy briefed us on what it was all about," giving his listeners a "sketchy idea of how it worked." It was obviously a vital source of information for the new air intelligence officer, but, after all, it provided only one kind of knowledge about the enemy. Vanaman wanted more. If he was ultimately responsible for selecting targets and sending men to fly over them, risking their lives, he himself ought to have the same kind of experience, see from the same perspective. He had already flown on a mission or two before being put in the Ultra picture; he felt a need to go again. He told Doolittle that "he thought he could do his job better if he had a chance to go overhead."[16]

It was, on the face of it, an impossible request. But it was not being made to just any commanding general, it was made to Doolittle the scientific daredevil, the master of the calculated risk. It was made to Doolittle the commander who believed that staff officers ought to fly combat missions so that they could understand the pressures under which flight crews did their job. It was made to Doolittle the "rebel about Ultra." And it was being made by a man of whom his closest boyhood friend was to say, "I would have thought that anything Art would do, he would do it completely and do it better than anyone else I knew."[17]

Doolittle thought Vanaman had a valid point. And it was not in the commander to discourage such spirit. He said okay.

THE 379TH BOMB Group (Heavy) took up residence at Kimbolton, on the plains of Huntingdonshire northwest of Cambridge, in November 1942. The bombers were parked around the field on dispersed paved areas called hardstands. Most of the living quarters for the men of the group were built south of the field, next to the town of Kimbolton, which had earned a footnote-level position in history as the final residence of Catherine of Aragon. Under the strong leadership of Col. Maurice ("Mo") Preston, tall, blond, a bit jowly, the 379th quickly became a crack outfit, and by the middle of 1944 it was well on its way to its ultimate record as the Eighth Air Force outfit that dropped the greatest weight of bombs (26,459 tons) on Germany and German-held territory. Its weapon was the Flying Fortress, the plane that delivered more bomb tonnage on European targets than any other Allied aircraft, American or British.

In the briefing hut at Kimbolton early in the morning of June 27, 1944, the crew of *Nightjar n-Nan* learned that they could expect a shorter day than usual, a mission to eastern France, not into the Reich itself. They had been fed the ritual pre-mission breakfast (real eggs—fried—instead of powdered eggs—scrambled), and digestion was getting under way as the briefing officer spoke. The Fort would be the lead ship of her flight, and hence would carry the H2X blind-bombing apparatus, an American higher-frequency refinement of the British

H2S. For this flight, the crew would include an extra officer, who would interpret the continuous radar picture unrolled on the screen by the H2X.

Trucks carried the fliers to their ships. On *Nightjar,* No. 1 engine coughed itself alive, but the noise from the engines was not raucous; the B-17 ran quietly.

The brigadier general, the "minor deity," was the twelfth, and last, man aboard *Nightjar.* The bomber began to roll.

THE DRAB BUILDINGS, brown or grayish-green, sprawled over a cleared area in the scraggly fir and pine forest just north of the town of Sagan, in Silesia about ninety miles southeast of Berlin. Actually, Stalag Luft III was not a single entity; by the middle of 1944 it had become a collection of six separate compounds holding altogether about 10,000 Allied airmen. Although the camp's full name, Stammlager Luft III, suggests that it was a prison for enlisted men, the great majority of those confined there were officers—thousands and thousands of highly trained, experienced Allied fliers—pilots, navigators, and bombardiers.

During 1944, Stalag Luft III experienced an ongoing population explosion, as the Allied air offensive sent even more bombers and their escorting fighters over German-held territory. In most of the compounds many of the prisoners had to live in tents until a third tier could be added to the double-decker bunks.

"We constantly talked of escape and made plans that were sometimes fantastic," one prisoner later wrote. "We had no idea of what might happen to us as the Germans reached the limit of their endurance and the idea that their cause was completely lost seeped into their minds. Our panic plans were to take care of the situation that might develop if it appeared to our senior officers that we might come up for extermination. We had heard stories of what had happened to the Poles and others at the hands of our hosts. Under the plans each prisoner was given a job to do, if and when the signal was given. Generally these plans included sudden and overwhelming attack on our guards with our bare hands. We knew that many of us would die in this mass uprising, but we also knew the guards couldn't kill us all and that a good many would break into the open to live off the land."[18]

Escape was not the only dream. The U.S. and British brass must surely realize what a valuable resource—what a concentration of skill and training—was sitting useless in these flimsy buildings in the Silesian forest. The war had been full of daring feats, of Commando raids and surprise landings, amphibious and airborne. What could be more likely than an attempt by the Allies to free the imprisoned 10,000 airmen and put them back where they belonged, in the skies bringing destruction to the Third Reich? The stroke might come as the result of a quick probing attack by units of the Red Army, now blistering the Germans in Poland perhaps no more than two hundred miles away. Others in the camp thought it more likely that the Americans and the British would drop an airborne force strong enough to seize the immediate area and hold it against any German counterattacks while transports evacuated the prisoners by air. If the need was obvious to the inmates of the camp, it was surely obvious to the Combined Chiefs of Staff.

The logical first step in a liberation operation would surely be the sending of an Allied advance man, an officer who would contrive to let himself fall into German hands precisely so that he would be brought to the camp; he would be a high-ranking airman, who could prepare the prisoners for mass action, encouraging them, telling them what to expect and what they must do. The men in Stalag Luft III were looking for a Moses, and one day in August 1944 they thought they had found him.

GENERAL VANAMAN CAUGHT some fragments of flak in his legs as he was descending toward the French countryside, and on landing he collided painfully with a tree. He managed to lie low through the balance of the day and during that first night behind the German lines, but he "was not fortunate enough to be picked up by the French underground." Instead, "I was picked up by German troops. I was taken to a little town called Boeuf, then to Frankfurt, to the hospital at Oberursel."[19] He spent four weeks in Hohemark hospital, while German doctors conscientiously treated his wounds and injuries; as a general, he was assigned an officer as an aide. But whatever the man was called, Vanaman realized, his underlying purpose was to pick up anything of intelligence value that the general might let slip. The aide could have no way of knowing that, just a few days earlier, this American general had been briefed on the biggest Allied secret of the war, but the general himself was acutely conscious of the fact; "unfortunately," he later said simply, "I knew about it."[20] As soon as he was in the hospital, Vanaman remembered that his wife had often commented on his habit of talking in his sleep. Just muttering the word "Ultra" or "Bletchley Park" might be enough to set his captors thinking. Since it would be impossible for him to go without sleeping for days on end, he had to devise another solution of the problem. "I kept awake until I was sure that everything had quieted down. Then I put a piece of adhesive tape on my mouth. I didn't go to sleep until then, because I didn't want them to catch me with any tape on my mouth. The guards could come into my room."[21]

As a general, Vanaman was told, he was to be sent to a castle near Dresden, a special camp for dignitaries. But first, he must go to Berlin. His many acquaintances in the capital wished to talk with him. The American was released from Hohemark Hospital on July 20, an extraordinary day in the bloody annals of the Third Reich. While the American general was on his way to Berlin, fury was breaking out across Germany. Shortly after noon on the twentieth, at his Wolf's Lair headquarters in the pine forest of East Prussia, amid a group of buildings not unlike a *Stalag*, Adolf Hitler barely escaped being killed in the explosion of Count Claus von Stauffenberg's time bomb. The ensuing days, while Vanaman was in Berlin, were a period of sadistic reprisals visited upon anyone suspected of belonging to a resistance group.

During this stay in the capital, always reminding himself of the danger of making the tiniest slip, Vanaman met an old acquaintance at the Air Ministry. Whatever the Germans might want from him, the American was determined to accomplish a purpose of his own. Having arrived in Germany inadvertently, he felt that he could best serve the Allied cause by living and working with the imprisoned flight crews; he had no wish to go to the VIP camp at Dresden. "Knowing German psychology, I just took the bull by the horns and pounded on the table and said you can't send me down there. I am going to the largest place that we have. I don't know where it is but that's where you're going to take me. I pounded on the table pretty hard . . ."[22]

The "largest place" was Stalag Luft III.

IN LONDON THERE had been a "bit of a panic."[23] Winterbotham's aide came with news that had reached him through channels from the Americans. An officer briefed on Ultra had disappeared in German-held territory and must be presumed to be a prisoner of the enemy.

The fact that it was an American who had committed the breach of security was awkward—two Americans, in reality: Vanaman, who had flown on the mission and Doolittle, who had approved his going. What could one do with Doolittle? Winterbotham had been acquainted with the famous flier's rebelliousness for perhaps a year and a half. In the nature of the game, the airmen, who could go anywhere, posed the biggest security problem. Pete Quesada, the energetic fighter-command and tactical-air commander, was another hard case. And the Vanaman affair was not the first flap involving Doolittle himself. Earlier, when Winston Churchill had dispatched Wing Commander Jim Rose to North Africa to check up on the doings of Ultra recipients, the officer from Bletchley had aroused Doolittle's ire by warning him that he must stop leading raids over such enemy-held territory as Sardinia. Doolittle had complained to Bedell Smith, who summoned Rose to Algiers and ordered him out of North Africa. "I pulled my rank (a lowly wing commander but *fondé de pouvoir* by Churchill) and managed to stay on!"[24]

The Vanaman case was discussed "at the highest level only,"[25] Winterbotham said. Unfortunately the stable was now empty—Vanaman could not be called back—but there was some thought that the chief of RAF Bomber Command, Air Chief Marshal Sir Arthur Harris (known everywhere as "Bomber" Harris), might give Doolittle some sort of reprimand (if one ally can reprimand another) in the hope that a stop would be put to any such moves in the future. But "it was thought best not to make too much fuss once the 'breach' had been made." Vanaman was beyond the clutch of discipline, and if any measures had been taken against such an illustrious figure as Doolittle, the fact in itself would have caused security problems because of the speculation that would inevitably have been stirred up.

At Eighth Air Force headquarters, Major Talbert, the Ultra officer, had been waiting to see Doolittle when an officer rushed past him and into the commanding general's office.[26] Talbert heard this officer say, "The Pentagon wants to know who authorized this trip of Vanaman's."

Doolittle waited a second or two, then said, "Tell them I authorized it."

When the news of Vanaman's disappearance had reached High Wycombe, there had been quite an outbreak of panic, matching that in Whitehall. Talbert now had the impression that in taking the responsibility, Doolittle was gamely grabbing a very hot potato, covering up for an erring subordinate. And the hottest thing about this potato was that the British "were always yelling that this was exactly what the Americans would do if they got Ultra."[27]

Actually, however, the British themselves did not come to the case with unsinged hands. Exactly a month before D-Day, a Lancaster bomber, No. 783 of No. 576 squadron,[28] crewed mostly by Australians, had as part of the preinvasion softening-up process taken off on a mission to bomb a German ammunition depot about twenty-five miles south of Le Mans. The mission was successful, the bomber stream turning the target into a spectacular fiery furnace, but after about five minutes on her homeward run No. 783 was riddled with cannon shot, and flames sprang up amidships. The captain gave the bail-out order. The bomb-aimer, an Australian sergeant, grabbed his parachute and was away. The man who had been crouching next to him, not a regular member of the crew, had seized his chute, started putting it on and headed for the bomb-aimer's exit when he was blown outward by an explosion that left him 15,000 feet in the air half-into his "brolly." The Lancaster had crashed in a ball of flame before this second man hit the earth with a bump, "badly shaken but otherwise all in one piece."

The man was Air Commodore Ronald Ivelaw-Chapman,[29] who for several months had commanded the Bomber Command base at Elsham Wolds in Lincolnshire. Exactly in the manner of General Vanaman, Ivelaw-Chapman thought that he "was not really being of much use as a base commander and was not likely to be" until he had at least one operational sortie to his credit. Forty-five years old, he was no purely desk-bound officer, however. He had been commissioned in the Royal Flying Corps in 1917 and the following year was awarded the Distinguished Flying Cross. Between the wars he held a variety of appointments, including four years as a test pilot at the Aeroplane and Armament Experimental Establishment. He also served two tours of duty in the Air Ministry directorate of operations and intelligence.

Wanting to have some first-hand experience of air missions in World War II, Ivelaw-Chapman had come aboard the Lancaster as surplus aircrew. He was, Group Captain Winterbotham observed, "brave but foolish."[30] His foolishness consisted in his flying on the raid even though, by virtue of his work as a planner at the Air Ministry, he was fully knowledgeable about Ultra.

After several days of hiding out in fields, trying to work his way toward the coast of Brittany, Ivelaw-Chapman made contact with farmers in the French underground, who first checked him out as thoroughly as they could (sheltering an Allied flier meant certain death if you were caught) and then kept him for some ten days. Another Frenchman, obviously an underground intelligence type, quizzed him on minutiae of English life and then contacted London with the news that the air commodore was alive in France.

In Whitehall, Winterbotham had the unhappy task of breaking the news of Ivelaw-Chapman's adventure not only to the Chief of the Air Staff, Air Chief Marshal Sir Charles Portal, but to Winston Churchill. Furious, the Prime Minister erupted in threats of court-martial, and there was "a bit of an up-and-downer with the Air Staff."[31] Some three weeks after his landing, after being moved about in disguise, Ivelaw-Chapman was told that a Lysander would fly in to pick him up. "The Prime Minister was anxious that I . . . should be extricated as soon as possible."[32] That was no doubt a fine bit of understatement.

But the morning before the rescuing Lysander was due, as Ivelaw-

Chapman lay on his farmhouse bed, there came a harsh whisper of "Gestapo!" The house was surrounded, the air commodore was taken into custody, and instead of being rescued he went first to a hospital for operations on his dislocated shoulder and then to the German interrogation center called Dulag Luft.

And now, within weeks, the same thing had happened to an American flying officer. Security seemed to have collapsed. But neither side could really do any finger-pointing. Bletchley Park simply had to watch Enigma intercepts with, if possible, even greater than normal care. If the enemy showed signs of suspecting the secret, the intercepts themselves would bring the message to BP, just as the Japanese in 1941 had used the Purple machine to discuss their worries about the security of that very machine. No such suspicions were voiced in the Enigma traffic. Summing it up, Winterbotham said simply, "We were lucky."[33]

THE AMERICAN GENERAL took up residence at Stalag Luft III, closely watched by the imprisoned fliers for signs that he was the anticipated Moses. He quickly won the approval of many, when word spread through the camp that he had refused to accept a truckload of handsome furnishings that his personal friend Reichsmarschall Göring had sent him for his room. But the captive airmen watched in vain for signs of a greater mission than the true one—the general's desire, once he was captured, to be of use to fellow Allied prisoners. In a strange way their watching and their expectations became translated into a kind of legendary fact. The belief grew up that an American general really had deliberately allowed himself to be captured by the Germans in order to prepare the way to freedom for thousands of Allied prisoners of war. No one who has heard that legend in all the years since has known that the full truth is even more remarkable.

THE CONCLUSION OF the Vanaman story suggests that it is unrewarding to be taken for a prophet or a deliverer, even if you have never made any such claim, and that one had better do one's best to satisfy expectations, even if one had no part in arousing them.

Access to each of the compounds that made up Stalag Luft III was gained through two great gates consisting of densely strung barbed wire fastened with heavy staples to pine logs taken from the surrounding forest. Late in the evening of January 27, 1945,[34] these gates began to swing open, and through them came a stream of prisoners, joining into a column that ultimately stretched for miles across the frozen country. The temperature was in the neighborhood of zero, and a blizzard-force wind drove a heavy snow before it. With the Russians nearing Sagan, orders had been given to march the Allied prisoners westward.

For eight days General Vanaman walked at the head of Center Compound's column. Even if he had not come to deliver them from captivity, most of the men were glad he was with them, because they felt that as a general he might well obtain various concessions from the Germans that would be refused if requested by a lower-ranking officer. But at the town of Spremburg, on the Spree River south of Cottbus, the prisoners were startled—and some were dismayed—when Vanaman and four other officers were ordered to leave the columns. Rumor flared up, and the fire was fed by the German announcement that the five men were being taken directly to Berlin to prepare them for early repatriation. Because of the orderly and efficient way in which they had led the prisoners during the march from Sagan, they were going to be sent home. It is not hard to imagine the bitterness with which the exhausted, famished, wind-chilled marchers saw Vanaman depart; the general hadn't panned out as a savior, and now he was callously deserting them in favor of a quick trip to the promised land.

Although he and his brother officers would have greatly preferred to stay with their fellow prisoners, Vanaman had no choice but to do as he was told. He was sure that the "repatriation" story was merely a cover cloaking other German purposes; his captors no doubt wished to make use of him in some fashion. Once in Berlin, however, he might well have opportunities of his own, a chance to influence policy toward the prisoners, whose struggling progress across Germany was showing signs of becoming a death march. Thus it was with mixed feelings that he parted company with the men he had known for almost half a year.

As it turned out, General Vanaman was sneaked into the capital and then out again to a camp about twenty miles south of the city, where SS General Gottlob Berger,[35] the chief of the Prisoner of War Administration, had convened a medical conference with the aim of alleviating some of the worst health problems facing prisoners. It was his idea that the presence of an American general would lend weight to the proceedings and could be capitalized on to hasten the arrival of relief supplies that the Allies had sent to Switzerland. It was an interesting venture for Berger, who is not otherwise remembered for saintly qualities. And in this instance, although he did in fact work directly with the Red Cross in an attempt to get the supplies shipped into Germany, he was playing a deeper game—nothing less than an attempt to negotiate a separate peace with the West so that the German armies still in the field could throw all their strength against the advancing Russians. It was an increasingly common idea in the latter part of the war, with adherents from many backgrounds and schools of thought, from Nazis like Berger and Himmler to bluff Junkers to devoutly religious intellectuals. But Berger was more daring than most of the believers.

What he wanted Vanaman to do was to carry special radio codes to General Eisenhower's headquarters so that secret negotiations could begin. Vanaman agreed, on condition that Berger continue to try to get relief for the prisoners and use his authority, whatever it was at this point in the collapse of Nazi Germany, to stop the movement of prisoners. Berger accepted the conditions, and on April 23 Vanaman and another American officer were slipped across the Swiss border, though in reality it was by now too late in the war for proposals like Berger's to have much significance. Yet, when Vanaman reached Supreme Allied Headquarters in France, General Eisenhower ordered his own aircraft made available to fly this surprising courier (never before had an Allied prisoner been used as an emissary by a German general) across the Atlantic to report directly to U.S. authorities. In two weeks, however, the war was over. Vanaman returned to Europe to serve briefly as deputy to the commanding general for POW affairs, the aim being to speed up the flow of freed prisoners back to the United States. But he never rejoined the group he left at Spremburg.

Everything about Vanaman's adventure, from the wrongly based eagerness with which he was welcomed at Stalag Luft III to the way in which he parted company with the other captive Americans, conspired to leave him for four decades not only a figure of mystery and the subject of legends but a focus of whispered resentments. And after he returned to the United States in 1945 he had to undergo a particular indignity; apparently for having embarrassed the Army Air Forces in the eyes of the other services and of the British, he was "busted" to colonel by the Commanding General, Hap Arnold, who in spite of his smiling public image is described by a close student of his career as "an unforgiving person."[36] One must suspect that it was the fact of this demotion that gave rise to the belief among even high Allied officials that Vanaman had gone on the fateful mission without seeking permission (and after the Ultra secret became publicly known in 1974, Vanaman's fellow ex-prisoners seem to have taken it for granted that he made the flight on his own; it was something else to hold against him). After all, Doolittle, Vanaman's superior, had encountered no problem, received no reprimand. But here, as often, Doolittle's uniqueness won out: the Commanding General of the Army Air Forces would have had to be wrathful beyond common understanding to disgrace the man who was one of the world's greatest pioneer fliers and whose raid on Tokyo in 1942 had brought the first light into a dark picture of American retreat and defeat. But somebody was going to pay—if not Doolittle, then Vanaman.

In England shortly after the end of the war, Vanaman was summoned by Bomber Harris,[37] but not for a dressing-down; the war was over. What the chief of Bomber Command wished to hear was all the details: how had the American managed to keep the Ultra secret from the Germans? There was much Vanaman could say about the way he had used the adhesive tape on his mouth, about the techniques he developed for self-hypnosis, about the discipline with which he emptied his mind so that he could go for long periods without even remembering that such a thing as Ultra existed.

But as Vanaman talked, he could see disbelief in Harris's eyes. Apparently you couldn't understand the story if you hadn't lived it.

13

"The Snow Must Be Dyed Red"

EARLY IN SEPTEMBER 1944 the Allied pursuit of the German armies reached its peak. Moving fast, General Dempsey's British Second Army had thundered across the Belgian border, taking Brussels, Antwerp, and Ghent by September 5. Flanking it, the Canadian Second Army had at the same time overrun the sites in the Pas de Calais from which V-1s—buzz bombs—were being launched against London. During the first eleven days of September,[1] the British moved 250 miles, from the Seine to the Belgian-Dutch border; to their right Courtney Hodges's U.S. First Army kept pace. On September 11 the Allies stood on a line that preinvasion planners had thought might not be gained until D+300—that is, May 2, 1945.

Before the landing in Normandy, the Allied plan of operations had called for a double thrust toward the "industrial heartland" of Germany, the Ruhr, with the main force striking north of the Ardennes and a "subsidiary axis" being maintained south of that gnarled country in the direction of the Saar. It was further explained in a SHAEF planning draft that this program meant that the Allies would advance on a broad front north and south of the Ardennes.

In August, as the enemy fled north and east, General Eisenhower included the U.S. First Army in the forces to advance north of the Ardennes. This would make the northern thrust embody the main weight of the continuing offensive aimed at the Ruhr. On September 2,[2] however, in consultation with Bradley, Hodges, and Patton, Ike reverted to the more strictly broad-front strategy, allowing Patton a thrust to the Moselle. The SHAEF intelligence chief, the British Major General Kenneth Strong, issued a G-2 summary glowing with optimism: "The August battles have done it and the enemy in the West has had it. Two and a half months of bitter fighting have brought the end of

251

the war in Europe within sight, almost within reach."[3] Monk Dickson at First Army predicted that turmoil and revolution might break out in Germany "within 30 to 60 days of our investiture of Festung Deutschland."[4]

These merry tunes evoked a responsive chord from Montgomery, who had just turned over direct command of the land battle to Eisenhower and, in compensation for his reduction in status, had been created a field marshal by Churchill. His reaction to the music, however, was somewhat different from Ike's. Where the Supreme Commander saw the greatest advantage to be reaped from a broad, remorseless advance, Monty began to wonder whether the Germans might not be so enfeebled now that they would crumble before a single powerful thrust aimed not only at the Ruhr but far beyond it, across the north German plain to Berlin.

Decisions of some sort had to be made because the advance that had swept like a grass fire across northern France and even into the Netherlands had brought its own problems. Logistics now constituted the great headache. Modern armies, it had been pointed out, "are exceedingly delicate, from the standpoint of logistics. They expire quickly of military anemia unless they receive almost daily transfusions of supplies."[5] Each GI, even if not in combat, required thirty-five pounds of supplies every day. One medium tank needed three-quarters of a gallon of gasoline for every mile it moved; the supply services had to make available 150,000 gallons to an armored division needing refills for its 3,000 vehicles.

For the time being, starting with the decision to bypass Brest and the other Brittany ports, the Allied command had wanted its armies to pursue the Germans as closely as possible rather than to advance in the kind of measured way that would have allowed the building up of a conventional logistic structure with its series of depots. The striking result was that at the end of August more than 90 percent of all the supplies on the Continent were still housed near the invasion beaches.[6] It was not a question of getting the material to France; the gap lay between depots near the coast and the army dumps now three hundred miles away. The damaged railroads could not fill it, nor did the lines of speeding trucks of the imaginatively improvised Red Ball Express provide sufficient supplies for the whole front.

One result of the logistical bottleneck had been the issuance by General Eisenhower of an order creating what Patton called "one of the critical days of the war."[7] Third Army was continuing its sizzling advance, now bringing it to Commercy and Verdun, the latter only fifty miles from the German border with not much enemy strength in the way. But on August 29 Patton found that 140,000 gallons of gasoline he had expected to get that day had not arrived; the fuel was being conserved for the northern operations. SHAEF was turning off Third Army's tap, and it kept it off for five days.

So it seemed that great prizes were offered to the Allies, although the logistical problems meant that not everybody would be able to collect one. In addition, the lighthearted view of the enemy's situation was not universally shared. Obviously the Germans ought to be sensible enough to acknowledge that they were beaten, but one observer produced a clear-eyed assessment of the enemy situation. In spite of all problems, said Col. Oscar Koch, "the enemy nevertheless has been able to maintain a sufficiently cohesive front to exercise an overall command of his tactical situation. His withdrawal, though continuing, has not been a rout or mass collapse." He went on to point out that clearly it was "the fixed determination of the Nazis . . . to wage a last-ditch struggle in the field at all costs."[8]

Although Antwerp, the greatest port in western Europe, had been captured on September 4, this produced no logistical results for the Allies. The city lies sixty miles from the open sea, and on either side of the Scheldt estuary leading to it the positions were held by German defenders, in conformity to Hitler's strategy of denying ports to the Allies. The Führer, too, was aware of logistical considerations. Instead of concentrating on clearing the approaches, however, Montgomery was developing further thoughts about the northern thrust (nor did Eisenhower exert any contrary influence). The Allied commanders could not be said to have had any excuse for this failure; on September 5 Bletchley Park distributed an order from Hitler emphasizing his intention of rendering Antwerp useless to the Allies.[9] Important as this information was, and faithful as Ultra was in making it available, it was simply ignored. The generals had their eyes on more distant, more glamorous targets.

Not one to stand on ceremony, whatever his feelings may have been, General Eisenhower on September 10 flew to Montgomery's tactical headquarters in Belgium; Monty sometimes had a lordly way of summoning others, whatever their rank. But, as Captain Butcher observed, Ike "never likes to have his battle-front commanders leave their jobs to come to see him. He much prefers to place himself at their convenience."[10] The Supreme Commander went almost the last mile, but not quite; suffering from a painful twisted knee, he received Montgomery in his aircraft. What emerged from this sometimes stormy meeting was a daring, dazzling plan to leap the lower Rhine and outflank the German West Wall—the Siegfried Line, as the Americans and the

British called it. Monty was not given everything he wanted (which was in truth just about everything—top priority for his operation, with the Americans to the south standing still; a political impossibility, regardless of what its merits otherwise might have been), but he was given the full use of SHAEF's special kind of strategic reserve, the three Allied airborne divisions, unemployed since the invasion and "coins burning holes in SHAEF's pocket."[11]

The plan as it was quickly developed had two phases. Between the Belgian border and the Rhine were a series of rivers and canals; the bridges across the waterways, Montgomery decided, must be seized by airborne troops who would, in effect, guarantee the existence of a highway through the Netherlands for the advance of British Second Army forces to the town of Arnhem and thence across the great river. Without such paratroop intervention, Montgomery believed, Second Army would simply become bogged down in fighting for one waterway after another; there would be no dash around the northern end of the West Wall.

Dash and daring! Was it really Montgomery proffering this plan—a high-risk venture from the apostle of caution, an operation to be mounted in only seven days from the hand of the most meticulous of planners? In Operation Market, the paratroopers were to seize the Dutch bridges as nearly simultaneously as possible; in Operation Garden, the British XXX Corps was to sprint from Belgium to Arnhem. Could it be done?

Success would depend on clear weather, which at that time of the year could hardly be counted on; on a lack of any considerable German resistance; on the capture of key bridges before German demolitions men could destroy them; on the arrival of XXX Corps at Arnhem within no more than forty-eight hours of the landing there of the British 1st Airborne Division. To accomplish this, XXX Corps would have to advance "across 64 miles of enemy-held territory on a one-tank front along elevated, unprotected highways, flanked by a soft and sodden tank-proof landscape, interspersed with waterways. Any delay—a blown bridge, an enemy ambush, a blocked road—and the entire column would be stopped."[12] Besides, a move on Germany by way of Arnhem would direct Montgomery's forces away from Hodges's U.S. First Army, thereby making the British advance a spearpoint instead of the "full-blooded thrust" Montgomery had advocated.

From the point of view of Montgomery's vanity, the plan made sense. George Patton had shown that one could get all kinds of headlines by moving fast;[13] the Americans had been credited with all the zip and dash in Normandy; it was time now to show them that somebody else could do it too. A scant week was allowed after the making of the decision for the launching of the attack, which went off on Sunday, September 17, in promisingly clear weather.

As the planning and preparations proceeded, where and in what strength were the Germans?[14] With their customary skill at improvisation (how their generals acquired their reputation for being rigid and unimaginative is a matter of some anthropological interest), the Germans had managed to ferry sizable forces across the Scheldt from Antwerp—remnants of the Fifteenth Army—and had put together, under the very capable General Kurt Student, a force cobbled from various elements that were on hand. This sort of opposition was expected by Allied planners, although it was far better organized than SHAEF suspected. On September 3, however, the energetic and strongly Nazi Field Marshal Walther Model, commanding Army Group B, had taken a step that no one could have foreseen. He ordered the Fifth Panzer Army, retreating before the continuing Allied advance from France, to release the 9th and 10th SS Panzer Divisions so that they could pause for rest and refit. Fatefully, the area he chose for their rehabilitation was Arnhem and the corridor leading to it.

Ultra had followed these divisions as they fell back through northeastern France and into Belgium. On September 5 it reported Model's order, and the next day it added the news that the field marshal had also directed the headquarters of II SS Panzer Corps, under SS-Obergruppenführer und General der Waffen-SS Willi Bittrich, to move to Eindhoven for the purpose of directing refit of the 9th SS and two panzer divisions. On September 15 Bletchley Park flashed the information that Model's headquarters had been established at Oosterbeek,[15] a village no more than three miles from the center of Arnhem. The escape of Fifteenth Army units from Antwerp was also reported by Ultra, so that whatever judgment SHAEF might make of the possible effectiveness of these forces, their existence in the general area of the corridor to Arnhem was known.

All these various CX/MSS messages from BP were distributed in the normal way, Hut 3 of course having no knowledge of the impending invasion from the sky and hence giving them no special emphasis. The emphasis had to come from the commanders and their intelligence staffs; nor were these staffs solely dependent on the umbilicus from Bletchley Park. In the field of intelligence, where much emphasis is laid on cover stories of one kind or another, it is not always possible to say categorically what is the exact source of a particular piece of information. But it appears that by September 10 the Dutch underground had got word to the Allies that panzer divisions had arrived for refit in the general area of Arnhem, Eindhoven, and Nijmegen. That the intelligence came to high-level attention was demonstrated by the reaction of Eisenhower's chief of staff, Lt. Gen. Walter Bedell Smith ("Beetle"). Smith, deeply perturbed—airborne divisions, though carrying some antitank weapons, were not designed to fight off panzer forces—obtained Ike's leave to fly to Montgomery's headquarters with an emphatic warning: the drop around Arnhem would have to be strengthened.[16] But Beetle's trip was made in vain. Montgomery "ridiculed the idea," Smith said later, and added, "he waved my objections aside." Ultra itself could not claim to have told the complete story, but it had certainly introduced the plot and characters, which generally was what it was best at. Montgomery turned the script down.

THE SUNDAY WAS, to quote General Student's description, "a remarkably beautiful late summer day,"[17] with the streets of towns along the fifty-mile corridor from Eindhoven north to Arnhem filled with Dutch civilians strolling home from church. Field Marshal Model was lunching at the Tafelberg Hotel in Oosterbeek, west of Arnhem, when the sky grew dark with airplanes and gliders and quickly filled with clouds of parachutes, many of which came to earth not more than two miles away. Rushing for his staff car, the German commander sped to the headquarters of II SS Panzer Corps and with no hesitation ordered the 9th SS Panzer Division into action; it was to hurry to Arnhem and hold the bridge across the Rhine. Model also ordered the 10th SS Panzer Division to Nijmegen and its bridge. Though the men of the British 1st Airborne Division who reached the bridge—only one of the three battalions of the 1st Brigade was able to do it—were to put up a stout struggle for three and a half days, as far as the outcome went the battle was settled at the outset. The Allies had allowed themselves to expect feeble opposition from dispirited and disorganized German troops. Instead, they ran into Model, panzers, and remarkable resilience.

XXX Corps could do nothing to save the Red Devils of the British 1st Airborne Division. The scheduled race along the causeway through Eindhoven and Nijmegen to Arnhem turned into a gigantic traffic jam that even General Patton, who liked to play cop, could not have straightened out.

Two U.S. airborne divisions took part in Market, the 101st dropping farthest south, around Eindhoven, the 82nd in the middle with the mission of capturing three bridges. Three American correspondents, including young Walter Cronkite of the United Press, flew in with the divisions in gliders. Ed Murrow, who was aboard a troop carrier plane, told his radio listeners that "it was the greatest operation of its kind in the history of warfare."[18] He described the drop: our men "will walk out onto Dutch soil. You can probably hear the snap as they check the lashing on the static line. There they go!"

A week later Murrow reported that the public imagination had "been captured by the daring of this great Allied airborne army which was thrown into Holland a week ago."[19] Daring and heroism were indeed present in abundance, and since Market-Garden did succeed in capturing some of its objectives, the commanders could say that the efforts it called forth had not been expended in vain. But in its strategic aim of leaping the Rhine and outflanking the West Wall, it was a misfire; the last bridge, after all, was the one that really mattered.

Ultra, the priceless oracle, had no way of seizing commanders and intelligence officers by the elbow and making them listen to its news.

And no one would have believed that it would take another six months for the Allies to cross the great river.

II

IN JULY 1944 Major Don Bussey had left Bletchley Park for his field assignment.[20] The first stop was Casablanca, and from there he hitched rides to Tunisia and then on to Naples. In Italy he visited army group and army headquarters, observing the working of Group Captain Winterbotham's Ultra system, and then he returned to Naples to board a convoy bound for the French Riviera.

Early in the morning of August 15, D-Day for Operation Dragoon (née Anvil), GIs of Lt. Gen. Alexander M. Patch's Seventh Army came ashore on the beaches between St. Tropez and Cannes; it was a beautiful day with a calm sea. At midday Bussey landed with the army headquarters contingent, which set up shop at a resort hotel in St. Tropez. Bussey's billet was a pup tent on the lawn; "the brass, of course, were in the hotel." The SLU, as usual, had its vehicles with wireless and decrypting equipment. Under the arrangement made with Bussey by the Army G-2, Col. Bill Quinn, the job of the Ultra representative was to receive signals from the SLU, process them, and post the information on a map. It appeared that Patch had paid no more attention than had any other general to the details of General Marshall's "SSO charter" letter as they were supposed to have been passed on by General Eisenhower's headquarters. No one at Seventh Army had any thought of Bussey's directly presenting Ultra intelligence "in useable form to the Commanding Officer and to such of his senior staff officers as are authorized Ultra recipients" or assisting "in fusing Ultra intelligence with intelligence derived from other sources."

But the facts of the battle quickly intervened. During the early days of the invasion "the quality of Ultra intelligence was unusually high and in the rapidly moving situation was the primary source of tactical information."[21] Adapting quickly, Colonel Quinn decided that Ultra needed a special war room and moved Bussey into an office adjacent to his own. Going further, Quinn concluded that, owing to the great dimensions of the Ultra flow, he could not personally absorb it all and brief General Patch. Accordingly, Bussey early in the game took on the responsibility for briefing all the recipients. He had, as he said, "six customers"—the commanding general, the chief of staff, the G-2, the G-3 (operations officer), the No. 2 in intelligence, and the officer in the G-2 section in charge of the German order of battle.

Because his customers said they hadn't time for it, Bussey rarely presented his Ultra information at a formal meeting, though he felt that such a procedure would have ensured the material's being worked up in the best form. The method he adopted was to brief Quinn every morning on the messages received overnight, and Quinn, if he deemed the information important, would call in Patch and the chief of staff, Maj. Gen. Arthur White. Actually, Patch, who was shattered from the loss of a son in Third Army fighting, had withdrawn from much of the ordinary routine and rarely came. He delegated much of his authority to White who, though he stood only a little over five feet and tended to plumpness and hence was "the most unprepossessing general you ever saw in your life," was "a wonderful chief of staff, and he kept his commander fully informed."[22]

What was the nature of the fast-changing situation that had brought about Colonel Quinn's appreciation of the importance of Ultra? Shortly after two in the afternoon of D+2, Bletchley Park transmitted a CX/MSS containing information from a decrypt picked up only that morning. Hitler was ordering Gen. Johannes von Blaskowitz, commander of Army Group G, to withdraw from southern and southwestern France. Normally, if Blaskowitz had shown signs of pulling out, Patch would have been faced with two questions: In view of the problems involved in supplying advance columns over a beach, to what extent could the enemy be pursued and outflanked? Was the enemy likely to counterattack on the right flank, from the Alpes Maritimes, thus endangering rear communications?

Since the evidence was supplied by Ultra, Patch could take a calculated risk, there being no suggestion that the enemy intended anything but defensive action on the flank. Impressed by the unusual military opportunities offered by the information from Bletchley Park, Colonel Quinn one day remarked to Bussey, "You know, this just isn't cricket."

Patch decided to give chase to the Germans, which meant that the army's unloading priorities had to be shifted. Precedence was being given now to fuel and vehicles. The 36th Division was sent to support a task force that had penetrated deep in the enemy's rear. This combined force formed a road block at Montélimar, about ninety miles north of the Mediterranean coast, where the main railroad and highway leading to Lyon passed through a defile. The German corps that ran into the roadblock fought with ferocity, suffering heavy losses in matériel but making its way through. Here again, as in Normandy, the Allies were reminded of the adage that he who has not fought the Germans does not know war. The highly professional Wehrmacht leaders at battalion and company levels were continually producing results that confounded their often-amateur British and American counterparts. The enemy might logically be defeated, but he still came onto the field with claws. Yet, led by Lt. Gen. Lucian Truscott's VI Corps, the chase was on. The Germans, increasingly exhausted, fell back, but toughened as they reached the foothills of the Vosges. On September 11, near Dijon, French forces from Patch's army met a patrol from a Third Army French armored division. The two Allied invasions had blended; there was now only one war in the west.

III

THE ERA OF spectacular movement had come to an end. As autumn advanced, the Allies struggled to impose a decisive defeat on the Germans west of the Rhine and hoped for an action that could give them that elusive goal, a foothold across the great barrier to the Reich. On October 18 General Eisenhower decided to make the principal push to the Rhine through the Aachen gap in the north; First Army and the new Ninth Army,[23] under the able Lt. Gen. William H. Simpson, pushed off on November 5. Third Army attacked toward the Saar five days later. But Hodges, "Big Simp" Simpson (tall and egg-bald, the general was as weathered as an Indian chief), and Patton were soon slowed by fierce rains and bogged down in mud; and the Germans fought back with everything they had. After a bitter month, 12th Army Group had moved forward only eight miles. North of the First and Ninth Armies, units of Field Marshal Montgomery's 21st Army Group had pushed across the Waal River above Nijmegen but were still below Arnhem and the Rhine. South of 12th Army Group the U.S. 6th Army Group, which had pursued the Germans from the Riviera, had reached the Rhine at Strasbourg and had liberated Belfort and trapped considerable enemy forces in the Colmar pocket.

At a high-level meeting convened by Eisenhower on December 7, the talk was all about the offensive to be staged early in 1945. A single strong thrust, Montgomery said, reprising the song he had sung since September; all other efforts should be limited to doing no more than holding the enemy. Not quite, Eisenhower said. Montgomery could make the main attack north of the Ruhr, and he could even have Simpson's Ninth Army, if he wanted it, but the Allies could not restrict themselves to one punch; Patton should continue attacking in the direction of Frankfurt. Montgomery felt that by ordering two actions, Eisenhower was biting off more than Allied manpower and logistics could chew.

Everyone at the meeting seems to have been exclusively offensive-minded. They were the actors; it was supposed to be the German role to react.

Stretching along a two-hundred-mile front, General Bradley's 12th Army Group numbered thirty-one divisions. With the main Allied efforts scheduled to be made in the north and to the south, the center of the line was left relatively undefended, being manned on a front of about eighty-five miles by only four divisions of VIII Corps, under Lt. Gen. Troy Middleton. That might be a risk, the generals acknowledged, but it surely was not a great risk. This central part of the Allied line ran through the famous Ardennes region, which was still, as it had been in 1940 when the Germans swept through it going west, heavily wooded, a land of narrow twisted valleys. What few good roads there were ran north and south; any force moving east or west had to take to sec-ondary roads through forests, and the many villages of the area re-stricted traffic to one lane.

Obviously, the Allied generals were not ignorant of the events of mid-May 1940; Montgomery had even played an effective part in their amazing sequel, the British retreat to Dunkirk. But the original German advance through the Ardennes had taken place in perfect summer weather, against feeble opposition. Now the twisting roads were at their winter worst; the German Army of 1944 was a ramshackle affair compared with the magnificent engine of war of 1940; and the Allied armies of 1944 bore little resemblance to the inexperienced and unready British and French forces of four and a half years earlier.

Since September the Allies—and the Germans as well (or so the Allies thought)—had been rotating new troops through this part of the line, giving them some seasoning before sending them for more active duty on the wings of the front; the Ardennes sector was to some extent regarded by SHAEF as a rest area. And aside from a general agreement that the Germans simply lacked the men and the resources to mount any kind of major offensive, the Allies had what they believed to be a very good reason to feel secure. After being removed by Hitler following the Normandy invasion, the veteran Field Marshal von Rundstedt had been reappointed Commander in Chief West in early September, and the field marshal, as everyone knew, was the essence of the professional soldier—no Rommel, no Patton, but conservative, cautious, orthodox.

THE SCENE IN Hut 3 was not always earnest, tight-lipped, full of heavy portent. The head of the hut, Wing Commander Eric Jones, was a sober and conscientious business type; "a man of firm good sense," Peter Calvocoressi said. "He delegated responsibility with generous assurance and most people in the Hut quickly saw how lucky they were to have him."[24] But he could provoke some unintended fun, too. "Every once in a while," Norland said, "he would commit himself to what I would call some rather turgid prose."[25] One evening it occurred to one of the watch chiefs that a directive from Jones, if translated literally, would make a perfect German order. A member of the watch was assigned the task. When the job was finished, the message was taken along to Hut 6, where it was dummied up with tape to resemble a genuine intercept, and then trundled back to Hut 3 and handed out to a member of Norland's watch to translate. This man was hard at work when someone came in and innocently began commenting on the absurdity of the new directive that Jones had issued. The mark looked up from his labors to say with feeling: "That sounds just like what I'm translating!"

Such moments were fun, but they were only occasional breaks in what was a grueling routine. As the autumn of 1944 progressed, a sort of generalized feeling of expectancy arose in Hut 3.[26] The Germans were doing little more than resisting the Allied push, yet they were engaged in a great deal of activity, which was reflected in numerous intercepts. Various units were being shuffled hither and thither; Norland was especially aware of these moves, because he had proved to have the kind of detailed memory that made him a valuable on-the-spot man for order-of-battle information—when and where a German unit had previously been placed. The Germans were building forward airfields for fighters. And a term not previously used began appearing in the traffic: *Blitzeinsatz* (lightning action). The new airfields, it seemed, might be related to the lightning action. Some of the advisers in Hut 3 speculated that in view of the airfields and of supply movements, the Germans might be preparing a surprise thrust in the area of Luxembourg. And the reading of railway Enigma yielded considerable information about troop movements to the western front, destinations sometimes becoming clear and all appearing to point to the middle of the Allied line. Luftwaffe signalers, free-talking as always, also let it be known that German fighter strength was being concentrated behind the front.

Particularly striking to the men in Hut 3 were German orders for radio silence. What plans were being cloaked? "By no means was everything clear," as Norland put it, "but I think a lot of us had the feeling that something was going to happen."[27] Many in Hut 3 wondered whether their customers, the Allied commanders, had succumbed to the idea that enemy had shot his bolt. Perhaps the Germans had, but they certainly seemed to be up to *something*.

As for Rundstedt being in command, whatever the generals and staffs in the field might choose to believe, members of Hut 3 watches knew better. The flow of *Führerbefehler* (orders from the Führer) showed that "there was no question who was calling the shots."

TO THE SOUTH of General Bradley's 12th Army Group lay General Devers's 6th Army Group, the northernmost component of which was the U.S. Seventh Army, operating in the general area of Strasbourg, south and east of the Moselle. Early in November Don Bussey began taking note of a series of Ultra messages in which the German Army Group B "was requesting counter-reconnaissance aerial missions over certain unloading points in the Eifel,"[28] the German region immediately east of the Ardennes and sharing many of its characteristics. A complex of hill ranges, thickly forested, the Eifel had one particularly interesting man-made characteristic—an extensive rail network, created before World War I for the concentration of the kaiser's armies west of the Rhine. What the Ultra messages were saying was that German army forces were asking the Luftwaffe to do its best to keep Allied reconnaissance flights from discovering what was happening at the unloading points mentioned. The first of these messages was probably Army Group B's request, reported on November 3, for fighter protection at various unloading points in the area of Cologne;[29] this was followed by some thirty similar signals dispatched by the middle of December. The most frequently mentioned area lay directly opposite the Ardennes. Although the whole Eifel area was well to the north of Seventh Army's front, and hence was not of Bussey's direct concern, he made a point of plotting the unloading points and marshaling yards mentioned in the messages, the question in his mind being simply, What are the Germans trying to hide?

Early in December, as these requests from Army Group B continued to pile up, Bussey sought out Colonel Quinn.[30] On the basis of the Ultra messages and his careful plotting, he told the army G-2, he was persuaded that the Germans were about to launch a major counteroffensive into Belgium on the Malmédy-Liége axis. Quinn listened carefully but then observed that, although what the Ultra representative was saying might be true, they in Seventh Army intelligence had only partial information with respect to the sectors of First Army and Third Army up to the north. SHAEF and 12th Army Group had much more complete intelligence, but they weren't making any such assertions in their estimates. "And that," Colonel Quinn said, "beats you!"

Nevertheless, Bussey, having based his hypothesis almost exclusively on the signals concerning the unloading points, began "watching non-Ultra sources just for little clues." A few days later a captured document identified a division as belonging to XLVII Panzer Corps, poised in the Eifel opposite northern Luxembourg, on the axis of the town of Bastogne. What was particularly provocative was the fact that this corps and another, the LVIII, had for two months disappeared from Allied eyes. Now here at least one of them had turned up, seemingly waiting for action. Not only did Bussey point this out to his G-2, he took the occasion of a trip to 12th Army Group headquarters to tell his counterparts at this higher level that he was expecting a major German counteroffensive. What kind of reception did they give his deduction? "They pooh-poohed it."[31] It was known fact that the Germans had out of desperation created units made up of men who were deaf, men who had only one eye, men who were ulcer victims and could eat only white bread. What kind of offensive had the Allies to fear from such as these?

IF, AS COLONEL Quinn had remarked to Don Bussey, higher headquarters were forecasting no German offensive, what, as December began, were the possibilities that *were* foreseen? On December 5, Bradley's intelligence chief, Brig. Gen. Edwin L. Sibert, reported that "the enemy's defensive plan has been quite clear for some time";[32] he would defend the Roer River so as to protect the Ruhr. But, Sibert conceded, the enemy had managed to "contain the drives of the Ninth and First U.S. Armies without committing any of the four SS panzer divisions of Sixth Panzer Army" that were "held in reserve presumably in the general area west of Cologne." These divisions, 12th Army Group G-2 thought, would be needed by the enemy to hold in the area of Aachen. Sibert offered no suggestion that this panzer force might have been set aside to constitute an offensive force.

As Ultra had told Sibert and other intelligence officers on September

27,[33] the establishment of Sixth Panzer Army had been ordered under the command not of a professional German officer but of General-oberst der Waffen-SS Sepp Dietrich. This was certainly a provocative appointment; Dietrich, a sergeant in World War I, was no student of war but he was something Hitler liked better, a fervent Nazi, and a veteran first of the Brown Shirts and then of the SS. In the Night of the Long Knives in 1934, he had wielded one of the biggest blades. So this new panzer force was being placed under the command of a man notable chiefly for his loyalty to Hitler. Might not the Führer have in mind a special task for this army?

A few days after Sibert's report, General Strong at SHAEF also commented on the Sixth Panzer Army, which, he said, "has been cleverly husbanded and remains uncommitted." His Delphic conclusion expressed at least a bit of concern: "Until this army is committed, we cannot really feel satisfied." Nevertheless, he saw "Rundstedt's problems"[34] as essentially defensive.

On December 11, Colonel Koch at Third Army summarized his thoughts in this fashion: "Although the Allied offensive is destroying weekly a number of German divisions, nevertheless the enemy has been able to maintain a cohesive front without drawing on the bulk of his infantry and Armor reserves, thereby giving him the capability of mounting a spoiling offensive in an effort to unhinge the Allied assault on Festung Deutschland."[35] On December 14, Third Army G-2 added that "Sixth SS Pz Army could constitute the reserve for a single large-scale counterattack against the major Allied threat to the Reich."[36] "Spoiling offensive" . . . "counterattack" . . . Koch showed some concern, but he clearly was not imagining the initiative being seized by the Germans, who had far greater strategic aims in view.

As his association with Monk Dickson had developed, Adolph Rosengarten had become concerned over his boss's habit of taking the ball and running with it[37]—seizing a fresh CX/MSS message from Bletchley Park and carrying it off to show to General Hodges without taking time to give it proper evaluation. In October an embarrassing incident of the sort had occurred, not, as it happened, with Ultra material but with a message in the less-sensitive Pearl category,[38] which consisted of messages from lower-level German formations. According to this intercept, which Dickson rushed to Hodges's van, Field Marshal von Rundstedt had shot an SS colonel, ordered Wehrmacht soldiers to disarm SS units, and had gone on to proclaim himself military governor of Cologne. He had followed this with a radio appeal to the German people, urging them to support him in negotiating an honorable peace with the Allies.

It was certainly sensational, even lurid, news, but after telling Hodges about it, Dickson returned to his radio monitors, who reported that unfortunately the broadcast had come not from Cologne but from Radio Luxembourg, which was a propaganda outlet of General Bradley's 12th Army Group. What Dickson had hurried to tell Hodges was a piece of U.S. disinformation—black propaganda. It was bad luck for the many-sided, sometimes self-contradictory Dickson.

On December 10 the First Army G-2 issued what became, within a limited circle, his celebrated Estimate No. 37. Like everybody else, Dickson bought the Rundstedt appointment at face value, making such observations as that "Rundstedt apparently is accepting defeats in the south rather than compromise his hope of a decisive success in the north." Neither to Monk nor to any other intelligence officer does it appear to have occurred that though the voice was that of the veteran field marshal, the brain and will were Hitler's. But this "decisive success"? What possibility was envisioned here? "It is plain," Dickson said, that the enemy's strategy "in defense of the Reich is based on the exhaustion of our offensive to be followed by an all-out counterattack with armor, between the Roer and the Erft, supported by every weapon he can bring to bear."[39] This counterattack, that is, would take place north of the Ardennes after the Allies had crossed the Roer. Rundstedt, who was obviously "conducting military operations without the benefit of intuition" (unlike Hitler), would probably choose as the focal point the area between Roermond and Schleiden; that is, it would include part of Dempsey's British Second Army front, all of Simpson's U.S. Ninth Army front, and the northern part of Hodges's U.S. First Army front. The blow would not fall on Middleton's "quiet" sector in the Ardennes.

Like everybody else who predicted any sort of German counteroffensive action, Dickson envisioned the attack coming expressly in response to Allied action, not at the weakest part of the Allied line but against "the Allied force judged by the German High Command to be the greatest threat to successful defense of the Reich."

Five days later—December 15—Dickson offered a new thought: "It is possible that a limited scale offensive will be launched for the purpose of achieving a Christmas morale 'victory' for civilian consumption. Many PWs now speak of the coming attack between the 17th and 25th of December..."[40] By selectively reading First Army G-2 assessments, one could have said that they forecast an all-out enemy counteroffensive on December 17 or shortly thereafter. But that was not the way matters were presented to General Hodges; and at no time could he have taken the forecasts to mean that the Ardennes front ought to be strengthened. In fact, on December 13 Hodges took a combat command out of that area and gave it to a corps preparing an attack elsewhere. And, having issued his "limited scale offensive" suggestion of December 15, Monk Dickson, who had enjoyed no time off since the Normandy landings, left the same day for a scheduled short leave in Paris.

The carefree mood at 21st Army Group was similar. General de Guingand, Montgomery's chief of staff, went off for leave in England on December 15, and the same day the field marshal told Eisenhower that unless there was some objection he would like to spend Christmas at home. In an estimate circulated by his headquarters the next day, December 16, Monty declared: "The enemy is at present fighting a defensive campaign on all fronts; his situation is such that he cannot stage major offensive operations. . . . The enemy is in a bad way."[41]

At 5:30 the next afternoon, December 17, SHAEF intelligence released its daily report. Taking up the front sector by sector, in its third paragraph it observed calmly that "a counter offensive has been launched in the German Seventh Army sector along the front in the Eifel . . . on the morning of December 16."

Was Rundstedt up to something?

FOLLOWING THE UNSATISFACTORY conference near Soissons in June, Hitler had removed Rundstedt as Commander in Chief West. One reason was supposed to have been that when the Führer's transcendently sycophantic chief of the high command, Field Marshal Wilhelm Keitel, telephoned him and asked plaintively, "What shall we do?", Rundstedt had replied, "End the war! What else can you do?" Or, as another report had it, "Make peace, you fools!"[42]

But now, on September 1, Hitler had reappointed Rundstedt to the chief command against the Allies. During this same week, the Führer entertained a caller—his long-time and unflagging admirer, Baron Oshima.[43] The course of the war in the west had been a disappointment, Hitler told his guest, because the German effort had been sabotaged by officers who were members of the July 20 conspiracy to assassinate him. It had been necessary to take the decision to withdraw most of the forces to the West Wall, aside from garrison troops in the important ports. But this did not at all mean that the Führer was conceding defeat. "From the beginning," he said, "we have realized that in order to stabilize the lines it would be necessary to launch a German counterattack." This, however, would be only a limited operation, to be carried out by General von Blaskowitz's Army Group G, which was falling back from southern France.

But Hitler had something much larger in mind than this sort of limited-purpose affair. "When the current replenishment of the air forces is completed and when the new army of more than a million men, which is now being organized, is ready, I intend to combine the new units with units to be withdrawn from all possible areas and to open a large-scale offensive in the West."

You could imagine Oshima's eyes popping. "When do you plan to launch such an offensive?"

"After the beginning of November."

Well, the baron said, "the present struggle has developed more and more into a real two-front war and Germany must, therefore, strike a deadly blow at the enemy on one front or the other." But was she in a position to do it? Had she the men and the resources?

Yes, the Führer said, he had planned how it could be done.

This conversation, like Oshima's other interview, was processed by the Magic team at Arlington Hall and passed on to G-2 in the Pentagon. Megalomania? Perhaps, but Hitler's career had been built on doing the unexpected and carrying out the impossible. And the fact that he might not be successful did not mean that he would not try. And why shouldn't he gamble? He had sold all the space he had to sell in the west; the Allies were now at the walls of the Reich itself. Certainly he was thinking on a far different plane from that of "spoiling attacks" to upset Allied plans. He had already made a good beginning, shrewdly appointing Rundstedt to preside over coming events in the west. In a way, the veteran soldier would serve a deceptive purpose: he would take attention away from his very real army just as George Patton had concentrated attention on the nonexistent First U.S. Army Group that he "commanded" in England.

On September 16, twelve days after his talk with Baron Oshima, Hitler interrupted a briefing at Wolf's Lair with a sudden demand for silence. Sitting in this austere citadel deep in the East Prussian pine forest—a strange place of barbed wire and concrete, described by one of his generals as a mixture of monastery and concentration camp—Hitler had earlier been studying a staff report he had ordered some days before. There was an interval of nervous silence. Then the Führer spoke. "I have just made a momentous decision. I shall go over to the counterattack"—he pointed to the map lying on the table before him—"that is to say, here, out of the Ardennes, with the objective . . . Antwerp."[44]

The group at Wolf's Lair was stunned by the scope of the proposed offensive. When the commanders in the field—Rundstedt, Model, and Hasso von Manteuffel—received their instructions some time later, their reaction showed them to be thinking in concert with Allied intelligence officers. "The available forces were far too small for such an extremely ambitious plan," Rundstedt said. Model, commander of Army Group B, agreed. Manteuffel, who would lead the Fifth Panzer Army, one of the three armies allotted to the operation, said that "the forces were not adequate to deliver an offensive on the lines laid down."[45]

Nevertheless, it was to be almost another Pearl Harbor for the Allies. Ultra and Magic had offered clues, indications of what was to come, but no one in power had thought of trying to see the picture through Hitler's paranoiac eyes.

Lt. Col. Edward K. Thompson, air intelligence officer at SHAEF (in civilian life he was an editor of *Life* magazine) put it this way: "More complete coordination of all types of Intelligence" would have the "advantage of providing more than one string for our bow. Our hold on Ultra is tenuous at best and the experience of the Ardennes offensive showed that we had become rather too dependent on having our information served on a platter."[46]

EARLY IN DECEMBER after performing various temporary duties, Langdon Van Norden arrived at Maastricht,[47] in the "appendix" protruding south from the Netherlands between Belgium and Germany, where he took up his assigned post as Ultra adviser to XXIX Tactical Air Command, headquartered in a large monastery. Each of the U.S. field armies had as its aerial partner one of these "Tac" commands, which served as a sort of especially mobile and flexible field artillery, hitting strongpoints, knocking out tanks, and giving in general valuable close support. XXIX Tac, commanded by Brig. Gen. Richard E. Nugent, worked in close touch with Bill Simpson's Ninth Army. The generals worked closely together as well, each of them being present at army headquarters for the morning briefing in which Van Norden participated by reporting Ultra information on the Luftwaffe.

Asleep in his billet on the top floor of a Dutch house a block from the monastery, Van Norden was awakened by Loftus Becker, his counterpart Ultra representative at Ninth Army. Becker said simply, "Lang, something's happening"—it was the opening barrage of Hitler's offensive. There was great concern in Maastricht that day and nonessential people were evacuated to the rear. Van Norden was among those who stayed, though he had a hand grenade with which, if necessary, he could blow up his box of Ultra secrets.

ON DECEMBER 22, when the offensive was six days old, a German lieutenant wrote his sister that "you cannot imagine what exciting days and hours we are living through. It looks as though the Americans cannot hold up our forceful push. Today we overtook a fleeing column and finished them off." It was, he said, "like an exercise. Their endless column arrived, two abreast, bumper to bumper, and every vehicle laden with soldiers. Then we started our concentrated fire from 60 guns and 120 machine guns. It was a most beautiful bloodbath and revenge for the destruction of our homeland . . . the snow must be dyed red with American blood. Victory was never as near as it is now."[48]

But he was wrong. For all the excitement on both sides of the front, the Germans could not reach the Meuse, let alone Antwerp. The Ardennes offensive represented a remarkable use of limited resources, but the lieutenant was not to see the realization of his wish to "push them into the sea, these strutting, boastful apes from the new world."

14

The Russian Fish

WHAT WAS GOING on? The rattle and crackle of small-arms fire echoed from the walls of the old rock quarry several miles out in the Buckinghamshire countryside from Bletchley. Was the local detachment of the Home Guard engaged in a sudden fire fight with German paratroopers who had landed in some kind of desperation late-war sneak attack on England? Machine guns clattered away; hand grenades arched through the air and exploded.

But it was no Home Guard action. Paul Whitaker, Art Levenson, Selmer Norland, and a number of other intelligence types from BP were the ones squeezing the triggers and lobbing the grenades—not at enemy invaders but at the stony walls of the quarry. Shortly before this, Whitaker, for one, had been feeling distinctly unmilitary in the pressured but nonviolent world of BP. An order had come down through channels from London that all U.S. military personnel were to wear leggings, field jackets, and helmets while on duty, whatever the duty was. It was the typical sort of "shape up" directive that military organizations are given to issuing from time to time; "probably," it seemed to Whitaker, "some colonel was sitting at his desk one day and didn't have anything to do, so he issued an order. Here I was working at a desk in the midst of a bunch of Britishers, and so I told Bill Bundy that I was damned if I was going to do any such silly thing as that. I was on night duty when the order came out, and so I just went on wearing my regular uniform. By the time I was back on daylight duty again, I think there had been enough pressure exerted so that the order was rescinded."[1]

Now, however, various kinds of specialists from Bletchley Park were engaged in some distinctly military action. "We had .45s," Whitaker said, "but I never could do anything with them, though I acquired a P-38 I really liked. And I couldn't hold one of our Thompsons on target;

271

it would simply rise right up. But what we concentrated on was the Sten gun. Those things looked like something you could buy in a dime store, and that bolt—when the gun was firing, it was going back and forth in a slot, and one of the first things they warned us about was not to get our fingers caught in it." Some people, it seemed, grasping the stock of the weapon, had had the ends of fingers chopped off by the fast-moving action of this mass-produced British submachine gun. "But," Whitaker said, "it seemed to me a silly thing to leave in there."[2] Others, as they pulled out their mangled fingers, may belatedly have thought so too.

Observing some of the goings-on in the quarry, a regular army officer remarked to a friend that "if they're sending those chaps, the war must really be over."[3]

Some days before the training began, Maj. Bill Edgerton, the Egyptologist who was much admired by Bundy and whose activities had seemed particularly secret, had summoned Whitaker and the others to private and very confidential meetings, one by one. These took place very early in the spring of 1945, in late February or the first days of March. The major had startling information to impart. The Allies were planning a very special operation, he said. A combined British-American team made up of men from all three services was to be sent into Germany to carry out a cryptological intelligence mission; the Allies wanted to find out as much as they could about the workings of German signal intelligence—who the knowlegeable people were and what kind of equipment they used—and they wanted some of this equipment brought back to England.

How did the officers from BP come in? This part was even more startling. The planners had proposed that a group from the Park be flown into Berlin and dropped by parachute into the middle of the city, right next to the cipher center across the street from the Tiergarten. The members of this team would be preceded by paratroopers of the U.S. 101st Airborne Division, who were to seize the building and seal it off. Then would come the turn of the intelligence officers, who would photograph the German equipment, scoop up any of it that seemed of special importance, grab all the likely looking documents, and even, if possible, round up some of the people working in the center.

As all this was going on, a flying tank column was supposed to be smashing its way into the city ("while," Whitaker said, "we poor signal-intelligence suckers were there and the paratroopers were protecting us"[4]). The armored force would then take over and carry the men of the Allied team and their booty and prisoners westward into the sunset. Here was a scheme that made Field Marshal Montgomery's Operation Market-Garden sound like a walk in the country. At the very least, the plan could not succeed without perfect timing; the tank column could not afford to be late even by minutes. Something else about the operation was notable: it was, so far as is known, the only definite plan that called for troops of the Western Allies to engage in any fighting in Berlin—the city that was about to become an East-West storm center.

"Oh, my gosh," Whitaker thought. "Why me?"

II

BY THE TIME the plan for this daring intelligence operation was being drawn up, the Battle of the Bulge was a piece of history. While it was being fought, Ultra was telling Don Bussey and the G-2 section of Seventh Army that the Germans were planning another offensive, for the Alsace front, presumably as a way of taking some pressure off the forces attacking in the Ardennes. Having extended its lines in order to free troops of Patton's Third Army for their great drive to relieve Bastogne, Seventh Army was vulnerable; but, as Bussey reported, in the sector between Saarbrücken and the Rhine, "Ultra provided information necessary for a proper estimate of the situation and preparations to meet the attack when it came." Luftwaffe Enigma messages from the German First Army were "being read consistently, and enemy order of battle and boundaries were thoroughly known." On the basis of this information, General Patch shifted two divisions; when the German attack was launched on January 1, the main effort collapsed completely, although as a result of the weakening of the eastern segment of the front the enemy made some temporary gains in the secondary thrust, in the area of Strasbourg. Without Ultra, Bussey felt, "it seems very doubtful whether the attack would have been repulsed, or whether other sources of information would have given advance warning."[5]

Although the battle in the Ardennes was by now lost, the Germans early in the morning of this same New Year's Day launched an air attack, nicknamed by the pilots "Operation Hermann," against Allied airfields. At Maastricht the Luftwaffe arrived during the morning briefing at Ninth Army headquarters. One fighter swooped low over the old monastery, strafing the whole building, and Generals Simpson and Nugent, along with Langdon Van Norden and everybody else in the session, hit the deck. But Van Norden, who as air Ultra representative had developed a sort of humorously proprietary interest in the dwindling Luftwaffe, said afterward to Loftus Becker, the military representative: "My poor little dog can still bite. Thank God for that!"[6] But he "didn't say it in front of all the generals." Operation Hermann was, however, the literal last gasp of the Luftwaffe; the Germans were running out of aviation fuel and out of pilots. Even the new jet Messerschmitt Me-262, about which the faithful Baron Oshima had informed the Allies by means of Magic, came too late to make any real difference.

III

IN EARLY FEBRUARY, Wing Commander Jim Rose had just moved from Bletchley Park to become deputy director of operational intelligence at the Air Ministry. At this time the Soviet drive from the east was leading Allied planners to look for ways to use their combined bomber force to help the Russian advance; Bomber Harris and some of his associates proposed raids against various cities in eastern Germany to create fresh hordes of refugees that would clog the roads and interfere with the movement of German troops and supplies. Rose learned one day that as part of this activity Bomber Command and the U.S. Eighth Air Force intended to mount a round-the-clock attack on Dresden. Rose was disturbed at this news. He could see "no tactical or strategic point in attacking the only beautiful and unbombed city left in Germany," and since the Russians had asked the Allies to bomb Leipzig but had made no mention of Dresden, he felt that as a target it was "even more irrelevant."[7]

Following up on his concern, he telephoned General Spaatz at his U.S. strategic air headquarters in Normandy to ask just why Dresden was to be bombed. Because, Spaatz said, he had been informed that two panzer divisions that had spearheaded the German offensive in the Ardennes were being transferred to Hungary by way of Dresden. Not so, Rose said; Ultra had supplied him with the complete movement order for those divisions. "They were going nowhere near Dresden," their route actually being through Gera, more than seventy miles to the west.

In that case, Spaatz said, he certainly would not want to bomb Dresden. He would call off the operation if the British agreed.

Rose immediately telephoned Bomber Command at High Wycombe, getting not Bomber Harris but his second in command, Air Marshal Sir Robert Saundby. The air marshal proved less responsive than Spaatz. "I don't care what you say," he told Rose, "we are going to bomb Dresden."

Why? Rose never got a satisfactory answer to the question, which continued to concern him. Ultra, so convincing to him, had failed to be persuasive with Bomber Command. Other considerations obviously were more important. The result was that, bombed in mid-February under weather conditions very favorable to the attackers, the "Florence on the Elbe," as the beautiful little city was once known, suffered what the British air historian Noble Frankland called "a comprehensive disaster greater than anything witnessed in any other European city during the Second World War."[8] Although no exact death toll could be calculated, it was very likely even greater than that caused by the aerial destruction of Hamburg in July–August 1943. Was it a lust for terror bombing that made Bomber Command ignore Ultra and for the Americans to go along? Certainly an outcry arose in the United States and even in Britain, where some people at least had "deluded themselves into thinking of bombing as surgery instead of what it was: an element in nearly total war."[9] The fact was that there was nothing aberrational about the Dresden attack. That only seemed to be the case because the war was obviously in its final stage; the wreaking of such destruction, popular enough earlier in the war, was losing its supporters. Disapproval was a luxury that many felt they could now afford. But it might be said that if you condoned this kind of bombing in 1943, you had little justification for objecting to it in 1945. That was clearly what the Air Staff thought; Jim Rose and his specific Ultra evidence were brushed aside in favor of one more big piece of area bombing.

IV

THE WAR HAD yet one more Ultra mishap to offer.[10] On April 7, Col. Robert S. Allen of Third Army G-2 was investigating captured German installations that, though fairly far forward, were behind U.S. lines. After this mission was completed, Allen, who had finally been briefed on Ultra some months earlier, entrusted himself and his party to another officer who was supposed to know the situation, but this man led the entire group so far into the danger zone that they were seized by a German unit. Fortunately, it was 1945 now, not 1944, and even if the Ultra secret had been divulged, military operations would hardly have been affected. As it was, Allen was soon liberated by advancing U.S. troops. He was never subjected to interrogation.

V

ALTHOUGH PAUL WHITAKER hardly welcomed the news of the proposed intelligence leap into the heart of Berlin, he was thoroughly accustomed to the Army and its ways. "What can you do when you're in the military? You just grit your teeth and go ahead."[11] The fact that nobody at BP was trained or conditioned for such commandoish heroics was simply one of those things.

The team and the operation were both called by the acronym TICOM,[12] standing apparently for Target Identification Committee (or perhaps Technical Intelligence Committee, either designation being conveniently vague). The plan was originally conceived by the British, but when word of it reached General Marshall in Washington he ordered General Eisenhower to see to it that Americans were included on an equal basis. Cryptological cooperation between the two western Allies had flourished increasingly as the war progressed; it was no time now for them to take separate roads. General Marshall certainly had no reluctance to sharing any crypto secrets with the British—and he certainly did not intend for the United States to be left out of any discoveries that anyone was going to make in Germany. There is no reason to believe that, at the time he instructed Eisenhower to deal Americans into the TICOM operation, the Chief of Staff made any suggestion or acknowledgment of any deeper purpose to the mission—that he was expecting the intelligence team to make any startling finds. But, as it turned out, when TICOM cast its net across the Reich, it hauled in a far greater treasure than it had sought.

Although members of TICOM were given a bit of instruction in the use of submachine guns and hand grenades, the authorities never got around to any kind of parachute drill. Detailed aerial photos of the Berlin intelligence complex were produced and studied. It was optimistically taken for granted that, having jumped from their aircraft, the men would reach the ground safely, and once there they would simply walk into the big several-storied building. But then, as preparations were being made, the picture changed. Even though the Soviet advance into Germany stalled at Küstrin, forty miles from Berlin, the rapid advance of the Allies in the west (the Ludendorff bridge at Remagen had been crossed by men of the 9th Armored Division, U.S. First Army, on March 7) earned the Bletchley team a reprieve. The double east-west pressure on the middle of Germany caused the enemy cipher operation to be dispersed north and south; important elements of it came to rest finally at Berchtesgaden, which by Hitler's choice had served as a sort of alternate capital throughout the strange history of the Third Reich.

In the waning days of the war, some Allied strategists and intelligence officers—particularly Americans—feared that Berchtesgaden would become the center of a so-called National Redoubt, where fanatical Nazi troops would hold out either to the disintegration of the Grand Alliance against them or until the final act of this Götterdämmerung. Although an official historian soberly stated that "most Allied intelligence officers discounted the likelihood of any formidable, self-contained fortress in the Alps, mainly because of limited agricultural and industrial resources in the region,"[13] the mountain country could logically be expected to provide the setting for the final actions of the war, even without the self-immolatory efforts of any fervid Nazis drunk on endless tankards of Wagnerian mead. And because Hitler had always spent a great deal of time at his retreat on the 6,400-foot Obersalzberg, the area already possessed its own Reichskanzlei, communications centers, and other facilities. It was in all ways a likely destination for important parts of the cryptological operation.

So, Whitaker said, "they were long gone from Berlin before we reached the Continent."[14] The members of TICOM were hardly rendered unhappy by this development, although by the time the mission was finally laid on the war was spinning out its last few days. The order transferring the TICOM personnel to the Continent was cut on May 3, only four days before the German surrender.

AFTER THE WAR broke out in Europe in 1939, Howard Campaigne, a young math instructor at the University of Minnesota,[15] had become interested in the principles involved in enciphering machines, and within a few months he had designed such a device and sent off drawings of it to the navy. His contribution was acknowledged by Laurance Safford, who thanked him but said that what the navy needed was not machines but people who could perform analysis of cipher systems. The result was that Campaigne took the navy correspondence course in cryptanalysis, did "very well," and received a commission as a lieutenant (jg) two days before Pearl Harbor. In 1942 he began working with others on the problems presented by German naval Enigma. The group benefited from information brought back by liaison persons sent to Bletchley Park.

In 1944, when the navy became aware that the British teams had made substantial progress against the German high-level on-line teleprinter called the Fish, the head of navy cryptanalysis told his top technical expert, Capt. Howard Engstrom, to send a man to join this British effort that held tremendous importance for the future. Engstrom picked Lieutenant Commander Campaigne, who went to work at BP under the eminent mathematician Max Newman, a short, bald, very donnish type from the University of Manchester. Through his hut (dubbed the Newmanry in parallel to the Testery of Major Ralph Tester) passed a variety of experimental electronic counting machines, leading at the end of 1943 to the imposing Colossus, the Fish-breaker.

In 1945, after a year's experience in the Newmanry, Campaigne was assigned to the TICOM team of which Whitaker, Norland, and Levenson were members. Another member of this team was Major Tester. The two groups that had attacked the Fish mathematically and linguistically were well represented in what was, after all, primarily a Fishing trip.

The team was instructed "to proceed to Kaufbeuren, Germany, and return to Paris, France, after approximately thirty (30) days."[16] Another group would probe the secrets of Flensburg, where Hitler's chosen successor, Grand Admiral Dönitz, had established his government. The groups arrived in Paris to begin operations on May 4. On this day troops of the U.S. 3rd Division crossed from Bavaria into Austria and moved through Salzburg and then south to Berchtesgaden without encountering any opposition, although only eighty miles away, around Linz, the enemy was pouring heavy fire on columns of the 11th Armored Division. Farther north, U.S. and Soviet generals were meeting, and at Field Marshal Montgomery's headquarters on Lüneburg Heath, southwest of Hamburg, Admiral von Friedeburg was signing the surrender of all German forces in the Netherlands, northwestern Germany, and Denmark.

The Kaufbeuren team consisted of nine officers, five British and four American, two British other-ranks radio operators and two drivers, U.S. enlisted men. Campaigne and Wing Commander Oscar Oeser were the respective senior officers. Since it was planned for the mission to send out smaller task groups from time to time, each of which might temporarily be joined by other officers, the American and the Briton would each serve as commanding officer. Oeser, who sported a proper RAF mustache, was a Bletchley Park veteran; a Cambridge psychologist and a friend of Winterbotham's, he had joined Hut 3 in the summer of 1940. Other members of the team represented the varied talents to be found at BP. One of the most notable was Maj. Angus McIntosh, who had come to BP from the Tank Corps; a linguistics expert whose specialty was Middle English, he held degrees from Oxford and Harvard. Capt. Lou Stone represented the U.S. Special Branch (and by now American military intelligence presented a more unified picture than previously, G-2 having in December won its long fight to take over the Signal Security Agency from the Signal Corps).

The TICOM cohort spent two nights in Paris and then, on May 6, went on to Heidelberg, staying at the Viktoria Hotel. "It was bleak and bare, but the Schloss Hotel, near the old castle ruins up on the hill, where we took our meals, was the last word in luxury," Whitaker noted in his journal. The team did not linger to enjoy this luxury, however; after breakfast the men piled back into the truck and set off south for Ulm.

While they had slept, Germany had surrendered unconditionally; at 1:41 Central European Time, at Eisenhower's Supreme Headquarters in Reims, Col. Gen. Alfred Jodl and Admiral von Friedeburg, the latter correct but profoundly morose, had signed the capitulation (shortly after affixing his signature to a third such document, at the Soviet-sponsored ceremony in Berlin, the admiral committed suicide), and orders had flashed across the Continent to silence the guns that had begun sounding at 4:45 in the morning on September 1, 1939, when the old German battleship *Schleswig-Holstein* fired a salvo from Danzig harbor on Polish troops in the detested corridor between East Prussia and the rest of Germany. The next day, May 8, would be officially proclaimed V-E Day.

The team's billet at Augsburg was a barrackslike building that had just ceased serving as a Luftwaffe headquarters, and in the basement the Allied officers discovered a *Hauptnachrichtenstelle*—a signals center. The rapidity of the Germans' departure was vividly revealed by the tape dangling from one of the teleprinters. After remarking that there were some Allied units not too far away, it had suddenly ended with the words: "My God, here they are now." On April 24, Whitaker was told, the Americans had appeared so quickly at one installation that the Germans had fled without destroying any equipment, and for two days while American soldiers were working in offices on the ground floor of the building, teleprinters in the basement were still clicking away, spewing out for Wehrmacht use yard after yard of weather information, reports on airfield conditions, details about the movements of various units, and general chitchat.

Next day, the TICOM team headed southwest from Augsburg for the town of Kaufbeuren, which was supposed to be the site of a major Luftwaffe signal intelligence installation. Hungry after several days of eating mostly field rations, they were delighted to come across a first-class American mess, where they had "a fine meal of chicken, mashed potatoes, peas, pineapple and so forth." Fortunately, they had already consumed the dinner before they encountered the colonel who ran the mess—*his* mess, he termed it. The colonel gave Whitaker a memorable chewing-out because, it seemed, the food was prepared primarily for the delectation of the U.S. 6th Army Group commander, General Jacob L. Devers, who might choose to pay a visit to Kaufbeuren some day or other.

When the TICOM team arrived at the airfield, which had formerly been Fliegerhorst Kommandantur A, they found a throng of 15,000 POWs milling about. Pushing their way through the crowds, they reached the objective, which they already knew was Wings 10 and 11 of a huge block of buildings. As they expected, these special sections had been sealed off when the Americans had occupied Kaufbeuren the previous week; a young lieutenant and a squad of GIs were keeping watch. In Wing 10 the men who had worked on Fish were fascinated to see masses of *Geheimschreiber* machines—this was indeed the original Fish—but their pleasure was limited: the machines were smashed up and their cipher wheels were gone. The *Geheimschreiber*, the T-52, made by the famous Siemens Company, was in fact the crowning achievement of the German efforts to create a secure encryption system. The word literally, and appropriately, means "secret writer."

On May 10 the team was rejoined by Major Tester, who had left it at Ausburg to go off on a special mission. He was accompanied by two Americans, a Major Eldridge and a Captain Forminiak. A quiet, down-to-earth Bletchley veteran, Tester had finally seen the other side of the hill. In 1942 he and others in the Testery had begun working on ways to solve the Fish problem—primitive ways they soon came to seem, pen-and-paper methods. Now he had just returned from a town called Pfunds, in Alpine country on the Inn River about forty miles southwest of Innsbruck, almost on the Swiss border. In that area in recent days, the war had not really come to a halt, it had simply unraveled. The Nineteenth Army of General Ernst Brandenberger was waiting to be disarmed and otherwise to complete its surrender. The Germans had been sitting patiently, still armed, their own officers in command.

The Allied officers were greeted and shown into a communications center where equipment was being inventoried and carefully stored, and there, along with Enigmas and other devices, was a *Geheimschreiber* in perfect working order—a late model of the Fish that Tester had been single-mindedly trying to land three years earlier. At last! When the Allied officers departed, the Fish, as well as an Enigma and other machines, departed with them.

That little side trip had been a great success. Campaigne was impressed by the German—the "authentic"—Fish.[18] More compact than the British-built version, which was "all spread out," as Campaigne said, the German original came in a rugged package about twenty-four inches high and thirty inches across. For a time Campaigne gazed at the machine, with its line of protruding wheels, in sheer wonder.

The next morning the TICOM team took over a small room in the Kaufbeuren town Rathaus to interrogate local people who had worked at the Fliegerhorst, the purpose being to elicit physical description of the men who had been their superiors; the search for them would be left to other military organizations.

That afternoon the team drove northeast to Munich, where Paul Whitaker had spent two years of his youth, and stopped for the night. "I knew Munich very well, of course," Whitaker said. "I took several pictures, standing in the midst of all the rubble, but I hadn't the slightest idea where I was. I just thought of what I was doing as making a kind of record of the mess I saw. It was only after I got back to England and developed the film that I discovered I'd been standing right at one of the main squares, where I'd been a hundred times. I didn't even recognize it. But in one of the pictures I saw the Frauenkirche—it's sort of the trademark of Munich, the twin towers with rounded tops—and by figuring back to where I had taken the picture, I knew exactly where I'd been standing."[19] Not long after Whitaker made his pictorial record, an impression of this same wasteland would be preserved in sound. One of Munich's greatest native sons, Richard Strauss, now an old man, brooding over the rubble, would be moved to work a minor-key in-memoriam section into his "commemorative waltz" called simply *München*.

The next day the TICOM team reached Berchtesgaden where they were billeted in the guest house of a sizable estate. Directly across the river was the mountain on which Allied officers could see the battered ruins of Adolf Hitler's Berghof. But this suburban living did not last long; Oscar Oeser, who had separated from the team at Kaufbeuren, arrived with news that the group had been booked into the Deutsches Haus hotel, which had been requisitioned by the Americans. Even though not much was left of the Berghof above ground, a visit to it revealed a "veritable maze of passages beneath and all around it, with provisions for months and months—hospital, dental clinic, huge stocks of wines and so forth." Perhaps the National Redoubt idea had not been merely the figment of overexcited or overcredulous OSS officers' brains. Inspection of the Reichskanzlei, on the outskirts of Berchtesgaden, revealed a similar picture. "We went deep down into the underground rooms, over a hundred feet below the surface. Everything was painted white, somewhat hospital-like; there was an emergency power station, sitting rooms, a telephone exchange, kitchen, baths, files of various kinds."[20]

A U.S. officer had arrived with a convoy of German signals trucks. These diesel trucks, driven by German drivers under the command of an *Oberleutnant,* were to carry the equipment that had been discovered to a port where it would be loaded onto a ship to be taken to England. The cargo consisted of four portable wireless teleprinter stations—Fish machines. This haul would appear to have been the great catch that TICOM was expected to make. Tester and Levenson were to accompany the equipment to England; in Germany, they would merely be passengers, serving chiefly to arrange passage for the trucks through the various military zones.

Then came May 21, a day that, most regrettably, Ralph Tester had to miss. To those devoted to cryptanalysis it possesses something of the quality of the moment in 1922 when Howard Carter, chiseling through the door of Tutankhamen's tomb, reported to the breathless Lord Caernarvon that through the aperture he had made he could see "wonderful things." On the morning of the 21st a party of seven left Berchtesgaden for Rosenheim, where Campaigne, Capt. Edward Rushworth of British intelligence, and Tom Carter, a U.S. officer who had joined the group, were to question an OKW-*Chi* (intelligence department of the High Command of the Armed Forces) cryptographer. Whitaker, Norland, and two British officers who were likewise newcomers to the team, Pickering and Cockrell, were to continue on in search of various wanted persons. (Pickering quickly proved a notable addition to the group, because of his marvelous Hitler act. One evening, with a lock of hair pulled over his face, he harangued the staff of a hotel with a Führer-style monologue—to such effect, Levenson said, that "they were ready to follow him anywhere.")

In the evening, after a fruitless search, Whitaker's group returned to Berchtesgaden. Here they found the rest of the TICOM team seething with excitement. A soldier had come to Campaigne, Rushworth, and Carter while they were at Rosenheim, with a message that some prisoners in the cage nearby wished to speak with the "proper people."

These prisoners had served at OKW-*Chi* headquarters. What they were burning to tell the "proper people" was that, fearing the advance of the Russians, they had buried a great mass of cipher equipment under the cobblestones in front of their headquarters. They were sure that this equipment would be of the greatest interest to the Western Allies and to the Russians, because by means of it the Germans could read Red Army signals—and not just any signals, but the most secret ones. It seemed that the Russians would split the message being sent into nine elements, transmitting it on nine different channels, and this German equipment could reintegrate it; having developed this capacity, the Germans had then succeeded in decrypting Russian traffic. The prisoners who were pouring out this news to Campaigne, Rushworth, and Carter had no way of knowing two facts: *a)* the western Allies very much wished to obtain information about the nature and significance of various Soviet troop movements in Germany, information which even then the Soviets were bluntly refusing to provide; and *b)*, the Allies had no capacity to decrypt this Soviet radio traffic. It was a momentous discovery, more of one, perhaps, than the TICOM team realized at the moment; "iron curtain" and "cold war" had not yet entered the language. Certainly the Germans' viewpoint was clear. Already, just two weeks after the surrender had been signed at Reims, the prisoners in their cage were hailing their American and British captors as comrades, men who must see the need to make common cause with them against the Russian hordes. They were eager to dig up the buried equipment and demonstrate its wonders to the TICOM team.

It was an offer the team could not refuse. The next day Campaigne's group returned to Rosenheim to supervise the recovery and sorting out of the equipment, and on May 23 Whitaker joined Campaigne and Carter on the sortie to Rosenheim. By the time the team arrived, "a little twenty-year-old German sergeant had the group well under control and working like beavers. They had one of the sets all set up and receiving traffic."[21] On studying and analyzing their find, the TICOM team realized that what they had been presented with was nothing less than a system that received and decrypted the Soviet equivalent of the German Fish traffic. And the Soviets, it was obvious, had no inkling that the Germans had developed this capacity. Nor could they know that the Western Allies had now inherited it. TICOM had made itself into a truly Top Secret operation.

The Germans "had put the equipment together down in the basement of part of this barracks complex. They were intercepting Russian traffic right while we were there. And pretty soon they had shown us all we needed to see."[22] The Allied team ordered the prisoners to dismantle the setup and return it to its crates along with the rest of the equipment. In sheer bulk the treasure was phenomenal. It filled twelve huge chests weighing more than 600 pounds each, fifty-three chests weighing about 100 pounds each, and about fifty more weighing 50 pounds each—some seven and a half tons altogether. It filled four large German trucks to capacity.

Rushworth and Norland were assigned to accompany the equipment and some of the technicians to England, where a highly select audience would see a demonstration. One wonders what General Marshall thought when he received word of this remarkable convoy.

He never put his thoughts about it on paper, and he died fifteen years before the existence of Ultra would even have been confided to his official biographer. TICOM and its amazing secret have remained unknown till this day.

On June 2 Whitaker was ordered to take six of the OKW-*Chi* prisoners to the Albrechtstrasse jail in Wiesbaden, where they were to be confined until official papers came through authorizing their being taken to England. "Those boys," Whitaker said, "were very down-hearted at being left in a prison after what they had done."[23] He assured them that their stay at Albrechtstrasse would only be temporary, and a week later they were flown to England, where the equipment was set up at an installation about twenty miles from Bletchley. It appears to have been put to work by the Allies immediately.

When Whitaker had arrived with his six prisoners at Wiesbaden on June 3, he discovered that the jail was housing a notable inmate, Julius Streicher, one-time editor of the newspaper *Der Stürmer,* a publica-tion so brutal and obscene that it had even disgusted some of the Nazis; Streicher was being kept in the prison pending the establishment of a procedure for dealing with war criminals. One of the guards asked Whitaker whether he would like to have a look at their notable guest; he indicated a small peephole. "I looked in and he was sitting there on his cot, with his head in his hands." As well Streicher might; he was to be hanged at Nuremberg.

It was a suitable farewell for the American to bid to Nazi Germany, which he had known in embryo, in triumph, and in utter desolation; its twelve-year life, now ended, would not have been believable had it not been fact.

For the teams at Bletchley Park there were no more intercepts from the Enigma and the Fish to decrypt and translate and put into the hands of forces fighting in the field. The Allied secret cipher army had waged a cooperative campaign successful beyond parallel and, in so doing, had won a victory that was no less great for being known only to a few. Three decades later, when the Ultra secret began to become public knowledge, it would be hard to believe.

Did the Allies really break the German code?

They did much more than that. It was not a question just of "a code." It was a way of encrypting, and messages had to be attacked anew every day. But the decrypters were consistently successful.

Well, if they were reading all those German messages, why wasn't the war over sooner?

A clever historian has supplied the definitive answer: It was.[24]

Epilogue

DID ULTRA WIN the war?

Nobody would make that claim. Men carrying rifles, driving tanks, fighting off U-boats, aiming bombs—these were the war winners: soldiers, sailors, fliers. But put the question a little differently. Did Ultra change the shape of the war? Even further, did Ultra keep the war from being lost? To each of these questions a distinct yes is possible.

Without Ultra, the German historian Andreas Hillgruber has said, the invasion of Normandy would have come later and the Russians would have advanced farther west. William Bundy has gone further than that: without Ultra, "the chances of any second front whatever would have been small."[1] If that is so, not only the length of the war but the look of the map of Europe afterward becomes a point to ponder.

Although granting that Ultra played only a small part in the great and pivotal air battle of Britain in 1940, an American historian, Harold Deutsch, has suggested that even a small part was important; here, when the outcome may well have been in the balance, Ultra took "a first step toward the eventual victory of the Grand Alliance."[2] A larger role was developing in another dimension; many who were involved with Ultra maintain that in the Battle of the Atlantic, the fight for the Allied lifeline, the work of the cryptanalytic teams was decisive. Deutsch cautiously says that "it appears at least plausible that this will be the ultimate verdict";[3] Don Bussey, whose involvement with the subject has continued through the years, holds the same view, and more strongly.[4] So, if the loss of the Battle of the Atlantic would have meant loss of the war, or at least the inability of the United States to win it, then Ultra has its own clear claim to primacy. And when to this point is added its influence in Normandy, both before the landings and afterward, you begin to wonder, very deeply, just how the war against

285

Hitler would have gone without the work of Bletchley Park and the supporting contributions of American Magic and Op-20-G. And if the generals had been listening at Arnhem and the Ardennes, the record would be even richer.

Quite apart from the Battle of Britain and the Battle of the Atlantic and Overlord, the work of Ultra, as this book has shown, was pervasive. As an incorruptible spy who said absolutely nothing for effect, Ultra provided a perfect check on other kinds of intelligence. It furnished information whereby the British could bag German human agents as they landed in England, making it possible for these spies to be turned against their Abwehr masters. Its battlefield importance was consistently high, as in the Cotentin, at Mortain, and in the New Year's Day 1945 attack in Lorraine. Ultra saved lives, both by means of tactical information—as in the example of the warnings to the 82nd and the 101st Airborne Divisions in the Cotentin peninsula—and through its overall shortening of the war.

It was, said Air Marshal Sir John Slessor, a "gift from the gods."[5]

Winston Churchill, perhaps speaking of intelligence in general but certainly giving prominent place to Ultra—whose leading supporter he was—declared: "We owe to the arm of General Menzies that we won the war."[6]

The deeds of Ultra and the testimonials they earned could make up a very long catalogue. Overall, no one would say that Patrick Beesly of the U-boat Tracking Room had overstated the case: "Ultra was *a* war winner" even if not "*the* war winner."[7] Many commentators would not stop there.

AS THE PRESENT author has observed to Group Captain Winterbotham, "Like a good many other persons, I shall never forget the stir made by *The Ultra Secret* when it appeared in 1974 . . . I cannot think of any other area of modern history in which a single book had so striking an effect." It actually amounted to an explosion in the world dwelt in by American and British students of World War II.

Yet the very fact of this great impact suggests a deficiency in these same students. Already, in 1973, two books had appeared that in very different ways lifted the lid on the secret. One was Gustave Bertrand's *Enigma*, which was a thorough and explicit story of the assault on the German enciphering machine as seen from the French side. That, apparently, was its great weakness; it was not in English and so it caused no stir in Britain or the United States. The reception of the other book suggests a different sort of cultural limitation; *The Infernal Grove*, a volume in Malcolm Muggeridge's autobiographical series, was unmistakably in English, some of it quite beguiling English, but Muggeridge was thought to be literary, not military-historical, and the story covered several periods of his life; hence his account of people at Bletchley Park reading high-level German cipher messages did not attract students of the subject—although the fact that Muggeridge adopts as his storytelling manner a jaded air, making it seem that no one he knows or nothing he encounters possesses much real importance, may have acted as a smoke screen, keeping even historically minded readers from sensing that they were being told something significant.

In earlier years Polish publications had contained some Enigma revelations, but if books in French and even English were ignored, journal articles in Polish had little chance of making even a ripple.

Actually, the vault had been opened on Ultra in 1969, in a conversation between "a distinguished military man"[8] and the British writer Anthony Cave Brown. For whatever reason, Cave Brown was told that the British and the Americans had been reading "German and Japanese command ciphers for the better part of the war." The Japanese side of it was no secret, of course; but German? This was a revelation. The "military man" was Brig. Gen. Edwin L. Sibert, who had been Omar Bradley's G-2. But with the agreement though not the active help of the British authorities, Winterbotham's book was rushed out before Cave Brown's *Bodyguard of Lies* could make its appearance, and thus the secret was secret from the public no longer.

A continuing mystery is how secret Ultra was from the Russians. They received the benefit of Enigma intercepts from the Western Allies, the intelligence being relayed to them through a mission in Moscow directed by the noted writer Edward Crankshaw. But the secret itself was deemed too precious to be shared directly; the source of the intelligence was disguised, just as it was to most British and American recipients. Security was the dominant consideration here. The Western Allies did not even have the sort of communication with the Soviets that made it possible to discuss such points in any reasonable fashion. And, apart from any other factor, Soviet signal security was worse than questionable. Besides, who knew what Stalin might decide to do tomorrow? No one should be surprised that the British authorities judged the risk far too great for any conceivable benefit, especially since information that was of use to the Russians was given them. But, through their penetration of British intelligence, did the Russians perhaps know the secret anyway? The finger has been pointed at Kim Philby. If Philby knew it, presumably he revealed it. He was cleared for Abwehr Enigma. But in the compartmented world of intelligence, exactly what else did he know? No one in the West now can be sure.

The Americans who took part in the Ultra operation—whether in Washington or in Europe, army or navy, as codebreakers, translators, advisers, or special security officers, Bundy's men or Taylor's—are uniformly proud of having kept silence all through the years, not only publicly but with family members and associates. That was the way it was supposed to be and that was the way it was. When the book was opened, they say, it was opened by the British; none of the Ultra Americans talked. This is perfectly true, but when you consider General Sibert's involvement the revelation, like the story, becomes an Anglo-American affair.

The ending of the secrecy has left a number of the Americans quite displeased. You can find one of these men in a small, comfortable house tucked behind a shopping center in Sarasota. The dean of American cryptanalysts, Frank Rowlett, a widower, lives simply. He greets you on the porch, not only looking exactly like Burl Ives but, astonishingly, speaking with the same gentle, pleasing quality. When Rowlett meets you, your thoughts immediately go back to 1930 and the beginning of the U.S. Signal Intelligence Service—and yet, here it is in the flesh, shaking your hand, all these years later. Inside the house you see ordinary items like coffee tables and a Barcalounger, but more important are densely packed bookshelves and what looks to a novice like a computerized command center, with screen and keyboard and printer and various extra devices, spreading along two walls.

Speaking of the work on Magic and how secret it was, Rowlett recalls the Pearl Harbor hearings after the war. When all secrecy was blown sky-high and the codebreakers were thrust into the spotlight for the first time, it was profoundly shocking for "some of us who had kept those secrets for so long."[9] He still feels "hypersensitive" about secrets, he says, and when he speaks to you about intelligence he considers his words very carefully. The Ultra secret, he believes, would have been best left untold. He will be wonderfully cooperative with you, but he will be careful, too.

In his own way, living in his very different world, Langdon Van Norden also deplores the revelation of Ultra. Churchill once described a visit to Roosevelt as having the same effect as opening a bottle of champagne. Welcoming you in the courtyard of his large house on one of the wooded roads of Greenwich, Connecticut, Van Norden is like that—exuding a sense of genuine cheer and well-being, a delightful sparkle. He was of the establishment before he went to the war, and he rose high in it afterward, serving for many years as president of the Metropolitan Opera Guild and later chairman of the Metropolitan

Opera Association. Ultra is now public knowledge, and so he will talk about it. He speaks in detail and amusingly about his experiences.

They are an impressive group, these American alumni of Bletchley Park. Lewis Powell, who as a justice of the U.S. Supreme Court receives you in his unostentatious summer chambers in Richmond, Virginia, gives you a thoughtful account, with notes, of his association with the Special Branch. Ed Kellogg during the latter part of the war moved from Bletchley Park to serve as Ultra adviser to Ambassador Jefferson Caffery in Paris and later became an assistant to Ambassador Robert Murphy on the Allied Control Council for Berlin (where at one function he saw Marlene Dietrich, whose mother was in the Soviet zone, practicing a bit of personal diplomacy by perching on the knee of a Russian general); sitting now in his old Vermont house in the village of Pomfret, Kellogg reflects on those days and on his great admiration for the British at Bletchley Park; after the war, Kellogg went on to a notable career in the diplomatic service, finishing as U.S. consul general in Dusseldorf (and, ipso facto, the busiest American diplomatic official in West Germany). Don Bussey, incisive and very thorough, is retired in Carlisle, Pennsylvania, near Carlisle Barracks and its military history collection. Telford Taylor's New York-based career as lawyer, author, and teacher is well known. Melvin Helfers is cozily retired near his alma mater, the Citadel. Adolph Rosengarten presides over a Main Line spread of mansion and gardens that gives fresh shine to the word "baronial" . . . These are only a few. The list of Alfred McCormack's recruits is a long one indeed, and their postwar achievements are impressive if not at all surprising. What else would you expect?

Of the original Signal Intelligence Service group, Abe Sinkov and Solomon Kullback have, like Frank Rowlett, chosen warm climates for retirement.

The men who came to Arlington Hall during the war went on to varied careers, Lou Smadbeck, for one, becoming a real estate tycoon in New York. But a number of them were attracted by the idea of continuing their careers in intelligence. Bill Bundy, having survived the fantastic charge by Senator Joseph McCarthy that he was a security risk (he had contributed to a defense fund for another member of the establishment, Alger Hiss), went on to rise high in the CIA before becoming an Assistant Secretary of State and later editor of *Foreign Affairs*. Selmer Norland and Art Levenson continued in the world of signal intelligence with the new National Security Agency, from which both have retired after long careers. As Norland still sees it, the work in intelligence at Bletchley was the most fascinating and exciting part of his life; it left him ready for more.

Paul Whitaker was given the same kind of opportunity. As he was being processed for discharge at the end of the war, he was asked—by Frank Rowlett, as he recalls it—whether he wished to stay on instead of returning to his professorship. The agency would like to have him.

But Whitaker declined. Remembering, he shakes his head—no, no: "I'd had all of that crap I wanted."[10]

Notes

Page numbers from books marked in the Sources with an asterisk are from book club editions whose pagination may be different from that in the original publication.

PROLOGUE—Assignment: "Something Special"

1. The description of the arrival at the Government Code and Cipher School is based on the author's interview with Whitaker of June 10, 1982, with added details from Levenson, December 30, 1983, and Norland, May 14, 1984. The personal information about Whitaker is from various interviews with him.
2. Whitaker.
3. Ibid.

1. Four Young Men

The description of the events of April 1, 1930, and the following days and of Frank Rowlett's background is based on the author's interview with Rowlett, December 27, 1983.

1. Rowlett's self-description.
2. Stock index figures are from *The New York Times,* April 1, 1930, September 4, 1929, and November 14, 1929.
3. *The New York Times,* April 1, 1930.
4. Quoted in Frederick Lewis Allen, *Only Yesterday* (New York: Harper, 1931), 340.
5. Goronwy Rees, *The Great Slump* (New York: Harper & Row, 1970), 86.
6. R. Ernest and Revor N. Dupuy, *The Encyclopedia of Military History* (New York: Harper & Row, 1970), 990.
7. Yardley, *American Black Chamber,* 219.
8. Abraham Sinkov interview, February 25, 1984.
9. Unfortunately for legend, Stimson made this famous remark later, not at the time of his action. McGeorge Bundy to the author, June 7, 1984.

10. Stimson and Bundy, *Active Service,* 454.
11. SRH-038, "Papers Pertaining to Herbert O. Yardley."
12. Ibid.
13. Friedman's background is described in many sources, e.g., Callimahos, "Legendary Friedman"; Kahn, *The Codebreakers*; and Clark, *The Man Who Broke Purple.* Chronological data are to be found in *Who Was Who in America* (1969-1973).
14. SRH-038, "Papers Pertaining to Herbert O. Yardley."
15. Arthur Levenson interview, February 28, 1984.
16. Sinkov interview, February 25, 1984.
17. Ibid.
18. Ibid.
19. Hannah, "Rowlett—Personal Profile," 7.
20. Ibid, 8.
21. This account from Rowlett, December 27, 1983 and March 22, 1984.
22. Sinkov interview, February 25, 1984.
23. The following conversation was reported by Rowlett.
24. The discussion of the 1930-32 period is based on Rowlett and Sinkov; also on Friedman, in SRH-029, "History of Signal Intelligence Service," and SRH-134, "Expansion of Signal Intelligence Service" and on Hannah.

2.   Enigma with Red and Purple

1. Memorandum by Rowlett to author, February 16, 1984.
2. Rowlett interview, December 27, 1983.
3. On this point see, for example, the testimony of Capt. Edwin T. Layton in *Pearl Harbor Attack (PHA),* 79th Cong., 1st sess., pt. 10: 4861.
4. Rowlett interviews, December 27, 1983, and March 22, 1984; and letter to the author, March 11, 1984.
5. Hannah, "Rowlett—Personal Profile," 14.
6. Rowlett interview, December 27, 1983. Previous accounts (e.g., Farago, *Broken Seal*) have credited the navy with breaking the Red machine. The navy's success, however, was enjoyed with the similar naval attaché cipher machine (see Safford in SRH-149).
7. Sinkov, interview with author, February 25, 1984.
8. Ibid.

9. Rejewski's background is recounted in Christopher Kasparek and Richard A. Woytak, "In Memoriam Marian Rejewski," (MAR-yahn Ray-EFF-ski), *Cryptologia* (January 1982), 19–25; and in Kozaczuk, *Enigma*.
10. Bertrand, *Enigma*, 24–25.
11. The Enigma machine is described in various sources; the author has also personally examined a machine. The figures given on the following pages are Rejewski's own, from Kozaczuk, *Enigma*, Appendix D.
12. The naming of the *bomba* is described in Kozaczuk, *Enigma*, 63, note 1. Polish problems at the time are discussed by Rejewski in a letter of October 26, 1978, to Richard Woytak (Kozaczuk, *Enigma*, Appendix B, 237).
13. Richard Woytak, "The Origins of the Ultra-Secret Code," *The Polish Review*, XXIII (1978): 84.
14. The dinner is described by Fitzgerald, *The Knox Brothers*, 234.
15. Bertrand, *Enigma*, 59.
16. Fitzgerald, *The Knox Brothers*, 234.
17. Ibid.
18. Rejewski in Kozaczuk, *Enigma*, Appendix D, 269.
19. *PHA*, 79th Cong., 1st sess., pt. 8: 3556.
20. Safford, 14.
21. Rowlett memorandum.
22. Friedman, SRH-159, "Solution of 'B' Machine."
23. The basis for this description of Friedman's mental state is provided by Rowlett. Many other persons and sources mention various aspects of Friedman's mental difficulties.
24. Hannah, "Rowlett—Personal Profile," 5.
25. Rowlett interview, December 27, 1983. Many previous accounts have credited Harry L. Clark with the idea of using switches instead of rotors; he is supposed to have said something like "What if those monkeys are using stepping switches instead of rotors?" However, Rowlett insists that Rosen, an electrical engineer from MIT, was the key person here.
26. Rowlett interview, December 27, 1983.
27. Some accounts credit the director of naval intelligence with applying the name "Magic" to the decrypts; Rowlett, however, recalls it as described here.
28. Safford, 13.
29. Stimson and Bundy, *Active Service*, 454.

3. Courtship

1. Smith, *The Shadow Warriors,* 37.
2. Snow, *Science and Government,* 39.
3. Ibid.
4. General Mauborgne's background from the program of a testimonial dinner for the general, Officers Club, Governors Island, N.Y., October 25, 1941 (courtesy of Frank Rowlett).
5. Clark, *Tizard,* 266.
6. Among those who do is Sinkov (interview).
7. Watson, *Chief of Staff,* 114.
8. André Morize, *France Été 1940* (New York: Éditions de la Maison Française, Inc., 1941).
9. Watson, *Chief of Staff,* 109.
10. Ibid., 114.
11. Ibid., 115.
12. Lee, *London Journal,* 61.
13. The comment was made by Laurance Safford in "Rhapsody in Purple, Part I," *Cryptologia* (July 1982), n. 193-228.
14. Sherwood, *Roosevelt and Hopkins,* 246.
15. The account of the Americans' mission is based on Sinkov interviews.
16. Sinkov interview, February 25, 1984.
17. Rowlett interview, December 27, 1983.
18. Sinkov interview, February 25, 1984.
19. This view is from an interview with Walter Fried, March 11, 1984.
20. Ibid.
21. Ibid.
22. Sinkov interview, February 25, 1984.
23. Lee, *London Journal,* 85.
24. Sinkov interview, February 25, 1984.
25. Ibid.
26. Ibid.
27. Some persons have speculated that Lord Halifax himself, in one of his last actions as foreign secretary, forbade the transfer of an Enigma to the Americans (although the Foreign Office normally played little part in the activities of the SIS).
28. Rowlett interview, December 27, 1983.
29. This point is made by Rowlett.
30. Sinkov interview, February 25, 1984.
31. Many stories have been circulated about the bounty with which the American team arrived in England; it is said to have included more than one Purple machine, Red machines, and numerous

codes and keys (see, e.g., Farago, *The Broken Seal,* 249-50, and "Rhapsody in Purple"). However, Sinkov asserts (March 29, 1984) that he and his associates delivered only a single Purple machine; this memory is supported by Rowlett.

32. *PHA,* 79th Cong., 1st sess., pt. 4: 1861.
33. Ibid., 1862.
34. Ibid.
35. Ibid., 1863.
36. Whaley, *Codeword BARBAROSSA,* 40.
37. Farago states categorically that Welles showed Magic material to Oumansky, making no attempt to disguise it, but adduces no source, saying that his informants insisted on anonymity. Farago, *The Broken Seal,* 192.
38. This calculation is made by Whaley, *Codeword BARBAROSSA,* 5.
39. U.S. Dept. of Defense, *"Magic" Background,* vol. 1, 22.
40. *PHA,* 79th Cong., 1st sess., pt. 11: 5475.
41. Rowlett memorandum.
42. *Report,* 182.
43. Ibid., 191.
44. Ibid., 193.
45. Ibid., 196.
46. Ibid., 204.
47. Ibid., 184.
48. *PHA,* 79th Cong., 1st sess., pt. 2: 911.
49. Ibid.
50. Ibid., 911-12.
51. The handling of the fourteenth part is from *Report,* 221.
52. *PHA,* 79th Cong., 1st sess., pt. 12: 245.
53. Ibid., pt. 11: 5273-74 (testimony of Rear Adm. John R. Beardall).
54. Ibid., pt. 12: 249.
55. Ibid., pt. 12: 248.
56. *Report,* 222 (testimony of Gen. George C. Marshall).
57. Ibid., 224.
58. The near-incredible handling of the message is from *Report,* 225. The time of delivery of General Marshall's telegram is from Farago, 401 (reexpressed in EST), from the letter of George Street. This evidence seems more likely than the time given in *Report,* 225.

4. The Purloined Pindar

1. The account of the development and demise of Arlington Hall is from Frances Jennings, interview with author, October 19, 1983.

2. Terrett, *Signal Corps: Emergency,* 72.
3. SRH-134, "Expansion of Signal Intelligence Service," 15.
4. Ibid., 21.
5. Ibid., 26.
6. Rear Adm. Joseph N. Wenger, SRH-197, "U.S. Navy Communication Intelligence."
7. Ibid.
8. Thompson, et al., *Signal Corps: Test,* 204.
9. Walter M. Whitehill, quoted in Lewin, *American Magic,* 133.
10. Details from SRH-152, "Historical Review of Op-20-G," 1-2.
11. Van Der Rhoer, *Deadly Magic,* 118-19.
12. Rowlett interview, December 27, 1983, and Clarke interview, July 24, 1984.
13. SRH-035, "History of Special Branch," 5.
14. Stimson and Bundy, *Active Service,* 342.
15. SRH-035, "History of Special Branch," 5.
16. Taylor interview, November 10, 1983.
17. Van Norden interview, August 1, 1984.
18. SRH-035, "History of Special Branch," 7.
19. SRH-185, "War Experience," 31-32. Although this document is considered to be of anonymous authorship—since it came from McCormack's files with no name attached—it contains changes and corrections by McCormack in his handwriting, and in style and tone it is typical of his work; hence the overwhelming likelihood, the author believes, is that he was in fact the original drafter of it.
20. SRH-035, "History of Special Branch," 7.
21. Ibid., 7-8.
22. Ibid.
23. Taylor interview, November 10, 1983.
24. SRH-035, "History of Special Branch," 11.
25. Ibid., 19.
26. Ibid., 12.
27. SRH-185, "War Experience," 7.
28. Truman Smith, *Berlin Alert,* 38.
29. Levenson interview, December 30, 1983.
30. SRH-029, "History of SIS," 14.
31. Callimahos, "Legendary Friedman," 2.
32. John Bryden interview, October 12, 1983.
33. Friedman to Edgerton, February 18, 1942, letter in the W. F. Friedman Papers, GCM.

34. William P. Bundy interview, November 30, 1983.
35. Background of Callimahos and quotations from his article "Legendary Friedman," 2–4.
36. Walter Fried interview, March 11, 1984.
37. Whitaker interview, September 1, 1981.

5.   To the Altar

1. SRH-116, "Problems of Special Branch," 43.
2. SRH-185, "War Experience," 6.
3. Ibid., 5.
4. Clarke interview, October 17, 1984.
5. Ibid.
6. SRH-185, "War Experience," 5.
7. Clarke interview, July 24, 1984.
8. Ted Hilles, SRH-110, "Military Intelligence," 36.
9. Clarke interview, July 24, 1984.
10. The theme of golf occurs frequently in Denniston's correspondence with Friedman, W. F. Friedman Papers, GCM. The quotations here are from Denniston to Friedman, October 4, 1943.
11. John M. Seaman interview, March 29, 1984.
12. This summary of the reasons for SIS's wanting "much more" owes much to Rowlett, December 27, 1983.
13. Hinsley, et al., *British Intelligence,* 2: 56, suggests this concern.
14. Quoted in Lewin, *American Magic,* 118.
15. SRH-110, "Military Intelligence," 10. The tenor of the discussions was described by Clarke, November 19, 1984.
16. Provisions of the U.S.-British agreement from SRH-110, "Military Intelligence," 39ff.
17. Taylor interview, November 10, 1983.
18. SRH-035, "History of Special Branch," 20.
19. SRH-185, "War Experience," 10.
20. The Yellow briefing and related details were described by Bundy, November 30, 1983, and August 8, 1984: in Whitaker's files.
21. Quotations from orders: SPSIS 311.5-Gen., Headquarters, Arlington Hall Station, Office of the Commanding Officer.
22. Murrow radio broadcast of July 11, 1943; quoted in his book *In Search of Light,* 65.
23. John Craig, *In Council Rooms Apart* (New York: Putnam, 1971; Paperback Library, 1972), 8.

24. Whitaker interview, June 10, 1982.
25. Norland interview, May 14, 1984.
26. Whitaker diary.
27. Ingersoll, *Top Secret,* 19.
28. Orders for Levenson, Norland, and Whitaker: AG 210.453, HQ SOS ETOUSA, 28 Aug 1943: in Whitaker's files.
29. Information on Miss Judge from Norland interview, May 14, 1984.
30. Landis Gores, "Princetonians in the Ultra Service," *Princeton Alumni Weekly,* May 27, 1975, 12.
31. Seaman interview, March 29, 1984.
32. Norland interview, October 26, 1984.
33. The scene in Welchman's office was described by him in interviews, November 14, 1983, and August 7, 1984; it is also referred to in Welchman, *The Hut 6 Story,* 135.

6.   "A Complete Meritocracy"

1. Innes (J. I. M. Stewart), introductory note to *Seven Suspects* (New York: Dodd, Mead, 1937).
2. Background information on the creation of the Government Code and Cipher School from Hinsley et al., *British Intelligence,* 1: chapter 1.
3. Calvocoressi, *Top Secret Ultra,* 9.
4. Martin Gilbert and Richard Gott, *The Appeasers* (Boston: Houghton Mifflin, 1963), 170.
5. Welchman, *The Hut 6 Story,* 11.
6. I. J. Good interview, August 16, 1984.
7. Welchman, *The Hut 6 Story,* 34.
8. Hinsley et al., *British Intelligence,* 1:54.
9. Quoted in Hodges, *Alan Turing: The Enigma,* 161.
10. Calvocoressi, *Top Secret Ultra,* 3.
11. Welchman interview, November 15, 1983.
12. Welchman, *The Hut 6 Story,* 54.
13. Ibid., 71.
14. Ibid., 72. Further information from Welchman, December 19, 1984.
15. *The Times* (London), June 16, 1954, quoted in Turing, *Alan M. Turing,* 47.
16. Hodges, *Alan Turing: The Enigma,* 97.
17. Turing, *Alan M. Turing,* 56.
18. Welchman, *The Hut 6 Story,* 81.

19. Welchman interview, November 15, 1983.
20. Ingersoll, *Top Secret,* 18.
21. Ibid., 8.
22. Ibid., 12.
23. Ibid.
24. Ingersoll, *Top Secret,* 5.
25. Ibid., 14.
26. Lewin, *Ultra,* n. 246.
27. Levenson interview, December 30, 1983.
28. Bundy interview, August 8, 1984.
29. The description on these pages of the working of Hut 6 is from an interview with Welchman, December 19, 1984.
30. Description of the work of the Central Party also appears in Welchman, *The Hut 6 Story,* 153-58.
31. Levenson interview, February 28, 1984.
32. Smadbeck interview, February 14, 1984.
33. Ibid.
34. Welchman, *The Hut 6 Story,* 132.
35. Welchman interview, December 19, 1984.
36. Ibid.
37. Ibid.
38. Bundy interview, August 8, 1984.
39. Smadbeck interview, February 14, 1984.
40. Information on General Strong's visit from Levenson interviews, December 30, 1983, and February 28, 1984.

7. Inside Hut 3

1. Smadbeck interview, February 14, 1984.
2. Hinsley et al., *British Intelligence,* 3: 461.
3. Description of Hut 3 from Whitaker interviews. See also Calvocoressi, *Top Secret Ultra,* for details about Hut 3 and its functioning.
4. Norland interview, November 1, 1984.
5. Somewhat discrepant accounts of the Polish work on the Green key appear in Bertrand, *Enigma,* 86; Hinsley et al., *British Intelligence,* 1: 493; and Kozaczuk, *Enigma,* 84.
6. Hinsley et al., *British Intelligence,* 1: 108.
7. For discussion of some of the problems encountered by the British at the time of Norway, see ibid., 115-25.
8. Derek Tangye, *The Way of Minack* (London: Michael Joseph, 1968; Sphere paperback edition, 119).

9. Winterbotham, *The Ultra Secret,* 15-16. The plan is developed in the following pages.

10. Winterbotham to the author, January 20, 1984.

11. Hinsley et al., *British Intelligence,* 1: 144.

12. Ibid., 184.

13. Winterbotham, *The Ultra Secret,* 39.

14. Winterbotham to the author, January 20, 1984. Colville, *Winston Churchill,* 81, provides a pleasant account of Boniface in action.

15. Colville, *Winston Churchill,* 81.

16. Parrish, *Encyclopedia of WW II,* 141.

17. Hinsley, et al., *British Intelligence,* 1: 316-19.

18. Ibid., 391.

19. Whitaker diary (cipher).

20. Hamilton, *Monty,* 765.

21. SRH-037, "Ultra in European Theater," 3.

22. Howe, *Northwest Africa,* 439.

23. Eisenhower, *Crusade in Europe,* 152.

24. Howe, *Northwest Africa,* 442.

25. Ibid., 447, quoted from 26th Inf AAR, 19-24 Feb 43.

26. Eisenhower, Crusade in Europe, 152.

27. Hinsley et al., *British Intelligence,* 2: 583.

28. The importance of this division is emphasized in Ambrose, *Ike's Spies,* 60.

29. Ibid.

30. Harry C. Butcher, quoted in Lewin, *Ultra,* 274.

31. Hamilton, *Master,* 144.

32. Deutsch, "Historical Impact," 20.

33. Bundy interview, August 8, 1984.

34. Ibid.

35. Description of the watch from Whitaker interview, September 1, 1981.

36. Norland interview, May 14, 1984.

37. Whitaker interview, September 1, 1981.

38. Whitaker diary.

39. Ibid.

40. CX/MSS of January 5, 1944, 9:44 A.M. (PRO).

42. Bennett, *Ultra in the West,* xi.

8. Dolphin, Shark, Frankfurt

1. Wolfgang Frank. *The Sea Wolves* (New York: Henry Holt, 1955; Ballantine, 1958), 108.

2. Jean Noli, *The Admiral's Wolf Pack,* trans. by J. F. Bernard (Garden City, N.Y.: Doubleday, 1974).

3. Ibid.

4. Dönitz, *Memoirs,* 60.

5. Frank, *Sea Wolves,* 108.

6. Cajus Bekker, *Hitler's Naval War,* trans. and ed. by Frank Ziegler (Garden City, N.Y.: Doubleday, 1974), 309.

7. Information on the U-boat totals from Rohwer and Hümmelchen, *War at Sea,* 1: 178.

8. Quoted in Morison, *Battle of the Atlantic,* 127-28.

9. SRH-185, "War Experience," 51.

10. Dönitz, *Memoirs,* 64.

11. Frank, *Sea Wolves,* 116.

12. Morison, *Battle of the Atlantic,* 130.

13. *New Republic,* May 11, 1942, 623.

14. *Newsweek,* March 30, 1942, 30.

15. Wolfgang Frank.

16. Kemp, *Decision at Sea,* 49.

17. Churchill, *Hinge of Fate,* 117.

18. Ibid., 119.

19. Loewenheim et al., *Roosevelt and Churchill,* 196.

20. Dönitz, *Memoirs,* 17.

21. Bekker, *Hitler's Naval War,* 184.

22. I. J. Good, *Cryptologia* (April 1979): 67.

23. Hinsley et al., *British Intelligence,* 1: 163, 336.

24. Reading the *Heimisch* settings is from Hinsley et al., *British Intelligence,* 2: 163.

25. Ibid.

26. Beesly, *Very Special Intelligence,* 114.

27. Quoted in Morison, *Battle of the Atlantic,* 53.

28. Ibid., 115.

29. Winn's success is reported by Beesley in *Very Special Intelligence,* and by Knowles, interview, March 16, 1985.

30. Beesly, *Very Special Intelligence,* 114.

31. Knowles interview, March 6, 1985.

32. Ibid.

33. Ibid.

34. Ibid.

35. Beesly, *Very Special Intelligence,* 114.

36. Knowles interview, March 6, 1985.

37. Muggeridge, *The Infernal Grove,* 129.

38. Hinsley et al., *British Intelligence,* 2: 657.

39. Muggeridge, *The Infernal Grove,* 129.
40. Good interview, August 16, 1984.
41. Welchman interview, August 7, 1984.
42. Hinsley et al., *British Intelligence* 2: 56-57.
43. Eachus interview, March 4, 1984.
44. Figures on the U-boat haul are from Kemp, *Decision at Sea,* 64.
45. Churchill, *Closing the Ring,* 6.
46. Quentin Reynolds, *Convoy* (New York: Blue Ribbon Books, 1942), 20.
47. Wilbur Von Braunsberg interview, December 27, 1982.
48. Information on the convoy from Rohwer and Hümmelchen, *Chronology of the War at Sea,* 308-10.
49. Quoted in Rohwer, "Ultra and the Battle of the Atlantic," 228.
50. Roskill, *War at Sea,* 2: 367.
51. "Rhapsody in Purple," Part II, *Cryptologia,* October 1982, 346.
52. Hinsley et al., *British Intelligence,* 2: 635-36.
53. Kahn, *Hitler's Spies,* 219.
54. Hinsley et al., *British Intelligence,* 2: 554.
55. Nicholas Monsarrat, *The Cruel Sea* (New York: Knopf, 1951), 506.
56. Information on the Atlantic toll is from Kemp, *Decision at Sea,* 171.

9. "I Don't Believe It"

1. Information on the Whyte residence is from the Whitaker diary.
2. Smadbeck interview, February 14, 1984.
3. Bundy interview, November 30, 1983.
4. Friendly, "Confessions of a Codebreaker," *Washington Post,* October 27, 1974, C-1.
5. Turing, *Alan M. Turing,* 69.
6. Lewin, *Ultra,* 136.
7. Winterbotham, *The Ultra Secret,* 15.
8. Information on the linguist and the mathematician from Friendly, "Confessions of a Codebreaker," *Washington Post,* October 27, 1974. C-1.
9. Ibid.
10. Norland interview, February 14, 1985.
11. Friendly, "Confessions of a Codebreaker," *Washington Post,* October 27, 1974, C-1.
12. Levenson interview, December 30, 1983.

13. Bundy interview, August 8, 1984.
14. Norland interview, May 14, 1984.
15. January 23 appears to be the date Hut 3 was given at the time, as reported in Whitaker's cipher diary. The first invasion wave actually landed about 0200, January 22.
16. Kenneth Macksey, *Kesselring* (New York: McKay, 1978), 196-97.
17. Hinsley et al., *British Intelligence,* 3: 198.
18. Eisenhower, *Crusade in Europe,* 219.
19. Sherwood, *Roosevelt and Hopkins,* 803, and Pogue, *George C. Marshall: Organizer,* 321. The quotations from Roosevelt differ slightly in detail but not in essence.
20. Eisenhower, *Crusade in Europe,* 219.
21. Ibid., 235.
22. Ibid., 223.
23. Ibid.
24. Nicolson, *Alex,* 239.
25. Lewin, *Montgomery,* 228.
26. Churchill, *Closing the Ring,* 444.
27. Ingersoll, *Top Secret,* 94.
28. Ibid., 101
29. Ibid., 102.
30. A good discussion of the implications of a failure of Overlord can be found in Ambrose, *Supreme Commander,* 331.
31. Eisenhower, *Crusade in Europe,* 245.
32. Description of Dudley Clarke from Mure, *Master of Deception,* 101.
33. Ibid., 215.
34. This point is well made by Deutsch, "Influence of Ultra," 10.
35. The story of Sydney Cripps and his bull is from Joseph Albright, Cox News Service, June 3, 1984.
36. Eisenhower, *Crusade in Europe,* 239.
37. Butcher, *My Three Years with Eisenhower,* 450.
38. Semmes, *Portrait of Patton,* 178.
39. Mure, *Master of Deception,* 257.
40. Enigma message of January 9 is from Bennett, *Ultra in the West,* 43.
41. SRH-185, "War Experience," 17.
42. Ibid., 73.
43. Ibid., 9.
44. Ibid., 11.
45. Van Norden background based on interview, August 1, 1984.

46. Kellogg background based on interview, August 1, 1984.
47. Rosengarten background based on interview, August 11, 1984.
48. Kitchen background based on interview, August 10, 1984.
49. Powell background based on interview, August 14, 1984.
50. Bussey background based on interview, July 28, 1984.
51. Taylor's activities from SRH-110, "Military Intelligence."
52. Ibid., 43.
53. Ibid., 12.
54. Ibid., 13.
55. SRH-035, "History of Special Branch," 23.
56. Bella Fromm, quoted in Boyd, *The Extraordinary Envoy,* 19.
57. Ibid., 131.
58. SRH-035, "History of Special Branch," 19.
59. Information on Colonel Ito's tour from SRH-066, "Intelligence Obtained from Cryptanalysis," 5-6.
60. Interview with Colonel Hayes and the trip to London: Van Norden interview, August 1, 1984.
61. Powell interview, August 14, 1984.
62. SHR-110, "Military Intelligence," 15.
63. Landis Gores, *Princeton Alumni Weekly,* May 27, 2975, 10.

10.   "The Largest Undertaking"

1. General Marshall letter with attached Tab SRH-026, "Marshall Letter to Eisenhower."
2. Lectures by British air advisers: personal notebook of Lewis Powell, lent to author.
3. Jim Rose conversation: memorandum from Edmund Kellogg to author.
4. Kitchen interview, August 10, 1984.
5. Campaigne interview, April 7, 1984.
6. The quotations and stories in this paragraph are from Kellogg memorandum.
7. Ibid.
8. Levenson interview, December 31, 1983.
9. Letter from Doris White to the author, May 25, 1984.
10. Doris White, *D for Doris, V for Victory* (Milton Keynes, England, Oakleaf Books, 1981), 59.
11. Ibid., 69.
12. Bundy interview, August 8, 1984.
13. Bundy Bible Belt comment is from Kellogg interview, August 1, 1984.

14. Oshima interview with Hitler: SRS-1320, June 1944.
15. Bundy on the night of June 5-6: interview, August 8, 1984.
16. David Howarth, *D-Day* (New York: McGraw-Hill, 1959).
17. Landing at Omaha Beach: Hugh Mulligan, Associated Press, May 27, 1984.
18. Roger Nesbitt, *Lexington Herald-Leader,* June 11, 1984.
19. Interview by Lisa Murray with Bob Tate, June 6, 1984.
20. Harrison, *Cross-Channel Attack,* 450.
21. Leigh-Mallory's views are from Harrison, *Cross-Channel Attack,* 186.
22. The troop movements are from Harrison, *Cross-Channel Attack,* 260 and 365.
23. Smadbeck interview, February 14, 1984.
24. SRH-185, "War Experience," 28.
25. Ibid., 29.
26. These traits and their significance are interestingly discussed at many points in Dixon, *Psychology of Military Incompetence.*
27. This and following quotations are from SRH-185, "War Experience," 30.

11. "We Are Advancing Constantly"

1. Bradley, in foreword to Eisenhower Foundation, *D-Day,* vii.
2. Bradley and Blair, *A General's Life,* 258.
3. Bernard Brungs interview, February 22, 1985.
4. Rosengarten interview, February 15, 1983.
5. Several quotations from Brungs interview, February 22, 1985.
6. Background facts on Dickson from interview with Mrs. Benjamin Dickson, July 29, 1984.
7. Brungs interview, February 22, 1985.
8. The story is from Brungs, who had been told it by others.
9. All the quotations in this paragraph are from SRH-026, "Marshall letter to Eisenhower."
10. Rosengarten in SRH-023, "Reports by U.S. Army ULTRA Representatives," Tab B, 8.
11. Ibid.
12. Rosengarten interview, August 11, 1984.
13. D'Este, *Decision in Normandy,* 122.
14. Rosengarten, "With Ultra from Omaha Beach," 128.
15. Liddell Hart, *The German Generals Talk,* 244.
16. Harrison, *Cross-Channel Attack,* 413.
17. Pogue, *Supreme Command,* 166.

18. Bradley and Blair, *A General's Life,* 234.
19. Recorded by Air Marshal Sir Philip Wigglesworth and quoted by Martin Blumenson in Eisenhower Foundation, *D-Day,* 208.
20. Ibid.
21. Four decades and more later, the literary battle at Caen continues to rage, leading recent combatants being Hamilton, D'Este, and Hastings.
22. Powell interview, August 14, 1984.
23. *Time* (May 1, 1944) saw Bradley that way.
24. Bradley and Blair, *A General's Life,* 232.
25. Blumenson, *Breakout,* 197.
26. Rosengarten, "With Ultra from Omaha Beach," 128.
27. Bennett, "Ultra and Some Command Decisions," 141.
28. Rosengarten, "With Ultra from Omaha Beach," 128.
29. Helfers interview, November 24, 1984, and memorandum dated November 1974 (Citadel archives, Charleston, S.C.).
30. Helfers memorandum.
31. Helfers interview, November 24, 1984.
32. Helfers memorandum.
33. Described, with quotations, in Allen, *Lucky Forward,* 18-20.
34. Helfers memorandum.
35. Ibid.
36. Ibid.
37. The quotations about Mont-St.-Michel are, of course, from Henry Adams, *Mont-Saint-Michel and Chartres* (Boston: Houghton Mifflin, 1936), 1.
38. Rosengarten, "With Ultra from Omaha Beach," 128.
39. Blumenson, *Breakout,* 313.
40. Weigley, *Eisenhower's Lieutenants,* 1: 251.
41. Bradley and Blair, *A General's Life,* 218-19.
42. Blumenson, *Breakout,* 310.
43. Widely quoted, as in Ladislas Farago, *Patton* (New York, Obslensky, 1963; Dell edition, 1965), 447.
44. Helfers interview, November 24, 1984, and his memorandum.
45. Message from Bletchley Park reproduced in Bennett, *Ultra,* 284.
46. Helfers memorandum.
47. Helfers interview, November 24, 1984.
48. SRH-108, "Third United States Army," 2-3.
49. Ibid., 3.
50. Helfers interview, November 24, 1984.
51. Helfers memorandum.
52. Incident with Willie described by Helfers, November 24, 1984.

53. Farago, *Patton,* 447.
54. Dickson-Brungs conversation from Brungs interview, February 22, 1985.
55. Bradley, *Soldier's Story,* 367.
56. Rohmer, *Patton's Gap,* 226.
57. Ibid.
58. Ibid., 209.
59. SRH-108, "Third United States Army," 3.
60. Ibid., 4.
61. Bundy interview, August 8, 1984.
62. From the scrapbook kept by Beverly Kitchen.
63. Kitchen interview, August 10, 1984.
64. Van Norden interview, August 1, 1984.
65. Ibid.
66. The Blank-Plank romance is recalled by Levenson.
67. The source for G-2's briefing activities is SRH-185, "War Experience."
68. Ibid., 33.
69. Ibid., 34.
70. Ibid., 35, 36.
71. Ibid., 72.

12. "A Bit of a Panic"

1. Information about the flight of *Nightjar n-Nan* from Major General (then Lieutenant) John W. Huston and from the report of the mission, courtesy of General Huston. Interview, May 20, 1982.
2. Millville Municipal League brochure, 1915.
3. Quotations descriptive of Vanaman from Leon Bard interview, April 4, 1982.
4. Vanaman's work in Berlin is admiringly discussed in Truman Smith, *Berlin Alert,* particularly 120-22 and 166.
5. Vanaman interview, May 12, 1983.
6. *Drexel University News,* December 1980.
7. Parrish, *Encyclopedia of WW II,* 557.
8. Winterbotham, *The Ultra Secret,* 89.
9. Eaker interview, April 2, 1982.
10. Doolittle interview, April 1, 1982.
11. Winterbotham to the author, June 1, 1982.
12. Doolittle interview, April 1, 1982.
13. Talbert in SRH-023, "U.S. Army Ultra Representatives."

14. *The Army Air Forces* (New York: Pocket Books, 1944), 28.
15. Vanaman interview, May 12, 1982.
16. Doolittle interview, April 1, 1982.
17. Bard interview, April 4, 1982.
18. Peaslee, *Heritage of Valor,* 249.
19. *Drexel University News,* December 1980.
20. Vanaman interview, May 12, 1982.
21. Ibid.
22. Durand, "Stalag Luft III," Ph.D. diss., 188.
23. Winterbotham to the author, June 1, 1982.
24. Rose to the author, March 29, 1984.
25. Winterbotham to the author, June 1, 1982.
26. Talbert at Doolittle's office: Talbert interview, March 27, 1985.
27. Ibid.
28. Description of the flight of No. 783 from an account by Air Marshal Sir Ronald Ivelaw-Chapman.
29. Ivelaw-Chapman background from Air Ministry Bulletin No. 33449, June 8, 1952 (PRO).
30. Winterbotham to the author, June 1, 1982.
31. Ibid.
32. Ivelaw-Chapman account.
33. Winterbotham to the author, June 1, 1982.
34. The description of the departure from the camp and the march is based on Durand, "Stalag Luft III," Ph.D. diss., 428-49.
35. Ibid., 451-52.
36. John W. Huston interview, May 20, 1982.
37. Vanaman meeting with Harris: Vanaman interview, May 12, 1982.

13. "The Snow Must Be Dyed Red"

1. MacDonald, *Siegfried Line,* 4.
2. Blumenson, *Breakout,* 686.
3. Pogue, *Supreme Command,* 244-45.
4. Ibid.
5. Limpus, *How the Army Fights,* 307.
6. Blumenson, *Breakout and Pursuit,* 689.
7. Patton, *War As I Knew It,* 115.
8. Pogue, *Supreme Command,* 245.
9. The Bletchley Park message on September 5 is from Bennett, *Ultra,* 149.

10. Butcher, *My Three Years with Eisenhower,* 661.
11. MacDonald, *Siegfried Line,* 119.
12. Dixon, *Psychology of Military Incompetence,* 146.
13. The author would not have had the temerity to put forward Montgomery's jealousy of Patton as a motivation for the field marshal's espousal of Market-Garden, had not Montgomery's compatriot and admirer, the eminently fair-minded Ronald Lewin, made such a suggestion. See Lewin, *Montgomery,* 299.
14. The moves of the German divisions are from MacDonald, *Siegfried Line,* 127.
15. Bennett, *Ultra,* 153.
16. Smith's warning to Montgomery is from MacDonald, *Siegfried Line,* 122.
17. Ibid., 140.
18. Radio broadcast, September 17, 1944: Murrow, *In Search of Light,* 84.
19. Radio broadcast, September 24, 1944: Murrow, *In Search of Light,* 86.
20. Bussey interview, July 28, 1984.
21. Bussey in SRH-023, "U.S. Army Ultra Representatives."
22. Bussey interview, July 28, 1984.
23. Information on the First Army and the new Ninth Army from SRH-112, "Ardennes Offensive."
24. Calvocoressi, *Top Secret Ultra,* 54.
25. Norland interview, November 1, 1984.
26. Ibid. and Whitaker interview, November 9, 1984.
27. Norland interview, February 14, 1985.
28. Bussey interview, July 28, 1984.
29. Bennett, *Ultra,* 194.
30. Bussey interview, July 28, 1984.
31. Ibid.
32. Weekly Intelligence Summary No. 17, Headquarters 12th Army Group, Francis Pickens Miller Collection—GCM.
33. Bennett, *Ultra,* 192.
34. General Strong's comments from Weekly Intelligence Summary No. 38, SHAEF, for week ending December 10, 1944, Francis Pickens Miller Collection—GCM.
35. Third U.S. Army G-2 Periodic Report No. 183, December 11, 1944, Francis Pickens Miller Collection—GCM.
36. Third U.S. Army G-2 Periodic Report No. 186, Francis Pickens Miller Collection—GCM.

37. Rosengarten interview, August 11, 1984.
38. Bradley, *Soldier's Story,* 419.
39. Quotations in this paragraph from G-2 Estimate No. 37, Headquarters First United States Army, December 10, 1944, Francis Pickens Miller Collection—GCM.
40. Pogue, *Supreme Command,* 370.
41. Bradley, *Soldier's Story,* 450.
42. Liddell Hart, *The German Generals Talk,* 245.
43. Information on the Hitler-Oshima meeting from SRS-1419.
44. Cole, *The Ardennes,* 2.
45. Reaction of the German generals from Liddell Hart, *The German Generals Talk,* 275-76.
46. Thompson in SRH-023, "U.S. Army Ultra Representatives."
47. Van Norden interview, August 1, 1984.
48. The German lieutenant's letter is from SHAEF G-2, Enemy Documents Section. Weekly Report 23—20 January 1945, Francis Pickens Miller Collection—GCM.

14.   The Russian Fish

1. Whitaker interview, January 3, 1982.
2. Ibid.
3. Levenson interview, December 30, 1983.
4. Whitaker interview, January 3, 1982.
5. Bussey in SRH-023, "U.S. Army Ultra Representatives."
6. Van Norden interview, August 1, 1984.
7. Rose to the author, March 29, 1984.
8. Noble Frankland, "Bombing: The RAF Case," in *History of the Second World War* (Marshall Cavendish USA Ltd, 1974), Part 79, 2186.
9. Ibid., 2197.
10. SRH-023, "U.S. Army Ultra Representatives," Tab D.
11. Whitaker interview, January 3, 1982.
12. The meaning of "TICOM": "Target Intelligence Committee" has also been suggested. "Technical Intelligence Committee" appears in the Friedman Papers (GCM) in a note in Mrs. Friedman's handwriting, but direct documentary evidence is not available.
13. MacDonald, *Last Offensive,* 407.
14. Whitaker interview, January 3, 1982.
15. Campaigne background based on interview, April 7, 1984.
16. SHAEF Orders, 3 May 1945.

17. The journal kept by Whitaker serves as the basis of the account of the TICOM mission in the following pages; it has, of course, the special value of being written day by day at the time of the events it describes.
18. Campaigne interview, April 7, 1984.
19. Whitaker interview, January 3, 1982.
20. Quotations from Whitaker's journal.
21. Ibid.
22. Ibid.
23. Whitaker interview, January 3, 1982.
24. The "clever historian" is Harold C. Deutsch.

EPILOGUE

1. Letter to the *Washington Post,* December 10, 1974, quoted in Deutsch, "Historical Impact," 32, note 27.
2. Deutsch, "Historical Impact," 19.
3. Ibid., 23.
4. Bussey interview, July 28, 1984.
5. Introduction to Winterbotham, *The Ultra Secret,* xii.
6. Quoted in Deutsch, "Historical Impact," 18.
7. Quoted, in slightly different form, in David Kahn, "The Significance of Codebreaking and Intelligence in Allied Strategy and Tactics," *Cryptologia* (July 1977): 210.
8. Cave Brown, *Bodyguard of Lies,* 922. That this military man was in fact General Sibert was confirmed by Cave Brown in a conversation with the author, April 1, 1985.
9. Rowlett interview, December 27, 1983.
10. Whitaker interview, September 1, 1981.

Sources

Substantive Interviews and Correspondence

Leon Bard
Col. Bernard Brungs
John R. Bryden
McGeorge Bundy
William P. Bundy
Col. Donald S. Bussey
Howard Campaigne
Col. Albert P. Clark
Brig. Gen. Carter W. Clarke
Lt. Gen. James H. Doolittle
Mrs. Benjamin A. Dickson
Joseph J. Eachus
Lt. Gen. Ira C. Eaker
Walter J. Fried
Landis Gores
Lt. Col. Melvin C. Helfers
Maj. Gen. John W. Huston
Rt. Hon. Roy Jenkins
Frances Jennings
Edmund Kellogg
Beverly Kitchen (Mrs. Harry Almond)
Capt. Kenneth A. Knowles
Kenneth A. Knowles, Jr.

Arthur J. Levenson
Ronald Lewin
Sir Stuart Milner-Barry
Selmer S. Norland
Justice Lewis F. Powell
Chalmers M. Roberts
E. J. B. ("Jim") Rose
Adolph G. Rosengarten
Frank B. Rowlett
John Russell
John N. Seaman
Abraham Sinkov
Louis Smadbeck
Ansel E. M. Talbert
Telford Taylor
Maj. Gen. Arthur W. Vanaman
Langdon Van Norden
Wilbur Von Braunsberg
Gordon Welchman
Paul K. Whitaker
Doris E. White
Group Capt. F. W. Winterbotham

Unpublished Materials

Abbreviations:

NA　　National Archives of the United States, Washington, D.C.
GCM　George C. Marshall Library and Research Center, Lexington, Va.
PRO　Public Record Office, London

MANUSCRIPTS
Melvin Helfers memorandum, 1974 (Citadel archives, Charleston, S.C.)
Edmund Kellogg notes, 1983
Lewis Powell lecture notes, Bletchley Park, 1944
Frank Rowlett memorandum and notes, 1984
Paul Whitaker. Diary, plaintext and cipher, 1944-45; journal of the
　　　TICOM mission, 1945

OTHERS
Bundy, William P. "The Literature of Spies and Code Breaking in World
　　　War II." Talk to the Friends of the Princeton Library, November 1,
　　　1981.
Durand, Arthur Aquinas. "Stalag Luft III: An American Experience in a
　　　World War II German Prisoner of War Camp." 2 vols. Ph.D. diss.,
　　　Louisiana State University, 1976.
Russell, Jerry C. "Ultra and the Campaigns Against the U-Boats in World
　　　War II." Research study, U.S. Army War College, Carlisle Barracks,
　　　Pa., 1980.

ARCHIVAL MATERIALS
List of Ultra recipients, March 25, 1945. Richard Collins Papers, U.S.
　　　Army Military History Research Collection, Carlisle Barracks, Pa.
CX/MSS (Ultra) messages and other documents (PRO)
Documents in the Francis Pickens Miller Collection (GCM)
Letters and documents in the William F. Friedman Papers (GCM)
National Security Agency documents in Record Group 457, NA
　　　SRH-005　　Use of (CX/MSS ULTRA) by the United States War
　　　　　　　　　Department (1943-1945)
　　　SRH-006　　Synthesis of Experiences in the Use of ULTRA Intelli-
　　　　　　　　　gence by U.S. Army Field Commands in the European
　　　　　　　　　Theater of Operations
　　　SRH-023　　Reports by U.S. Army ULTRA Representatives with
　　　　　　　　　Army Field Commands (with Tabs)

SRH-026   Marshall Letter to Eisenhower on the Use of ULTRA Intelligence

SRH-029   A Brief History of the Signal Intelligence Service, by William F. Friedman

SRH-033   History of the Operations of Special Security Officers Attached to Field Commands

SRH-035   History of the Special Branch, MIS, War Department

SRH-037   Reports Received by U.S. War Department on the Use of ULTRA in European Theater

SRH-038   A Selection of Papers Pertaining to Herbert O. Yardley

SRH-042   Third Army Radio Intelligence History

SRH-061   Allocation of Special Security Officers to Special Branch Military Intelligence Service

SRH-062   History of Military Intelligence Service, MIS, War Department

SRH-066   Examples of Intelligence Obtained from Cryptanalysis

SRH-107   Problems of the SSO System World War II

SRH-108   Report on Assignment with Third United States Army, Major Warrack Wallace

SRH-110   Operations of the Military Intelligence Service, War Department, London

SRH-112   Post Mortem Writings on Indications of Ardennes Offensive

SRH-116   Origin, Functions and Problems of the Special Branch, MIS

SRH-117   History of Special Branch, MIS

SRH-132   History of the Special Distribution Branch, MIS

SRH-134   Expansion of the Signal Intelligence Service from 1930-December 7, 1941, by William F. Friedman

SRH-141   Papers from the Personal Files of Alfred McCormack, Colonel, AUS (Parts 1 and 2)

SRH-146   Handling of ULTRA within the Military Intelligence Service 1941-1945

SRH-149   A Brief History of Communications Intelligence in the United States, by Laurance F. Safford, Captain, USN

SRH-152   Historical Review of OP-20-G, United States Navy

SRH-153   MIS, War Department Liaison Activities in the UK, 1943-1945

SRH-159   Preliminary Historical Report on the Solution of the "B" Machine

SRH-185   "War Experience of Alfred McCormack

SRH-197   U.S. Navy Communication Intelligence, by Rear Adm.
             Joseph N. Wenger
SRH-221   SIS Activities of Captain Harrison and Captain Koerner,
             ETO, 1944-1945
SRH-276   Correspondence Concerning the Possible Transfer of
             the Signal Intelligence Service from the Signal Corps to
             the Military Intelligence Service
SRS series   "Magic Diplomatic Summaries"
Special Research History 197. U.S. Navy Communication Intelligence;
     Organization, Liaison and Collaboration 1941-1945 (prepared at
     the direction of Capt. J. N. Wenger; from *NCVA Cryptolog,* Winter
     1984)

Reports

U.S. Congress. *Pearl Harbor Attack: Hearings Before the Joint Com-
     mittee on the Investigation of the Pearl Harbor Attack.* 79th
     Cong., 1st sess., 1946. 39 vols.
U.S. Congress. *Investigation of the Pearl Harbor Attack: Report of the
     Joint Committee on the Investigation of the Pearl Harbor Attack.*
     1946.
U.S. Department of Defense. *The "Magic" Background of Pearl Har-
     bor.* 5 vols., with Appendixes. Washington, D.C.: U.S. Government
     Printing Office, 1977.

Articles

Bennett, Ralph. "Ultra and Some Command Decisions." *Journal of
     Contemporary History,* 16 (1981): 131-51.
Callimahos, Lambros D. "The Legendary William F. Friedman." NSA
     in-house publication.
Campbell, John P. "The 'Ultra' Revelations." *Canadian Defense Quar-
     terly* (Summer 1976): 36-42.
Calvocoressi, Peter. Three radio talks on Enigma. *The Listener,* January
     20, 1977, p. 70; January 27, 1977, p. 112; February 3, 1977, p. 135.
Cochran, Alexander S., Jr. "'MAGIC,' 'ULTRA,' and the Second World
     War: Literature, Sources, and Outlook." *Military Affairs* (April
     1982): 88-92.
Davies, Donald W. "The Siemens and Halske T52e Cipher Machine."
     Cryptologia (October 1982): 289-308.
Deavours, C. A. "Analysis of the Hebern Cryptograph Using Iso-
     morphs." *Cryptologia* (April 1977): 162-74.

_____ and James Reeds. "The Enigma." *Cryptologia* (October 1977):

Deutsch, Harold C. "The Historical Impact of Revealing the Ultra Secret." *Parameters,* VII, 3, pp. 16-32.

_____. "The Influence of Ultra on World War II." *Parameters,* VIII, 4, pp. 2-9.

Friendly, Alfred. "Confessions of a Codebreaker." *Washington Post,* October 27, 1974, p. C-1.

Good, I. J. "Early Work on Computers at Bletchley." *Cryptologia* (April 1979): 65-77.

Hannah, Theodore M. "Frank B. Rowlett—A Personal Profile." NSA in-house publication.

Kahn, David. "The International Conference on Ultra." *Military Affairs* (April 1979): 97-98.

_____. "The Significance of Codebreaking and Intelligence in Allied Strategy and Tactics." *Cryptologia* (July 1977): 209-222.

_____. "The Ultra Conference." *Cryptologia* (January 1979): 1-8.

Knowles, Kenneth A. "Ultra and the Battle of the Atlantic: the American View," in *Changing Interpretations and New Sources in Naval History,* Robert W. Love, Jr., ed. New York: Garland, 1980, p. 444.

Kruh, Louis. "Reminiscences of a Master Cryptologist." *Cryptologia* (January 1980): 45-50.

"Rhapsody in Purple: A New History of Pearl Harbor." *Cryptologia* (July 1982): 192-228.

Rohwer, Jürgen. "Ultra and the Battle of the Atlantic: the German View," in *Changing Interpretations and New Sources in Naval History,* Robert W. Love, Jr., ed. New York: Garland, 1980, p. 42C.

Rosengarten, Adolph. "With Ultra From Omaha Beach to Weimar, Germany—A Personal View." *Military Affairs* (October 1978): 127-32.

Spiller, Roger J. "Some Implications of ULTRA." *Military Affairs* (April 1976): 49-53.

Stafford, David A. T. "Ultra and the British Official Histories: a Documentary Note." *Military Affairs* (February 1978): 29-31.

"Ultra Sidelights." *NCVA Cryptolog,* Fall 1984, p. 7.

Official and Semiofficial Histories

Blumenson, Martin. *Breakout and Pursuit.* The U.S. Army in World War II. Washington, D.C.: Office of the Chief of Military History, 1961.

_____. *Salerno to Cassino.* The U.S. Army in World War II. Washington, D.C.: Office of the Chief of Military History, 1969.

Coakley, Robert W., and Leighton, Richard M. *Global Logistics and Strategy.* The U.S. Army in World War II. Washington, D.C.: Office of the Chief of Military History, 1968.

Cole, Hugh M. *The Ardennes: Battle of the Bulge.* The U.S. Army in World War II. Washington, D.C.: Office of the Chief of Military History, 1965.

Craven, Wesley Frank, and Cate, James Lea, eds. *The Army Air Forces in World War II.* Volume II: *Torch to Pointblank.* Chicago: University of Chicago Press, 1949. Volume III: *Argument to V-E Day.* Chicago: University of Chicago Press, 1951.

Garland, Albert N., and Smith, Howard McGaw. *Sicily and the Surrender of Italy.* The U.S. Army in World War II. Washington, D.C.: Office of the Chief of Military History, 1965.

Harrison, Gordon A. *Cross-Channel Attack.* The U.S. Army in World War II. Washington, D.C.: Office of the Chief of Military History, 1951.

Hinsley F. H.; Thomas, E. E.; Ransom, C. F. G.; and Knight, R. C. *British Intelligence in the Second World War.* Vols. I and II and Vol. III, Part 1, published to date. London: Her Majesty's Stationery Office, 1979-84.

Howe, George F. *Northwest Africa: Seizing the Initiative in the West.* The U.S. Army in World War II. Washington, D.C.: Office of the Chief of Military History, 1957.

MacDonald, Charles B. *The Siegfried Line Campaign.* The U.S. Army in World War II. Washington, D.C.: Office of the Chief of Military History, 1963.

Matloff, Maurice, and Snell, Edwin M. *Strategic Planning for Coalition Warfare 1941-42.* U.S. Army in World War II. Washington, D.C.: Office of the Chief of Military History, 1953.

Morison, Samuel Eliot. *The Battle of the Atlantic.* History of the U.S. Navy in World War II. Boston: Little, Brown, 1947.

Pogue, Forrest C. *The Supreme Command.* U.S. Army in World War II. Washington, D.C.: Office of the Chief of Military History, 1954.

Roskill, S. W. *The War at Sea.* Vol. II. London: Her Majesty's Stationery Office, 1956.

Terrett, Dulany. *The Signal Corps: The Emergency.* U.S. Army in World War II. Washington, D.C.: Office of the Chief of Military History, 1956.

Thompson, George Raynor; Harris, Dixie R.; Oakes, Pauline M.; and Terrett, Dulany. *The Signal Corps: The Test.* U.S. Army in World War II. Washington, D.C.: Office of the Chief of Military History, 1957.

Watson, Mark S. *Chief of Staff: Prewar Plans and Preparations.* U.S. Army in World War II. Washington, D.C.: Department of the Army, 1950.

Ziemke, Earl. *The German Northern Theater of Operations,* 1940-1945. Washington, D.C.: U.S. Government Printing Office, 1960.

Other Books

Allen, Robert S. *Lucky Forward.* New York: Vanguard, 1947.

Ambrose, Stephen E. *Ike's Spies.* Garden City, N.Y.: Doubleday, 1981.*

————. *The Supreme Commander.* Garden City, N.Y.: Doubleday, 1970.*

Bamford, James. *The Puzzle Palace.* Boston: Houghton Mifflin, 1982; Penguin edition, 1983.

Barnett, Correlli. *The Desert Generals.* New York: Viking, 1961.

Bauer, Cornelius. *The Battle of Arnhem.* New York: Stein and Day, 1967.

Baxter, James Phinney III. *Scientists Against Time.* Boston: Little, Brown, 1946.

Beesly, Patrick. *Very Special Intelligence.* Garden City, N.Y.: Doubleday, 1977; Ballantine edition, 1981.

Bekker, Cajus. *Defeat at Sea.* New York: Henry Holt, 1955; Ballantine edition, n.d.

————. *Hitler's Naval War.* Garden City, N.Y.: Doubleday, 1974.

Bell, Ernest L. *An Initial View of Ultra as an American Weapon.* Keene, N.H.: TSU Press, 1977.

Bennett, Ralph. *Ultra in the West.* New York: Scribner, 1979.*

Bertrand, Gustave. *Enigma: ou la plus grande enigme de la guerre.* Paris: Plon, 1973.

Blackett, P. M. S. *Studies of War.* New York: Hill & Wang, 1962.

Boyd, Carl. *The Extraordinary Envoy.* Washington, D.C.: University Press of America, 1980.

Bradley, Omar N. *A Soldier's Story.* New York: Holt, Rinehart & Winston, 1951; Popular Library edition, n.d.

———— and Blair, Clay. *A General's Life.* New York: Simon & Schuster, 1983.

Brereton, Lewis H. *The Brereton Diaries.* New York: Morrow, 1946.

Bryant, Arthur. *Triumph in the West.* Garden City, N.Y.: Doubleday, 1959.

————

*Books marked with an asterisk are from book club editions whose pagination may be different from that in the original edition.

————. *The Turn of the Tide*. Garden City, N.Y.: Doubleday, 1957.

Buchanan, A. Russell. *The United States and World War II*. New York: Harper & Row, 1964.

Busch, Harald. *U-Boats at War*. Translated by L. P. R. Wilson. New York: Ballantine, 1955.

Bush, Vannevar. *Modern Arms and Free Men*. New York: Simon & Schuster, 1949.

Butcher, Harry C. *My Three Years with Eisenhower*. New York: Simon & Schuster, 1946.

Calvocoressi, Peter. *Top Secret Ultra*. New York: Pantheon, 1980.

Cave Brown, Anthony. *Bodyguard of Lies*. New York: Harper & Row, 1975.*

Churchill, Winston S. *The Second World War*. Vol. I: *The Gathering Storm*. Vol. II: *Their Finest Hour*. Vol. III: *The Grand Alliance*. Vol. IV: *The Hinge of Fate*. Vol. V: *Closing the Ring*. Vol. VI: *Triumph and Tragedy*. Boston: Houghton Mifflin, 1948-53.

Clark, Ronald. *The Man Who Broke Purple*. Boston: Little, Brown, 1977.

————. *Tizard*. Cambridge, Mass.: MIT Press, 1965.

Coffey, Thomas M. *Hap: The Story of the U.S. Air Force and the Man Who Built It*. New York: Viking, 1982.*

Colville, John. *Winston Churchill and His Inner Circle*. New York: Wyndham, 1981.

Colvin, Ian. *The Chamberlain Cabinet*. New York: Taplinger, 1971.

Deacon, Richard. *A History of British Secret Service*. London: Frederick Muller, 1969; Granada edition, 1980.

D'Este, Carlo. *Decision in Normandy*. New York: Dutton, 1983.

Divine, Robert A. *Roosevelt and World War II*. Baltimore: Johns Hopkins Press, 1969; Penguin edition, 1970.

Dixon, Norman F. *On the Psychology of Military Incompetence*. New York: Basic Books, 1976.

Dönitz, Karl. *Memoirs*. Cleveland: World, 1959; Leisure Books edition, n.d.

Draper, Theodore. *The Six Weeks' War*. New York: Viking, 1944.

Eisenhower, Dwight D. *Crusade in Europe*. Garden City, N.Y.: Doubleday, 1948; Dolphin edition, 1952.

Eisenhower Foundation. *D-Day: The Normandy Invasion in Retrospect*. Lawrence: University Press of Kansas, 1971.

Ellis, John. *The Sharp End*. New York: Scribner, 1980.*

Essame, H. *Patton: A Study in Command*. New York: Scribner, 1974.*

Farago, Ladislas, *The Broken Seal*. New York: Random House, 1967.

_____. *The Tenth Fleet*. New York: Ivan Obolensky, 1962; Paperback Library edition, 1964.

Fest, Joachim C. *Hitler*. New York: Harcourt Brace Jovanovich, 1974. *

Fitzgerald, Penelope. *The Knox Brothers*. New York: Coward, McCann and Geoghegan, 1977.

Frankel, Nat, and Smith, Larry. *Patton's Best*. New York: Dutton, 1978; Jove edition, 1984.

Freidin, Seymour, and Richardson, William. *The Fatal Decisions*. New York: William Sloane Associates, 1956; Berkley edition, 1958.

Garlinski, Jozef. *The Enigma War*. New York: Scribner, 1980. *

Hamilton, Nigel. *Master of the Battlefield*. New York: McGraw-Hill, 1983.

_____. *Monty*. New York: McGraw-Hill, 1981.

Hastings, Max. *Overlord: D-Day and the Battle for Normandy*. New York: Simon and Schuster, 1984.

Haswell, Jock. *D-Day: Intelligence and Deception*. New York: Times Books, 1979. *

Hodges, Andrew. *Alan Turing: The Enigma*. New York: Simon & Schuster, 1983.

Ingersoll, Ralph. *Top Secret*. New York: Harcourt, Brace, 1946.

Jackson, W. G. T. *The Battle for North Africa 1940–43*. New York: Mason/Charter, 1975. *

Holmes, W. J. *Double-Edged Secrets*. Annapolis: Naval Institute Press, 1979.

Johnson, Brian. *The Secret War*. New York: Methuen, 1978.

Kahn, David. *The Codebreakers*. New York: Macmillan, 1967.

_____. *Hitler's Spies*. New York: Macmillan, 1978.

Keegan, John. *Six Armies in Normandy*. New York: Viking, 1982. *

Kemp, Peter. *Decision at Sea: The Convoy Escorts*. New York: A Talisman/Parrish Book—Elsevier-Dutton, 1978.

Kirkpatrick, Lyman, Jr. *Captains Without Eyes*. New York: Macmillan, 1969.

Kozaczuk, Wladyslaw. *Enigma*. n.p.: University Publications of America, 1984.

Lee, Raymond E. *The London Journal of General Raymond E. Lee*. Edited by James Leutze. Boston: Little, Brown, 1971.

Lewin, Ronald. *The American Magic*. New York: Farrar Straus Giroux, 1982.

_____. *Montgomery as Military Commander*. New York: Stein and Day, 1971. *

_____. *Rommel as Military Commander*. New York: Van Nostrand,

1968; Ballantine edition, 1970.

———. *Ultra Goes to War*. New York: McGraw-Hill, 1978.

Liddell Hart, B. H. *The German Generals Talk*. New York: Morrow, 1948.

Limpus, Lowell M. *How the Army Fights*. New York: D. Appleton-Century, 1943.

Loewenheim, Francis L.; Langley, Harold D.; and Jonas, Manfred, eds. *Roosevelt and Churchill: Their Secret Wartime Correspondence*. New York: Dutton, 1975.

MacDonald, Charles B. *A Time for Trumpets*. New York: Morrow, 1985.

Macintyre, Donald. *The Naval War Against Hitler*. New York, Scribner, 1971.

Marshall, S. L. A. *Bringing Up the Rear*. San Rafael, Calif.: Presidio Press, 1979.

Masterman, J. C. *The Double-Cross System in the War of 1939 to 1945*. New Haven, Conn.: Yale University Press, 1972; Avon edition, 1972.

Morison, Samuel Eliot. *The Two-Ocean War*. Boston: Little, Brown, 1963.

Muggeridge, Malcolm. *Chronicles of Wasted Time*. Chronicle 2: *The Infernal Grove*. New York: Morrow, 1974.

Mure, David. *Master of Deception*. London: William Kimber, 1980.

Murphy, Robert. *Diplomat Among Warriors*. Garden City, N.Y.: Doubleday, 1964; Pyramid edition, n.d.

Murrow, Edward R. *In Search of Light*. Edited by Edward Bliss, Jr. New York: Knopf, 1967.

Nicolson, Nigel. *Alex*. New York: Atheneum, 1973.

Nimitz, Chester W.; Adams, Henry H.; and Potter, E. B., eds. *Triumph in the Atlantic*. Englewood Cliffs, N.J.: Prentice-Hall, 1960.

Parrish, Thomas, ed. *The Simon and Schuster Encyclopedia of World War II*. New York: Simon & Schuster, 1978.

Patton, George S., Jr. *War As I Knew It*. Boston: Houghton Mifflin, 1947; Bantam edition, 1980.

Peaslee, Budd J. *Heritage of Valor*. Philadelphia: Lippincott, 1964.

Philby, H. A. R. *My Silent War*. New York: Grove Press, 1968.

Pogue, Forrest C. *George C. Marshall: Ordeal and Hope*. New York: Viking, 1966.

———. *George C. Marshall: Organizer of Victory*. New York: Viking, 1973.

Rohmer, Richard. *Patton's Gap*. New York: Beaufort Books, 1981.

Rohwer, Jürgen, and Hümmelchen, Gerhard. *Chronology of the War at Sea, 1939-1945*. Translated from the German by Derek Masters. 2 vols. New York: Arco, 1973.

Ruge, Friedrich. *Der Seekrieg.* Translated by M. G. Saunders. Annapolis: U.S. Naval Institute, 1957.

Ryan, Cornelius. *A Bridge Too Far.* New York: Simon & Schuster, 1974.

Semmes, Harry H. *Portrait of Patton.* New York: Appleton-Century-Crofts, 1955; Paperback Library edition, 1964.

Sherwood, Robert E. *Roosevelt and Hopkins.* New York: Harper, 1948; Grosset & Dunlap edition, 1950.

Shirer, William L. *The Rise and Fall of the Third Reich.* New York: Simon & Schuster, 1960.

Smith, Bradley F. *The Shadow Warriors.* New York: Basic Books, 1983.

Smith, Truman. *Berlin Alert.* Edited by Robert Hessen. Stanford, Calif.: Hoover Institution Press, 1984.

Snow, C. P. *Science and Government.* Cambridge, Mass.: Harvard University Press, 1961.

Stevenson, William. *A Man Called Intrepid.* New York: Harcourt Brace Jovanovich, 1976.

Stimson, Henry L., and Bundy, McGeorge. *On Active Service in Peace and War.* New York, Harper, 1948.

Strawson, John. *The Battle for North Africa.* New York: Scribner, 1970.

Strong, K. W. D. *Intelligence at the Top.* Garden City, N.Y.: Doubleday, 1969.

Tedder, Lord. *With Prejudice.* Boston: Little, Brown, 1966.

Toland, John. *Adolf Hitler.* 2 vols. Garden City, N.Y.: Doubleday, 1976.*

———. *Infamy.* Garden City, N.Y.: Doubleday, 1982.*

Trevor-Roper, H. R. *Blitzkrieg to Defeat.* New York: Holt, Rinehart & Winston, 1965.

Turing, Sara. *Alan M. Turing.* Cambridge, Eng.: Heffers, 1959.

Van Der Rhoer, Edward. *Deadly Magic.* New York: Scribner, 1978.

Von der Porten, Edward P. *The German Navy in World War Two.* New York: Crowell, 1969; Ballantine edition, 1974.

Weigley, Russell F. *Eisenhower's Lieutenants.* 2 vols. Bloomington: Indiana University Press, 1981.*

Weinberg, Gerhard L. *World in the Balance.* Hanover, N.H.: University Press of New England, 1981.

Welchman, Gordon. *The Hut 6 Story.* New York: McGraw-Hill, 1982.

Whaley, Barton. *Codeword BARBAROSSA.* Cambridge, Mass.: MIT Press, 1973.

Winterbotham, F. W. *The Ultra Secret.* New York: Harper & Row, 1974.

Wohlstetter, Roberta. *Pearl Harbor: Warning and Decision:* Stanford, Calif.: Stanford University Press, 1962.

Yardley, Herbert O. *The American Black Chamber.* Indianapolis: Bobbs-Merrill, 1931.

Index

Acheson, Dean, 90
Adlertag, 129
"A" Force, 172-73
Afrika Korps, 131, 132, 133
Air Force Intelligence School, 179
Air Ministry, 127, 149, 184, 191, 239, 246, 274
Air Staff, 126
Aitken, Alexander, 194
Alexander, Gen. Hugh, 116, 138, 170, 194, 215
   takeover of Hut 8, 155
Allen, Col. Robert S., 220, 223, 275
Allen, Yorke, 187
Allied bombing, 216, 236, 239, 241, 242, 245
   of Tokyo, 237
Allied Force Headquarters
   Algiers, 133, 185
   integrated intelligence staff of, 132
Allied forces, 10, 128, 131
   advance forces to Berchtesgaden, 278
   advance toward Berlin, 276
   eastward across France, 228
   arrival at Normandy, 257
   assault on Festung Deutschland, 264
   attacks on German aircraft plants, 191
   change during course of war, 260
   Continental invasion armies, 171-72, 215, 216-17, 220-23, 236, 237, 239, 241, 251, 252, 253-57, 258, 259, 262-69, 273, 274, 276, 278
   casualties in North Atlantic, 161
   control of air over Normandy, 233

   crytological intelligence mission to Berlin, 271-73. *See also* TICOM
   in the Mediterranean, 116-17, 168
   on French Riviera, 257
   Naval ciphers used, 160
   in North African campaign, 85, 133-35
   number of, to land on Cotentin peninsula, 201
   peak of offensive, 251
   plan of operations, 251
   in Tunisia, Sicily, and Italy, 116
   unification of armies at Dijon, 259
Allied Intelligence
   capacity to decrypt Soviet radio traffic, 283
Allied Powers, 9, 22, 52, 60
   war effort, 102
Allied shipping
   convoy protection of, 154, 158
   losses to U-boats, 143-46, 156, 159
Allied strategists
   view of Germany as primary target (1942), 80
Almond, Beverly Kitchen. *See* Kitchen, Beverly
Alpes Maritimes, 258
American Black Chamber, 35, 36, 63
   archives of, 38, 39
   consolidation into SIS, 33
   corporate front, 32
   establishment of, 31-33
   Yardley publishes book about, 39
American Expeditionary Force, 35
American Intelligence Service, 180
Anderson, Lt. Gen. Sir Kenneth, 133, 134